D0996519

career education

220557

The Third Yearbook of the

American Vocational Association

career education

edited by Joel H. Magisos

LC 1044
M33

American Vocational Association
Washington, D.C.

Published 1973 by
THE AMERICAN VOCATIONAL ASSOCIATION, INC.
1510 H Street, N.W., Washington, D.C. 20005

Copyright © 1973 by The American Vocational Association, Inc.

*No part of this Yearbook may be reproduced
in any form without written permission
from the publisher*

Printed in the United States of America

PREFACE

This yearbook is the third in a significant series of educational literature commissioned by the American Vocational Association. It brings to one volume both the scholarly thought and the practical experience of competent educators and others interested in some aspect of the yearbook theme.

The theme of the third yearbook, *Career Education,* is especially fitting because of widespread interest and activity in development and implementation of career education concepts. Career education promises to become the educational milieu within which vocational education will flourish. It already has begun to bridge the false gap between vocational and academic education, thereby promising to make all education relevant and useful for the majority of the nation's youth and adults.

The American Vocational Association has shown its vital interest in career education in resolutions by the AVA House of Delegates in 1966 and 1971, the formation of the AVA Task Force on Career Education, articles in the *American Vocational Journal,* and the program content of AVA conventions and meetings. The Association will continue this interest because vocational education is an essential component of career education.

The authors of the yearbook chapters represent several educational specialties, all of the occupational areas, diverse educational settings, and almost every educational level. All gave their efforts unselfishly and many expressed the hope that their own chapter would contribute to the usefulness of the yearbook for the profession. It is believed that *Career Education* will be a volume that will have utility both initially and over time.

Joel H. Magisos, editor of this yearbook, has been involved in vocational, technical, and career education as a student, teacher, state supervisor, teacher educator, researcher, and administrator. Added to this professional background has been early work experience on the farm and in the shipbuilding, aircraft, and food-processing industries. He has authored or co-authored more than 30 research reports, bulletins, monographs, journal articles or chapters and served on the AVA Task Force on Career Education. His experience, combined with his objective overview of education, his perception and his energy, enabled Dr. Magisos to bring together a sound work that provides a needed comprehensive look at career education. Dr. Magisos is an associate director of The Center for Vocational and Technical Education and an associate professor at The Ohio State University.

LOWELL A. BURKETT
Executive Director
American Vocational Association

INTRODUCTION

Career Education, the third yearbook of the American Vocational Association, is a volume of contrasting and complementary ideas. It explains the foundations of career education, describes evolving career education concepts, recommends the development of programs and processes, relates efforts to develop operational and conceptual models, and presents the perspectives of a diverse group of people.

A carefully-chosen group of 34 authors independently developed the 31 chapters in the yearbook. The organization of the chapters into five parts is intended to help the reader explore and study some major facets of career education.

Part I focuses on the foundations of career education by exploring its evolving definition, tracing historical antecedents, analyzing the underlying value structures, describing the theoretical framework, and reviewing legislative aspects.

Part II treats career development in depth and provides descriptions of six related concepts. Career awareness, career exploration, and occupational preparation stages of career education are described from theoretical, developmental, or operational points of view. Concepts related to occupational clusters, career information, and career ladders and lattices are considered.

Part III provides direction for processes and programs that facilitate the conceptualization, development, and implementation of career education. Programs for personnel development, research and development, and information dissemination are recommended. Leadership and administrative processes needed to carry out the programs are explained.

Part IV gives attention to the school-based, employer-based, and home and community-based career education models under development. Description of local and state level implementation efforts provides both topical and fundamental information.

Part V shares the valuable perspective on career education of teacher, counselor, local director, principal, area vocational school superintendent, school district superintendent, university professor, university president, and labor specialist. The nature of career education requires that diverse groups have a part in shaping the program.

While most professional educators must concentrate on some aspect of education, career education should be thought of as a comprehensive approach to meeting the special needs of individuals at each stage of their career development. The evolving concept of career education offers a new and exciting opportunity to:

> Concentrate on the *development* of individuals, rather than on sorting and remediation,

Increase the *relevance* of learning, knowledge, and the educational enterprise,

Actualize *continuing, self-initiated education* by facilitating unpenalized reentry to the educational system,

Broaden and increase, rather than narrow, career options through well developed programs for awareness, exploration, and preparation,

Utilize home, community, and industry *resources* in the educational process, and

Provide youth and adults with the means to obtain satisfactory and satisfying *employment.*

The realization of these opportunities will require the commitment of many individuals. As the third yearbook goes to press, there is mounting evidence that career education is being accepted as a viable concept, developed in various forms, and implemented in the nation's schools. Where implemented, it is being favorably received by students, parents, and educators. As new career education curricula and related products are disseminated, personnel development programs modified, and further research and development conducted, the prospects for success improve.

The authors of the yearbook are among the leaders who will contribute to the further development of career education. Their splendid cooperation is recognized and it is hoped that the editor has been able to optimize their selfless contribution to the profession. Recognition also is due the legion of AVA members who reacted to tentative outlines of the yearbook and suggestions for authors.

J.H.M.

Columbus, Ohio
August 1973

CONTENTS

foundations for career education

*Definitions, History, Philosophy,
Theory, and Legislation*

Career education became a national priority during the early 1970s. It was a new concept for some. Others recognized it as the amalgamation of several powerful theoretical and philosophical ideas that had been under development for some time. Some of the foundations of the career education concept have undergirded vocational education and some of the earlier educational reform movements.

That the foundation is still being laid can be seen in the chapter by Hoyt who describes current effort to define the total career education concept. He analyzes current conceptual and operational definitions and identifies areas of consensus and disagreement. Special attention is given to the problems of validity for elements of the definitions.

Barlow contends that a principal framer of vocational education, U.S. Senator Carroll S. Page, identified many of the tenets of career education in a three-hour speech before the Senate 61 years ago.

Swanson analyzes the values served or the values employed to justify a career education emphasis. He maintains that such an emphasis requires institutional commitment and the expression of individual and institutional values.

Herr and Swails maintain that career education synthesizes elements and concepts that have been advocated during the past century. They trace the beginnings of career education in several theoretical approaches to vocational behavior and show how these approaches have been incorporated into present models.

Burkett reviews the legislative path from whence career education emerged and makes an appeal for adequate legislative support for the total concept.

These leaders recognize career education as the result of years of labor by many to make education meaningful and purposeful for all Americans. Each knows that the success of the movement will require an increased effort from all educators.

TOWARD A DEFINITION OF
CAREER EDUCATION

Kenneth B. Hoyt

Great growth in both vision and perspective is currently evident among those who profess to be definers of career education. Nowhere is such growth more easily demonstrated than in two 1971 statements made by former U.S. Office of Education Commissioner Sidney P. Marland, Jr.

In January 1971, Marland said:

> *All* education is career education, or should be. And *all* our efforts as educators must be bent on preparing students either to become properly, usefully employed immediately upon graduation from high school, or to go on to further formal education. Anything else is dangerous nonsense (Marland, 1971a, italics added).

By November 1971, Marland had changed considerably in his thinking, and in an interview with editors of *American Education,* he said:

> . . . what the term "career education" means to me is basically a point of view, a concept—a concept that says three things: first, that career education will be *part* of the curriculum for all students, not just some. Second, that it will continue throughout a youngster's stay in school, from the first grade through senior high and beyond, if he so elects. And third, that every student leaving school will possess the skills necessary to give him a start to making a livelihood for himself and his family, even if he leaves before completing high school (Marland, 1971b, italics added).

Obviously, great differences exist between a point of view that sees *all* education as career education and one that sees career education as *part* of the curriculum. Many current definitions of career education will be referred to here. Thus, it seems appropriate to begin with a reminder that some of the definers may have changed their minds before these words appear in print. Readers who wish to associate a particular definition with a particular individual are warned that they should look for his *latest* "definition." Career education truly is an *emerging* concept.

Hopefully, this chapter can contribute positively towards the emerging definition of career education through systematically reviewing some of its major dimensions. This can best be done through noting both those areas of apparent current consensus and those areas where basic disagreement appears to still be present. The goal of this chapter is to help the reader move towards developing a thoughtful definition of career education for himself or herself. No pretense will be made here that final consensus has been reached or that all now agree on a single definition of career education.

In September 1972, Dr. Sidney C. High, Jr., Chief, Exemplary

Programs Branch, U.S. Office of Education, attempted to collect, with the assistance of the various regional USOE offices, all of the official definitions of career education. He found 19 such "official" state definitions and has made them available for use in preparation of this chapter. These, with a variety of others found in the published literature liberally sprinkled with biases of the writer, form the basic background material for this chapter.

Two subtopics seem appropriate for use here: (a) definitions, and (b) components of career education. The first subtopic will be discussed by noting the extent to which consensus appears to have been reached and the extent to which disagreement appears to still be present. The second subtopic will present two alternative approaches to identifying components of career education.

DEFINITIONS OF CAREER EDUCATION

Definitions *do* make a difference in describing and delimiting the basic nature and purposes of any concept. While definitions have limited usefulness in helping one understand *how* a program is to operate, they are of central importance in specifying *what* the concept is intended to accomplish. The words that are used and the ways in which words are joined together combine to form the basic rationale and justification for the concept itself. Each of the following definitions represents an official statement on the part of some recognized educational agency and/or some authority in the field of career education. Some definers have used, in effect, several pages to state what they mean by career education. In such cases, an attempt has been made to use only what appear to be key words in the total statement. Where an agency or an individual has stated a definition in three sentences or less, the complete definition is given.

Definitions from State Educational Agencies

Arizona—In Arizona, we have defined career education as combining the academic world with the world of work. It must be available at all levels of education . . . Career education is not an add-on . . . it is a blending of the vocational, the general, and the college preparatory education . . . Synonymous with "all education," "career education" must become the term. When we say "education," we must mean "career education" (from a speech by Dr. Weldon P. Shofstall, State Superintendent of Public Instruction, November 1971).

California—Through . . . career education, each student will develop positive attitudes about himself and others, make sound decisions regarding alternative and changing careers, acquire skills leading to employment, and pursue a life style which provides self-fulfillment and contributes to the society in which he lives (from a statement of the California State Department of Education Career Education Task Force, May 4, 1972).

Maine—Career education . . . signifies a concerted effort to educate youth as early as kindergarten in exploring careers and acquiring the skills necessary for transition to a job. Career education is a melding of diverse curriculum efforts into a unified whole that requires the academic, vocational and guidance specialists to plan integrated learning events. In summary, it is a planned, sequential, orderly curriculum effort (from a state department of education bulletin entitled "Career Development in the Elementary Schools," September 1972).

Minnesota—Career education is an integral part of education. It provides purposefully planned and meaningfully taught experiences for all persons, which contribute to self-development as it relates to various career patterns. Career education takes place at . . . (all) . . . levels of education. Emphasis is placed on career awareness, orientation and exploration of the world of work, decision making relative to additional education, preparation for career proficiency . . . and understanding the interrelationships between a career and one's life style (adopted by State Board of Education, May 2, 1972).

Nevada—Career education is a comprehensive education program focused on careers and an educational process where people gain knowledge, attitudes, awareness, and skills necessary for success in the world of work (career success) (adopted by State Board of Education, July 1972).

New Hampshire—Career education is a concept of relevant and accountable education centered on the individual which provides the opportunities for educational experiences, curriculum, instructions and counseling leading to preparation for economic independence. The development of this concept is a lifelong process which involves a series of experiences, decisions and interactions that provide the means through which one's self-understanding can be implemented, both vocationally and avocationally (draft presented to State Board of Education for possible adoption, October 1972).

New Jersey—Career education is an integral dimension of the nursery through adult curriculum which provides for all students a sequential continuum of experiences through which each individual may develop a more realistic perception of his capabilities and prepare him for entry and re-entry into employment and/or continuing education (from "Answers to Five Basic Questions About Career Education" by Patrick Doherty, Director of Career Development, New Jersey State Department of Education).

North Dakota—Career education is an integral part of education. It is a concept that includes as its main thrust the preparation of all students for a successful life of work by increasing their options for occupational choice and attainment of job skills, and by enhancing learning achievement in all subject matter areas . . . a total effort of the home, school, and community to help all individuals become familiar with the values of a work-oriented society, to integrate these values in their lives in a way that work becomes useful, meaningful, and satisfying (from Dr. Larry Selland, Assistant State Director of Vocational Education, North Dakota State Department of Education).

Tennessee—Career education is all the learning experiences through which a student progresses in an educational program regardless of the length of the program . . . not an additional or separate phase of the educational program . . . a comprehensive, dynamic, programmatic, and integrative educational program . . . it must utilize the common and unique contributions of all educators and the resources of home, school, and community (prepared January 1972, by the state staff of Vocational-Technical Education, State Department of Education).

Texas—Career education is coordinated instruction, integrated into the entire curriculum, K-12, and designed to assist students in (a) understanding both the world of work and attitudes toward it; (b) understanding the relationships which exist between education and career opportunity; (c) understanding the economic and social structures of our society and how they influence the ways people support themselves; (d) making informed decisions concerning how they will earn a living and taking responsibility for making those decisions; and (e) acquiring marketable skills as preparation for earning a living (from Texas Education Agency, April 1972).

Utah—Career education is defined as a comprehensive, correlated educational system . . . focused on individual career needs . . . begins in grade one or earlier and continues through the adult years . . . is not separate and apart from total life education . . . calls for a united effort of the school and community to help all individuals become familiar, with the values of a work-oriented society; to integrate these values into their lives; and, to implement them in such a way that work becomes useful, meaningful, and satisfying (adopted by State Board of Education, May 12, 1972).

Washington—Career education is a term currently used to describe a sequentially developed education program offering career orientation, exploration, and job preparation for all students. Programs begin in the first grade, or earlier, and continue through adult life (publication of State Department of Education, 1972).

Wyoming—Career education is one of the key purposes of education. It is a concept through which we instill a sense of self-identity and self-awareness within each student. It is individualized and geared to the 168-hour living week, not just the 40-hour work week. This concept motivates children to want to learn and makes them capable of economically supporting themselves and their families (statement of Dr. Dean P. Talagan, Wyoming Department of Education).

Other Commonly Quoted Definitions

BAVTE, U.S. Office of Education—Career education is a comprehensive educational program focused on careers, which begins in Grade 1 or earlier and continues through the adult years (from "Career Education: A Model for Implementation," May 1971).

American Vocational Association—Career education is needed by and intended for all people. . . . It is a lifelong process which extends from early childhood through adulthood . . . based upon the premise that all honest work and purposeful study is respectable . . . provides the means by which the educational system can focus on career development . . . provides a unifying core for the total educational enterprise with intensive occupational preparation as a significant aspect . . . it will be necessary to utilize the common and unique contributions of all educators and the resources of home, school and community. . . . (from "Task Force Report on Career Education," AV JOURNAL, January 1972).

Keith Goldhammer and Robert E. Taylor—Specifically, career education is designed to capacitate individuals for their several life roles; economic, community, home, avocational, religious, and aesthetic. . . . Designed for all students, career education should be viewed as lifelong and pervasive. . . . Career education is a systematic attempt to *increase* the career options available to individuals and to facilitate more rational and valid career planning and preparation. Through a wide range of school and community-based resources, young people's career horizons should be broadened. Their self-awareness should be enhanced (in *Career Education: Perspective and Promise.* Columbus, Ohio: C. E. Merrill Publishing Company, 1972).

Rupert Evans—Career education is the total effort of the community to develop a personally satisfying succession of opportunities for service through work, paid or unpaid, extending throughout life (in *Career Education: What It Is and How to Do It.* Salt Lake City: Olympus Publishing Company, 1972).

Kenneth Hoyt—Career education is the total effort of public education and the community aimed at helping all individuals to become familiar with the values of a work-oriented society, to integrate these values into their personal value systems, and to implement these values into their lives in such a way that work becomes possible, meaningful, and satisfying to each individual (in *Career Education: What It Is and How to Do It.* Salt Lake City: Olympus Publishing Company, 1972).

Wesley Smith—Career education is a comprehensive, systematic and cohesive plan of learning organized in such a manner that youth at all grade levels in the public schools will have continuous and abundant opportunity to acquire useful information about the occupational structure of the economy, the alternatives of career choice, the obligations of individual and productive involvement in the total work force, the intelligent determination of personal capabilities and aspirations, the requisites of all occupations, and opportunities to prepare for gainful employment. . . . It is a priority objective of public education, with achievement measured by employability in occupations, both gainful and useful, that are a reasonable match of both talent and the ambition of every citizen (Director of Vocational Education, California State Department of Education).

John Coster—Career education has as its mission the attainment of an optimum level of work proficiency for each individual within the context of the social, individual, and work systems. Career education (1) facilitates the acquisition and processing and integration of information by the individual; (2) enhances the decision-making process; (3) provides the individual with salable skills to start his/her career; and, (4) provides for continuous recycling of information, decision making, and action through retraining and upgrading of skills (Director, Center for Occupational Education, North Carolina State University).

Those readers who are willing to study, compare, and think about this wide variety of definitions will discover that general consensus has been reached with respect to some concepts of definition. They will also discover that wide areas of disagreement are apparent. The following is intended to concentrate on both the areas of consensus and of disagreement in these definitions.

AREAS OF CONSENSUS

General consensus is still rare enough to be rather readily identifiable. Most definers seem to be in agreement that career education: (a) is a conscientious *effort,* not merely an attitude or point of view (The important thing here is that, as an effort, career education is going to take some time and cost some money.); (b) is a program that begins no later than grade one and continues through all of adult education; (c) is a program that is intended to serve all individuals rather than some special segment of the population; and (d) emphasizes education as preparation for work. On these four basic points of definition, there appears to be general consensus.

There also appears to be general consensus that vocational education, as we have known it, is but one of several important parts of career education. None of the above definitions specifically exclude vocational education from the definition of career education. Indeed, several make vocational education an explicit part of their total definition of career education. None of these definitions makes vocational education synonymous with career education.

Fairly general consensus seems to exist concerning the notion that career education is to be viewed only as part of education and that the term "career education" is not synonymous with the term "education." Further, among those who agree with this concept, there seems also to be general agreement that the substance of career education is to be integrated into the total educational program rather than "added on" as a new subject, curriculum, or separate body of knowledge to be assimilated by students.* The fact that no consensus exists regarding the kind or amount of substance associated with career education is beside the point here.

AREAS OF DISAGREEMENT

Three basic and serious areas of disagreement appear to be present among the definers of career education.

Primary Rationale for Career Education

The first concerns itself with the primary rationale behind emergence of the career education concept. The controversy here, stated in perhaps an oversimplified form, centers around whether the career education movement was born because of a need to restructure American education, because of a need to improve the quality of transition from school to employment, or because of a need to restore

---

* While it is natural to expect educators to feel that career education belongs in education, it is important to keep in mind that of the four career education models currently being funded by the National Institute of Education only one is a *school* based model. Further, those readers who believe this issue has already been settled are urged to study carefully plans now under development in the U.S. Department of Labor for career education. It is not at all settled yet whether or not career education represents a movement whose basic policies and actions will be centered within public education.

work as a vital and viable personal value among our citizens. Of all the areas of current disagreement, this one is, by far, the most basic and the most serious. It deserves and requires special discussion.

Some definers of career education place their primary definition emphasis around the need to restructure the patterns of educational experiences and opportunities available to students. Such persons emphasize the need to blend the academic, general education, and vocational education programs of American education in ways that provide a completely integrated pattern of educational opportunities from which students can choose. They seem intent on doing away with the fallacious notion that some high school students (those in the college preparatory curriculum) are working toward college entrance, some (those in vocational education) are preparing for work, and that others (those in general education) are working toward obtaining a diploma. Instead, they wish to see *education as preparation for work* become an important goal of all who teach and of all who learn. While this is a concept that would have the enthusiastic support of almost all definers of career education, there are many who would disagree that this forms the basic rationale for career education.

Other definers have oriented their rationale for career education around the need to help those who leave our educational system, at any level, to find paid employment that is satisfying to the individual and beneficial to society. Such persons base much of their efforts to implement career education programs around current national, state, and local statistics related to employment, unemployment, and underemployment of youth and adults in our society. Recognizing that, in a post-industrial society such as ours, the relationships between education and employment become closer and closer each year, they plead for career education as a means of helping students plan and prepare for, enter, and progress in the occupational society. For such individuals, paid jobs for all who leave the educational system is the "pot of gold" at the end of the career education "rainbow." Again, few would disagree with the desirability of such a goal. However, several of the definers of career education would disagree that this goal forms the basic rationale for career education.

Still others have formulated their definitions around a basic rationale that emphasizes the need to make work possible, meaningful, and satisfying to each individual. To them, distinctions between "work" and "making a living" are of basic importance. Whether work is paid or unpaid is not nearly so important as whether it is personally meaningful to the individual and beneficial to society. To such individuals, the concept of *productivity* is central to a meaningful definition of "work." It is the need to restore the personal meaning and meaningfulness of work to the individual citizen that these persons see as the basic, underlying rationale for the career education movement. They would see both the need to restructure American education and the need to reduce unemployment and alleviate under-employment as a means to the end of helping each individual discover and internalize a set of work values as a vital and viable part of his or her total personal value structure.

The first basic disagreement is currently very strong and pervasive. Until and unless it can be resolved, we will continue to find the case for career education, and so the nature of career education itself, made in quite different ways. It is an area of disagreement deserving of careful thought.

Long-range Goals

The second basic area of disagreement is found in perceptions of the long-range goals of career education. This area, too, is of basic importance in that it implies criteria appropriate for use in evaluating the results of career education. It can be seen by those who study the definitions of career education presented here that some would effec-tively limit the long-range goals of career education to post-educa-tional job experiences of former students. For these persons, the long-run effectiveness of career education can be evaluated by such criteria as the appropriateness of career decisions, the proportion of former students in training-related employment, the relative success of former students in their chosen occupations, and the relative degree of satisfaction these persons find in their jobs. Few, if any, of the definers of career education would argue about the necessity for applying such criteria in evaluating career education. At the same time, many would argue that because such criteria are *necessary,* this in no way means they are sufficient for use in evaluating effects of the total career education effort.

Careful study of the definitions presented earlier will reveal in-dividuals' use of such terms as "total life style," "self development," "total life education," "economic, community, home, avocational, religious, and aesthetic life roles," and "enhancement of the decision-making process." Such perceptions of the career education mission go far beyond either concern for helping school leavers find jobs or an emphasis on work values as part of one's total personal value system. Those arguing for a broad-based definition of career education have available almost all the criteria that could be used to evaluate the total educational program. While few are unaware that a career education effort holds potential for influencing many aspects of an individual's life, many are worried about the potential danger of presenting the concept so broadly that it is difficult to distinguish "career education" from "education" itself. Those having this concern contend that career education is big enough and important enough to have a finite set of goals and criteria for evaluation that makes it clear career education is but one of a large number of worthy goals for the total educational system.

Definers of career education who see the goals of career education directed toward making work possible, meaningful, and satisfying to all individuals would apply still another set of criteria in evaluating the career education effort. They offer the three key words, "possible," "meaningful," and "satisfying." When other words are applied to a concept that allows work to be either paid or unpaid in nature, these key words take on additional meaning. While endorsing and supporting all of the evaluative criteria proposed by those who see paid jobs as the end point of career education, these definers extend the concept to include criteria used in evaluating the efficacy of work for volunteers, for full-time homemakers, for those on welfare, and for those retired from paid employment. In addition, they would place great emphasis on criteria related to the development and internalization of various kinds of work values that can bring meaning and meaningfulness to the individual. They are concerned about ways in which a person can increase his feelings of self-worth, self-identity, and accomplishments through work he performs—whether or not that work is in the form of a paid job. Finally, such definers of career education are concerned about conditions of the work setting that affect worker satisfaction and would value criteria appropriate to this aspect of career education. In short, they would limit evaluative criteria to those demonstrably related to the concept of work. In this sense, their criteria would be broader than those concerned only with paid employment, but considerably more narrow than those concerned with such concepts as "religious and aesthetic life roles."

School or School, Home, Community

The third basic area of disagreement concerns itself with whether career education should be pictured as an effort of the schools alone or whether it should involve the home and community as well. Seven of the 21 definitions of career education presented earlier specifically include the home and community in their statements of definition. Of those remaining, nine appear to define career education as an effort of the schools alone while five definitions are unclear as to whether or not the home and community will be involved. This is a serious area of disagreement because it speaks to both the scope and locus of control of career education. As with the preceding two areas of basic disagreement, there appear to be three divergent positions emerging. Some individuals define career education as an effort controlled and existing only within the system of public education.

Others picture it involving the occupational community and the home, but with control and direction resting within the educational structure. Still other definers are viewing both the home and the broader community as active *participants* in career education with public education as just one of several agencies involved. Who will determine the goals of career education? Who will control it? Who will direct its efforts? Where will career education take place? Who will pay for it? These are only some of the key questions to ask with reference to this area of basic disagreement.

There is little doubt but that these three areas of basic disagreement do exist among the definers of career education. If all current definers could gather in a single place to discuss these areas of apparent disagreement, considerable progress could probably be made towards arriving at a greater degree of consensus. The areas of disagreement are probably not as sharp as they have been presented here. No single definition of career education can be said to be lacking in wisdom or in thoughtful consideration. Wide divergence in definitions of career education can help career education grow and gain in strength by virtue of attempts on the part of the definers to convince others of the validity of their particular point of view.

COMPONENTS OF CAREER EDUCATION

Career education will continue to be operationally defined through the activities of institutions purporting to operate career education programs. How is a school system to know if it has a comprehensive career education program? Answers to this question are currently appearing in a variety of forms and from a variety of perspectives. In hopes that further clarification of the meaning of career education can be obtained, two divergent means of answering this question are presented.

One comprehensive approach to this question is found in the Comprehensive Career Education Model (CCEM) under development at The Center for Vocational and Technical Education at The Ohio State University. The project staff has identified eight broad elements and terminal characteristics which, taken together, serve as one operational means of defining career education. The complete model involves 32 subordinate themes, 1,500 goals, and 3,000 general performance objectives associated with eight elements. This is perhaps the most comprehensive operational definition of career education yet developed. The eight broad elements and terminal characteristics are to be found in the chapter, "The School-Based Comprehensive Career Education Model," by Aaron J. Miller elsewhere in this yearbook. An outline of these eight elements is found in a recent publication by Keller (1972) entitled *Career Education In-Service Training Guide.*

CCEM provides a viable way of defining career education through expected student outcomes that have been stated in behavioral terms. A model such as this does not speak to *how* these outcomes are to be attained or *who* is responsible for their attainment. This does not detract at all from the viability of these eight career education elements. CCEM has made a valuable contribution to the definitional debate.

A second significant contribution to defining career education programs in operational terms is found in a paper presented by Duane J. Mattheis (1972), Deputy Commissioner for School Systems, U.S. Office of Education, to a statewide conference on career education called by the Oklahoma State Department of Education. In his paper, Mattheis presented a set of 11 operational objectives for career education recently set forth by the U.S. Office of Education. Both because of their usefulness in providing an operational definition and because these objectives provide clues to ways in which some of the arguments regarding the definition of career education have apparently been resolved by USOE (at least for the moment), these objectives are presented here. They include:

1. Provide students with a more unifying, relevant curriculum; infuse academic and general curriculum course offerings with career relevance; end channeling of students into tracks.

2. Provide educational experiences to give students increasing knowledge of occupational alternatives and the world of work. This experience should begin in elementary school and continue as long as needed.

3. Provide nonacademic career options (at secondary, postsecondary, and adult levels) which have equal status with academic career options. The unfairly discriminating distinctions between the academic track and the vocational track must be eliminated.

4. Provide students with a comprehensive and flexible program of career-qualifying opportunities—one that will allow students to progress at their own pace and yet will not lock them into a particular track. It should increase the options available at the secondary and postsecondary levels through greater breadth of course offerings, more meaningful content (jobs with a future), and availability of different types of learning modes.

5. Provide for greater involvement of employers in the educational experience of all students. Employers can make an important contribution through work-study and cooperative education programs, involvement in occupational guidance, career orientation, and placement activities, and in employer conducted alternatives to the "in school house" education.

6. Provide students with career counseling that begins early in the educational program and follows through to job placement or further education. While the system should be built on the principle of maximizing individual choice, students should be provided with options that are realistically related to labor market conditions. A job placement function should be located in the schools.

7. Provide opportunity for counseling, for re-entry, and retraining for those who have exited the system—both for those who have failed to gain employment and for those in the world of work. Individuals whose skills are no longer marketable, those in dead-end jobs, and those who want a career change for personal happiness should be able to re-enter the system.

8. Provide graduates from the secondary level and each level there-after with either the skills to enter the world of work or to embark on additional education. Many career options will require education beyond the secondary level, and the system should provide this experience. The criterion should be that at the exit point for each career option the student is qualified to enter that career.

9. Provide students with some notion of what is wrong with the world of work, particularly the way jobs are structured. Simply preparing students to accept the occupational system is insufficient.

10. Provide the consumers of career education with a role in its design and implementation. If individuals are to gain greater self autonomy and control over their destinies, it is important they be involved in the planning and development of career education.

11. Provide students with credentials that overcome discriminating distinctions both in school and in the society at large. Give credits for vocational courses that are of equal value to those given for college preparatory courses. For those whose work performance qualifies them, give credentials of competitive value for educational or career options. This will require an active role in seeking to change the credentialing procedures for entry into the world of work.

It will be noted that each of these USOE operational goals for career education begin with the word "provide." It is clear that this view of career education is one that will require time, effort, and funds. It is a very long way from earlier USOE statements that referred to career education as an "attitude" or a "point of view." School systems that wonder whether or not they are offering a comprehensive program of career education would do well to view their efforts in light of these 11 basic operational goals for career education (Mattheis, 1972).

VALIDITY OF DEFINITIONS

So long as one limits oneself to the task of conceptualizing, any definition of career education can be considered "valid." However, when people attempt to convert a given concept into an operational program of action, "validity" is determined by how well the action program works. This chapter would be incomplete were the problem of validity of definitions ignored.

There is little doubt that those who are defining career education in terms of needed, basic changes in the K-12 system of public education could demonstrate the validity of their definition through operational program results. The two basic claims being made by these definers are that a career education emphasis will (a) make school more enjoyable and meaningful to both students and teachers, and (b) result in increases in pupil achievement. We know enough about educational motivation, about curricular methodology, and about worker satisfaction so that both of these claims could be readily validated through action program results.

This is not to say that it would be easy nor that these claims could be validated by the embryonic career education programs now in existence. If these claims are to be validated, major curricular and school organizational changes must be made—including initiation of an open entry/open exit system of education, performance evaluation, the year round school, expanded career guidance programs, and changes in teacher certification requirements. Moreover, major changes in classroom teaching procedures, incorporating teacher and student ingenuity and creativity, would have to take place. All of these things could be done if the needed investments of time, effort, and money were to be committed.

A more serious problem of validity must be faced by those definers who emphasize career education as a concept through which each student leaving school will either be prepared to (a) find gainful employment, or (b) continue his education. As of today, many persons still leave the secondary schools and can find neither a paid job nor the funds required to continue their education. So long as this situation continues, the operational validity of this concept of career education is open to serious question.

The career education concept can be validated only if massive changes take place. One such needed change will be a great expansion of vocational education at both the secondary and post-secondary school levels. Present vocational education programs, even though staffed by persons with unusually high dedication and commitment, are simply inadequate in size and scope to serve all persons who need vocational education. A second required change will involve major revisions in child labor and minimum wage laws. These laws are currently preventing employers from creating jobs that could appropriately be entered by persons of secondary school age. A third, and related, change will be the creation of comprehensive financial aid programs so that any person who desires to prepare himself for work at the post high school level will be able to do so. Unless these kinds of changes come about, the operational validity of career education must be seriously questioned.

The most serious problems of operational validity are faced by those definers, including the author, who conceptualize the goals of career education as ones of making work possible, meaningful, and satisfying to each individual. For this concept to be validated by action programs, it will be necessary for vocational education to be expanded, and laws to be changed. In addition, basic changes will be required in the work setting itself. The basic causes of worker alienation and worker satisfaction have been studied and researched for many years. There has been a tacit assumption, and some evidence, that a positive relationship exists between worker satisfaction and productivity in the work place. Yet, the work place, for many employed persons, continues to lack those ingredients that would cause work to be personally meaningful and satisfying. It is fruitless to picture work as a *pleasure* to students as long as it continues to be regarded as a *punishment* by many workers. To continue this would simply invalidate this concept of career education.

The basic problem to be resolved is one of making workers happier with their work while maintaining the basic and essential discipline of the work place. It will not be easy to give the individual worker more autonomy while simultaneously retaining the concept that every worker has a "boss." Again, therein resides a problem that is capable of solution but one that does not, as yet, appear to be solved.

Those who formulate conceptual definitions of career education cannot avoid responsibility for considering how their concepts can be translated into action programs. Conceptual definitions are essential because one cannot efficiently reach a destination unless he knows where he is trying to go. At the same time, those who chart the road to success for career education must include, in their "road map," some indication of obstacles to be overcome along the way. Unless this is done, career education will be a dream that is not realized.

CONCLUDING REMARKS

The definition debate concerning career education is well underway. Here, an attempt has been made to provide the reader with selected examples of career education definitions that have been officially adopted by some state agency, professional organization, the U.S. Office of Education, or by recognized leaders in the career education movement. An attempt was made to provide a brief discussion of basic areas of apparent consensus and continuing disagreement found among those who have attempted to define "career education." Two contrasting approaches to defining career education in more operational terms were presented. Finally, questions were raised regarding the validity of various career education concepts. It is hoped that this diversity in approaching the problem of definition may be helpful to those seeking to understand the meaning of career education.

In the long run, of course, "career education," like any other educational concept, will be defined by individual school systems and communities across the nation. Several hundred such local units have already completed initial versions of this definition task for them-selves. Had space and resources been available, these are the defini-tions that would have formed the substance of this chapter. The real leadership in the career education movement has come from those local communities throughout the country that have undertaken to define career education in terms of action programs they run. It is hoped that this chapter may help communities move forward in con-tinuing attempts to bring meaning and meaningfulness to the career education movement. It is in the communities where the "action" is, and where it should be.

REFERENCES

Goldhammer, Keith; and Taylor, Robert E. *Career Education: Perspective and Promise.* (Columbus, Ohio: Charles E. Merrill Publishing Company, 1972)

Hoyt, K.; Evans, R.; Mackin, E.; and Mangum, G. *Career Education: What It Is and How to Do It.* (Salt Lake City: Olympus Publishing Company, 1972)

Keller, Louise J. *Career Education In-Service Training Guide.* (Morristown, New Jersey: General Learning Corporation, 1972)

Marland, Sidney P., Jr. "Career Education Now." Speech delivered before the Convention of the National Association of Secondary School Principals, Houston, Texas, January 23, 1971a.

————. "Marland on Career Education," *American Education,* VII, (Novem-ber, 1971b).

Mattheis, Duane J. "Career Education—What It Is and What It Seeks to Accomplish." Speech presented at a statewide conference on career edu-cation called by the Oklahoma State Department of Education, Central State University, Edmond, Oklahoma, September 20, 1972.

HISTORICAL ANTECEDENTS TO CAREER EDUCATION

Melvin L. Barlow

PROLOGUE

It is my firm belief that the founders of the vocational education movement were so thorough in their analysis of America's needs that in effect they defined the principles of vocational education—principles that are as valid today as they were then.

One day of that early period has captured my attention—that day was June 5, 1912, when Senator Carroll S. Page (Vermont) laid before the United States Senate his bill on vocational education. The quotations that follow are taken from the *Congressional Record* (U.S. Congress, 1912). The essence of the career concept is found in these quotations.

BACKGROUND FOR LEGISLATION

Senator Page's bill addressed itself to a great public question that involved the welfare of boys, girls, mature vocational workers, and homemakers "as has no other [bill] which has been before the Congress for more than half a century." The answer to this question would "settle in a great measure the quality of our citizenship in the generation upon which we are now entering." The intent of this vocational education bill was to "broaden out our school system by the addition of education for the basic vocations on the farm, in the shop, and in the home."

Fifty years earlier, in 1862, the Morrill Act had provided a beginning of vocational education at the college level by establishing agricultural and mechanical colleges. Subsequently, in 1887, 1890, and 1906, other acts of Congress had aided the college level program substantially. But only 1.7 percent of the total school population were in college, 5.3 percent were in secondary school, and 93 percent were in elementary school through the eighth grade. "That something is very badly needed to supplement the Morrill bill is universally conceded," Page pointed out to the Senate.

That "something" was a vocational education bill designed to provide a larger percentage of eighth grade graduates with reasons for continuing high school, and to add a new purpose to their education.

PAGE'S NATIONAL STUDY

Senator Page had introduced his bill in the Senate on April 6, 1911, and the bill was referred to the Committee on Agriculture and Forestry. Toward the end of the legislative session (prior to August

22, 1911), the Committee considered the Page bill and in general gave its approval, but asked Page, "as a subcommittee of one," to correspond with prominent people throughout the United States about provisions of the bill and to rewrite the bill accordingly.

Page wrote to every superintendent of public instruction, to prominent educators, to governors, to labor leaders, to representatives of business, industry, agriculture, and to many other persons. The response was an overwhelming endorsement of the idea of his bill and replies were received from every state in the nation. When Senator Page made his presentation in the Senate on June 5, 1912, he included in his remarks the endorsements received in favor of the bill, some of which were as follows:

> The very root of the matter is reached through our schools. If teachers are competent and enthusiastic in such work, they have an opportunity to arouse an interest in the homes of grammar school pupils, which represent the great mass of the pupils of our public-school system. . . .

> The practical value of agricultural courses in high schools is apparent, and if our agricultural colleges are to do work of the highest quality and breadth, they should be supplemented by such preparatory courses in the high schools. . . .

> This measure specifically recognizes the most important duty that rests upon the nation as well as upon the individual, community, and state, the duty of training for citizenship through public schools. . . .

> The people throughout this state are thoroughly alive to the benefit to be derived from aid of this sort, and they are watching the acts of their representatives with a great deal of interest to see that every effort is put forth for the passage of this bill, which seems to us to be best adapted to our needs at the present time. . . .

> It will inevitably raise the standard of living of the masses through instruction in the use of resources. . . .

> The nation-wide movement now on foot for correcting this evil [the curriculum in the high school] is what I have been hoping for all of my life, and I welcome most warmly the initiative taken by you in giving national aid to this important subject provided the states will do so themselves. . . .

> I do not know of anything that the United States Congress could do that would so directly aid in the development of the general intelligence of the people through an educational process as the passage and carrying into effect properly this bill. Education for efficiency must, first, train an individual to earn a living to secure and own a home; second, to be of service to others in making life better and richer; and, third, in having an abiding interest in the development of our institutional life, as the home, the school, and the state. These mark the efficiency of the school system. Our school system has not been such as to attain these ends. It seems to me this bill will lead more directly to it than any other means apparent at the present time. . . .

> The need of greatly extended opportunities for vocational education is felt by nearly everyone who is connected with the schools. It seems to me that the matter is of great importance to the country at large. . . .

After considerable study of the subject, with particular attention to Germany, which is far ahead of other countries in training for the industries, I am forced to the conclusion that a satisfactory system of industrial education in this country must include a working over of the elementary school curriculum in such a way as to make the industrial activities of the community the vitalizing factor in it. . . .

I am in favor of working out further the idea of introducing vocational subjects into the curriculum of the schools. People are beginning to realize that boys and girls must be taught to earn a living and that they can not spend their entire time in studying so-called classical subjects. All children must be educated for their ethical side and must be taught about the higher things of life, but they must also be taught that they must support themselves and be given lessons in how to earn money. Our schools should be well balanced, with both these ideas kept well to the front. . . .

Too many boys are being turned loose in the world to live in a makeshift way; turned loose without any one desirable thing having been well enough learned to make a living at it. . . .

It is the best bill yet offered having for its purpose the training of the sadly neglected masses. It is socially and economically sound. Congressional action is necessary to draw out backward states. . . .

Too long has our educational system been at fault in that it did not prepare our boys and girls for useful citizenship. We need to educate them for the farm and the trades rather than away from them. . . .

You are right in believing that the people are demanding vocational education, and I will believe that it will be a mistake for their representatives in Congress to neglect this demand. . . .

The public school system of America is lamentably weak in failing to make provision for this kind of education. The United States cannot hope to hold a leading place among the industrial nations without the training of young men for efficient service in industrial work. . . .

In every village, town, and city there are many young people to whom the public schools are distasteful because they do not offer work that is of vital interest in fighting the battle for bread. . . .

Education to serve the highest purposes of the republic, must keep very close to the life of the people. When an educational institution is out of touch with the life of the community in which it exists, its days are numbered. . . .

I approve most heartily of any effort tending to advance the practical and vocational studies. . . .

I should not want any reflection made upon the old idea of education —the study of the classics and mathematics—but I quite agree with you that wider educational opportunity should be offered in elementary education. . . .

Our schools do not now meet the needs of society. The tendency is now, and has ever been, to place emphasis upon the so-called art studies at the expense of industrial training. This is forcing thousands of bright boys and girls out of school annually. They become impatient to become breadwinners, because they recognize that the average high school or college course does not qualify them for a competence. . . .

Page received hundreds of replies ranging from a simple, "I approve," to many pages of rationale concerning either the total bill or specific provisions within. The replies provided the resource needed to revise the bill so it would fit a variety of school conditions and state organizations for education. In short, Page had received a mandate to move ahead with all possible speed to secure passage of the bill.

CAREER ELEMENTS IN
THE NATIONAL STUDY

Although the term *career education* was not used in the Senate discussions in 1912, elements of the career motif were present in the Senate's rationale.

The Elementary School

For the most part, schooling for the masses in 1912 consisted of completion of the eighth grade or attempts to complete the eighth grade. The dropout rate was appalling—few young people continued their education beyond grade eight and many not that far. ". . . a vast army . . . leave the school discredited, unsuccessful, aimless, most of them having gotten no further than the sixth grade." They had learned little beyond the three R's. "They had been, in a way, schooled early in how to fail."

The junior high school had been invented, but its impact upon education was scarcely noticeable. The concern expressed in the Senate was about the plight of elementary school graduates being projected upon society unable to compete on the basis of their full talents, which the school had not in any way helped the student to discover.

In effect, the elementary school was the transition point from school to social life. The appeal to the Senate on June 5, 1912, strongly emphasized education's responsibility for the student's future life as a producer of goods and services that society needed and wanted.

The critical posture of the Senate in relation to the elementary school was unquestionably also a critical posture toward the society that allowed such conditions to exist. Somewhere within the early schooling of the individual, some job intent must be developed for youth. This is largely the essence of the career awareness emphasis for the elementary school in contemporary programs of career education, providing, of course, that one takes into account the extended nature of schooling today. What was said in 1912 about the elementary school is being said in the 1970s about the high school.

Vocational Guidance

Inherent in the vocational education theory was the idea that the school should help students "find themselves" in relation to their occupational future; and this was to be done "before compulsory education ceases." Hence, the strong push for action in grades seven and eight.

A few schools had tried to integrate elements of vocational guidance into the educational experience of students, but most had not. Meyer Bloomfield, Director of the Boston Vocation Bureau, expressed the situation as follows:

> The rediscovery of the child in school and shop has become the task of our agents. Too long have children been living and learning and working together as fractions of selves. Personality is subordinated to system. Excessive organization is stifling child energies struggling for self-expression. Vocational guidance looks to the whole child, to its past, present, and future. Through its efficacious interest and cooperating agencies it demands the utmost investment of all that a child is and may become (U.S. Congress, 1912).

Senator Page was impressed by vocational guidance and the opportunities it offered to boys and girls, and was convinced that the schools were the best means of providing this guidance. The scope of vocational guidance was broad and later would incorporate the opportunity to explore, to select, to prepare for, and to enter the occupation of a person's choice; in short, to find the job for which a student was best fitted.

Society and Educational Need

Page was sensitive to the "widening gulf" between capital and labor and reported the summary observations of social experts as follows:

> The old vertical lines of social division—by income, profession, and family—are gone. The new line is horizontal. Above it are all those who live by dividends and below it are all those who live by labor. Already it is more than a line—it is a crack, a cleavage. And I tell you that unless that cleavage is bridged in the next 10 years it never will be bridged in our time.

This was not a threat, but rather a statement of fact. Page wanted to reach below the horizontal line and give an educational hand (through vocational education) to those who were denied the right to a proper transition from school to work.

> I am ready to give the benefit of the doubt to the cause of the sons of the men who toil, even though the expense of doing so to the Federal Government might be even more than 15 cents per capita per annum of our population, the amount called for by this bill. [Note: The appropriation recommended by the Page bill was $14,752,000, roughly twice the appropriation of the Smith-Hughes bill, five years later.]

The costs to society for various aspects of education were compared. Senator Page disclosed that splendid care was given to those in college, somewhat reasonable care to those in high school, but "we are not doing our duty to the other 93 percent." The costs quoted as the social investment in education were: for students in the elementary schools, $22 per capita; for those in high schools, $45 per capita; and for college students, $280 per capita.

> Practically all of these boys who are in the 93 percent class are today deprived of any kind of vocational or industrial training. And because of this fact they are swelling the ranks of our outcasts and criminals and filling our jails and asylums with the flotsam and jetsam of our social life. They form the very scum which rises to the top of the great seething caldron of uneducated humanity and is forming that uncontrollable element which is the natural outgrowth of the injustice which is today being practiced on the sons of our toiling millions in the matter of withholding from them a decent measure of vocational and industrial training.

> Mr. President, there is no truer saying than that talent should lay its tribute upon the altar of human need. If there is any human need demanding tribute from the best talent of this Senate more than the need of the average American boy, I do not know where it is.

Society was not providing properly for the educational need of the masses; evidence of the inequality of opportunity was overpowering. The Senate had before it a social condition to reckon with, not a theory. Senator Page concluded this section of his remarks to the Senate with strong convictions.

> If our citizens in the generation ahead of us are not able to earn a decent livelihood and give their children such an education as will equip them to run the race of life with a fair measure of success, it will be impossible to convince them that they are receiving that equality of opportunity to which they are entitled and without which they can not be loyal citizens.

Community Resources

In one way or another, the great ideas in education have fostered concepts of student-community involvement. In career education, conscious effort is directed toward the advantages of utilization of the "real world" in the education of the individual. The essential element is to take the classroom to the community, or bring the community to the classroom, in such a way as to reinforce schooling and living in the social order.

So, when Senator Page made his survey, he turned to the outside world for support. Page was trying to get support from the community at large in efforts to add vocational subjects to the curriculum, which in 1912 was almost totally devoid of such subject matter.

Samuel Gompers, of the American Federation of Labor, responded to the need for vocational education, saying, "The prosperity of a nation depends upon its industrial and commercial success, and in respect to this success depends upon the training and intelligence of its citizens. It is plainly evident that a national educational system determines its destiny." Continuing his remarks about the youth who leave school, Gompers said:

> They seek employment largely in unskilled industries because they are fitted for nothing better . . . the prospects of emergence from unskilled to skilled industries is so small, [and] is attracting attention to the problem and demanding solution (U.S. Congress, 1912).

H. E. Miles, of the National Association of Manufacturers, hailed the movement toward vocational education as imperative. "The need of industrial education is coming to be seen in all quarters, and the movement has a tremendous impetus." (Vocational education was one of the few matters the American Federation of Labor and the National Association of Manufacturers could agree upon in 1912.)

Many other examples emerged from Page's testimony before the Senate, emphasizing the strong support existing among the agricultural, business, and industrial community for the addition of vocational education to the curriculum. Furthermore, that support pledged the readiness of these communities to help the schools in their efforts to make the elements of instruction more appropriate. In a sense, what emerged from the survey was that while industry alone, or the schools alone, could do a good job of vocational preparation, it was only by combining the two that the best job could be provided. Years later, the union of the school and the community was to become a hallmark of quality in vocational education. The essence of community involvement in the career education program of the 1970s does indeed have deep historical roots.

Educational Criticism

Criticism of education in 1912, in relation to the lack of vocational education, reads much like the criticism of the 1970s, in relation to the lack of career education. Senator Page was deeply concerned about such criticism because he visualized the great need for vocational education (the career preparation stage of career education), and at the same time was aware of educational gains in general. It was a fact that illiteracy had been reduced by 39 percent during the first decade of the twentieth century. Page repeatedly apologized to the Senate about the nature of the criticism.

> But I submit, not as a criticism but as a suggestion for the consideration of the Senate, that there is something wrong in a school system which drives the average boy away from school life at the very time when he should be just beginning to realize the great importance of education. It is absolutely futile to argue that it is the boy's own fault. If there is any criticism to offer upon our system of education it is that the curriculum repels rather than attracts the average boy, and worse still, the father of the average boy.

Senator Page quoted many letters from business, industry, and education concerning the failures of education. In his view, vocational education must include, and contribute to, "a general cultural education." The foundations of education—reading, writing, and arithmetic—must be strongly developed for each student; otherwise he would not be able to perform the skills needed in work and would not possess the basic knowledge required of a successful worker. Page cited data which indicated that when skilled workmen attended evening vocational schools they enhanced their capacity to improve their earnings.

> Let me repeat that the average so-called skilled mechanic received from fifteen to twenty-five dollars per week, while these graduates from the . . . school averaged $66 per week, thus showing that the men who were sufficiently enterprising and ambitious to take the training at this school rose to positions as managers, foremen, and overseers.

Page was convinced that the vocational preparation of the youth of the nation was a school responsibility; he made reference to those persons working below their capacity (due to the lack of preparation for work) as idlers.

> We must convert the idlers of this nation into producers; and, in my judgment, we may do so if we will take the hundreds of thousands of boys, now almost running wild in our larger cities, and, by industrial education, by instruction along the lines of the trades and industries, and by finding them places to labor, turn them from vicious paths into self-respecting, self-supporting, contented producers.

An area of education referred to as domestic science or home economics had gained a small foothold in the public school curriculum. Page had developed a conviction that this area of education needed to be enlarged and it was natural that it should accompany the general proposal for vocational education.

> Mr. President, thousands of homes are wrecked, tens of thousands of lives ruined, and hundreds of thousands are made unhappy because the home-keepers of our country have no training in that greatest of all professions, the profession of homemaking and motherhood. All must live in some sort of a home, for everyone finds his chief happiness there. Character is developed there. No great advance, spiritual or mental, is possible which does not begin with the home. The home-makers of America have the making of a nation.

Page's nationwide study was thorough and did much to pinpoint areas of educational need—areas that could be improved by adding programs of study with vocational significance. Entirely too many students were leaving school unprepared for the work society required of them. The problem, as presented in Page's testimony, was clearly an educational one requiring high priority.

Adult Instruction

It is interesting to note the parallels between the career education concept of lifelong learning and Page's point of view regarding adult instruction. In case after case, Page cited the values of vocational instruction for adults. Increased earnings for workers was consistently a result, as was the opportunity to move into higher positions. Repeatedly, Page talked about the opportunity afforded adults to "make up" for the "failures" of early schooling. Adult programs in vocational education provided many opportunities for women and for the development of citizenship among the population as a whole. "It will inevitably raise the standard of living for the masses," Page insisted.

America was rapidly becoming an industrialized nation, creating a need for adult learning far beyond any previous need. However, despite the need of specific groups for vocational education, an element of totality appeared in the thinking of the promoters of vocational education. As early as 1908, the idea that vocational education services were independent of restrictions concerning race, creed, color, sex, or national origin had been firmly established. In fact, the words in the *Vocational Education Amendments of 1968* that vocational education is for "all persons of all ages in all communities" found their origin in this early historical period. Page pointed out to the Senate that "the movement for vocational education is not confined to any one section, nor to any class of people, but has taken deep hold upon our agricultural, our commercial, and our manufacturing population." In this plea for totality is strong evidence for including the most forgotten person of the time—the working adult.

EPILOGUE

The antecedents to career education reach deep into the historical past—the Hebrews, circa 64 A.D., for example, had well defined laws relating to career preparation. Many other examples abound throughout early history.

This analysis of the antecedents to career education is limited to a three-hour speech in the United States Senate by Senator Carroll S. Page of Vermont in 1912, for two reasons. First, few people seem to be aware of this rich resource material and, consequently, its values have been largely unsung. Second, the principles of education involved in Page's speech are directly related to principles of career education. Although Page did not refer to career education in the terminology of today, the intent of his rationale for vocational education bears a striking resemblance to elements of career education. The following concepts in career education are listed as they relate to his testimony:

Career education has strong social and economic value;

Education can be improved by attention to the future work responsibilities of youth;

Most of the youth in school are shortchanged in vocational preparation;

Career awareness, exploration, and preparation must be provided;

Career education is generally more acceptable to business, industry, agriculture, and the public at large than to educators;

Career education has a strong citizenship component;

The place to begin career education is in the elementary school;

Vocational guidance over a prolonged period is imperative;

Earning potential is increased;

The community is the laboratory of career education;

Career education is needed to maintain pace with economic and technological needs;

Career education is a lifelong process.

REFERENCE

U.S., *Congressional Record,* 62nd. Cong., 2nd. Sess., 1912, XLVIII, 7662-7669.

PHILOSOPHICAL BASES FOR CAREER EDUCATION

Gordon I. Swanson

Anyone who purports to educate is eventually involved in justifying his action, and any justification becomes philosophical. This is true to the degree that the standards for justifying any educational program are ultimately in a philosophical domain. Philosophy may refer to an academic discipline that is concerned with the logical behavior and meaning of knowledge. It may also refer to a set of beliefs or values held by individuals for guiding and justifying their behavior or that of institutions. Such beliefs and values may be held by persons who are not necessarily aware that they have them; they emerge, nevertheless, when actions or patterns of action are in need of justification.

Social anthropologists have urged us to distinguish between the ideal values of a culture, as enunciated by its teachers, clergymen and lawmakers, and the actual values exemplified in people's daily behavior. They have alerted us, for example, to the considerable gap between the ideal values of a nominally Christian culture and the way that people actually behave. With a little effort, it is possible to identify the largely unformulated but consensually validated rules that govern everyday living. While truthfulness, honesty, altruism and equality rank high among our ideal values, a stranger to our culture would soon note that dominant motives also embrace values that justify acquisition, personal ambition, and almost any rationalization for an interpretation of the survival of the fittest.

These baser motives may not be openly admitted but they are shown clearly in the orientation and expression of advertising, the problems in merchandise labeling, the way people spend their time and money, and in the purpose and content of the educational system. The educational system is, after all, geared to perpetuate the main features of the social structure including its differentials in income, occupation and in education itself.

Education, in particular, is a value-oriented activity. For society and for individuals, it involves choices among many alternatives requiring some assessment of worth. Every choice is ultimately a choice of value to be realized or served. A concern for career education is an attempt to exercise a choice of values or, alternatively, to create conditions in which values may be clarified and realized. Confronting such values requires individuals in some way to change their lives, even if only their private commitments. It provides a focus for the concentration of vision and identifies where moral and intellectual priorities must be assigned. Values are rarely neutral; they provide individuals with allies and they identify adversaries. In short, educational values impose an interest in their own ultimate realization that goes far beyond the realm of detached contemplation.

STRUCTURE AND HIERARCHY OF
VALUE ORIENTATIONS

Structure, as used here, means a system of relations in which the constituent units exist mainly as aspects of such relations. In any structure, there is a structural principle by which the relationship between elements is expressed. A common principle of this kind is that of distinctive opposition. Examples important to career education include values related to generality as opposed to those related to specialization, values related to work roles as opposed to those related to leisure, and values related to instruction included in the school curriculum as opposed to instruction ordinarily excluded.

Distinctive opposites, as illustrated above, are not necessarily dichotomous; it is possible to choose some middle ground between individual pairs. But, combinations of pairs often begin to describe patterns of preference; it is possible to detect patterns of choice that endorse values consistent with career education and other patterns that reject such values. The patterns of choice can be viewed, thus, as an acceptance or rejection of values to justify an educational program embracing career education. Schools do, in fact, reflect values for justifying the inclusion or exclusion of certain types of instruction. Vocational education, for example, entered the American school system as an intruder, seducing its way with financial incentives, and often winning its way as a compromise of values. It endorsed the value of work-orientation and of specialization. These values are essential to an individual or institutional interpretation of career education, and they are necessary as a pattern of interrelated values, not convenient choices of distinctive and dichotomous opposites.

A second notion of structure and hierarchy follows from the work of Louis Dumont (1970:20), a French anthropologist, who has stated his ideas about value hierarchies in his study, *Homo Hierarchicus*.

> Man does not only think, he acts. He has not only ideas but values. To adopt a value is to introduce hierarchy, and a certain consensus of values. A certain hierarchy of ideas, things and people, is indispensable to social life. This is quite independent of natural inequalities or distribution of power. No doubt, in the majority of cases, hierarchy will be identified in some way with power, but there is no necessity for this. Moreover, it is understandable and natural that hierarchy should encompass social agents and social categories.

Dumont, it appears, argues that action implies intent, that intent requires thought, and that thought requires categories through which to think. Such categories embrace the classifications of society and an evaluation of the classifications.

Not all individuals go through such a mental exercise before they act. But the values related to career education are not fully available to students unless they do so. What, then, are the appropriate categories or classifications? The occupational hierarchy and its various clusters are of central importance. The classifications that describe social class structure may also be appropriate. It is important to recognize that values are, indeed, related to the hierarchies and classifications of society and that values tend to reflect one's view of the structure and hierarchy of society's categories, particularly its occupational hierarchy. Policy decisions can be made that permit students to relate to the entire range of such classifications and hierarchies or they can be made to restrict the view that students have of society.

There is a third way in which value orientations are related to structure and hierarchies. Professionalism in all fields has created platforms that must be mounted before one can be heard or can demonstrate his ability to perform. Pathways fashioned mainly by the trades and professions provide access to these platforms. Although the educational community is proud of its preoccupation with the intellect and with various interpretations of competency, it is a willing guardian of the accepted routes to success established initially by the guild system. At all levels, educational institutions are custodial to the licensing, credentialing, and certifying practices in the society that surrounds them. They almost always endorse longer and longer periods of schooling as the best path to the rewards of society. Value orientations are most vigorously defended where the paths are long and well worn. Career education does not easily fit such a model. For most occupations in the occupational structure, the pathways are not well marked and educational institutions are not well tooled-up to guide students along an appropriate path nor even to make their choice of paths a completely instructive experience. The most easily described paths are, however, the ones that become the most easily justified by the value orientation of the school. These combine to reflect the value hierarchies espoused.

TYPES OF VALUE ISSUES

Almost every educational issue involves, ultimately, a concern with values. When people argue about educational issues, they are ordinarily addressing questions of value, not of fact. When people make up their minds, they choose words to convey their preferred values. Those who choose to dismiss problems as being merely semantical are usually disregarding the important values associated with meaning.

Career education is burdened with such excess baggage of preferences and tastes employed to accommodate particular routes to the justification of values.

It is not possible to explicate all of the types of value issues that surround the complex concepts involved in career education. In the following analysis, several types of issues will be chosen to illustrate the range of value choices that may be identified by such an encompassing theme.

The Distribution of Society's Tasks and Roles

Educational philosophy is often regarded as an expression of lofty idealism—as an examination of an utopian level of perfection, after the style of Plato's *Republic*. Career education is not a late-comer on the scene of educational discourse. It has attracted very little reaction or response from educational philosophers even though it is closely related to major ideas and forces that have been at work for centuries.

The way in which jobs, statuses and rewards are divided up among members of a society has been sufficiently important as an ideology to alter the boundaries of nations and to change the balance of power among them. Career education deals specifically with statuses, rewards, jobs and the values that determine how these shall be rationed among the people of society. It introduces refinements in the rationing process and to appreciate them it is important to understand the antecedent rationing mechanisms.

In 1776, Adam Smith published *An Inquiry Into The Nature and Causes of the Wealth of Nations*. It became a classic of western economies. It described a justification for allocation of statuses, jobs, and other highly-sought rewards or roles. Smith saw this justification as an expression of natural differences that were, somehow, divinely sanctioned. He recognized the hierarchical divisions in society but accepted these, too, as being wholly neutral. It seemed clear to Smith that God harmonized the selfish interests of individuals to promote the general good. He frequently appealed to theological premises in attempting to justify the division of labor interpreted as (a) the division of jobs into detailed tasks for increasing output and, (b) as the hierarchies that allowed some individuals to be in jobs of higher status than others. Smith's contribution to the Calvinist roots of the Protestant Work Ethic were great. The educational system responded dutifully in reflecting a view that reinforced the differences accepted as natural. The divine plight of serfs was not regarded as less natural or less preordained than the divine right of kings.

A secular view began to emerge when Charles Darwin (1872) published his *On the Origin of Species by Natural Selection*. It was a controversial treatise, not solely because of its argument but also because of its title. Theologians elevated the volume to a position of prominence by their attacks on the title. Darwin ushered in a new era of science by offering scientific legitimacy to the process that had become the speculative observation of many. The phrase "survival of the fittest," which is often credited to Darwin, had already been coined by Herbert Spencer, but Darwin's work gave it the credibility of a natural law.

Darwin had not intended his biological theory of natural selection to have application in the social or political realm. But applications had already begun. Spencer had opposed state assistance to the disadvantaged on the grounds that it would tend to sustain the weaker and less successful members of the race. The idea of competition as a fundamental social principle grew simultaneously with rugged individualism at the outset of industrial development. Darwin's concept of the fittest described those most adapted to their environment, not necessarily the best. There was continued confusion and disagreement regarding an appropriateness of distinguishing the fittest from the best. Those who wanted to distinguish between them did not wish to accept biological evidence as a basis for ethical principles. The importance of distinguishing between them is easily seen in a twentieth century expression of fascist elitism, in the growing expressions of ethnicity, and in such movements as Jensenism.

Needless to say, the social implication of Darwin's work had a significant effect on the system of allocating statuses, rewards, and jobs. Adopting their own interpretation of the concept of survival and their own definition of fitness, educational systems easily accommodated a competitive rationale without clearly distinguishing between the fittest and the best or between biological and ethical principles. The educational system is a self-perpetuating environment as well as a social system. It selects some individuals to remain in the environment and determines others as unfit to remain. Those chosen to remain are regarded as the best candidates for positions in the upper strata of the occupational hierarchy, the levels toward which the educational system continues to provide an extended preparatory environment. The casualties are neither the best nor well fitted to the environment provided by the system. Many of them soon discover that the educational system is not anxious to create an environment for preparing individuals to compete in the complete range of jobs, statuses and rewards of the occupational hierarchy. The educational system does, accordingly, choose the fittest and the best. "Fitness" is determined by the degree of adaptation to an environment created to promote individuals to advanced preparation and the concept of the "best" is a reflection of the level at which individuals perform in that environment.

Darwin's intent was merely to describe a biological process. In its application to the social scene, Darwinism assisted in creating a value system that was easily institutionalized and one in which it was easy for individuals to accept the notion that the best of the rewards, statuses and jobs were an available choice for the "fit" and only a hope for the unfit.

An even more secular view was advocated by Karl Marx in 1867 in *Das Kapital,* subtitled, "A Critical Analysis of Capitalistic Production." Marx was critical of both Smith and Darwin. He criticized Smith for relating the hierarchical order of society to God-given harmony. He chided Darwin for establishing a parallel between the beasts and plants, and the individual competition in English society. But Marx later acquiesced to the Darwin thesis by accepting a basis in natural science for his interpretation of the class struggle in history. Although much of Marx's work has been discredited, it represents a full swing of the pendulum from the earlier views of Smith. Smith's argument was that the jobs, statuses and rewards of society were preordained and natural. Marx's argument was that they were conventions invented by humans and about which classes of humans would continue to struggle.

The brief and incomplete analysis above does not include the important contributions of such men as Compte, Malthus, Veblen, Huxley, and others to the value orientations that have affected the process of allocating roles and rewards in society. It is sufficient, however, to illustrate that career education has antecedents representing a wide range of value orientations.

How is this important to current views of career education? Clearly it is important to recognize that career education is a refocus on a theme to which Adam Smith addressed himself more than 200 years ago, namely the process of rationing the privileges and responsibilities within society. It can be accepted on Smith's terms that the rationing process will involve the need for everyone to, somehow, learn to see and accept his natural place in the occupational hierarchy. It can also be accepted as the need to create conventions, including schools, which allow individuals and groups to involve themselves in the process of allocating the roles and rewards of society. If career education becomes available to all students, it will justify a view or a value that obligates the educational system to make the entire occupational hierarchy available to every student, not merely as an academic exercise, but as opportunities to be realized.

The Work Ethic

Career education has introduced much discussion about the validity of a work ethic and also with the possibility that career education is a kind of conspiracy to insure obedient and compliant workers for an industrial establishment. It is clear that the values implicit in a technological society have come under widespread challenge because technology itself has been viewed as inimical to important aspects of some preferred life styles. Many aspects of an alleged Puritan ethic— hard work and postponement of gratification—are often seen as overvalued virtues. Even the sense of satisfaction that comes from occupational accomplishment is often viewed by many as of lowered value. The change, if there is one, is toward feeling and away from *pro forma* exercises.

Young people continue to have heroes with whom they identify and explore frontiers. In common, they prize inner-freedom and the realization of their personalities. Self-fulfillment and self-discovery are seen as important accomplishments. Neither career education nor the work ethic is inconsistent with such values. Interpreted as useful activity, work may be gratifying and fulfilling whether regarded as an end or a means. In fact, career education offers unique opportunities to explore frontiers of self-discovery and fulfillment.

To those who would argue that career education is a devious system for insuring an obedient work force within the occupation structure, it should be pointed out that the opposite value may also be realized. Job enrichment, which is jargon for redesigning jobs to allow more scope for interest, initiative, discretion, responsibility, and personal achievement is an effort to redress the trend toward breaking work into its simplest and most repetitive components. It seeks to build up jobs to raise the level of skill and conceptual agility demanded in the work setting. Career education seeks another form of job enrichment, namely the opportunity for recurrent education, the chance to move successively and repeatedly from educational programs to the work force, being instructed in both as one moves toward work roles that are satisfying and fulfilling.

The validity of the work ethic is hardly available for refutation. Work continues to ration the goods, services and satisfactions of society. It is an accepted medium of exchange for which money is merely a proxy. Although work may have many forms and be amenable to many interpretations, it remains the most important global currency for exchanging values, statuses, and rewards.

Schools or Non-schools

Widespread discussion has recently emerged to question the value of schools in carrying out the roles traditionally assigned to them. With arguments favoring the "deschooling of society," Illich (1970) has included himself among the spokesmen for a diminishing role for formal education. The argument is that nonformal education, along with various forms of familial and para-familial intervention, would provide a better alternative. Career education must confront the type of values issue introduced by these arguments although it may not need to choose among the extremes presented in many of them.

As mentioned earlier, the educational system is highly preoccupied with organizing various categories of knowledge. In doing this, there is a tendency to include some information at the expense of other information—to emphasize some types of instruction at the expense of others. Since a school tends to deal with highly conventionalized forms of knowledge and with highly conventionalized approaches to scheduling, instruction and evaluation, it can be expected to reflect patterns of inclusion and exclusion, emphasis and subordination, which support its conventions (Swanson, 1967:104). To the extent that such patterns tend to diminish the stature or range of career education, it can be expected that the school exercises significant control over the way great numbers of people judge the importance of work or the degree to which education for work, an important part of society, is already deschooled.

The question of school versus non-school arrangements has other dimensions for viewing the values of career education or of the school itself. Community interaction is held to be an important element of career education. Much of this interaction involves work experience and other activities that are essentially nonformal. Most people would regard their nonformal educational experiences as extremely important to their total education. It is possible, indeed desirable, for formal and nonformal education to be linked together to provide credibility to each other. The initiative for doing this must come from the institutions providing formal education. They have more control of the conventions relating to credentialing, accreditation, and certification.

The values employed in justification of school versus non-school programs or in formal versus nonformal education are available to career education. Their availability, however, is determined by the choice of means as well as the choice of ends.

Equality of Opportunity

The demands of justice are the most important demands in any community. Ordinarily this is thought of as something in the domain of judges, lawyers, or courts. It is most important for it to be present in all of democracy's institutional forms. Inequalities should not be regarded as natural or predestined.

Justice is inextricably linked with equality of opportunity and thus with education. In education, it should be regarded as the most stringent of virtues, the one to be the least sacrificed for any kind of convenience. Only after the demands of justice have been met should educators or policy-makers begin to think about the implementation of other goals or values.

Justice demands adherence to two principles: first, that each person should have an equal right to the most basic liberty compatible with a similar liberty for others; and, second, that such inequalities as exist should be (a) to everyone's advantage and (b) attached to roles available to all (Rawls, 1971). The second principle justifies inequalities only by promoting the well-being of the least advantaged and by insuring equality of opportunity. Justice, therefore, does not guarantee ends or equality of results, it merely puts a major focus on instrumental value of means.

The types of values represented by the demands of justice are of crucial importance to education and particularly to career education. They justify access to opportunity and self-development as a function of the institutional forms for providing career education. They also require that all other claims be subordinate to the demands of justice.

SUMMARY

The philosophical bases for career education identified in this chapter are largely in the area of values to be served or values employed to justify a career education emphasis. Such an emphasis requires institutional commitment and an expression of individual and institutional values. People and institutions often refuse to leave the shelter of a value pattern that justifies their current behavior. Career education requires a reexamination of these value patterns.

The types of value issues involved in career education include those which require a view of the educational system engaging in the process of allocating and rationing the statuses, rewards and jobs available to members of a society. This view requires a subset of values to justify the nature of hierarchies considered, the patterns of inclusion and exclusion evidenced in school programs, the degree of endorsement of the work ethic, the acceptance of the credibility of nonformal educational experiences, and the acceptance of the demands of justice.

Schools were once regarded as merely an expression or a reflection of the nation's culture. Increasingly they are being called upon to produce that culture. The outcome will depend upon the values that society regards as important as it chooses what to do with its energy, its wealth, and its children.

REFERENCES

Dumont, Louis. *Homo Hierarchicus.* (Chicago: University of Chicago Press, 1970)

Illich, Ivan. *Deschooling Society*. (New York: Harper and Row, 1970)

Rawls, John. *A Theory of Justice*. (Boston: Belknap Press of Harvard University Press, 1971)

Swanson, Gordon. "The World of Work," *Designing Education for the Future*. ed. Edgar L. Morphet and Charles O. Ryan. (New York: Citation Press, 1967)

THEORETICAL AND CONCEPTUAL FRAMEWORKS FOR CAREER EDUCATION

Edwin L. Herr and Richard G. Swails

In January 1971, then U.S. Commissioner of Education Marland introduced "career education" as a priority concern with implications for all educational levels. Since then, considerable national, state, and local effort has been expended in defining the term and in developing model programs to implement the assumptions and concepts underlying the definitions.

It has become clear that this "new idea" is, in fact, a synthesis or amalgamation of many concepts already familiar to American educators, but within a framework that draws heavily upon the literature and research related to decision-making behavior and the career development process. Indeed, the U.S. Office of Education has indicated that the roots for what is now coming to be known as a K through 12 "career education system" go back into many years of basic research on career development theory (Exemplary Programs and Services Branch, USOE, 1971).

Career education can be described as a combination of education for choosing and education for productivity (Herr, 1971). As such, it depends heavily upon vocational education although the two terms are not synonymous (National Association of State Directors for Vocational Education, 1971). Clearly, however, the vocational education legislation of the 1960s, particularly Part D of the Vocational Education Act Amendments of 1968, served as the stimulus for prototype models and conceptual development that have now come to an evolutionary fusion in career education.

It is the intent of this chapter to examine career education and some models currently being developed in terms of theoretical belief systems that give career education construct validity. Since the early 1950s there has been a rapidly expanding body of literature and research directed toward vocational behavior. This material provides a multitude of useful concepts that can serve as unifying themes upon which to design educational programs of the future (Herr, 1972b). The following sections describe some of these.

THE CLUSTER CONCEPT

The cluster concept, which is now an integral part of many career education models, can be indirectly traced to the components of the 1968 Amendments that call for the development of new ways of conceptualizing vocational education. An excellent example of how the cluster concept can be incorporated into an educational program is the Cluster Concept Program developed by the University of

Maryland's Industrial Education Department. The objectives of the
Maryland model are:

1. To broaden the student's knowledge of available opportunities in the occupations found in each cluster.
2. To develop job entry skills and knowledge for several occupations found in a cluster.
3. To develop safe habits and a favorable attitude toward work required in the occupations in a cluster.
4. To develop a student's insight into the sources of information that will be helpful to him as he moves through the occupational areas (Industrial Education Department, University of Maryland, 1972).

The Maryland model is much broader in scope than traditionally
oriented vocational education programs that have attempted to provide intensive skill training for a narrowly focused occupation, such
as carpentry or masonry. Under the cluster concept, the intent is to
provide students with skills, knowledge, and attitudes required for
entry into a family or cluster of occupations, i.e., the construction
occupations cluster.

Implicit in the cluster concept is the integration of academic areas
with the world of work. Thus, the so-called academic subjects (e.g.,
English, mathematics, science) help prepare the student to acquire
the skills, knowledge, and attitudes necessary to perform the cluster
tasks rather than functioning as separate entities. The importance of
this cannot be overemphasized, particularly since education is undergoing a period in which students are increasingly questioning the
relevancy of the educational experiences to which they are being
exposed. In this sense, the cluster concept provides the opportunity
to link real work problems directly to ways by which basic education
skills—communication, computational, and reasoning skills—are
necessary to their solutions.

The cluster concept has also been adapted as a structure for prevocational and articulated career education experiences beginning
with the elementary school and becoming increasingly comprehensive
in the secondary schools. For example, the Comprehensive Career
Education Model (CCEM) being field-tested nationally under the
supervision of The Center for Vocational and Technical Education
at The Ohio State University has used the cluster arrangement shown
on the next page to guide instructional objectives and learning experiences (Reinhart, 1972).

THEORETICAL APPROACHES TO
VOCATIONAL BEHAVIOR

While the cluster concept represents a structure describing occupational differences on different criteria, it has become increasingly

CCEM CLUSTERS FOR K-12

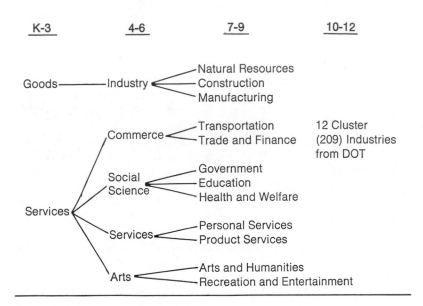

K-3	4-6	7-9	10-12

Goods———Industry —< Natural Resources, Construction, Manufacturing

Services —< Commerce —< Transportation, Trade and Finance

Social Science —< Government, Education, Health and Welfare

Services —< Personal Services, Product Services

Arts —< Arts and Humanities, Recreation and Entertainment

12 Cluster (209) Industries from DOT

obvious that one's transactional behavior with regard to that structure is also important. The recent surge of findings and theoretical speculation from vocational psychology, developmental psychology, occupational sociology, and decision theory has cast into increasingly bold relief the factors that facilitate or impede individual aspirations and plans of action that lead to placement in the labor market and to development of vocational identity.

Because career development has been found to differ among people and groups, it is evident that such development is modifiable; it can be learned. Thus, career development theory represents a reservoir of ideas and constructs that can be brought together to create programmatic responses designed to help students acquire attitudes, knowledge, and skills essential for effective planning, choosing and employability.

The theoretical approaches that describe career development or some aspect of it can be organized in several ways. For the purpose of this chapter, the following classification will be used: trait and factor approaches; decision theory; sociological emphases; psychological emphases; and, developmental emphases.

Trait and Factor Approaches

Inherent in most career education models, as they are now being developed, is an emphasis on the importance of the development of self-awareness on the part of the student—in terms of his abilities, interests, and values; and, how these self-characteristics relate to the process of decision-making. This concept has its roots in the so-called trait and factor approaches to occupational choice.

From a historical perspective, the trait and factor approach has been one of the first and most consistent of the various ways of viewing occupational choice. Derived from the psychology of individual differences, trait and factor approaches have been known by a variety of different labels—trait-measurement psychology, differential psychology, and the actuarial approach. But perhaps the most commonly applied term over the years has been trait and factor approach to occupational choice. Regardless of the terminology applied, the basic assumptions that underlie this approach are that individual differences can be observed and classified in terms of variables such as aptitudes, interests, and values; requirements for occupations can be classified in analogous ways; and, thus the individual can be "matched" to the right occupation. These assumptions have remained a major component of the process of vocational counseling since Frank Parsons first described it in 1909.

Since Parsons first articulated this approach, it has changed only in level of sophistication. This has resulted chiefly because of the increasing improvements in the field of psychometrics. The trait and factor approach has provided insights into the importance of certain specific factors as they relate not only to occupational choice, but also in respect to job satisfaction and job success. Through the use of this approach, it has been possible to examine and identify the interaction of variables such as occupational aspirations, occupational stereotype, and occupational prestige as they influence personal value systems and their effects on limiting an individual's focus on occupational fields of study. In recent years, it has also helped demonstrate that the Parsonian concept of one right job for everyone has little foundation in reality. Most individuals have multipotentiality. This gives validity to the concept in most career education models of exposing students, particularly through the late elementary and junior high school years, to a wide variety of occupational families or clusters. This is further reinforced by the evidence from trait and factor approaches to suggest that there exists in most occupations latitude to tolerate a wide range of individual differences on the part of workers.

While trait and factor approaches have significantly contributed to an understanding of occupational selection, they furnish a rather narrow perspective on the process of vocational development. Trait and factor approaches to occupational choice have usually been directed toward a specific point in time in which the individual must make an occupationally oriented decision. However, vocational development is an ongoing process but also a process by which such choices can be purposefully integrated with a patterning of decisions. It thereby maximizes freedom of choice and implements the personal meaning of the ways one conceives his traits, or his self-concept. The successful integration of these behaviors throughout constitutes the operational meaning of career.

Decision-making Approaches

Another basic concept in career education is that the student should develop understanding of the decision-making process and be equipped to implement decision-making strategies as they relate to his personal development. A number of theoretical approaches have been focused upon the matter of decision-making itself.

Most of the approaches that attempt to theorize about vocational choice through the use of decision models have incorporated the assumption, based upon Keynesian economic theory, that one chooses a career or an occupational goal that will maximize his gain and minimize his loss. The gain or loss is, of course, not necessarily money but can be anything of value to the particular individual (Herr and Cramer, 1972). Implicit in such an approach is the idea that an individual can be assisted to predict the advantages and disadvantages of each alternative and the possibility of his achieving each of the alternatives. He will then choose the alternative that promises the most reward for his self-investment with the least probability of failure.

Among the variety of inputs to such an approach are the following concepts:

1. Choice occurs under conditions of uncertainty or risk (Brayfield and Crites, 1964).

2. A choice between various possible courses of action can be conceptualized as motivated by two interrelated sets of factors: the individual's valuation of different alternatives and his appraisal of his chances of being able to realize each of the alternatives (Blau, et al., 1956: 533).

3. The process of making a decision between uncertain outcomes requires reconciliation of several general factors: the relative valuing of the outcomes, the cost of attaining the outcomes, and the probability that each outcome may occur (Davidson, et al., 1957).

4. Decision-making includes the identifying and defining of

one's values; what they are and what they are not, where they appear and where they do not (Katz, 1966).

There appears to be growing evidence to support the contention that an understanding of the decision-making process and decision-making skills can be taught to students in a classroom setting by applying one of many decision models through the use of a simulated decision-making situation (Boocock, 1967; Krumboltz, et al., 1968). Strategies such as the use of a life career game or job experience kits incorporate various theoretical assumptions about decision-making. They also provide the learner with vicarious experiences in the decision-making process without his having to accept the immediate consequences of those decisions so made, thus allowing him to develop the skills needed prior to making similar decisions in real life.

Sociological Approaches

Another concept built into most career education models is that a student needs an understanding of the social structure of which he is a part and the implications of this structure for his future choices. Increasingly, research findings have shown that the place one occupies in the social structure has much to do with the viability of the choices one makes, considers, or can implement. Thus, there are limitations placed upon career development by restricted social class horizons. Much floundering in decision making is a result of limited avenues of career choice or limitations upon the knowledge of opportunities available to the individual so restricted. The individual cannot choose or prepare for that about which he does not know.

Lipsett (1962) has pointed out that we must understand the implications for a particular individual of the following social factors as they interact with vocational development:

1. Social class membership—e.g., occupation and income of parents, place and type of residence, and ethnic background.
2. Home influences—e.g., parental goals for the individual, influence of siblings, family values and counselee's acceptance of them.
3. School—e.g., scholastic achievement, relationship with peers and faculty, values of the school.
4. Community—e.g., the "thing" to do in the community, group goals and values, special opportunities or influences.
5. Pressure groups—e.g., the degree to which an individual or his parents have come under any particular influence that leads him to value one occupation over another.
6. Role perception—e.g., the individual's perception of himself as a leader, follower, isolate, etc.; the degree to which

his perception of himself is in accord with the way others perceive him.

Two occupational sociologists, Miller and Form (1951), have woven the above factors into a theory of occupational choice that has had considerable influence on other theorists' conceptions of vocational development. Other concepts they emphasized include work stages and career patterns. According to Miller and Form, an individual's vocational development can be divided into five work stages: preparatory stage (beginning in childhood and continuing into the school years); initial work stage (which includes the individual's experiences with part-time and full-time work prior to the completion of his formal education); trial stage (in which there is an exploration of several jobs of short-term duration); stable work period (in which the individual stabilizes in a particular job); and, the retirement stage.

The work of Miller and Form has provided a framework by which to view the various ways in which individuals enter and progress through the world of work. One can conclude from these efforts that there is no such thing as one "correct career pattern," but rather many different patterns of work periods. Based on their research, Miller and Form have identified 14 such patterns, with men and women exhibiting distinctly different career patterns. This has important implications as we attempt to develop career education syllabuses that will meet the needs of both male and female students. It would seem to suggest that boys and girls may need slightly different experiences at different times in order to maximize their career development.

LoCascio's (1967) concepts of delayed and impaired vocational development as a function of the richness or scarcity of one's past experiences complement the Miller and Form work. These concepts also provide us with greater insight into the importance of individualizing career education programs according to the varying readiness levels of students.

LoCascio suggests that there are four basic steps in accomplishing the various vocational developmental tasks associated with normal or continuous vocational development: (a) the individual must become aware of the task to be mastered, i.e., selection of an appropriate program of study; (b) he must draw upon previously learned and related responses; (c) he must learn new behaviors in his attempt to deal with the confronting task; and (d) he must incorporate these new responses into his behavioral repertoire for use with future tasks.

Delayed vocational development occurs when an individual displays a deficiency of prior vocational behaviors necessary to master the particular task now confronting him, thus causing a delay in the successful completion of that phase of his development. Once he learns the necessary behaviors he can master the task, incorporate the behaviors, and move forward in his development.

Impaired vocational development stems from the fact that certain individuals fail to recognize the task confronting them, or, if aware of the task, refuse to deal with it. The vocational development of such individuals is characterized by gaps or deficiencies that, in some cases, may seriously diminish their employability potential.

Psychological Approaches

Psychological approaches to vocational choice stress intrinsic individual motivation to a greater degree than the other approaches discussed thus far. The major assumption of these approaches is that differences in personality structure reflect different need predispositions, the satisfaction of which is sought in occupational choices. Thus, different career areas are populated by persons of different need or personality type (Herr, 1972a).

Within this context, Roe (1956) has attempted to wed personality theory to vocational development. Much of her work stresses the influence of early parent-child interactions and the emotional climate of the home or the development of a need structure, which she contends is a major determinant of occupational choice. Roe has integrated her theoretical concepts into a well-known field and level classification of occupations. She contends that people enter one of eight occupational fields primarily as a result of their value structure, interest pattern, and orientation toward or away from people. Roe's fields include: service, business, contact, organizations, technology, outdoor, science, general culture, and art/entertainment. The occupations found within each field may be subdivided into various levels, based on work complexity and responsibility, such as: professional and managerial, semiprofessional, skilled, semiskilled, and unskilled.

Maley (1967) has pointed out that, at a psychological level, such a theoretical position validates the increased concern for dealing with occupational clusters. The cluster scheme developed by the U.S. Office of Education, and now being incorporated into numerous career education efforts, is compatible with the original field and level concept of Roe and consistent with the recent U.S. Department of Labor classification of jobs by intensity of their relationship to data, people and things.

Developmental Approaches

Most people charged with the responsibility of developing and implementing a program of career education recognize the importance of providing students with an integrated set of learning experiences beginning with the student's initial contact with the school and continuing until he enters the labor market as a full-time worker. Support for this can be found within the developmental approaches to vocational behavior and decision-making.

Developmental emphases on vocational behavior and decision-making differ from the emphases previously discussed—trait and factor, decision-theory, sociological and psychological—not because they reject the others, but rather because they are typically more inclusive, more concerned with longitudinal expressions of vocational behavior, and more inclined to focus on the individual's self-concept (Herr and Cramer, 1972).

The early work of Ginzberg, Ginsburg, Axelrod and Herma was the first attempt at theorizing about occupational choice from a developmental perspective. Ginzberg, et al. (1951) suggest that occupational choice represents a series of decisions made over a period of time, not a single choice made at a specific point in time; the process becomes increasingly irreversible; the act of choosing represents a compromise between what is considered to be the ideal and that which is realistically available; and, that the vocational choice process could be divided into various stages of development labeled fantasy, tentative and realistic.

To date, Super and his colleagues (Super, et al., 1957; 1963) have formulated the most comprehensive vocational development theory which is essentially based upon a phenomenological approach within a developmental framework. Super, et al. have characterized vocational development as ongoing, continuous, and generally irreversible; a process of compromise and synthesis within which his primary construct—the development and implementation of the self-concept—operates. The basic theme is that an individual chooses an occupation whose characteristics will furnish him with a role that is consistent with his self-concept, and that the latter conception is a function of his developmental history.

Drawing on the earlier work of Buehler (1933), and Ginzberg, et al. (1951), Super has divided the vocational development continuum into five stages: Growth Stage (birth to 14 years), Exploration Stage (15 to 24 years), Establishment Stage (25-44 years), Maintenance Stage (45-65 years), and the Decline Stage (65 years to death). Within each, he has applied the developmental task concept of Havighurst (1953) and others. The vocationally-oriented developmental tasks of each stage as outlined by Super suggest a skeleton upon which to build themes for career development at different educational levels. Table 1 provides an example of various themes for a career education program (Herr, 1972a).

The various factors under each of the general themes or "prime considerations" can easily be translated into specific statements of desired behavior using any one of a number of approaches to the

EXAMPLES OF THEMES FOR CAREER DEVELOPMENT AT DIFFERENT EDUCATIONAL LEVELS

Elementary School

Prime Considerations: Formulations of self-concept, developing a vocabulary of self and environmental alternatives.

Factors:

Formulating interests
Developing a vocabulary of self
Developing a vocabulary of work
Developing rudiments of basic trust in self and others
Developing rudiments of initiative
Developing rudiments of industry
Developing rudimentary knowledge of fundamentals of technology
Differentiating self from environment
Formulating sex social role
Learning rudiments of social roles
Learning fundamental intellectual, physical and motor skills

Junior High School

Prime considerations: Translation of self-concept into vocational terms; dealing with exploratory needs with purpose and intent.

Factors:

Using exploratory resources
Relating interests and capacities
Identifying personal strengths which one wants to exploit in formulating a vocational preference
Understanding the interdependence of the educational and occupational structures
Differentiation of interests and values
Developing implications of present-future relationships
Accepting one's self as in process
Relating changes in the self to changes in the world
Learning to defer gratification, to set priorities
Acquiring knowledge of life organizations
Preparation for role relationships
Preparation for level and kind of consumption

Senior High School

Prime Considerations: Formulating plans to execute implementation of self-concept and generalized preference.

Factors:

Refine and particularize as necessary junior high school factors
Relating interests and capacities to values
Planning for specific occupation or intermediate educational alternative
Acquiring information necessary to execute specific plans
Achieving mature relationships with peers of both sexes
Achieving emotional independence of parents and other adults

Table 1

writing of behavioral objectives such as Mager (1962), Krathwohl (1965), or Gronlund (1970). This is the basic approach that has been utilized in some of the initial career education efforts at the federal, state, and local levels.

EXAMPLES OF CAREER EDUCATION MODELS

The school-based Comprehensive Career Education Model (CCEM) is under development by The Center for Vocational and Technical Education at The Ohio State University in cooperation with six local school districts selected by the U.S. Office of Education. CCEM is based on a developmental time line beginning in kindergarten and running through senior high school. The model is designed to assist students in moving from a level of primary self-awareness toward the more complex levels of development associated with vocational-identity.

After an extensive review of career development and human development literature, the CCEM staff identified what they believe to be the major elements of career education: Self-Awareness, Educational Awareness, Career Awareness, Economic Awareness, Appreciations and Attitudes, Decision-making Skills, Skill Awareness and Beginning Competence, and Employability Skills. These have been translated into various themes with specific goals for each grade level. These, in turn, have yielded over 3,000 student performance objectives that will become the bases for the various learning experiences employed at the different grade levels (A. Miller, 1972).

Various efforts at the state level have produced numerous career education materials. One of the earliest of these efforts and perhaps the best developed at this point in time is the Wisconsin model developed by Drier, et al. (1972).

The Wisconsin model has three basic components—the self, the world of work, and career planning and preparation—from which 16 career development concepts have been developed. These various concepts are introduced, further developed, or given specific emphasis roughly correlating with the various periods of educational development—middle childhood (K-3), late childhood (grades 4-6), early adolescence (grades 7-9), and adolescence (grades 10-12). The concepts translate into a series of sample behavioral objectives for each of the developmental periods. This model along with a comprehensive listing of resource materials has been incorporated into a K-12 guide for integrating career development into local school curriculum within the state of Wisconsin (Drier, et al., 1972).

There have also been numerous efforts on the part of local school districts in the past few years to develop programs related to career education. Two of the earliest and perhaps the best known are the

Career Development Activities for grades five to seven of the Abington School District, Abington, Pennsylvania (1967-1968), and the Cobb County Occupational and Career Development Program, Marietta, Georgia (Cobb County School System, 1969-1970).

The Abington program was an attempt to design learning experiences that would facilitate the vocational development of middle school students. A theme based on the research of vocational development literature is assigned to each grade. This provides the central focus for the activities of the grade but is not a limiting factor. The learning experiences were also developed with attention to innovations in methodology: simulation, gaming, role-playing, problem-solving, decision-making, and dramatics. In designing the activities, effort was made to emphasize the process through which one can arrive at a career decision (Abington School District, 1967-1968).

The Cobb County program consists of orientation and information at the elementary level, information and exploration at the middle school level, and exploration and preparation at the secondary level. All of these are built around a career development theme that includes: (a) the student's evaluation of self-characteristics, (b) exploration of broad occupational areas, (c) introduction to the economics and social values of work, (d) introduction to the psychological and sociological meaning of work, (e) exploration of educational avenues, and (f) development of the students' process of decision-making (Cobb County School System, 1969-1970).

CONCLUSION

When one views the current efforts in career education, such as those discussed here and numerous others, it becomes apparent that the foundations for these efforts are deeply embedded in the collective findings of the various theoretical approaches to career development. It is also clear that many of the elements and concepts that have been incorporated into present descriptions of career education have been advocated in one form or another for at least the past century. However, the uniqueness and major contribution of the current career education movement lies in its attempt to synthesize these concepts and utilize their emphases upon planning, decision-making, and informal choice as a unifying theme for a comprehensive educational program designed to make all students effective decision makers and productive workers when they enter the labor market.

Some similarities are apparent among the currently developing career education models that suggest they rest on similar foundations. One can identify the following:

1. The assumptions or objectives of current programs suggest the importance of developing self-awareness, decision

making prowess, planning as well as preparation for employability as the focus of our educational efforts.

2. Career development theories have been instrumental in stimulating concepts and programs that have a prevocational character placed earlier in the life of children. Rather than assuming that the educational experiences dealing with vocational preparation should be confined to secondary or post-secondary school, the current models are encompassing the implications for career orientation, career identity and knowledge that reside in the early life of the child. Career development is a continuing process of integrated learning experiences and decision making moving from simple to complex behaviors.

3. A further assumption is that by introducing concrete, "hands on" or manipulative vocationally oriented opportunities early in the school life of children, the meaningfulness or relevance of education will be enhanced.

4. Since vocational behavior is learned, it is modifiable through an integrated, systematic educational program. Such a program must involve all aspects of the school and the community in providing experiences and resources to foster vocational maturity on the part of the learner.

Clearly, career education may be viewed as an affirmation of the importance of preparing man well for his work and extending to him the dignity and self-esteem which comes from managing his life through effective decision making.

REFERENCES

Abington School District, Abington, Pennsylvania. "Career Development Activities, Grades V, VI, VII." 1967-1968.

Blau, P. M., et al. "Occupational Choice: A Conceptual Framework," *Industrial Labor Relations Review,* IX, (1956).

Boocock, S. S. "Life Career Game," *Personnel and Guidance Journal,* XLVI, (1967)

Brayfield, A. H., and Crites, J. O. "Research on Vocational Guidance: Status and Project," *Man in a World at Work.* ed. H. Borow, (Boston: Houghton Mifflin. 1964)

Buehler, Charlotte. *Der Menschliche Lebenslau als Psychologicles Problem.* (Leipzig: Hirzel. 1933)

Carkhuff, R. R.; Alexik, Mae, and Anderson, Susan. "Do We Have a Theory of Vocational Choice?" *Personnel and Guidance Journal,* XLV, (1967)

Cobb County School System. "A Developmental Program of Occupational Education." Series of unpublished papers. Marietta, Georgia: Cobb County School System. 1969-1970.

Davidson, D., et al. *Decision-making: An Experimental Approach.* (Stanford, California: Stanford University Press. 1957)

Drier, Harry N., Jr., et al. *K-12 Guide for Integrating Career Development into Local Curriculum.* (Worthington, Ohio: Charles A. Jones Publishing Company. 1972)

Ginzberg, E.; Ginsburg, S. W.; Axelrod, S.; and Herma, J. L. *Occupational Choice: An Approach to A General Theory.* (New York: Columbia University Press. 1951)

Gronlund, N. E. *Stating Behavioral Objectives for Classroom Instruction.* (New York: Macmillan Company. 1970)

Havighurst, R. J. *Human Development and Education.* (New York: Longmans Green. 1953)

Herr, Edwin L. "Contributions for Career Development to Career Education," *Journal of Industrial Teacher Education,* IX, (1972a)

————. *Decision-making and Vocational Development.* (Boston: Houghton Mifflin. 1970)

————. *Review and Synthesis of Foundations for Career Education.* (Columbus, Ohio: The Center for Vocational and Technical Education, The Ohio State University, 1972b)

————. "Unifying an Entire System of Education Around a Career Development Theme." Paper presented at the National Conference on Exemplary Projects and Programs of the 1968 Vocational Education Amendments, Atlanta, Georgia, March, 1969.

————. "What is Career Education?" Paper presented at Career Education Conference for Cochise County School Administrators, Casa Grande, Arizona, August, 1971.

————, and Cramer, Stanley H. *Vocational Guidance and Career Development in the Schools: Toward a Systems Approach.* (Boston: Houghton Mifflin. 1972)

Holland, J. H. *The Psychology of Vocational Choice.* (Waltham, Massachusetts: Blaisdell Publishing Company. 1966)

Industrial Education Department, University of Maryland. "The Cluster Concept." Product Development Report No. 18. Palo Alto, California: American Institutes for Research. 1972.

National Association of State Directors for Vocational Education, *Position Paper on Career Education,* Las Vegas, Nevada, September, 1971.

Katz, Martin R. "A Model of Guidance for Career Decision-making," *Vocational Guidance Quarterly,* XV, (1966)

Krathwohl, D. R. "Stating Objectives Appropriately for Program for Curriculum and for Instructional Materials Development," *Journal of Teacher Education,* XVI, (1965)

Krumboltz, J. D., et al. *Vocational Problem Solving Experiences for Stimulating Career Exploration and Interest: Phase II, Final Report.* (Stanford, California: School of Education, Stanford University. 1968)

Lipsett, L. "Social Factors in Vocational Development," *Personnel and Guidance Journal,* XL, (1962)

LoCascio, R. "Continuity and Discontinuity in Vocational Development Theory." *Personnel and Guidance Journal.* XLVI, (1967)

Mager, R. F. *Preparing Instructional Objectives.* (Palo Alto, California: Fearson. 1962)

Maley, Donald. "Cluster Concept: Change for Occupational Exploration." *American Vocational Journal.* XLII, (1967)

Miller, A. J. "Strategies for Implementing Career Education: A School Based Model." Paper presented for Annual Meeting of American Educational Research Association, Chicago, Illinois, 1972.

Miller, D. C. "Industry and the Worker," *Man in a World at Work.* ed. H. Borow, (Boston: Houghton Mifflin. 1964)

Miller, Delbert C., and Form, William H. *Industrial Sociology: The Sociology of Work Organizations.* (New York: Harper & Row, Publishers, 1951)

Reinhart, Bruce. "A Comprehensive Career Education Model: A Bridge between School and Work." Paper presented to Southwide Research Coordinating Council, Clearwater, Florida, May, 1972.

Roe, Anne. *The Psychology of Occupations.* (New York: John Wiley and Sons, Inc. 1956)

Stefflre, B. "Vocational Development: Ten Propositions in Search of a Theory," *Personnel and Guidance Journal,* XLIV, (1966)

Super, D. E. *The Psychology of Careers.* (New York: Harper and Row, 1957)

———, et al. *Career Development: Self-concept Theory.* (New York: College Entrance Examination Board, 1963)

———, et al. *Vocational Development: A Framework for Research.* (New York: Bureau of Publications, Teachers College, Columbia University, 1957)

U.S., Office of Education, *Background on the Design, Development and Implementation of Vocational Exemplary Projects, Funded Under Part D, section 142(c) of the Vocational Education Amendments of 1968.* Washington, D.C., Exemplary Programs and Services Branch, Division of Vocational and Technical Education, U.S. Office of Education, 1971.

LEGISLATING CAREER EDUCATION

Lowell A. Burkett

The failure of America to govern itself under the Articles of Confederation taught the young country some important lessons about federalism—lessons that leaders in the United States have tended to forget periodically in subsequent years. In advancing the concept of career education today, it seems we are again forgetting what governmental action and machinery are required to accomplish a job for the country.

The following is an effort to retrace the legislative path that has led to career education—not so much in order to point the way to the future, but rather to provide a firmer grounding concerning the essential role of government in carrying out the objectives of a unified nation.

Four basic premises will serve as an introduction:

1. People band together under a social contract to do that which they cannot do alone.
2. Smaller governmental units, no matter how autonomous, confederate to accomplish what they cannot as separate entities.
3. The most practical way for these united peoples and governments to work together is through the legislative process.
4. The legislative process is an orderly, developmental process, with subsequent actions depending on previous precedents and experiences.

From the vantage point of these premises, one can see a distinct line of legislative action that has led to the concept of career education as the next giant step forward. In the same sense, to ignore this foundation and set the development of career education off on a tangential slope would be taking a giant step backward.

HISTORIC SETTING

Colonial America

To start close to the beginning, education in colonial America was based on religious teaching. This education was not as irrelevant as we may now think, because religion was the basic order of society, and the teachings reflected the "life realities" of the day. However, in the course of a century, church control of education proved to be increasingly inadequate as related to community needs.

Eventually, public opinion in the democracy paved the way for young people to have a chance at the education their parents could not have. A whole generation worked to develop systems of free and common schools. There were idealists in this movement, to be sure, but the major thrust was by working people and their organizations. Perhaps they could have banded together and formed education corporations, and built schools in their spare time, but they felt this should be a function of the government. If the government didn't serve the will of the people, why was it there? The government was to be the obvious instrument for advancing and supporting public education.

The immediate results of this move had far-reaching implications. What this told us, in effect, was that government, even at state and local levels, could do what individuals and corporate bodies could not do. The public education movement of the nineteenth century put government into the education business.

The Nineteenth Century

By the beginning of the Civil War, considerable progress was made in providing free and nonsectarian secondary education in tax-supported facilities. A great boost to public education came when the Federal Government passed the Morrill Act of 1862. Under the Act, Congress provided a grant of public land to each state for the foundation of colleges of "agriculture and mechanical arts." Many of the states variously used the grants to establish new institutions, or redirect existing public or private institutions.

The Morrill Act provided for the establishment of some of the world's great universities, and influenced all of American education. Higher education became less elitist in nature, or at least gave more people an opportunity to become members of a democratic elite. The educational aspirations of children from working families could be accommodated.

The demands for more and better education at the elementary and secondary levels were met by schools of education. A continuum ranging from the elementary schools to the universities could be seen. The higher one went up this educational ladder, the better off one was. Education began to have value in itself, although the trappings of education were becoming confused with true learning.

Twentieth Century

John Dewey began calling for education to be more closely attuned to the preparation for practical, modern life rather than for perpetuation of academic tradition. Perhaps, he foresaw the problem of scholars creating more scholars and teachers creating more teachers until the practice would reach the present saturation point.

Meanwhile, President Woodrow Wilson, himself an educator of note, was standing under a cloud of war and perceived more immediate problems. In 1914, America was almost certain to become the arsenal of democracy and the hope of the western world. There was work to be done, there were breadbaskets to fill. The industries that helped us to establish and maintain a way of life were becoming increasingly sophisticated. They must be supplied with skilled workers.

President Wilson established the National Commission on Vocational Education that resulted in the Smith-Hughes Act of 1917. Under the terms of this Act, the Federal Government would directly and specifically provide funds for job skill preparation. Congress was in the education arena once again, doing what state and local governments apparently could not do for themselves.

The Smith-Hughes Act opened the way for a new role for education, relating it more closely to the needs of the national job market and economy, but the Act still set vocational education apart from the mainstream of public schooling. A succession of amendments to the Act followed. Even so, there was little or no change in the dual concept of education for many years.

This dual concept was unfortunate for both the nation and for education itself. The nation was living under a misconception about the relative values of work and human worth. The education community was becoming less relevant to educational needs. These distortions were being reflected in a reliable mirror, the people themselves. Those who could not achieve academically were shunted off to vocational courses. Those who had the aptitude and natural preference for skilled work were denied the opportunity to choose what they wanted because social and parental pressure forced them automatically into the academic track. Many students fell in-between because the educational system either could not understand or refused to understand their special problems.

These remarks are not intended to disparage the American educational system of the past. Under the circumstances, it can be said that both academic and vocational education served the nation rather well in the first half of the twentieth century—but not in the second half.

By the late 50s, both social and economic needs were changing, and education was not keeping up, on either track.

In 1962, President John F. Kennedy appointed a panel on vocational education that resulted in the Vocational Education Act of 1963. The important contribution of this Act was that it formally recognized the work experience concept and provided the federal money and leadership to implement it. The Act authorized grants to states to "provide part-time employment for youths who need the earnings from such employment to continue their vocational training on a full-time basis." This included "persons of all ages in all communities of the state—those in high school who have completed or discontinued their formal education . . . those who need to upgrade their skills . . . special educational handicaps. . . ."

Quite definitely, the Act was a step in the right direction, a solid link in the chain leading toward career education.

The full concept, however, didn't emerge until the 1968 Amendments to the Vocational Education Act were passed. Those Amendments called for the establishment of "exemplary programs and projects" to give "the same kind of attention" to persons entering the so-called vocations as to persons entering college. Again, as in the 63 Act, this section of the law called for bridging the gap between formal education and life. The programs established have, indeed, been exemplary. Operating in all the states and territories, they developed such career education concepts as occupational awareness, occupational orientation, occupational exploration, specialization and job clusters, and much more. Each exemplary project developed its own unique program to meet local needs. Additional funds were made available for research and development of program models. Contracts were let for career education curriculum development.

Legislation in 1972 went even further conceptually, even though the concept was not backed up by financial support. The Act called for integration of vocational education into the world of work as a continuing service for all segments of the community. Throughout their lives, people could enter and exit the system in order to develop new skills, adapt to change, and even change careers and develop new modes of recreation.

But despite these many years of progress, the rift still exists between vocational and academic education—even though there is a growing recognition of the need for integrating life, employment and education.

FUTURE TRENDS

The foregoing has addressed the matter of where we have been. Although the past should certainly teach us something about how to proceed, the questions of where we are now and where we are going are more pertinent.

Definition

Still at issue is the matter of definition. What are we talking about when we say "career education"? The definitions we have come close to describing it only in part. Therefore, because it cannot, as yet, be described as a whole, our legislative bodies are unable to develop it, except indirectly, as a part of the undefined whole.

Descriptive titles are necessary, and the title "career education" has certainly stuck. However, from the legislative standpoint, many people, including the author, wish we could take it all back and call career education something else. We are so used to treating new concepts in categorical terms and as "programs" or "projects" that we look at a reform movement like career education as a new and separate entity to be funded and operated in a virtual vacuum.

Career education is a reform, or change, or revolution in the total public education system. It is not a part of the system, it is the system.

Legislation

The major issue in legislation, of course, is legislation itself. Historically, we have seen how it has been necessary to legislate in the field of education when cooperative and informal means proved to be ineffective. The situation becomes confused on occasion, but, generally, it can be said that where local legislation didn't work, there was state legislation and when that didn't work, there was federal legislation.

At this writing, the current federal administration is making every effort to reverse this legislative process in education as well as in other areas of domestic concern. It remains to be seen whether this represents innovation or an abdication of responsibility. The current administration's approach would strip the states and communities of national legislative support and mandate and expect them to do what they could not do before. Nothing in the historical records says that it will work. The fact remains that, increasingly, education has become a matter of national concern, a national problem, a national priority.

In education, as in other domestic matters, there is legislation to be written and carried out at all levels of government. However, the political realities at the local and state levels are different from those of the national. There is every possibility that recognized national priorities cannot be met at lower levels of government, partly because of political situations, but to a greater extent because the state and local governmental machinery is not geared to deal with such matters with dispatch.

This is not to say that local and state governments cannot meet the needs of the people. Rather, returning to the evolution of legislative activity again, the federal level of government has an established and recognized role in the overall governmental process. It is doubtful if the roles of federal, state, and local governments can be switched from one to the other quickly or without grave crises or internal upheavals.

Sometimes, a crisis can be foreseen and averted at the national level, whereas in a state or community the crisis usually has to occur before something is done. Even in that event, higher levels of government are often called upon to bail out the smaller entity.

Funding

Such a crisis has been brewing for some time with the advent of changes in revenue collection. Many districts have already had crises because of upheavals caused by desegregation, outmigration of higher income population and resulting reduction in the tax base. For years, federal assistance has been crucial to the survival of these districts. If the trend continues, federal legislation will play an increasing role in pulling the school districts over the rough spots in the next series of crises.

Under consideration here are schools in general rather than vocational education in particular, because the existence of common problems may eventually lead to mutual salvation no matter how painful these problems may be for a time. The institution of career education will require a turnabout of the entire system, forced by critical circumstances, and probably implemented by the highest legislative body—the United States Congress.

The most vital legislative issue at the national level continues to be revenue and expenditure. The administration and the Congress would obviously like to see more results for less money. The taxpayers express the same sentiments.

Will career education increase costs? The conventional thinkers, including those in the U. S. Office of Education, think that it should and that it will. The case is already being made for the lost cause of "temporary" increase in cost to eventually reduce the total costs. This is nonsense. Initiate a high cost program, and it will stay a high cost program until it dies; that is the legislative experience.

The mistake that is now being made and perpetuated considers career education as a separate program or thrust. As such, of course, it will result in increased cost because it is an add-on, an imposition on the present system.

In point of fact, career education need not cost more than the present system and could serve to reduce costs. A solid curriculum would require fewer frills when the educational system is made a part of the total community, when it would not be required to attempt to duplicate existing resources and facilities.

Leadership

The need, it appears, is for a new kind of legislation, a new kind of legislative leadership. It is not so much a matter of pouring more money into new kinds of programs in the old programmatic fashion as it is redirecting present resources in an imaginative way toward career education. The opposition to such legislation will be strong, but the rewards for successfully legislating education reform will be worth the fight.

relevant concepts

*Career Development, Awareness,
Exploration, Preparation, Occupational
Clusters, Knowledge About Work, and
Career Ladders and Lattices*

Several persuasive concepts are being incorporated into the operational models for career education, especially in the school-based models. Part Two treats a number of these concepts.

According to Drier, career development is serving as the theory or construct to direct the career education movement. He recommends that awareness, orientation, exploration and preparation be the structure for career education planning, together with development factors and life stages.

Peterson describes a project in which career awareness concepts are being developed for a K-6 curriculum. She specifies major concepts and subconcepts at seven levels for attitudes and appreciation, coping behaviors, decision making, life style, self-development, educational awareness, and career information.

Tennyson traces the genesis of career exploration as a concept and shows how it fits into the modern career education program.

Rasmussen shows how the occupational cluster can be incorporated into an occupational preparation program at the high school level.

Taylor illustrates the occupational cluster concept, pointing out that "cluster" can have a variety of meanings. He reveals the rationale behind the clustering system that he recommended for career education.

Adams shows how knowledge about work can be structured for educational purposes and describes a career information model that can serve as the framework for a career information system.

Kintgen discusses the concept of career ladders and lattices and makes a case for the utility of these concepts in the total career education program.

CAREER DEVELOPMENT: CONSTRUCT FOR EDUCATIONAL CHANGE

Harry N. Drier

Throughout the history of the nation, changes have emerged in educational programs because of national crises, legislative dictates, or public criticisms. Educational critics presently are attacking education with a new fervor. Lack of relevancy, disunity, ineffectiveness, and excessive cost are some of the most common concerns of these critics. While American education is charged with providing a well-rounded education for all youth, some believe that present instructional programs are producing insecurity, disillusionment, and frustration because former students lack the employment skills necessary to survive in the competitive world of work. These charges are well documented. (Holt, 1964; Coleman, 1972; Silberman, 1970).

Educational planners are looking for new ways to refocus and redirect education. This focus will center primarily on the needs of students in relation to an ever changing society. Career development is serving as the theory or construct to direct the current education renovation. Career development, while relatively new, has a history and has been advocated by leading educators, but without much impact until late (Herr, 1972). With the advent of serious consideration of career development theory, an analysis and description are necessary. The purpose of this chapter, then, is to describe at least one such useful construct, its concepts, possible structure and stages, and clues for placing responsibility for its use as an organizing theme in revitalizing education.

Career development is seen in the context of one's total self-development. It is viewed as the process of preparing a person for his total life that includes a distinct number of roles to be played. Others have singled out the social, personal, vocational, avocational, and educational aspects of life and dealt with them separately. This has caused fragmentation in theory and practice. Goldhammer (1972) probably describes this concept best by delineating the broad concept of career into five meaningful roles:

1. Worker,
2. Member of a family unit,
3. Participant in social and practical life of society,
4. Participant in avocational pursuits,
5. Participant in regulatory functions involved in aesthetic, moral and religious concerns.

Intervention strategies can be organized and structured to assist development in a systematic way of describing a person's career in terms of his major life roles. The total educational program could be organized around the basic roles expected in society. Education would come alive and be meaningful because students could relate their learning to life roles that they are playing or will assume in adulthood. Career development in this sense is not merely occupational development in isolation, but purposeful advancement toward the total style of life one is striving to achieve.

Much of today's literature attempts to define the possible range of careers one can choose and prepare to enter. Such material tends to emphasize only the work role. This could give students the feeling that all one has to do is select an occupation at random, accumulate a set of educational experiences, and obtain a position in the field. Career, in this sense, tends only to be concerned with one's work, for a period of time. This limited connotation of career has been associated with the more glamorous occupations and has falsely implied that the core maker in a foundry, as an example, has less than a career. Individuals have careers, the world of work has occupations (Gysber, 1972). An employer provides job experiences that individuals utilize to develop a career.

An individual's work role is extremely important, but is only one way that an individual can express himself and find satisfaction. All decisions that must be made regarding expected or assumed roles need to be considered in totality rather than in isolation. One's career, in this context, should not be viewed as dependent upon outside forces for its own unique growth pattern. It should be viewed as the total mixture of a person's decisions and experiences tempered by his own values, feelings, attitudes, knowledge, achievements, and skills. A career is developed through continuous assessing of one's present position in relation to what he now values as life goals and acceptable means of attainment.

Career development is lifelong, all inclusive, uninterrupted and an irrevocable process. All inclusive means that all experiences are included in a continuum. Uninterrupted means that they are experienced without voids throughout life. Irrevocable indicates that each experience is important to one's development and none can be overlooked. One can interrupt his education or employment; adjust or reverse his values, attitudes, or interests; but the total amalgamation of all these decisions and experiences makes up his career. In this sense, one's career should never be viewed as complete at any point in life, but always evolving.

STAGES OF DEVELOPMENT

Many theorists agree that there are clearly defined life developmental stages that are useful in program development. Such stages have been labeled fantasy (birth to age 11), tentative (age 11 to 17), realistic (age 18 and beyond) (Ginzberg, et al., 1951). Super (1963) titles the stages as growth (birth to age 14), exploration (years 15 to 24), establishment (years 25-44), maintenance (years 45 to 65), and decline (years 65 and beyond). Another way of classifying the stages to enable educational planners to infuse career development into the total educational experiences of students in elementary, secondary, and postsecondary schools could be organized as depicted in Figure 1.

In varying degrees, all are going through phases of awareness, orientation, exploration and preparation. Career development theory suggests that this is the sequence in which one learns and experiences. The structure allows us to stress appropriate goals for all children and adults. All are constantly searching, becoming aware, exploring and learning new skills. All have different needs at various stages, as well as different capacities to meet them. Educators can assist individuals through this process by appropriately intervening and providing options to facilitate meaningful career development.

Interventions must be carefully selected and formulated. Career educators must not overwhelm students so they do not experience and decide for themselves. Career education cannot be led by those who see themselves, or instructional content, as primal. An educational environment and staff must exist that guides, rather than decides, that emphasizes learning more than teaching and that associates learning and living.

"How continuously on the watch we must be in order not to help too much, not to help to the point of interfering where we are not wanted or needed" (Benjamin, 1969). "The responsibility for what life expects of a person is ultimately and undisputedly his, and his alone. Genuine choices he must be given and mistakes he must be allowed to make. It is he who must reach a decision and it is he who must suffer the consequences" (Yamamoto, 1972). Education developed around career development concepts permits the student to make his own decisions in order to achieve personal life expectations.

Application of career development concepts to public education demands a model that provides scope, sequence and direction to assure broad coverage of developmental goals. If education is to be infused with career development goals, all staff, students, parents, and the community in general need to understand when and how to play their role.

Utilizing Super's four basic stages (awareness, orientation, exploration, and preparation) as a frame of reference, we must determine a finer breakdown before we can apply goals and objectives in a developmental way. For this purpose, nine different factors are offered in Figure 2 to bring into perspective and focus the recommended

CAREER DEVELOPMENT STRUCTURE FOR EDUCATIONAL PLANNING

STAGES	GRADE AND AGE LEVELS	GOALS
Awareness	Middle Childhood Grades K-3 Ages 6-9	To become *conscious* of themselves, others, workers and the environment in which they live
Orientation	Late Childhood Grades 4-6 Ages 10-12	To begin conceptualizing and putting into life goal perspective the previously and presently acquired knowledge and experiences arranged in a usable form
Exploration	Early Adolescence Grades 7-9 Ages 13-15	To begin generalizing about past experiences and through real life discovery learning acquire sufficient preparation knowledge to influence career decision-making
Preparation	Adolescence and Early Adulthood Grades 10-16 Ages 16-and beyond	The internalization of experiences with emphasis on skill acquisition, sufficient to step into life roles as an adult

Figure 1

design for restructuring education. These factors, being either introduced, developed or emphasized at any of the stages in a developmental way, will result in an honest and realistic career identity. The individual will thus be able to make appropriate self-assessments, decisions and adjustments. Career identity is *always* present, not merely an event. Career education can assist the individual in accomplishing self-assessment and application.

Awareness

The application strategy used at the awareness level is one of initially introducing five of the nine basic career development factors using sensory stimulus. Children in grades K-3 should begin to achieve a perception of themselves, understand how similar or different they are from others they know, differentiate between work and play, understand the economic structure that exists in their home and community, identify the many workers in their lives and the importance of all workers to their environment, and identify other societal factors that exist around them and which affect their lives.

Orientation

At the orientation level, education should continue to develop the factor learnings previously introduced at the awareness level with the emphasis shifting to a formulation of personal conceptualizations. As the child matures, new factors, such as career planning, occupational preparation, leisure, and avocational planning, are also introduced. Through instruction and guidance, students should have the opportunity for successive, successful learning experiences related to self, workers, decision making, society, characteristics, economics and the process of career planning. Through closer examination and more active participation (visitations, role playing, and experimentation), the student will be better able to sort out the apparent differences between individuals in terms of what they do and how they plan and prepare. They will also begin to gain a perspective of society.

Exploration

In early adolescence, exploration should be stressed to provide the individual needed experiences and knowledge to begin internalizing and drawing initial general conclusions about himself in relation to possible life careers. Through intensified opportunities to test decision making capabilities, students begin to put into perspective what they have learned. They begin to see purpose and realize capabilities to plan and prepare for projected life roles. Educational and guidance programs need to be organized in a way to enable students to check initial career plans against reality in an environment that allows both success and failure to be perceived as positive. It should be positive in the sense that trial and error leads to a better self-concept, thus allowing for intelligent planning. Through exploration, the need for

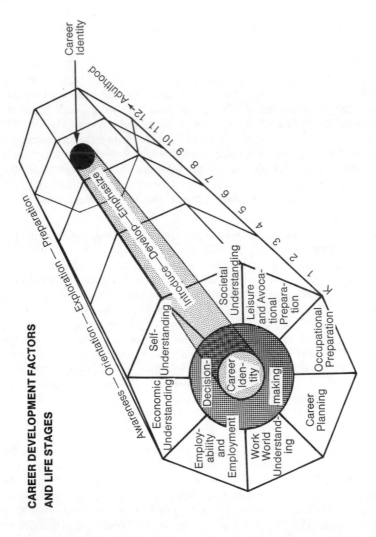

**CAREER DEVELOPMENT FACTORS
AND LIFE STAGES**

Career Identity

Awareness — Orientation — Exploration — Preparation

Adulthood 12 11 10 9 8 7 6 5 4 3 2 1

Introduce — Develop — Emphasize

Self-Understanding

Societal Understanding

Leisure and Avocational Preparation

Economic Understanding

Decision-making

Career Identity

Occupational Preparation

Employability and Employment

Work World Understanding

Career Planning

Figure 2

occupational preparation is introduced. Traits necessary for employment become meaningful and one begins to perceive the work opportunities that exist, and become inquisitive about preparing for job entry.

Preparation

When a student has been introduced to and has developed basic understandings and skills necessary for his career development, he has matured to the point of making specific conclusions concerning himself and his perceived life style. Through educational preparation programs that permit role testing, he can try out his plans and dreams and begin to construct a tentative life plan developed for work, leisure, community involvement and other aspects of his life.

In order to allow individuals the freedom to design and test their projected life plans, secondary and postsecondary schools must permit an atmosphere that encourages individuals to plan, decide, test, evaluate and replace. Each student should be given the opportunity to plan, with proper guidance, his educational program. Educators' major roles will be to guide, advise, and coordinate the various educational and work experiences deemed necessary by the individual. This educational stage permits a positive test of a student's decision making skills and his educational and occupational competence before formal ties to the school are severed.

INFUSION OF CAREER DEVELOPMENT GOALS
IN EDUCATIONAL PROGRAMS

Figure 3 portrays a scope and sequence to use in infusing career development into curriculum and guidance programs. While the chart shows a limited number of factors being introduced at certain stages, it is intended to show where the major formal emphasis should be placed at a given point in time. The chart should not be interpreted as suggesting that the factors can be introduced only during the period of time indicated. The terms "introduce," "develop," and "emphasize" are used to guide those who must design sequential program goals, objectives in a programmatic and pragmatic way.

Factors for Infusion

The factors in Figure 3 are but one way of identifying the developmental concepts that could provide for an understanding of the career development process. Each factor could be defined more specifically for clarity.

Self-understanding involves how one perceives himself in relation to his individual characteristics and the relationship he has with others within his intervening environment (Drier, et al., 1972b).

Economic understanding identifies the ability to define relationships between occupations and personal economics, how economic wealth

CAREER DEVELOPMENT PROGRAM PLANNING
SCOPE AND SEQUENCE

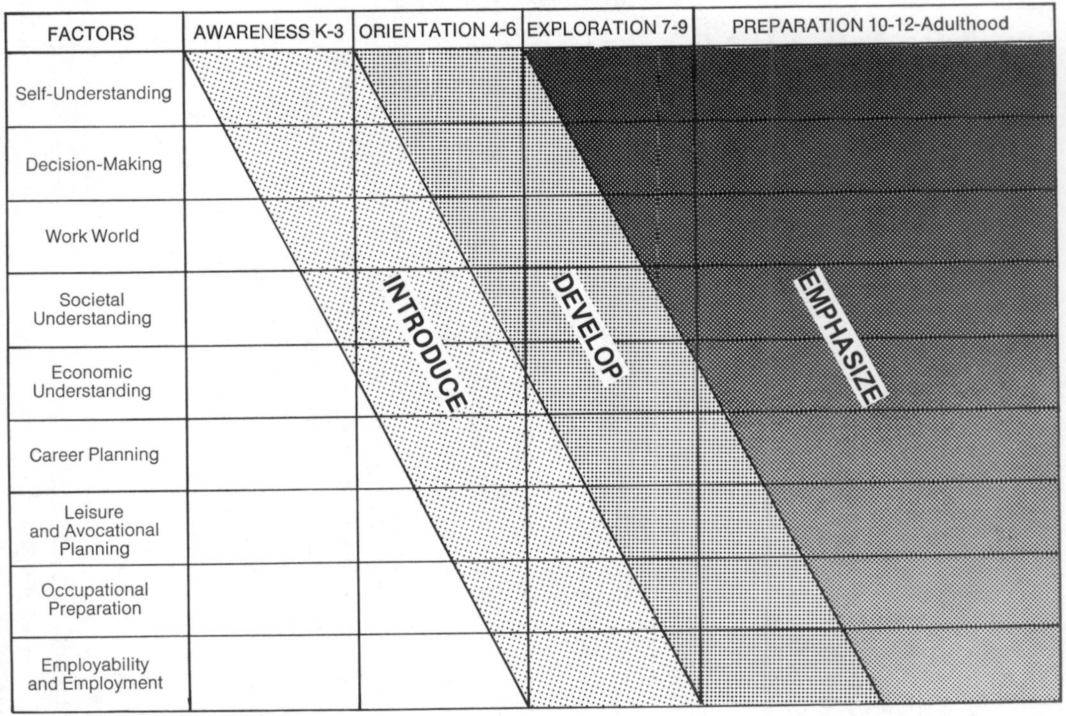

FACTORS	AWARENESS K-3	ORIENTATION 4-6	EXPLORATION 7-9	PREPARATION 10-12-Adulthood
Self-Understanding				
Decision-Making				
Work World				
Societal Understanding				
Economic Understanding				
Career Planning				
Leisure and Avocational Planning				
Occupational Preparation				
Employability and Employment				

INTRODUCE

DEVELOP

EMPHASIZE

Figure 3

is accumulated other than through work, and how to relate effectively one's present and anticipated economic status to that present in his total environment and its possible effect on his career.

Employability and employment is the ability to locate, analyze, compete for and procure occupational opportunities, as well as those attitudes and interpersonal skills necessary for job retention, progression and adjustment.

Work world understanding includes the ability to see work as an integral part of self-expression and self-realization; to view the work world considering such factors as the working conditions, social aspects, impinging economic impact, psychological considerations, its structure and nature, its change and effect as well as the benefits and restrictions related to the different kinds of work available.

Career planning relates the ability to see career (life) planning as an informational, experiential and decision making process. Planning serves as a way of preparing for change. One needs to consider the kinds of information needed for acting, understand the impact that one's family, peers and community have upon his planning and realize the reservoir of opportunities available to him to assist in decision making.

Occupation preparation identifies the ability to be in a state of employment readiness (tool and process) at the point of exiting from school. One's occupational preparation is exhibited by his being able to apply successfully job competencies acquired in school to his initial occupation. He should also be able to analyze the additional skills and understandings necessary to mature in the occupation.

Leisure and avocational preparation is the ability to recognize that leisure is one major aspect of life that needs to be considered and to understand that much personal satisfaction can be achieved if appropriate preparation is gained. The importance of seeing how one's avocational interests and skills can often be utilized in his choice of work may bring a higher level of satisfaction in both.

Societal understanding includes the ability to analyze society through the study of physical and social sciences, language arts, mathematics, humanities, etc. While there are many nonwork related ways of acquiring basic communication skills and understandings of society, past, present, and future, there are also numerous relationships to how one plans, chooses and participates in work.

Decision making involves the ability to understand a logical process for such decision making and the possession of sufficient skills to achieve internalization of the experiences in all aspects of life. It includes the ability to see the relationship between cause and effect and a willingness to shoulder the responsibilities for decision results; and, the ability to detour where necessary, for appropriate life adjustments.

Changing the Program

How does one take a program at this point and begin to modify the instructional program for which he is responsible? How can career development concepts be infused into the total educational program utilizing current staff to accomplish the task? An instructional imperative such as career education is powerful as an incentive, but alone it remains a pressure. Its development and implementation are hollow if there are no curriculum or guidance programs. However conceptually sound and well designed it may be, the program is inert until it reaches the student through interested and prepared persons who bring it to life. What is needed is the help of local staff in authoring the text for educational change. Such involvement will not only build commitment, but increase staff skills and knowledge needed to execute the program with students. We can claim arrival of career education when education functionally includes the broad career dimension; when it has career development goals implanted into its materials, processes, policies, budget and information systems; when career development is integral to the daily instructional experiences of students; when it is a demanded expectation of parents and patrons; when career development education occurs in our schools, communities and homes as a regular, not special curriculum or guidance program, we will then be able to state with confidence, "Career education has arrived" (Drier, 1972a).

Involvement of Staff

How does one involve all staff to permit individual and local ownership? A process must be developed that allows full staff participation, using their accumulative knowledge and skills. A first step might be to establish a community wide task force, with representatives from education, industry/business, youth and parents. This committee could be charged with forming a conceptual model for determining programmatic goals for each factor and grade level. During this period, each task force member, using a simplified Delphi process should gain the reactions of other peers. This approach not only utilizes their advice, but begins the process of multi-staff involvement. A second responsibility of the task force would be to design an infusion process that would clearly describe how one could take career development goals and integrate them with the curriculum and guidance program. One tested method involves use of the Cubistic Model Approach (Figure 4) that identifies each of the necessary steps one must follow.

With this approach, staff can use either of two infusion methods. One would be to design, somewhat in isolation, a separate career education program that would be taught intermittently with the present curriculum. The other would involve total integration. To

FACTOR ECONOMIC UNDERSTANDING

Teacher and Counselor Model
for Infusing Career Development Concepts,
Goals, and Objectives into all Learner Experiences

Example illustrated
in Figure 5

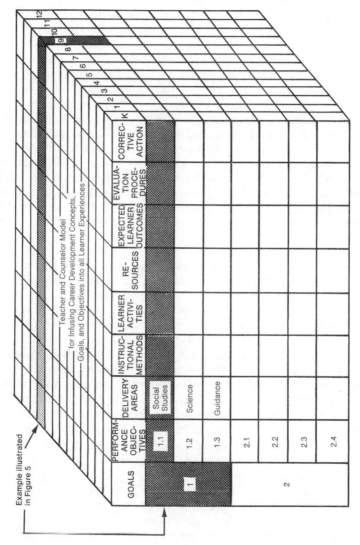

Figure 4

avoid program fragmentation, the latter is by far the wiser choice. This demands that staff take their present instructional program guide materials and seek new ways to incorporate the newly developed career development goals for each grade and discipline. At this point, there needs to be an articulation check to assure that there is little unplanned overlap between goals between grade levels. Once this assurance is made, staff in small groups utilizing community and student assistance can begin to make decisions about delivery, methods, learner activities, resources, performance objectives, outcomes expected, evaluation procedures and strategies for pilot testing and revising their work (see Figure 5).

These decisions should be made in reference to the total educational experience to be provided the individual and in reference to the specific grade and life stage being studied. The resulting outcome should be a comprehensive instructional plan both at a specific grade or discipline level as well as for the total district. Careful analysis must be made at specified milestones throughout the process to allow sorting out possible duplications that could exist because of the many persons utilized in this type of program development work.

This approach may be viewed as requiring massive duplication, poor utilization of staff time and educational-financial resources when done by every school system across the country. Some critics suggest that we should instead develop a national career education curriculum with the necessary resources for its implementation. Educational planners could then purchase the nationally developed curriculum and install it with a minimum of in-service training for their staff. The suggested method outlined does not delimit the potential of utilizing the various materials being developed and tested at research and development centers, state departments, universities, commercial firms or in other local districts. This approach suggests that educators want, and in fact insist on, a voice in program development and revision at the local level. Through a local development effort that includes careful study of resources available, staff benefits are many.

First, they feel their professional competencies have been utilized in program decision making and development. This also tends to stimulate a feeling of ownership. Second, it personalizes their instructional programs, taking into account the educator's understanding of the local environmental conditions, student interests and achievement potential. Third, this process can involve many key factors in the community to permit students, parents and employers an opportunity to play more than a token role in educational decision making. Through this type of involvement, installation has a greater chance for success because it is the community's program, not one developed in isolation. Fourth, the process itself provides comprehensive in-service training and community involvement program necessary for

FACTOR Economic Understanding
GOAL STATEMENT The student will understand that occupations can develop in different ways.
PERFORMANCE OBJECTIVE Through teacher-directed class projects and discussions, students will recognize that their community's awareness of the need to preserve the environment will create a demand for new occupations.

DELIVERY AREA	INSTRUC-TIONAL METHODS	LEARNER ACTIVITIES	RESOURCES	EXPECTED LEARNER OUTCOMES	EVALUATION PROCEDURES	CORRECTIVE ACTION
SOCIAL STUDIES	Invite visitors representing (2) local manufacturers into the classroom to discuss the synthetic process and their products	List products that have been replaced by synthetic products because of a concern for natural resources	Local plants Periodicals in media center	Knowledge of 5 products that have been replaced by synthetic substitutes	Student check-list and student report observation	New periodicals needed Select new speakers
	Make contact with (1) local manufacturer to arrange for a guided tour	Field trip to recycling plant	Visitors Samples of products	Be able to describe verbally the recycling process	Each student will write a field trip report paper on the process they witnessed	Cut down on leaflets Report writing task
Possible aid from the gu dance, science, art and English departments	Provide a basic outline on how to construct a bulletin board display and make appropriate materials available	Make a bulletin board to display new ecology products, e.g. new 7-UP returnable bottles, garbage compressor	Construction paper and pictures	Ability to follow directions and to know the kinds of display materials that are available because of their knowledge of recycled products	Observation of bulletin board displays	None

Figure 5

program adoption and implementation. It allows the dissemination of information, the rationale, intent, factors, concepts, objectives and delivery strategies of career education. It develops commitment, positive attitudes through interaction and involvement, participation and identification, as well as competency. The opportunity to observe, to practice, to experiment, to prepare, to transact and to evaluate are provided. Lastly, it will demonstrate educators' responsiveness to systematic planning and accountability, it also demands the program be all inclusive, one in which all are involved and all are uniquely accountable (Drier, 1972a).

The responsibility and accountability issue is one that is dealt with during the program development process. While it has been implied that all members of the school community have shared responsibility, decisions must be made in a systematic way about who is the most appropriate specialist to assume responsibility for each aspect of program delivery. A suggested sample set of competencies—that existing instructional and guidance staff may already possess—that would help in delivering career education follows:

Teacher

Provide easy transition from home to school,

Demonstrate relationships between learning and occupational requirements,

Assist parents in understanding the child's career development needs,

Provide curriculum based decision making experiences,

Understand group processes and interpersonal techniques,

Analyze student cumulative career development experiences,

Provide exploratory experiences in the world of work,

Assist in student understandings of capabilities, interests and limitations,

Provide occupational preparation experiences sufficient for one's career development,

Provide work experiences in a non-threatening environment.

School Counselor

Understand career development process,

Understand individual differences and process for self-appraisal,

Understand process of human growth and development,

Understand methods of obtaining necessary data for self-appraisal and world of work,

Possess skills in individual and group counseling and guidance,

Possess consulting skills necessary to interact with staff, parents and community,

Possess skills in the use of assessment tools and techniques and methods of information storage and use,

Identify role models for individuals to use,

Understand curriculum and relationship to individual needs.

Other key individuals such as administrators, community members, parents, peers and the individual himself may also have some of the unique skills needed by a career education program. The teacher and counselor examples serve only to suggest that once program functions have been identified, competencies of all those involved should be analyzed and specific roles identified for each participant. They imply that existing roles must be restructured to fit the new program and be modified as program, students, society and staff change.

CONCLUSION

Career education cannot be viewed as a frill or an add-on to the present educational program. It must be viewed as total education—education for life—not an intervention that occurs periodically. Career development must be woven into the ongoing substantive procedural and organizational fabric of the system. The thoughts expressed in this chapter are intended to describe a process for infusing career development into education at all points, involving all those persons who are eventually responsible for its outcomes.

REFERENCES

Benjamin, Alfred. *The Helping Interview*. (Boston: Houghton Mifflin Co. 1969)

Coleman, James. "The Children Have Outgrown Our Schools," *Psychology Today*, V, (February, 1972)

Drier, Harry N., Jr. "In-service Preparation—Key to Career Education Delivery." Paper presented at the 6th Annual National Vocational and Technical Teacher Education Seminar, Columbus, Ohio, 1972a.

———, et al. *K-12 Guide for Integrating Career Development Into Local Curriculum*. (Worthington, Ohio: Charles A. Jones Publishing Co. 1972b)

Ginzberg, E.; Ginsburg, S. W.; Axelrod, S.; and Herma, J. L. *Occupational Choice: An Approach to A General Theory*. (New York: Columbia University Press. 1951)

Goldhammer, Keith. *A Careers Curriculum*. (Columbus, Ohio: The Center for Vocational and Technical Education, The Ohio State University. 1971)

Gysber, Norman C. "Foundations of Career Education." Paper presented at the 5th Annual National Leadership Development Seminar for State Directors of Vocational Education, Columbus, Ohio, 1972.

Herr, Edwin L. *Review and Synthesis of Foundations for Career Education.* (Columbus, Ohio: The Center for Vocational and Technical Education, The Ohio State University. 1972)

Holt, John C. *How Children Fail.* (New York: Pitman. 1964)

Silberman, Charles E. *Crisis in the Classroom.* (New York: Random House. 1970)

Super, D. E.; Starishevsky, R.; Matten, N.; and Jordon, J. P. *Career Development: Self Concept Theory.* (New York: College Entrance Examination Board. 1963)

Yamamoto, Kaoru. "Better Guidance for the Individual," *Educational Leadership,* XXIX, (January, 1972)

A CAREER AWARENESS PROGRAM UNDER DEVELOPMENT

Marla Peterson

THE RELATIONSHIP OF CAREER AWARENESS, CAREER DEVELOPMENT AND CAREER EDUCATION

In the recent literature concerning elementary school curriculum development, the terms "career awareness," "career development," and "career education" are sometimes used interchangeably. This is one sign that an educational movement is in its formative stages. But as various public school exemplary projects and career education curriculum projects progress, definitions of career-related terminology are beginning to become more explicit.

The Enrichment of Teacher and Counselor Competencies in Career Education Project (ETC Project), a career awareness curriculum project funded by the Curriculum Center for Occupational and Adult Education, U.S. Office of Education, is being conducted by The Center for Educational Studies in the School of Education at Eastern Illinois University. The project staff has established the following definitions for the project:

> *Career awareness* is the term generally assigned to the pre-school through sixth grade career education program when referring to a comprehensive pre-school through adult career education program.
>
> *Career development* includes those concepts which are related to: Attitudes and Appreciations, Coping Behaviors, Career Information, Decision Making, Educational Awareness, Lifestyle, and Self Development.
>
> *Career education* in the elementary school is the curriculum which results when career development concepts and subject matter concepts are brought together in an instructional system that has meaning for children.
>
> *Career education activities* (1) emanate from the concepts that are related to the seven dimensions of career development cited above, (2) act as synthesizing agents to bring subject matter and career development concepts together, (3) revolve around life-based experiences, and (4) are intended for use by all students throughout their educational programs.

An examination of the above definitions reveals the ETC staff's beliefs about the "content" of career development and also a philosophy regarding the placement of career development concepts within a total elementary school program.

The "Content" of Career Development

One of the first questions that must be asked when career education programs are being developed is, "What career development concepts should be included in a career education curriculum?" The

ETC staff has identified career development concepts that should be a part of a K-6 career education program, following an extensive review of career development theory and a look at concepts that had been identified by these career education projects:

> Comprehensive Career Education Model (CCEM)
> The Center for Vocational and Technical Education
> The Ohio State University
>
> Anne Arundel County Career Education Project
> Anne Arundel County, Maryland
>
> Ohio's Career Continuum Program
> Division of Vocational Education
> State Department of Education
>
> EPDA Institute: Career Development and the Elementary
>   School Curriculum
> College of Education
> University of Minnesota
>
> OCCUPAC Project
> Eastern Illinois University
> Charleston, Illinois

The concepts were divided into seven dimensions (Attitudes and Appreciations, Career Coping Behaviors, Career Information, Decision Making, Educational Awareness, Lifestyle, and Self-development). Within each of the dimensions, major concepts that spiral through the curriculum have been identified. Within major concepts, main ideas for each experience level have been developed. Teaching units will be written for each experience level for five of the dimensions—Attitudes and Appreciations, Career Coping Behaviors, Decision Making, Lifestyle, and Self-development. The other two dimensions, Career Information and Educational Awareness, will be integrated with the materials that are devised for the other five dimensions. Teacher resource units will be devised for the dimensions.

Each teaching unit will (a) emphasize certain career education main ideas, (b) be tied directly to a subject matter area (mathematics, science, language arts, or social studies), and (c) relate to an occupation or occupational cluster area. The units will tend to emphasize the use of manipulatives and concrete objects.

The K-6 career development concepts that are serving as the basis for the development of ETC curricular materials will be presented here. With these concepts, as well as with other attempts that have been made to identify career development concepts, *it must be remembered that these attempts, for the most part, are still being validated.* Concepts are being revised, moved to different grade levels, etc. The concepts are presented so that other groups may test them, validate them, and select from them in order to help build career development programs.

ATTITUDES AND APPRECIATION

Major Concept

Society is dependent upon the productive work of many people.

Subconcepts

Readiness: Men and women work in many different jobs

First experience: The community is dependent upon various workers

Second experience: Work has importance and value to society

Third experience: The work of many people is needed to produce goods and services consumed by society

Fourth experience: The work of one individual depends on the work of other individuals

Fifth experience: Specialization creates an interdependent society

Sixth experience: A wide range of specialized occupations is necessary for the well-being of society

Major Concept

Every worker has responsibility to himself and to society.

Subconcepts

Readiness: Completing a task is important

First experience: An individual may be relied upon by others to complete an accepted task

Second experience: There are common expectations such as punctuality, avoidance of excessive absence, etc., that apply to almost all occupations

Third experience: An individual should appreciate that policies and procedures are needed in work settings and that these policies and procedures vary from one setting to another

Fourth experience: Honesty in work takes many forms

Fifth experience: Upon successful completion of a task one may receive various rewards such as self-satisfaction, recognition from others, etc.

Sixth experience: An individual must determine what career-related rewards are important to him

COPING BEHAVIORS

Major Concept

Certain identifiable attitudes, values, and behaviors enable one to obtain, hold, and advance in a career.

Subconcepts

Readiness: An individual should learn to cope with authority exercised by others

First experience: An individual should learn to cope with the rights and feelings of others

Second experience: An individual should learn how to take and give criticism

Third experience: A contribution to group effort can be made by demonstrating ability to both compromise and exercise influence in achievement

Fourth experience: Certain behaviors are appropriate to specific job settings

Fifth experience: There is a universality of feelings and aspirations of all people—regardless of physical appearance, nationality, creed, sex, or ethnic background

Sixth experience: There are effective interpersonal relations skills for giving or evaluating instructions

Major Concept

Individuals can learn to perform adequately in a variety of occupations and occupational environments.

Subconcepts

Readiness: Different skills and knowledges are required for different tasks

First experience: Several skills may be required to perform a given task

Second experience: Some skills can be transferred from one job to another

Third experience: Performance requirements for a job will vary with the work setting of the job

Fourth experience: Performance requirements for a job may change with time

Fifth experience: It is important for a person to be able to make the transition from one job to another

Sixth experience: There are characteristics which differentiate between occupations—both within and between job families

DECISION MAKING

Major Concept

Life involves a series of choices leading to career commitments.

Subconcepts

Readiness: Choice means "making up one's mind" and there are certain situations where one can make choices

First experience: Things change and these changes influence the choices and decisions one makes

Second experience: An individual's decisions affect himself and others

Third experience: People change and these changes influence the choices and decisions one makes

Fourth experience: Decision making involves risk

Fifth experience: Decision making can precipitate chain reactions

Sixth experience: Previous decisions, peers, gratifications, needs, interests, and career information influence present and future decisions

Major Concept

Basic components of the decision-making process can be applied to the establishing of personal goals and the making of career-related decisions.

Subconcepts

Readiness: An individual should recognize what "a goal" is and learn how to set one's own goals

First experience: An individual should consider alternative ways to reach a given goal

Second experience: Problems which conflict with one's goals can be identified and assessed

Third experience: Decision making plays a role in the setting of immediate and long-range goals

Fourth experience: The decision-making process can be used to set priorities in developing personal goals

Fifth experience: Setting goals can be enhanced by analyzing decision-making processes

Sixth experience: The decision-making process can be used to determine one's preferences between various job families at that point in time

LIFESTYLE

Major Concept

Work affects an individual's way of life, in that a person is a socioeconomic being, a family being, a leisure being, and a moral being.

Subconcepts

Readiness: Most people work and there are many reasons why people work

First experience: Family members perform work they are capable of performing, responsibilities are shared, and the family is an interdependent unit

Second experience: Family life is affected by work

Third experience: Occupational choice affects the amount of leisure time an individual has

Fourth experience: Moral principles are an integral part of one's work life

Fifth experience: Relationships exist between desired lifestyles and career monetary rewards

Sixth experience: Leisure-time activities and interests may lead to a career

SELF-DEVELOPMENT

Major Concept

An understanding and acceptance of self is important.

Subconcepts

Readiness: Awareness of oneself within the context of the family structure is important

First experience: An individual plays various roles—friend, student, group member, etc.

Second experience: There are certain physical, social, and emotional characteristics which make an individual unique

Third experience: An individual's feelings relative to happiness, fear, anger, loneliness, etc., are diverse

Fourth experience: Conclusions may be drawn about how one person's membership in a group affects the group and how the group affects him

Fifth experience: There is a relationship between an individual's developing interests and his abilities

Sixth experience: There is a relationship between an individual's knowledge and acceptance of self and his career preference

Major Concept

Social, economic, educational, and cultural forces influence self-development.

Subconcepts

Readiness: An individual is influenced by other people

First experience: The school can provide an opportunity to enhance self-development

Second experience: An individual is influenced by economic forces

Third experience: Groups outside of school influence an individual's personal development

Fourth experience: An individual's feelings and the feelings of others relate to commonly held beliefs and customs

Fifth experience: Changes in an individual influence his environment and changes in environment influence him

Sixth experience: An individual's values and personal goals are influenced by the values of other people

Major Concept

Individuals differ in their interests, aptitudes, values, and achievements.

Subconcepts

Readiness: An individual should be aware of the tasks that he performs and begin to determine his interests in these tasks

First experience: An individual has the ability to perform various tasks

Second experience: An individual's interests and abilities are not always the same as his peers,

Third experience: An individual's values are not always the same as his peers,

Fourth experience: Achievements in school and out of school are often dependent upon interests, aptitudes, and values

Fifth experience: An individual can differentiate between himself and others in terms of interests, aptitudes, values, and achievements in and out of school

Sixth experience: There is a relationship among interests, aptitudes, achievements, values, and occupations

Educational Awareness and Career Information are two dimensions of career development that will be integrated with each of the other five dimensions as curricular materials are being developed. In other words, no separate units on career information are being planned. Rather, career information is interspersed throughout other career education activities. This integration of career information with other career education concepts prevents the development of a career education program that is built solely on an "occupational information" approach.

Concepts related to Educational Awareness and Career Information are presented below:

EDUCATIONAL AWARENESS

Major Concept

Educational skills and experiences are related to the achievement of career and life goals.

Subconcepts

Readiness: There are reasons for going to school

First experience: Learning and performing various tasks are related

Second experience: Language arts skills and mathematics skills are required in many occupations

Third experience: There may be a relationship between one's in-school experiences and out-of-school experiences

Fourth experience: People continue learning throughout their lives

Fifth experience: Skills learned in the classroom can be related to those skills used in specific careers

Sixth experience: Desire and capability to learn influence learning and career directions

CAREER INFORMATION

Major Concept

Basic career information will aid in making career related decisions.

Subconcepts

(Note: Career information has not been broken out into subconcepts at the various experience levels. Instead, each subconcept is appropriate for all experience levels. Activities will be designed so the subconcepts are presented at increasingly higher levels of sophistication as the experience levels increase.)

Occupations may have certain *dress* requirements.

Some occupations require the use of *specific materials and equipment.*

Some occupations have their own *vocabulary.*

Some occupations have their *unpleasant as well as* their *pleasant* aspects and these are determined by the individual worker.

Occupations have their own *work environment,* i.e., indoors-outdoors, quiet-noisy, individual-group, daytime-nighttime hours, factories-offices, etc.

Some occupations require *special aptitudes.*

Earnings vary with occupations.

Occupations have *training requirements.*

There are different *sources of training* for occupations.

Cost of training for an occupation varies.

Career development includes *progression through stages of educational and occupational training.*

Technological, economic, social, and political factors influence job *supply and demand.*

A wide variety of occupations exist which may be classified in several ways.

There are *many sources* of career information—past experience, family, friends, community, school, commercial materials, etc.

Sources of information *need to be validated.*

Placement of Career Development Concepts
Within the Elementary School Curriculum

There are several philosophies regarding the placement of career development concepts in the elementary school curriculum. Some career education leaders maintain that career development concepts should be organized into a career education program that can stand by itself alongside the other subject matter that is traditionally taught in the elementary school. Others maintain that career development concepts are the unifying force that can make other subject matter more meaningful, and that career development concepts ought to be infused into them. There is need for experimentation with both types of curriculum organization plans.

Regardless of which plan is used, there are basic planning functions to be taken into consideration. Have career development concepts been identified? If so, is the number of concepts so unwieldy that almost any school curriculum would be hard pressed to incorporate all the concepts into its curriculum? Quantity does not necessarily imply quality. Has child growth and development data been taken into consideration? Are suggested activities good activities for children? Can the career development concepts be tied to subject matter in a meaningful way? Or, is the relationship an artificial one?

ELEMENTARY SCHOOL CAREER EDUCATION CURRICULUM EFFORTS

There are several major career education curriculum projects currently in progress that have implications for elementary school programs. Five of these projects are funded directly by federal agencies and are among the better known elementary school and pre-school career education curriculum projects:

1. *The School-based Comprehensive Career Education Model (CCEM),* one of four models being supported by the National Institute of Education; conducted by The Center for Vocational and Technical Education, The Ohio State University, Columbus, Ohio; Dr. Aaron Miller, Director.

2. *Career Education Curriculum Development for Awareness (Grades K-6),* funded by the Curriculum Center for Occupational and Adult Education, U.S. Office of Education; conducted by The Center for Educational Studies, School of Ed-

ucation, Eastern Illinois University, Charleston, Illinois; Dr.
Marla Peterson, Director.

3. *Career Education Curriculum Development for Awareness
   (Grades K-6),* funded by the Curriculum Center for Occupational and Adult Education, U.S. Office of Education; conducted by American Institutes for Research Center for Research and Evaluation in the Application of Technology in
   Education, Palo Alto, California; Dr. James Dunn, Director.

4. *Curriculum for Career Awareness for Children's Television
   Programs,* funded by the Curriculum Center for Occupational and Adult Education, U.S. Office of Education; conducted
   by Sutherland Learning Associates, Los Angeles, California;
   Alan Sloan, Director.

5. *Objectives, Content, and Evaluation of TV Career Aware-
   ness Program for 3-6 Year Olds,* funded by the Curriculum
   Center for Occupational and Adult Education, U.S. Office of
   Education; conducted by Division of Vocational Education,
   University of California, Los Angeles, California; Dr. Melvin
   Barlow, Director.

The CCEM project is the most comprehensive of the five projects
in that it involves the development of a comprehensive education program focused on careers, beginning with the entry of the child into a
formal school program and continuing into the adult years. (CCEM is
discussed more fully by Miller in another chapter in the Yearbook.)

The two Career Education Curriculum Development for Awareness
(Grades K-6) projects described here have similar objectives:

1. To develop, evaluate, and disseminate career education curriculum guides that are applicable to any school with grade
   levels functionally equivalent to K-6 and which result in the
   integration of positive values and attitudes toward work, self-
   awareness, development of decision-making skills, and awareness of occupational opportunities in career lines within major occupational fields;

2. To develop, implement, evaluate, and disseminate sample
   teaching learning modules for the K-6 career education curriculum guides achieved by fusing and/or coordinating academic and occupational concepts and utilizing multi-media
   instructional tools;

3. To develop, evaluate, and disseminate a design of a K-6 career education instructional system which is adaptable to any
   elementary instructional program and which may serve as an
   alternative to present career education instructional systems.

The two career education curriculum projects for 3-6 year olds described previously complement each other in that the UCLA project is providing the objectives, content, and evaluation procedures for a multi-media learning system that is being devised by Sutherland Learning Associates.

An innovative part of the multi-media system is the distribution and dissemination procedures. A series of two-minute films, one product of the multi-media system, were aired on the CBS children's program, "Captain Kangaroo" during the spring of 1973. Development of study guides, books, records, etc., that complement the films is also envisioned. The complete system is intended for use with pre-school, kindergarten, and first grade children.

The objectives for the multi-media system are:

1. To develop in the child (age 3-6) an awareness of occupational opportunities.

2. To enlarge the vocational self-concept of children—that is, to enable the child to see himself in a variety of occupational roles.

3. To begin to develop a responsibility ethic within the child— that is, responsibility to self and others.

In addition to the five career awareness projects that have already been cited, it should be noted that some elementary school curriculum materials will be devised by the various "cluster" projects that have been funded by the Curriculum Center for Occupational and Adult Education, U.S. Office of Education. K-6 career education materials will be developed by projects such as the "Curriculum Development Basic to the Training of Individuals for Employment in Agri-Business, Natural Resources, and Environmental Protection" project, which is being conducted by the Ohio Career Education and Curriculum Management Laboratory in Agriculture Education at The Ohio State University, and the "Development of Comprehensive Career Education Curriculum Guidelines for Recreation Hospitality and Tourism Occupations Cluster" project, which is being conducted by the Research Foundation, University of Kentucky.

SUMMARY

Elementary school career education programs have progressed from the stage of being essentially an occupational-information type program to the stage where career development concepts that relate to areas such as self-development and decision making are also an integral part of a K-6 career education program. Federal and state-administered funding has permitted experimentation with career education programs at the elementary school level. This represents a truly developmental approach to career education.

CAREER EXPLORATION

W. Wesley Tennyson

The genesis of career exploration dates to 1895 when the California School of Mechanic Arts, under George Arthur Merrill, introduced exploratory activities into its curriculum. In addition to pursuing general education subjects, the student was exposed to two years of "sample exercises drawn from simple work in each of the trades taught by the school . . . followed by two years of preparation in a specific trade" (Brewer, 1942:49).

Later, certain elements of career exploration were formally explicated in a posthumously published classic entitled *Choosing a Vocation* (Parsons, 1909). Parsons' book outlined the steps he believed necessary to make an informed vocational choice. His formulation acknowledged the place of self-information along with information about job characteristics and opportunities in making a choice. Occupations were to be explored through both reading and direct observation.

The value of exploratory and tryout experiences was again emphasized with the passage of the Smith-Hughes Act of 1917. This act provided matching funds for states to set up vocational training in agriculture, home economics and industrial education. Supervised work experience and placement aids were viewed as principal strategies for career exploration.

Until the early 1930s, the need for providing career exploratory experiences for youth continued to be advocated. Brewer (1932), speaking from a guidance point of view, saw career activities as a way of helping students discover their interests and abilities. He argued for:

1. Exploratory courses offering sample tasks from a number of occupations,
2. Student activities requiring work resembling that of certain occupations,
3. Observations of work, with possible participation in simple tasks,
4. Clubs, scouting, recreational experiences outside of the school, and activities in the home,
5. Work experiences, with or without pay.

This early interest in providing career exploratory activities receded, however, during the late thirties and the years ensuing. The evolving psychology of individual differences focused upon development of tests to measure various traits and abilities. Use of these tests to establish aptitude patterns for a variety of occupations became the *modus operandi* for facilitating a match between self-characteristics and occupational requirements. Not only was the exploratory experience played down, but the assumptions underlying the trait-and-factor approach led to a narrow perspective of career development, with attention focused primarily upon choice of an occupation.

The use of tests and inventories in vocational guidance and career education can, of course, offer a strategy for facilitating career exploration. Whether or not they will be used in this way depends upon the intention of the counselor or vocational educator, and the manner in which the tests are interpreted. Most often, tests have been used for the purpose of predicting the outcome of career decisions rather than to promote the exploration of self and/or career. Furthermore, the classical prediction strategies typically have not included performance measures and assessments based upon work samples. The student is asked to make his decisions upon the basis of a paper and pencil performance and a faith in statistical findings and probability statements of a normative nature. His decisions and choices are not made as affirmations of identity developed from insights into himself, his values, or any real understanding of the world of work. Educators are coming to recognize that it is a narrow conception of vocational guidance, and indeed an ineffective one, that fails to build into the curriculum those kinds of "real world" experiences that will enable the student to try himself out and test his abilities and values.

RENEWAL OF INTEREST

Several developments converge today to stimulate a renewal of interest in career exploration and to provide some new conceptions about it. Of these, the most important is the increasing interest being given by vocational psychologists to the processes by which vocationally relevant behavior is developed and expressed. Much of the current theory construction and empirical research in vocational psychology shows a fundamental shift in emphasis away from specific decision making to preparation for decision making (Tennyson, 1970). The developmental emphasis in research on vocational behavior, beginning about 1950, has served to bring the concept of exploration once again to the fore.

Career development theory assumes that expressions of vocational behavior become evident in early childhood; that this behavior continues to express itself in an on-going, progressive way throughout life; that this life-long process can be studied and described in terms of developmental life stages; and, that each stage presents the individual with critical developmental tasks that are mastered in various ways and to varying degrees.

Ginzberg, et al. (1951) were early leaders in treating exploration within a theoretical framework. They postulated three gross phases in the process of vocational development: a stage of fantasy choices, a stage of tentative choices, and a stage of realistic choices. Exploration was seen as a component of the realistic stage, a period in which the individual would test himself in new experiences. It is important to note that Ginzberg, et al. saw exploration as a prominent feature of late adolescent development.

Without question, the developmental thrust that has received the most attention and generated the most significant research is that of Super and his colleagues (Super, 1957; Super, et al., 1957, and 1963). According to this theoretical schema, exploration begins at about the age of 15, the age at which needs, interests, abilities and values are considered and tentative choices are made and tried out in fantasy and discussion. Exploration continues through the early twenties when one or more beginning jobs are found and tried out. In his earlier writing, Super (1957) presented a detailed explanation of the process of exploration and the role that various activities (e.g., leisure, part-time work, courses) might play in development of self-awareness and awareness of the work world. His later writings specify the developmental tasks and behaviors he considers appropriate to the exploratory stage; however, his formulations, while suggestive and helpful, do not lend themselves directly to development of an exploratory curriculum.

Because the work of these researchers, as well as that of others such as Gribbons and Lohnes (1968), has been directed at explicating the process of exploration as it occurs during adolescence, vocational educators often hold the notion that exploration is a discrete event occurring after the student has achieved career awareness and prior to his engaging in preparation. In a paper that offers a significant theoretical analysis of vocational exploratory behavior, Jordaan (Super, et al., 1963:51) made the observation that development psychologists have not "taken sufficient note of the fact that exploration may occur in any life stage, and particularly during the period preceding and following entry into a new life stage." Tiedeman (1958) seems to agree, as reflected in his statement that each decision concerning the occupancy of a position involves exploration, establishment and maintenance. Super (Super, et al., 1963) has acknowledged that the exploratory process that goes into self-concept formation continues throughout life.

Any distinction implied in the use of the terms career awareness and career exploration apparently then loses some import when looked at theoretically. The distinction, however, will be maintained as a matter of convenience in pursuing the career education theme of this Yearbook. The remainder of this chapter will be concerned primarily with career exploration as it is manifested during adolescence.

THE NATURE OF CAREER EXPLORATION

As we have seen, career exploration has often been defined as a life stage in vocational development. Frequently, it has been talked about in vocational education circles as a series of activities and experiences designed to provide an exploration of occupations and the world of work. Currently some psychologists talk about the concept in terms of outcomes expected. Consider, for example, the following definition:

> Vocational exploration is the process of clarifying the self-concept and translating it into occupational terms . . . (Super, 1957).

The shortcomings of each of these conceptualizations of career exploration are, as Jordaan (Super, et al., 1963) has pointed out, that they tend to be vague about the process engaged in by the individual. According to Jordaan, a behavior can be considered to be exploratory only when it involves the qualities of search, experimentation, investigation, trial, and hypothesis testing. By hypothesis testing, he means that the behavior is engaged in for the purpose of validating some more or less clearly formulated belief or expectation concerning the self or the environment. Therefore, a first requirement of career exploration is that at least some of the above mentioned qualities be present in the individual's behavior.

It is readily recognized that not all behavior that may be called exploratory will necessarily relate to career. Thus, the purpose for which the exploratory activity is undertaken becomes a second important consideration. That purpose must relate to career.

How one defines career, therefore, determines the scope of career exploration. At one extreme, career may be defined simply as those activities the individual engages in for monetary remuneration; at the other, it may denote a general life pattern that includes virtually all of one's activities. For practical reasons, a compromise position seems warranted. The joint Commission on Career Guidance and Vocational Education of the American Vocational Association and the National Vocational Guidance Association in a recently completed position paper on career development* attempted such a compromise:

> . . . the term "career" means a time extended working out of a purposeful life pattern through *work* undertaken and engaged in by the individual. The meaning of the word "career," then, is directly dependent upon the meaning one attaches to the word "work." Work, as conceived for purposes of this paper, may be defined as an expenditure of effort designed to effect some change, however slight, in some province of civilization. It is not simply arbitrary or gratuitous action, but something

---

* At this time, the Policy and Planning Committee of the AVA Guidance Division has not acted on the paper and it has not been released for circulation.

which, from some viewpoint within society, *ought* to be done. The concept carries the intention that an act of human effort will lead to an improvement of one's own condition or that of some element of society.

The Commission went on to state:

> Viewed in this way, work is not directly attached to paid employment, but it may include also efforts of an educational or avocational nature. Thus, education for work and certain elements of leisure which are undertaken to benefit society or which contribute to a sense of individual purpose and achievement are included in the definition.

With these considerations in mind, it seems clear that career connotes a process internal to the individual and that career exploration implies a proactive rather than a reactive person. Career exploration, therefore, may be defined as those activities, both mental and physical, that purposely utilize the stimuli and information provided by work and the work world to perpetuate a continuing clarification of self, including one's needs, interests, attitudes, values, and work role perceptions and competencies.

PROGRAMMING FOR CAREER EXPLORATION

Traditional methods of facilitating career exploration (e.g., occupational units, career days, field trips, and other special programs), though not without some value, have generally fallen short in developing vocational maturity in the majority of young people. The weaknesses of these traditional approaches can be attributed to their short term, hit-or-miss nature, their lack of coordination, and their neglect in providing a sequential set of educational experiences designed to develop career understandings and career competencies. Career development theory and research indicate that exploratory activities need to be programmed developmentally; that such activities must begin in the elementary grades and become more intensified during the secondary school years when the youngster begins to grapple with reality considerations.

Career exploration may be thought of schematically as an inverted pyramid in which career options available to the individual are deliberately kept open as he moves through adolescence. The primary objective of career exploration is not career selection, but rather to provide the student with experiences that enable him to look at himself and clarify his motives. When he is called upon later to make choices about his future, he will, as Super (1957) suggests, likely be ready and able to do so.

There is emerging in the career development literature a set of constructs and propositions that hold value for organizing and structuring career exploratory activities in a systematic way. At the University of Minnesota, a group of vocational teacher and counselor educators is attempting to utilize these concepts in the development of a performance based career exploration curriculum (Tennyson, Klaurens and Hansen, 1970). The Minnesota project, called Career Development Curriculum (CDC), is directed at deriving a conceptualization of career development and specifying objectives and exploratory activities that can be implemented through the traditional subject areas, grades K-14. Those parts of the conceptualization pertinent to career exploration at the junior and senior high life stages are reported here. Similar projects are underway at The Ohio State University, the University of Missouri, and in other parts of the country.

OUTCOMES OF CAREER EXPLORATION

It is appropriate to ask, "What are the areas of self and environment that weigh significantly in career exploration?" The question comes down to identifying the instructional dimensions for which exploratory activities are to be provided. From widely scattered propositions, the CDC project staff identified 10 dimensions that are translated here into broad instructional outcomes for a career exploration program. The objectives of the program are aimed at assisting the student to:

Self Dimensions
1. Develop a positive image of himself and clarify that image through continuous evaluation of his interests, abilities, values and needs as they relate to occupational roles.
2. Develop interpersonal and basic skills and see the relationship of such skill development to career.
3. Acquire a sense of agency or the belief he does have a degree of control over his life.
4. Acquire a concept of self as a productive person and a responsible worker in society.
5. Exhibit planfulness in striving to achieve occupational goals and objectives.

Work Dimensions
6. Examine occupational fields in terms of opportunities, potential satisfactions, roles and life styles of different workers, along with related considerations.
7. Examine the psychological and economic meanings of work and determine how he wants to use work in formulating a life style.
8. Acquire a sense of community relatedness and an appreciation of the value of his work and the work of others.

9. Understand how work is structured and how power operates within a work organization.

Self in Relation to Work

10. Integrate self-knowledge with environmental knowledge in furthering the person's career and his career development.

Together these instructional outcomes suggest the content areas of career exploration as defined by the Minnesota CDC project. Although self and work outcomes have been grouped separately, one should understand that they are not treated as separate entities in career exploration. Pritchard's (1962) phrase "self-at-work exploration" conveys the integration intended.

Perhaps the severest criticism that may be leveled at schools purporting to have a program for facilitating career exploration is that they almost universally neglect to tie exploratory learning activities to specified objectives. Drawing from many sources, including the National Assessment Program, the Minnesota CDC team assembled and classified over 100 performance objectives in accordance with the instructional outcome dimensions. It seemed essential as a beginning step in this project that objectives be identified or formulated to cover all of the instructional outcome dimensions assumed to have some relationship to career exploration. While this procedure accomplished its intended purpose of delineating the domain of career exploration, it left unanswered the question of how to arrange these objectives into a curriculum or program having some relevance to vocational development and maturity.

CAREER DEVELOPMENT TASKS

If career development is considered to be an on-going process of growth and learning, then the timing of exploratory activities may be crucial. Maturing in a vocational sense involves mastering the developmental career tasks of a given life stage. Herr and Cramer (1972) explained it well when they said:

> . . . the assumption can be made that the developmental task concept is useful both as a description of the changing demands on individuals as they move through life, as well as a means of organizing those demands—whether knowledge, attitudes, or skills—into a systems approach to vocationalization.

The value of the concept of developmental task is that it enables one to order objectives and exploratory learning activities sequentially.

Although a number of theorists have employed the concept of developmental tasks related to life stages in studying human growth and behavior, the tasks they have identified are for the most part too large to be usable in developing curriculum. Drawing upon the work of Havighurst (1953), Erikson (1963), Piaget (1962), Super (1957), Gribbons and Lohnes (1968), and Super, et al. (1963), University of Minnesota staff members have delineated a schema of career development tasks related to school life stages that appears to have value for a systems approach to career exploration. While they have been specified for four life stages, only those appropriate for the adolescent are presented here.

Junior High Life Stage:
1. Clarification of a self-concept,
2. Assumption of responsibility for vocational planning,
3. Formulation of tentative career goals,
4. Acquiring knowledge of occupations and work settings,
5. Acquiring knowledge of educational and vocational resources,
6. Acquiring awareness of the decision-making process,
7. Acquiring a sense of independence.

Senior High and Post Two Years Life Stage:
1. Reality testing of a self-concept,
2. Acquiring awareness of preferred life style,
3. Reformulation of tentative career goals,
4. Increasing knowledge of and experience with occupations and work settings,
5. Acquiring knowledge of educational and vocational paths,
6. Clarification of the decision-making process as related to self,
7. Commitment with tentativeness within a changing world.

Career development stages, like physiological and moral development stages, are sequential and cannot be equated directly with chronological age. The stages and tasks presented here reflect those periods of curricular change that bring new demands and expectations with which the student must deal. While it may be possible to accelerate the accomplishment of these developmental tasks, such may not be desirable. Antholz (1973) said "there seems to be what Piaget terms the 'optimal time' for mastering tasks, a time when learning is easiest and most efficient." Havighurst (1953) calls this the teachable moment, "when the body is ripe, and society requires, and the self is ready to achieve a certain task."

A principal value of the concept of developmental task (DT) is that it permits one to lock performance objectives (PO) and exploratory learning experiences to a developmental system. For example, objectives related to decision making can be directly tied to this junior high life stage task as follows:

DT—Acquire awareness of the decision-making process.

PO #1—Construct a definition of the term value and describe the valuing process.

PO #2—Identify the decisions one must make prior to entering an occupation and list the options available to him.

If the educator chooses to do so, he may work directly from the developmental tasks in formulating objectives. He should, however, assure himself that objectives are written that cover all of the instructional outcomes expected of career exploration.

PROCESSING THE WORLD OF WORK

Very little is known about the processes people use to acquire and utilize data about the world of work. But in growing up, each person does construct and reconstruct a picture or map of the external world that he uses to clarify certain aspects of himself. That the dynamics involved are highly individualized, varying from person to person, seems evident. Yet educators often fail to take account of this fact when structuring experiences for the adolescent.

To assist the growing youngster to organize the work world in a meaningful way, the educator has used a number of occupational classification and clustering schemes. The sheer number of occupations found in the economy and the complexity of the occupational establishment necessitate grouping occupations that have some similarity along one or more dimensions. A variety of criteria have been used in forming these classifications. The problem has been that one cannot know which criteria best fit an individual's unique cognitive pattern. Speaking to counselors, Pritchard (1962) addressed this problem in the following way:

> To rely solely on one standard classification system . . . to suggest fields of work or occupational groupings for exploration is to assume that the kinds of factors and relationships "built into" the system are the most significant and fruitful for all counselees. As a result, such a practice tends to limit "occupational hypotheses," explicit or implicit, to those inherent in the system as given—to "cut" the individual counselee's pattern to fit the stereotyped dimensions *assumed* significant and valid by the "across-the-board" models conveniently available.

Pritchard argues for a self-created system in which the student, with the help of a counselor, draws upon a number of classifications to find occupational factors relevant to his exploration. The approach is highly individualistic and difficult to accomplish outside of the counseling relationship. Obviously when an educator considers providing for career exploration through the curriculum, he cannot "custom-tailor" occupational classification in the manner Pritchard suggests. But there is no reason why the educator cannot or should not teach the student several methods by which others have structured and formed a meaningful picture of the work world. The structuring system used, however, should be selected to serve specific purposes.

To provide a rationale for determining which classification systems to teach, it is helpful to examine those dimensions that together constitute the world of work. Van Rooy and Bailey (1972:10) have said that "the sum of all occupational establishments is the world of work." These theorists identified seven components of the basic world of work unit called the occupational establishment. Their several components may be identified as follows:

> *Personnel*—all of the individuals who participate directly to achieve the goal of the establishment.
>
> *Organizational Structure*—the internal social system, including the patterns of human interaction both formal and informal which exist within the occupational establishment.
>
> *Activity*—the goal oriented activity that takes place in the occupational establishment.
>
> *Expertise*—that knowledge and skill brought to bear upon the task of achieving the goal.
>
> *Capital*—the real and potential material utilized within the occupational establishment, including tools, machines, buildings, and money available.
>
> *Goal*—the initial justification for the creation of the establishment, expressed in the form of an object to be produced or an activity to be undertaken.
>
> *Socioeconomic Function*—the effect made by the occupational establishment upon the socioeconomic environment.

This model reveals the infinite complexity of the occupational establishment. However, it is conceivable that with a little investigation one could identify an occupational classification appropriate to each of the model's components, though each would have varying significance for any given individual exploring a career. Even if carried out, the idea would be unmanageable, from both the standpoint of teacher and student. A more realistic proposal is to suggest that we identify some fewer classifications that would allow the student to interact with all components of the occupational establishment. Some further discussion of occupational classification will clarify how this connection might be made.

Fine's (1967) theory of work performance identifies three types of skills—adaptive, functional, and specific content. His adaptive skills are "those competencies that enable an individual to accept and adjust to the physical, interpersonal, and organizational arrangements and conditions in which a job exists." Functional skills are "those competencies that enable individuals to relate to Things, Data, and

People in some combination to their personal preferences and to some degree of complexity appropriate to their abilities." Specific content skills are "those competencies that enable an individual to perform a specific job according to the specifications of an employer and according to the standards required to satisfy the market."

Fine's approach provides a bridge for relating occupational classifications to the several components of the occupational establishment as conceptualized by Van Rooy and Bailey (1972). The way these might relate and possible classifications appropriate to each are shown below:

Components of the Occupational Establishment	Skill Competencies and Illustrative Classifications
Organizational Structure Goals Socioeconomic Function	ADAPTIVE SKILLS Standard Industrial Classification, 1967
Personnel Expertise	FUNCTIONAL SKILLS Dictionary of Occupational Titles, Functional Classification, 1965 Roe's Field-Levels Classification
Activity Expertise Capital	CONTENT SKILLS Vocational Education Cluster Approaches Based Upon Job Analysis

Classifications related to each of Fine's three types of skill will facilitate a differential exploration of career. An adaptive skills classification (e.g., industry, enterprise, or establishment) will enable the student to examine himself in relation to the nature of the environment in which work takes place and the way occupational establishments interrelate in serving societal needs. Functional skills classifications permit the student to examine personal characteristics such as interests, values and other personality variables in relation to occupational requirements. Certain functional systems also allow the student to explore himself in relation to educational expectations and requirements of different occupations (e.g., Roe's classification). Content skills classifications, reflected in vocational education clusters, enable the student to test his performance against skill requirements of the various fields of work. Each of the three ways of organizing the work world contributes something of value to career exploration; together they more nearly assure an examination of self in terms of the total character of work as a social institution.

THE TEACHER AS FACILITATOR

There is an abundance of special methods, materials, media and technologies available to the teacher who will facilitate self-exploration through work. A number of these have been described in recent articles by Hansen (1967, 1972). Among special techniques that lend themselves to incorporation in the curriculum, she mentions activities such as:

1. Decision-making experiences,
2. Industry and education visits,
3. Career games,
4. Learning modules,
5. Simulations,
6. Career logs,
7. Career information interviews,
8. Career development contracts,
9. Exploratory work experiences.

Hansen's work has been complemented by Olson (1970) who has provided a comprehensive review of career exploration instructional materials and innovative strategies. It is beyond the scope of this chapter to elaborate further upon techniques and specific strategies. Instead, the chapter concludes with a discussion about how the teacher may effectively use such techniques and methods in furthering the adolescent's career exploration.

Traditional approaches to career exploration have given little recognition to the network of attitudes, feelings, needs and value commitments that interact upon and affect the individual's vocational development. Personality needs and the ideas and feelings the individual holds about himself affect the way he looks at occupations and occupational fields. When the teacher comes to recognize this interaction and embrace the more dynamic characteristics of students and vocational life, he makes a more significant contribution to the students' career exploration.

To regard career exploration as a process that is developmental in character opens fascinating possibilities for implementing guidance in the classroom, particularly in the area of vocational education. As vocational programs expand, supervised occupational experiences can be expected to be more prominent in the young person's school experience. A further assumption is that vocational educators will increasingly employ the exploratory techniques described in the separate reviews by Hansen and Olson. Whether or not these exposures to work and work-related activities will prove instrumental in helping youth clarify self or in assuring that wise decisions regarding career be made, will depend upon what the teacher makes of the experiences.

If the vocational educator is to maximize the young person's career development, he must discover how to draw upon the observations and stimuli provided by the work experience in enabling the student to acquire meanings about himself and the overall milieu in which he lives and will work. This will require looking at occupations in his field within the broader context of the work situation. It is not enough to pursue a limited investigation into the economic aspects of occupations, i.e., material rewards, functions and duties performed, skills required, physical conditions, and the like. For the teacher to permit the needs of the individual to become an instrumental part of the learning process, he and the student must learn to observe subtle, psychosocial aspects of the work situation and the person performing in the occupation. This will involve observing the role expectations and the role relationships, the value commitments of those engaged in the occupation, and the power and status arrangements within the work setting.

To further maximize the learning value of the exploratory work experience or simulation, observations made in the field or laboratory must then be brought back into the classroom, discussed and analyzed in relation to self. The objective is to bring awareness of self through work to a conscious level. There are many proper questions the teacher can ask: What roles do the various workers play? What kind of lives do they live? Which activities performed appeal to you most? Do the workers seem to have a range of available satisfactions? How are they handicapped by controls imposed by the organization? What does this experience mean to you, as a student, and as the kind of person you wish to become? Can you accept the roles subscribed to in this or that occupation? To what extent will you be able to reject the prescribed roles, if necessary, to meet your unique needs for self-esteem?

These questions enable the student to project himself into different roles and thereby discover a little more about himself. At the same time, they serve also to help him identify behavior patterns and roles that will do him justice. Meaning for the individual is developed as he is helped to understand the actions of others and encouraged to choose for himself who he will *be* in different situations.

REFERENCES

Antholz, Mary B. *Conceptualization of a Model Career Development Program, K-12.* Master's Colloquium Paper. Minneapolis: Department of Counseling and Student Personnel Psychology, University of Minnesota. 1973.

AVA-NVGA Commission on Career Guidance and Vocational Education. *Position Paper on Career Development.* (Washington, D.C.: American Personnel and Guidance Association Archives. 1973)

Brewer, John M. *Education As Guidance.* (New York: Macmillan Company. 1932)

————. *History of Vocational Guidance.* (New York: Harper and Bros. 1942)

Erikson, Erik H. *Childhood and Society.* (New York: W. W. Norton and Company, Inc. 1963)

Fine, Sidney A. "Nature of Skill: Implications for Education and Training." *Proceedings, 75th Annual Convention, APA.* (Washington, D.C.: American Psychological Association. 1967)

Ginzberg, Eli, et al. *Occupational Choice: An Approach to General Theory.* (New York: Columbia University Press. 1951)

Gribbons, Warren D., and Lohnes, Paul R. *Emerging Careers.* (New York: Teachers College Press, Columbia University. 1968)

Hansen, Lorraine S. "Theory Into Practice: A Practitioner Looks at Career Guidance in the School Curriculum." *The Vocational Guidance Quarterly.* XVI, (December, 1967)

————. "A Model for Career Development through Curriculum." *Personnel and Guidance Journal.* LI, (December, 1972)

Havighurst, Robert J. *Human Development and Education.* (New York: Longmans, Green. 1953)

Herr, Edwin L., and Cramer, Stanley H. *Vocational Guidance and Career Development in the Schools: Toward a Systems Approach.* (New York: Houghton Mifflin Company. 1972)

Olson, Levene A. *Career Exploration: Instructional Materials, Evaluative Results and Innovative Programs.* (Huntington, West Virginia: Department of Vocational-Technical Education, Marshall University. 1970)

Parsons, Frank. *Choosing A Vocation.* (Boston: Houghton Mifflin Company. 1909)

Piaget, Jean. *The Moral Judgment of the Child.* (New York: P. F. Collier. 1962)

Pritchard, David H. "The Occupational Exploration Process: Some Operational Implications." *Personnel and Guidance Journal.* XL, (April, 1962)

Super, Donald E. *The Psychology of Careers.* (New York: Harper and Bros. 1957)

————, et al. *Vocational Development: A Framework for Research.* (New York: Teachers College Press, Columbia University. 1957)

————, et al. *Career Development: Self Concept Theory.* (New York: College Entrance Examination Board. 1963)

Tennyson, W. Wesley. "Comment." *The Vocational Guidance Quarterly.* XVIII, (June, 1970)

————; Klaurens, Mary K.; and Hansen, Lorraine S. *Career Development Curriculum.* (Minneapolis: Career Development Curriculum Project, University of Minnesota. 1970)

Tiedeman, David V. *The Harvard Studies in Career Development in Current Perspective.* (Boston: The Harvard Center for Career Development, Harvard University. 1958)

Van Rooy, William H., and Bailey, Larry J. *A Conceptual Model of the World of Work.* (Carbondale: Career Development for Children Project, Southern Illinois University. 1972)

PREPARATORY PROGRAMS IN CAREER EDUCATION

Marvin Rasmussen

The intent of this chapter is to deal directly with some of the practical aspects of occupational preparation from the point of view of a local educator, rather than to delve into a theoretical and philosophical examination of career education preparatory programs.

Vocational education must be viewed as the core of career education. In turn, occupational preparatory programs can be considered the heart of vocational education. In these programs, the student acquires the competencies required for entry into the world of work or for entry into advanced training. While there is no clear-cut separation between the different phases of career education, it is generally considered that entry into the occupational preparatory phase is appropriate after the student has made a tentative career choice. Figure I illustrates a career development model with a cluster-based preparatory program in grades 11 and 12 and occupational specialization at the high school level.

While there are local, state, and national models for career education and occupational preparation, the need for further development and refinement remains. It may be "educational heresy" for a local educator to suggest national unity in the development of a model and curriculum for occupational preparation. However, more unity in efforts being made throughout the nation should be welcomed. This would still allow local institutions the flexibility necessary to fit programs to students and to particular regions in which these students live and work. Although there have been several developmental programs funded at the national level, the short timelines inherent in getting the instructional programs operational appear to have precluded carrying out sound and extensive manpower and occupational analyses on which to base the grouping of occupations into families or clusters and the development of appropriate curriculum.

HIGH SCHOOL PROGRAMS

In order for the concept of a total career education program to be implemented, significant changes will need to occur in vocational education programs at the secondary school level. Students who have made a tentative career choice require the availability of preparation opportunities. These opportunities accommodate as wide a selection of career goals as possible in keeping with available resources. The comprehensive high school appears the logical setting for such a program.

CAREER EDUCATION

This career education model provides for comprehensive program development at the elementary, mid-school, secondary and post-high school levels. The articulated, continuous curriculum design is based upon a strong emphasis on guidance and counseling at every level.

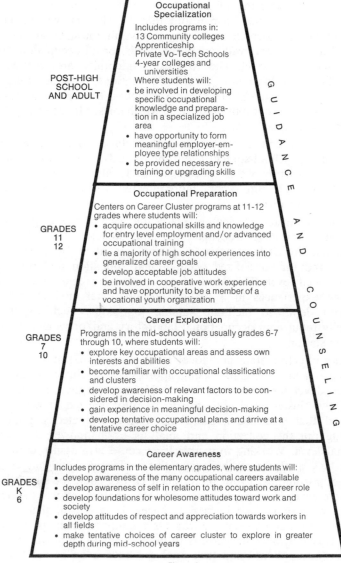

POST-HIGH SCHOOL AND ADULT

Occupational Specialization

Includes programs in:
13 Community colleges
Apprenticeship
Private Vo-Tech Schools
4-year colleges and
    universities
Where students will:
- be involved in developing specific occupational knowledge and preparation in a specialized job area
- have opportunity to form meaningful employer-employee type relationships
- be provided necessary re-training or upgrading skills

GRADES 11 12

Occupational Preparation

Centers on Career Cluster programs at 11-12 grades where students will:
- acquire occupational skills and knowledge for entry level employment and/or advanced occupational training
- tie a majority of high school experiences into generalized career goals
- develop acceptable job attitudes
- be involved in cooperative work experience and have opportunity to be a member of a vocational youth organization

GRADES 7 10

Career Exploration

Programs in the mid-school years usually grades 6-7 through 10, where students will:
- explore key occupational areas and assess own interests and abilities
- become familiar with occupational classifications and clusters
- develop awareness of relevant factors to be considered in decision-making
- gain experience in meaningful decision-making
- develop tentative occupational plans and arrive at a tentative career choice

GRADES K 6

Career Awareness

Includes programs in the elementary grades, where students will:
- develop awareness of the many occupational careers available
- develop awareness of self in relation to the occupation career role
- develop foundations for wholesome attitudes toward work and society
- develop attitudes of respect and appreciation towards workers in all fields
- make tentative choices of career cluster to explore in greater depth during mid-school years

GUIDANCE AND COUNSELING

Figure 1

Occupational Clusters

The primary focus at the secondary level should be on those occupational clusters that offer a wide choice of occupational fields, while also facilitating further occupational exploration within each cluster. Each instructional program centers on the competencies common to the occupations that comprise a cluster. The clusters need to be structured in such a manner so that it is economically feasible to offer programs covering a high percentage of potential career choices. Developers in Oregon have found that 13 clusters will encompass approximately 80 percent of occupations within the state, and estimate that 18 to 20 clusters will satisfy the needs for all occupations at the secondary school level. The 13 clusters identified are: Agriculture, Forest Products, Marketing, Health Occupations, Food Services, Construction, Electricity-Electronics, Accounting-Bookkeeping, Clerical Occupations, Stenography, Industrial Mechanics, Metals Occupations, and Service Occupations.

Preparation for employment in a properly identified career cluster helps the high school student avoid the hazards of premature commitment to a narrow work specialization. It also provides sufficient breadth to enable him to cope more effectively with occupational and employment changes.

A career cluster curriculum leads the way to the acquisition of skills and knowledges (occupational competencies) that will qualify the student for at least entry-level employment in the cluster occupations and for specialized occupational education and training at an advanced level. This kind of occupational preparation demands learning experiences in a realistic occupational environment with sufficient depth to facilitate salable job skills. Such experiences normally require an occupational laboratory and/or work experience training station.

Many effective state and local level cluster programs have been developed and several promising approaches to clustering and curriculum development have appeared. However, if the potential benefits of the cluster curriculum are to be fully realized, it would seem essential that there be a more massive, coordinated approach to carrying out the collection and analysis of manpower data at the national level. Working from this level could also assure uniform in depth task analyses of the occupations offering significant employment opportunities. From there, such efforts could be paralleled at the state level by occupational and task analysis efforts to identify significant regional and local differences. It is critical that the task analyses be based on what the workers actually do in the performance of their jobs if the instruction is to be relevant to employment.

Once occupational and task analyses have been completed, it is possible to determine the competencies needed to perform the identified occupational tasks. Implicit in this regard is a consideration of all recognized aspects (cognitive, affective and psychomotor) of the tasks performed. The competencies identified for key occupations can provide the basis for refining and expanding the occupational clusters, and, perhaps of greater importance, can serve as the basis of instructional units or learning modules that could be used flexibly by local institutions. The units or modules need to be small enough to insure this flexibility and numerous enough to give a great amount of latitude and local option to the educator developing programs for his school.

Occupational Specialization

Instructional programs should accommodate students with differing capabilities, interests and needs. Students whose career goals require completion of extensive educational programs in post-high school institutions will benefit from that instruction that prepares them to pursue further education. On the other hand, students whose capabilities and interests direct them toward employment upon leaving the high school may require instruction directed toward specific occupational skills.

Specialized occupational instruction can be provided within a cluster program by (a) arranging for appropriate cooperative work experience as a part of the individual's instructional program, or (b) concentrating the instruction in specific occupational areas in keeping with the individual's needs. A comprehensive occupational program in a larger high school may well supplement the cluster offerings with such programs as:

1. Diversified occupations cooperative work experience programs.
2. Specialized programs on a district-wide or area basis when warranted by an adequate number of students who have appropriate well-established goals and identified employment opportunities.
3. Intensive short-term courses for students who are about to graduate or leave school without previous employment preparation.

POST-HIGH SCHOOL PROGRAMS

A comprehensive career education system provides a number of options for education and training for specific occupations and jobs. Prominent at this level are: (a) postsecondary programs in community colleges and area vocational schools, (b) apprenticeship and other on-the-job training programs, (c) 4-year colleges and universities, and (d) private vocational schools.

Generally, occupational instruction at this level focuses on specific tasks rather than on the broader cluster-based competencies of the high school program. Such instruction should be designed to accommodate efficiently the student with secondary level occupational preparation as well as provide for students with little or no prior training. Emphasis is needed on individualization in order to permit open-entry/open-exit scheduling and adaption of the instruction to student needs.

CURRICULUM BASES

Implementation of new, and expansion of existing, career education preparatory programs at the secondary and post-high school levels should be based on valid information about students' career goals and employment opportunities. A functional career exploration program, supplemented as needed by surveys of student interest, will supply adequate information about potential enrollment.

Four components comprise a thorough analysis of manpower needs: (a) a detailed listing of occupations included in the occupational group or cluster, (b) employment data and projected needs relating to the identified occupations, (c) output data from existing and planned training programs, and (d) information about current hiring practices. Once these components have been completed, preferably for the local, state and national levels, some basic decisions about the implementation or alteration of the proposed program can follow. Identification of key occupations or occupational areas for task analysis and curriculum construction purposes, and current data for career guidance activities represent added outcomes of the manpower analysis.

MEETING INDIVIDUAL NEEDS

Occupational instruction at all levels ought to permit each student to (a) proceed at his own pace, (b) have available instruction that is suited to his individual learning style, and (c) progress through learning experiences that are directly related to occupational goals. Inherent in this requirement is a need for curriculum materials that not only are suited for learner use on an individual basis, but also provide for a variety of learning modes and learning levels. The occupational competencies identified through occupational and task analysis can, most likely, provide the most satisfactory base for the development of such materials.

A rapidly increasing number and variety of "learning packages" designed for student use in individualized instruction are becoming available and are being used in both secondary and postsecondary programs. Unfortunately, the nature of some of these materials poses problems that seriously impair their effectiveness. These include:

1. Materials based primarily on reading and limited to one reading level.
2. Instructional personnel not adequately prepared to use materials.
3. Materials requiring expensive instructional hardware.
4. Different, compatible materials.
5. Purchasing, duplicating, handling and storing large numbers of individual "packages."
6. Materials limited in variety of learning modes.

The solution to these and other problems will only be possible if sufficient commitment exists to provide personnel and financial resources to carry out extensive developmental work, either through allocation of new resources or reallocation of existing ones. Results of experimental and pilot programs strongly indicate that individualized instructional delivery systems, when fully implemented, can not only make available greatly improved instructional effectiveness but also greatly increase program efficiency through improved staff utilization, equipment utilization, management techniques and instructional technology.

In designing and producing the system, primary emphasis can well be placed on improving the match between student learning styles and teaching styles through student-centered learning materials developed on a multi-level, multi-media basis. The production and distribution of the volume of materials needed will demand the development of new methods of making these materials available to all schools at a reasonable cost.

Key factors in improving the efficiency with which a student can move between programs or between program levels will consist of concentration of instruction on the mastery of identified competencies, and provision of an adequate system of compiling, storing, and reporting information on student achievement. The program design should also include adapting the instruction to the individual through consistent attention to interdisciplinary approaches to developing the identified occupational competencies, and developing the competencies the student needs for other life roles.

SUMMARY

With its supportive guidance and counseling, articulation and interdisciplinary emphasis, and its emphasis on complete career preparation, the career cluster curriculum provides extensive possibilities as the focal point in the broad concept of career education. Not only does it offer an expanded approach to occupational preparation, but it also provides a strong basis for further career preparation through a variety of post-high school options. In this capacity, it becomes the key element in an educational system that can offer to each student the opportunity to acquire the basic skills and knowledge required to function successfully in the various "life careers" in which he will engage as a member of society.

OCCUPATIONAL CLUSTERS FOR CAREER EDUCATION

John E. Taylor

Other chapters provide detailed information on the foundation, perspectives, and definitions of career education. Several describe the current operational models of career education: the School-Based Model, the Employer-Based Model, and the Home-Community-Based Model. This chapter discusses various occupational clustering systems and describes the clustering system that was synthesized specifically for the Comprehensive Career Education Model (CCEM). Although it was designed to be integrated into a K-12 public school sequence, this clustering system can be employed with any model.

This system was the end product of HumRRO Project S72-12 (P72-20), *The Validation of a Set of Occupational Clusters for Use in the Comprehensive Career Education Model (CCEM)*. The project was performed for The Center for Vocational and Technical Education of The Ohio State University by Taylor, Montague, and Michaels (1972). Its purpose was to provide a set of occupational clusters to be used for career education in grades K through 12.

CRITERIA AND PREMISES FOR A CLUSTERING SYSTEM FOR CAREER EDUCATION

The term "cluster" has taken on a variety of meanings. It may refer to a simple grouping of like jobs, to broad institutional groupings such as transportation or manufacturing, to groupings based on similar job products, to groupings based on analysis of work tasks, and so on. The type of cluster developed depends upon the particular purposes and requirements of the agency doing the clustering. Overall, the field of occupational clustering is marked by a diversity of criteria and variables, and a paucity of *comprehensive* frameworks.

The *criteria* for the project require that the system be:

1. *Inclusive.* The clustering system must encompass most existing jobs.
2. *Operational.* The clusters must be capable of being used for training. They must be congruent with labor-market entry jobs, and must be translatable into curricular materials and instructional strategies, so that a person trained in the basic skills of a cluster would have entry-level job potential in a variety of jobs within the cluster.
3. *Viable.* The recommended system must have clear advantage over other systems for use in career education.

From these general criteria, *premises* were developed to guide the selection or synthesis of a clustering system for career education. A clustering system should:

1. Permit career preparation to be flexible, generalizable, and relatively comprehensive, allowing students to acquire broad skills and capabilities for entry into a range of related jobs. It must not handicap the student in exercising the option of further education by narrowing his training around too specific skills.

2. Serve as a means of introducing students to the great variety of jobs within a format that is easily comprehensible.

3. Provide means for organized exploration of career possibilities that exist within an occupational area.

4. Contain dimensions that provide students with a clear conception of important attendant variables related to career choice and development. Such variables include—educational and training requirements; expected income and economic projections; working conditions to be expected; the degree of power, personal freedom, and responsibility inherent in broad strata of occupations; the presence or absence of lateral and vertical avenues of mobility; the present and projected influence of institutional organization and stratification in industries and unions; and, the life styles attending various strata of occupations.

5. Be usable in the design of curricula meeting the general goals of awareness, orientation, exploration, selection, and entry preparation.

6. Take into account the markedly different natures of the age populations being served. Maturity level and fantasy/reality orientations change sharply over the 12 school years.

7. Be related to and be able to draw upon the more organized and detailed work that has been done in the field; the system cannot stand alone. Many current systems are isolated and unique and cannot draw support from present bodies of information.

Attending to these criteria and premises constitutes a large order. No past system, to our knowledge, attempted to develop a comprehensive curriculum-related clustering system. Yet, the envisioned curriculum requires such a model.

A REVIEW OF CLUSTERING SYSTEMS

Through Educational Resources Information Center (ERIC), library research, correspondence, and the project staff's past experience, current clustering systems were studied. Because of the unpublished status of many attempts, complete coverage cannot be claimed. Nevertheless, all major and relevant efforts were at least typified in the search.

General Review

Although the term "cluster" has many meanings, it is felt that the great majority of past work may be fitted into three groups without undue damage to any. These three groups may be characterized as *descriptive, sociological-psychological,* and *task-analytic.* Like the clusters or families they cover, they possess many inconsistencies, mixed categories, and blanks.

Descriptive Approaches. These approaches are based primarily upon an informational approach to occupational families rather than on analysis and synthesis of broad job needs and their relationship to student characteristics.

Such systems are intended for employment market information and vocational guidance and are exemplified by a joint publication of the U.S. Department of Health, Education, and Welfare and U.S. Department of Labor (1969), entitled *Vocational Education and Occupations,* or by various Department of Labor publications, such as the *Occupational Outlook Handbook* (1970-71) and like publications. To a certain degree, the draft of 15 occupational clusters developed by the Division of Vocational and Technical Education of the U.S. Office of Education (1971) falls into this descriptive approach, although its implications are considerably broader.

Sociological-Psychological Approaches. A second broad class of systems comes from social scientists interested in various aspects of worker characteristics as these relate to life styles and occupational choices. A great range of personal attributes, such as job satisfaction, mobility, personality traits, work attitudes, personal value systems, vocational interests, and the interaction of total life style and work, have been studied.

In an attempt to systematize these wide-ranging variables, some writers have developed one-, two-, or three-dimensional matrices of occupational families arranged in order of vertical (status) and horizontal (occupational areas) position (Roe, 1956; Super, 1957). The *Dictionary of Occupational Titles* (DOT) (U.S. Department of Labor, 1966) represents one such categorization. Robinson, Athanasiou, and Head (1969) have performed a detailed and valuable task in attempting to describe and draw together some of the many approaches.

Task-analytic Approaches. The development in recent years of two approaches to occupational training results in another means of classifying job or occupational characteristics.

The first is typified by Smith's several publications (1964, 1965,

1971), in which he described methods for analyzing job and task needs and requirements, and for carrying these job-functional characteristics back to the training site for the purpose of defining training objectives, means, and equipment in preparing workers or students for specific jobs or job families. This approach led to emphasis on highly functional preparation, fixed mastery levels, variable training-time schedules, and other properties of a job-function approach to training.

The second approach is that of Maley (1966c) and others (Oregon State Department of Education, 1967; Bakamis, et al., 1966; Rahmlow, et al., 1966; Rahmlow and Winchell, 1966; Perkins and Byrd, 1966) in utilizing a similar rationale to study the common task requirements and characteristics of a wide range of skill families.

Specific Review

Every clustering scheme is a judgmental arrangement, selecting from a wide variety of dimensions those that are most important to the purpose at hand. The HumRRO project's purpose was to meet the needs of total curriculum change, and the staff's needs went beyond the dimension of any system reviewed.

Three basic assumptions or predictions, developed from the staff's general experience and from early review, should be noted:

1. It was assumed that no one system would answer all needs; that development of a quite new system would require prolonged, extensive effort; and, that current systems would provide only partial answers—fitting in some places and not in others.

2. It was felt that any system to be used could neither be entirely newly devised nor based on lone efforts that were limited in scope and not widely disseminated. That is, there was an underlying feeling that a system intended for a broad curricular purpose and for widespread use should somehow be related to the broadest, most useful of materials readily available to workers in the field.

3. There was concern regarding the number of necessary dimensions that could be handled in a single system without rendering it so complex as to be unworkable.

The remainder of this section provides a more detailed review of the more systematic occupational categorizations considered. It does not include local systems for which little rationale could be obtained (Shelby, 1971). Nor does it include military systems. While the military occupational specialties are well systematized, they are more narrow in range than present purposes require, tend to be written in general terms, and are not easily available.

Descriptive Systems

U.S. Department of Labor Publications. The most complete system to come to attention was that made up of the many related component parts of the Department of Labor publications. These are the volumes of the third edition of the DOT with supplements, *Occupational Man-power and Training Needs* (1971), *Occupational Employment Statistics, 1960-1969* (1970), *Vocational Education and Occupations* (DHEW and DOL, 1969), and related publications. The DOT volumes present a wide coverage of occupations, and a systematic way of considering the important variables of functional job relationships, worker characteristics, job conditions, training time, and the important factor of functional levels in dealing with people, data, and things.

On the positive side, the DOT and other Department of Labor publications provide the only widely disseminated body of materials on which an immeasurable amount of work has already been accomplished and within which are based well-rationalized clustering or grouping systems.

On the negative side, there are a number of factors. The DOT is, at first glance, a complex system and requires familiarity and training to use it.

As DOT, Volume I states (pages iii and ix), the descriptions and information given therein are of a typical and general nature, not specifically applicable to an individual situation, and are based on 75,000 observations of 45,000 jobs, some of these based on data other than actual interviews with workers. Experience indicates that information from job holders may vary from that given by supervisors, employers, and industrial organizations. Consequently, conclusions regarding the grouping of seemingly similar tasks are somewhat weakened.

For some purposes, as Maley points out, some DOT groupings are too narrowly defined for easy inclusion in a task-analysis cluster system or, on the other hand, are duplicated in separate divisions because of mixed categorization. Maley, and Altman and Gagne, as quoted by Maley (1966a) felt that DOT groupings were not appropriate for developing occupational families, and that new job and task analyses based upon new sampling would be required.

U.S. Bureau of Census. The Bureau of Census (1960) has long used a coding system for occupations and industries. This was reviewed, along with associated studies of socioeconomic variables. Two major headings, "Industrial Classification" and "Occupational Classification," are subdivided into appropriate categories. While these listings are fairly comprehensive, they are intended for the information storage and retrieval purposes of the Bureau of the

Census and do not appear easily translatable into curricular terms.

U.S. Office of Education. The Division of Vocational and Technical Education of the U.S. Office of Education responded to the need for clustering systems adaptable to educational use by issuing a draft of 15 comprehensive, but skeletal, headings that were primarily functional in their implications (transportation, environment, communication, etc.), but included some traditional institutional groupings (public services, marine science, agri-business and natural resources). The internal construction of many of the clusters is mixed. Some, such as business and office occupations, are fairly consistent in dealing with subclusters of jobs with similar task descriptions (e.g., secretarial, clerical, records maintenance). Others, such as manufacturing or transportation, tend to mix or blur lines of family distinction so far as job or task training is concerned.

Sociological-Psychological Systems. Roe (1956) and Super (1957), among others, have been concerned with the vertical dimension of occupations. These studies bring into play personal and occupational characteristics that cannot be ignored in student orientation to the world of work. Some of these are: (a) work as the determiner of status (and, conversely, status as a determiner of occupation); (b) work as the source of other than livelihood—power, autonomy, way of life, security, group belonging, self-determination, and others; (c) work as a necessary, but not integral, part of a life scheme, for a growing number of people.

For these writers, emphasis is placed on socioeconomic or other indices of status and on a horizontal dimension variously called "situs" or, in Super's term, "enterprise." In Super's model, a distinction is made among (a) *level,* which defines prestige, income, authority, freedom of action; (b) *field,* which uses a functional definition of the general type of work accomplished; and, (c) *enterprise,* which corresponds to our definition of institutionally defined industrial or business areas. These same distinctions are made by Roe, although she emphasizes field rather than enterprise as a horizontal dimension. In a study of situs, or horizontal status equivalence of work areas, Morris and Murphy (1969) differentiate occupations into 10 functional areas (e.g., commerce, education and research, manufacturing) and four prestige strata.

Although these models were designed as exemplary rather than exhaustive coverage of occupational areas, they are of particular value in showing the necessity for considering several broad dimensions in one way or another, and for calling attention to other than purely job-training dimensions.

Task-analytic Systems. The systems to be treated in this section are based on an approach to the development of training courses that has been well described by Smith (1964), and Ammerman and Melching (1966). They are characterized by detailed study of the skills and knowledges found in the various tasks making up a job, determining the common skills and knowledges that cross the boundary lines of a given cluster of tasks (or jobs), and constructing objectives and courses that provide skills for a range of related tasks or jobs. It is important to note that the relating thread is not the geographical area of the jobs, not the common aspects of job product, not traditional academic partition, but, rather, the common skills and knowledges defined by what is done to what recipient (person, datum, thing), to what criterion of completion, and with what equipment. Finally, it must be noted that these systems are job-training related, and are intended only for job preparation, once job choices have been determined.

Basing their efforts on the above approach, researchers for the Oregon State Department of Education (1967) analyzed a number of occupations and jobs and established the broad areas of mechanical, electrical, spatial-structural, chemical-biological, symbolic, and people. They defined hierarchical levels of functioning similar to those described in the DOT, and defined a hierarchy of mental processes ranging from simple chaining (association) to problem solving. With these tools, they developed similarity indices between basic tasks, two at a time, and through statistical grouping developed related clusters.

The Oregon study was not broad enough to satisfy the premises set for the CCEM clustering project. It was concerned only with job preparation for high school students. As far as can be determined, it was tried out on only one basic task in each occupation, not on the range of tasks comprising a job. While it provides a compelling example of the great detail and time required to construct even a few clusters, it seems bound to those few clusters. Its generalizability is not readily apparent.

The works of Maley (1966) and his staff at the University of Maryland, conducted over a period of several years, provide information regarding the task-analysis approach. Maley's reports incorporate a review of work (much of it unpublished) to 1966, and a thorough coverage of the requirements, pitfalls, and advantages of task-analysis clustering. As he points out, this approach is aimed solely at the final preparation of a prospective worker for a family of similar jobs, and is not necessarily a feasible approach for a national or regional program of general occupational education.

Maley's original approach was not unlike the Oregon approach. General criteria for job inclusion, on such bases as mobility, favorable employment outlook, and advancement, were established, along with more specific criteria such as being within the traditional scope of vocational industrial education and being capable of immediate job entry.

At this point, it is well to note a difference between Maley's approach and the DOT approach. Essentially, the DOT and like systems are based upon job function or product; the task-analysis approaches are based on worker properties (skills, knowledges, actions). There is no question of the value of the task-analytic approach as an avenue to more efficient training for selected and specific entry-level clusters of occupations. Yet, in many ways, it is severely self-limiting. The population of clusters to be thus analyzed and developed is endless and the process laborious. It is not conceptually developed with relation to a comprehensive 12-year curriculum. It does not at this time, or in the foreseeable future, provide a means of creating a general system covering many occupational areas and their vertical and horizontal interrelationships. Many of the limitations of the approach were discussed or portrayed by participants in a symposium on clustering reported by Cunningham (1969).

Related Systems. A number of institutions and individuals have been developing limited clustering systems for vocational and technical purposes for several years. Maley reviews programs in Pennsylvania, Massachusetts, Michigan, North Carolina, Nebraska, Missouri, and Indiana. Cunningham and his symposium members critically review others. Rahmlow (Rahmlow and Cavanagh, 1966; Rahmlow, et al., 1966) describes procedures for identifying knowledge and competence clusters in a number of areas of work. Schill (1964) describes curricular content for technical education in terms of core courses, while Altman (1966) has been concerned with the appropriate development of such courses. Gagne (1962, 1965) has long been concerned with the hierarchical nature of such learning.

Other similar schemes were noted in our review of the literature or in personal correspondence. The Dallas Independent School District (1971) has instituted, for high school students, a major and extensive program around 27 occupational clusters.

All the schemes that have been noted are, by virtue of their basic concepts and purposes, aimed at late vocational and technical preparation for job entry, and *are not suited to a comprehensive curriculum*. Furthermore, perusal of these systems shows a fundamental lack of agreement on conceptual variables and criteria underlying their development, a point strongly made in Cunningham's discussions. In brief, in terms of project requirements, the task-related structures are seen as adjunct tools rather than conceptual systems.

From this review it was concluded that no single system would cover the premises set up. Three approaches showed some promise in providing ideas or partial frameworks for needs: (a) the DOT system and related publications, (b) the USOE set of clusters, and (c) certain aspects of the Super and Roe categories. The development of these into a framework that could be integrated along the K-12 time line is described below.

CLUSTERING SYSTEM SYNTHESIZED
FOR THE CCEM

Development of Institutional and Occupational Matrices

While reviewing cluster systems and making initial attempts at constructing a multi-dimensional system, the research staff began to develop a *changing* total curricular system that would reflect the needs of the differing age populations and would reflect the changing objectives of the educational time span.

Gradually, a single multi-dimensional matrix came to be seen as too complex, too static, and as not responding sufficiently to the changing objectives for the different age populations. It was decided to construct two systems of bi-dimensional matrices, each to be integrated, in turn, with the ascending K-12 grade levels.

With the emphasis in the lower grades on general awareness and information being provided very young children, the first matrix is structured upon what may be termed an *institutional* approach. Here, the emphasis is not on job or occupation, but on the broad—in some ways regional—complexes such as public service, manufacturing, natural resources, commerce, communications, construction, and others. Such a broad orientation allows the most general and descriptive approach in early years; allows, but does not require, the selection of regional characteristics (agriculture, manufacturing, commerce, etc.) if these are to be seen as familiar starting points; and, allows for the spiraling development of basic skills and knowledges on an increasingly wider scale in the accompanying curricular processes.

Twelve broad institutional areas make up one dimension, seven socioeconomic or status levels make up the other. This two-way table allows development of occupations or groups of occupations, in as much detail as desired, using available sources from USOE, Department of Labor, and other emerging "world-of-work" publications. Importantly, it clusters these broad or narrow occupational groups along the status dimension, allowing early development of a general appreciation of both the presence of general levels and some of the important concomitants of differing statuses. The actual number of institutional areas and status levels proposed for use in the curricular process ranges from two wide groupings in each dimension in early years to the full 12 x 7 matrix in later years.

The 12 institutional areas are derived from common sources, including the USOE headings, Bureau of the Census headings, and DOT classifications, as are the major sub-headings in each. They have been cross-checked against the several sources and include present and emerging fields.

Like the originals, this system is mixed in some respects, sometimes stressing type of work, sometimes work-product, sometimes location or nature of the institution. The common thread, however, remains broadly institutional rather than occupational.

The second matrix, intended to be integrated with curricular processes for upper-level students, is more closely allied to an *occupational* or job-functional approach. It was strongly felt that this matrix must be based upon material widely available and well worked out. There is little question that Volume II and Supplements I and II of the DOT, with admitted deficiencies, provided the only categorizing system that even approaches this requirement. It provides a comprehensive, inclusive general framework; it provides considerable detail; it takes personal characteristics and preparation into account; it is open-ended enough to allow for the addition of clearly emerging occupations, many of which will be variations of older skills; and, it in no way hinders the development of empirical and specific skill-clusters of the Maley type, should these later be deemed necessary.

Major divisions of each of the nine Occupational Categories of Volume II, DOT, represent one dimension, the seven status levels represent the other. This portrays clearly the consistent clustering of broad families of occupations within given ranges of the status dimension.

The matrix allows early and easy identification of important implications regarding preparation for these different levels. It is intended that this matrix begin to complement the institutional matrix in the middle school years, providing a similar, but different, way of cross-cutting occupational groups, and allowing a counselor or student to note rather easily the place of a job cluster, such as a structural craft grouping in both the general field of construction (planning, architecture, engineering, crafts, labor) and in the specific array of crafts included in structural work (masonry, metal fabrication, electrical installation, etc.). In both instances, curricular and career implications are brought readily into focus.

The DOT system, with its nine major categories, 80 or more divisions, and over 600 groups, allows as detailed a grouping as is desired. It further allows for consideration of worker function, worker characteristics, and level of activity. It is geared to other publications. This matrix is intended, as the other matrix, for integration with the ascending K-12 grade levels.

Description and Functioning

The clustering system proposed for the CCEM is a progressively developing one that incorporates three factors—(a) the main institutional job areas, (b) the career levels dimension, and (c) the DOT functional occupational categories—with the Awareness—Entry time dimension. Figure 1 provides a general representation of the system laid out along the K-12 grade levels.

As shown in Figure 1, the system calls for rather simple combinations of factors (a) and (b) at the Awareness level, a somewhat more detailed combination of the same two factors at the Orientation level, a detailed breakout of these two and a blending in of the third factor at the Exploration level, and a shift of emphasis loading heavily on the third factor, and deemphasizing the first two, at the Selection level. The grade levels corresponding to Awareness—Entry on the vertical dimension are intended to be illustrative rather than hard and fast. The demarcation between Exploration and Selection, particularly, should be determined by the readiness of a given individual student to select and to begin specialization rather than by his particular grade level.

Figure 2 shows that, at the Awareness level, the system calls for collapsing all institutional areas into a simple dichotomy according to their involvement with the production of goods or services, and for collapsing all career levels into another dichotomy depicting their place ("lower" to "higher") along the continuum describing responsibility/income/status. All possible careers can be clustered in such dichotomous fashion without taxing the ability of elementary children to comprehend. An unlimited array of careers can thus be treated with coverage being expanded or contracted, depending upon various careers' relevance to the local socioeconomic context. Local option would determine where along the K-6 time line specific careers should be introduced into the system.

Figure 2 also shows that at the Orientation level the system calls for a somewhat more detailed clustering of careers along both the institutional area and career levels dimensions. By this time, the students will have been provided with a broad awareness of the spectrum of careers and of the general place of these careers on the levels dimension. Now they are ready for more detailed orientation as to the specific place of particular careers in the five general job areas and along the now trichotomic career level dimension.

At about this level, students begin to formulate their romanticized and idealized concepts of what they "want to be." This 3 x 5 clustering of the world of work provides a simple structure so that any student can become oriented as to where his metamorphosing career interests and income aspirations might place him in the overall socioeconomic structure.

CLUSTERING SYSTEM FOR THE CCEM

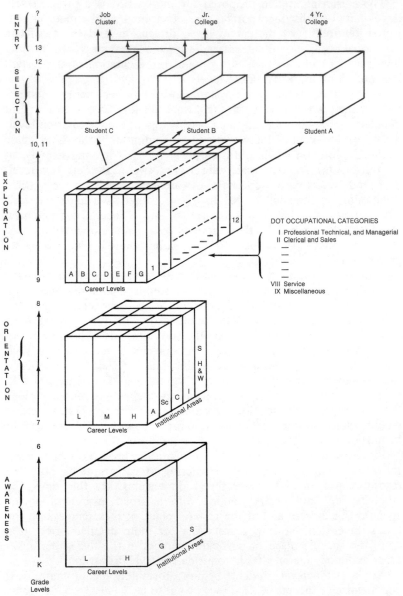

DOT OCCUPATIONAL CATEGORIES

I Professional Technical, and Managerial
II Clerical and Sales
—
—
—
—
VIII Service
IX Miscellaneous

Figure 1

This simple clustering, still not overly categorized and subcategorized, and not beyond the ability of the typical student to comprehend, provides the potential for explicating the long-term implications (activities, life style, income, status, autonomy) of the universe of career choices. This clustering provides the student with a realistic and systematic way of orienting himself (his interests, abilities, and aspirations) to the available world of work, and with a simple way of conceptualizing various possibilities for his own career development. The application of the system through the Awareness and Orientation levels calls for *all* students being provided the same exposure and learning experience about the world of work.

Figure 3 depicts the system at the next levels of student development. At the Exploration level, the clustering system expands to its most detailed form. Here all 12 institutional areas (1-12) are employed, and the career level dimension is subdivided into seven levels (A-G) ranging from laborer to executive or planner. At this level, then, careers are clustered according to a 7 x 12 matrix. It is sufficiently comprehensive that any job can be rather precisely located and described both as to institutional area and career level. This matrix, then, provides the student with a somewhat detailed, though still not complex, clustering system to use as a conceptual framework for viewing the world of work and for undertaking more detailed career exploration in the areas of his choice.

It is at this level that the need for the incorporation of the third factor, the nine DOT Occupational Categories (I-IX) becomes apparent. It is at this level (where detailed exploration of selected career options will occur) that the student must also have the information provided by overlaying the DOT categories, which group occupational areas by function, upon this structure.

Figure 3 also depicts how incorporation of the DOT functional categories provides another way of viewing broad possible career areas. Each DOT category, when laid over the other two factors, encompasses certain unique combinations of the other two. For instance: (a) the DOT category, "Professional, Technical, and Managerial" (DOT I) ranges across all 12 of the institutional job groupings and over the upper cells of the career levels dimension; (b) the DOT category "Clerical and Sales" (DOT II) includes almost all of the 12 institutional job areas and the lower-to-middle career levels; and, (c) many occupations from the DOT "Miscellaneous" category (DOT IX) include only one job grouping and the lowest career levels.

Further, and possibly most important, this phasing-in of the DOT functional categories at the Exploration level brings the student to grips with what the DOT authors have termed "Worker Traits Components." These components describe the abilities, personal traits,

AWARENESS AND ORIENTATION LEVELS OF CCEM

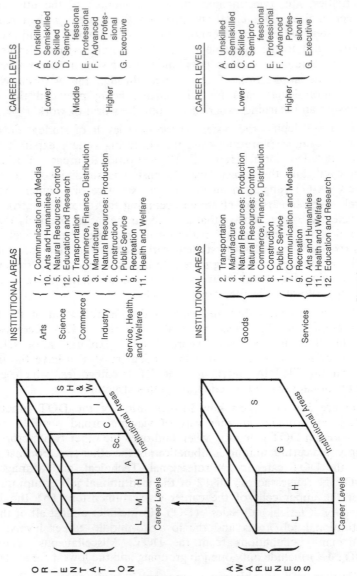

INSTITUTIONAL AREAS

Arts {
  7. Communication and Media
10. Arts and Humanities

Science {
  5. Natural Resources: Control
12. Education and Research

Commerce {
  2. Transportation
  6. Commerce, Finance, Distribution

Industry {
  3. Manufacture
  4. Natural Resources: Production
  8. Construction

Service, Health, and Welfare {
  1. Public Service
  9. Recreation
11. Health and Welfare

CAREER LEVELS

Lower {
  A. Unskilled
  B. Semiskilled
  C. Skilled
  D. Semiprofessional

Middle {
  E. Professional

Higher {
  F. Advanced Professional
  G. Executive

INSTITUTIONAL AREAS

Goods {
  2. Transportation
  3. Manufacture
  4. Natural Resources: Production
  5. Natural Resources: Control
  6. Commerce, Finance, Distribution
  8. Construction

Services {
  1. Public Service
  7. Communication and Media
  9. Recreation
10. Arts and Humanities
11. Health and Welfare
12. Education and Research

CAREER LEVELS

Lower {
  A. Unskilled
  B. Semiskilled
  C. Skilled
  D. Semiprofessional

Higher {
  E. Professional
  F. Advanced Professional
  G. Executive

Figure 2

and individual characteristics required for successful job performance. Thus, the student learns the requirements of the various career options for education and training, aptitudes, interests, and so forth.

Figure 3 also illustrates how a given student might exercise his Exploration options. A student who knows he is job-bound after high school may elect to explore narrowly within one functional occupational category (DOT V), honing his career plans more and more finely as he proceeds (V' to V''). Another, less decided, might explore in depth across two or more of the broad functional occupational categories (DOT I and II). All students would be encouraged to explore widely, keeping numerous options open as long as possible, rather than becoming committed prematurely to circumscribed, specific jobs.

At the Selection level in Figure 3, the diagram depicts how instructional content-module combinations unique to a particular student might develop from the exploration activities of the preceding level. Each of the three-dimensional stacks of cells represents the two-year Selection level program of study chosen by three hypothetical students who have formulated quite different career plans for themselves.

Student A has determined that his career interests are in the architecture and engineering group of the Professional, Technical, and Managerial Category (DOT I). He is undecided between studying architecture and civil engineering, but he knows that he has a good chance of going to college to become a professional. Therefore, he pursues the broadest possible curriculum to ensure that he meets the academic junior or four-year college entrance requirements. At the same time, he is including in his curriculum those specific technical and interpersonal subjects that will qualify him for immediate entry-level employment as a technician with architectural, engineering, and probably a variety of industrial firms upon leaving high school if his college plans don't materialize. Thus, Student A keeps all his career options open, preparing himself at a minimum for entry-level employment in his chosen career area, with the possibilities for paraprofessional technical training or professional training being available—depending upon the development of his interests, motivation, or finances.

Student B has determined that her career interests are likewise in the Professional, Technical, Managerial Category (DOT I), but in the medicine and health group. Her explorations have led her to seriously consider nursing, dietetics, or medical or dental technology as equally possible careers. The knowledge she has acquired regarding the worker trait components required in these fields, matched up with her own interests, motivation, and financial prospects for education, have led her to aim for the paraprofessional level, envisioning no more than two years of post-high school training (junior college,

EXPLORATION AND SELECTION LEVELS OF CCEM

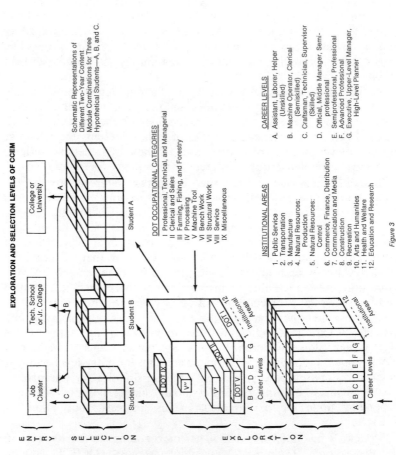

Schematic Representations of
Different Two-Year Content
Module Combinations for Three
Hypothetical Students—A, B, and C.

DOT OCCUPATIONAL CATEGORIES

I Professional, Technical, and Managerial
II Clerical and Sales
III Farming, Fishing, and Forestry
IV Processing
V Machine Tool
VI Bench Work
VII Structural Work
VIII Service
IX Miscellaneous

INSTITUTIONAL AREAS

1. Public Service
2. Transportation
3. Manufacture
4. Natural Resources:
   Production
5. Natural Resources:
   Control
6. Commerce, Finance, Distribution
7. Communication and Media
8. Construction
9. Recreation
10. Arts and Humanities
11. Health and Welfare
12. Education and Research

CAREER LEVELS

A. Assistant, Laborer, Helper
   (Unskilled)
B. Machine Operator, Clerical
   (Semiskilled)
C. Craftsman, Technician, Supervisor
   (Skilled)
D. Official, Middle Manager, Semi-
   professional
E. Semiprofessional, Professional
F. Advanced Professional
G. Executive, Upper-Level Manager,
   High-Level Planner

Figure 3

hospital, or technical school). Although she has eliminated four-year college study as a possibility, she wishes to keep all her other options open, and selects those subjects that will enable her to enter a junior college to pursue nursing (RN or LVN), dietetics, or medical/dental technology upon being graduated from high school. At the same time, to ensure that she has post-high school employability, whether or not her plans for advanced training materialize, she selects those specific subjects (biology, health, etc.) that will prepare for her entry-level employment as a home health aide or as an aide in a hospital or clinic. Thus, Student B has chosen to limit her options by excluding the possibility of attending a four-year college, but, at a minimum, she will prepare herself for entry-level employment in the career field of her selection. For her, the possibility of paraprofessional training beyond high school is highly probable, with the final choice of specific job cluster to be determined by where her developing interests lead.

For some time Student C has known what her choice of career would be and has explored and selected accordingly. For many years, she has spent her summer and holiday vacation time working in the family retail business. It is her firm intention to enter the business full-time upon leaving high school, to continue to learn all aspects of the business on the job, and to take over the business upon her father's retirement. Her career explorations have led her to con- sciously eliminate both junior and four-year college study as unneces- sary for her career plans. She includes those courses of study in her curriculum (business mathematics, retail merchandising, communica- tion, interpersonal processes, etc.) that will afford the broadest array of specific business-related skills and knowledge. Thus, Student C consciously restricts her post-high school career/education options to one. Her entry-level employability and long-range career objectives are isomorphic.

General Curriculum Implications

The above described model for systematizing the world of work is seen as providing a basic curriculum framework for career education. It is viewed as a significant step toward the solution of the following problems in our current public schools:

1. Traditional vocational training is oriented toward a static job market and job preparation that is too narrow and single- job specific.
2. The public schools generally do not provide a comprehensive variety of broad and flexible career development options.
3. Young adults of school age perceive disparities between school activities and the world in which they will be func- tioning. To them there seems to be a great deal of irrelevance in their educational programs.

4. Students are generally required to choose between vocational and academic goals, thus making career decisions too early and without sufficient knowledge of their own abilities, interests, and the world of work.
5. Vocational education, as currently offered, does not enjoy full acceptance among many educators, students, or parents. Minority groups, particularly, tend to shun that which they perceive to be second-class educational preparation.

This structure is in consonance with the objective of the CCEM to revise the public school curriculum to fit the unique requirements of individuals. It is intended to serve as a structure that will make the curriculum flexible and adjustable so that all students can find employment with or without the benefits of college study. It will provide the real-world context through which integrated and comprehensive curriculum processes will flow, providing all high school graduates with the qualifications for maximum post-high school flexibility. Its salient feature is that no option—four-year degree study, community college, technical school occupational training, or entry into the job market—is arbitrarily closed to any student prior to high school graduation.

Student Information and Guidance

The discussion of the previous section treated the general implications of the system for curriculum content and process exclusively. Consideration of the proposed system leads to the conclusion that it is equally useful as the basis for organizing student information and guidance programs. It provides a systematic, comprehensive, and not too complex framework for organizing job-market information, for charting trends, and for comparing local, regional, and national opportunities. At any point along the educational growth line, the student has a framework for comprehending, sorting, and storing his growing body of information about the world of work, his developing aspirations, and the guidance he receives in regard to bringing them together.

REFERENCES

Altman, James W. *Research on General Vocational Capabilities* (Skills and Knowledges). Final Report. (Pittsburgh, Pennsylvania: American Institutes for Research. March, 1966)

Ammerman, Harry L., and Melching, William H. *The Derivation, Analysis, and Classification of Instructional Objectives.* Technical Report 66-4. (Alexandria, Virginia: Human Resources Research Organization, The George Washington University. May, 1966)

Bakamis, William A., et al. *Identification of Task and Knowledge Clusters Associated With Performance of Major Types of Building Trades Work.* Report No. 7. (Pullman: Washington State University. December, 1966)

Bloom, B. S., ed. *Taxonomy of Educational Objectives.* I. (New York: David McKay Company, Inc. 1956)

Cunningham, J. W., ed. *The Job-Cluster Concept and its Curricular Implications: A Symposium.* Center Monograph No. 4. (Raleigh: Center for Occupational Education, North Carolina State University. 1969)

Dallas Independent School District: "Skyline Center." Brochure. 1971.

Fine, S. J. *The Nature of Automated Jobs and Their Educational and Training Requirements.* Research Report 6416-Ae. (McLean, Virginia: Human Sciences Research, Inc. 1964)

Gagne, R. M. "The Acquisition of Knowledge." *Psychology Review.* LXIX, (1962)

————. *The Conditions of Learning.* (New York: Holt, Rinehart and Winston, Inc. 1965)

Maley, Donald. *Construction Cluster—An Investigation and Development of the Cluster Concept as a Program in Vocational Education at the Secondary School Level.* (College Park: University of Maryland. August, 1966a)

————. *Electromechanical Installation and Repair Cluster—An Investigation and Development of the Cluster Concept as a Program in Vocational Education at the Secondary School Level.* (College Park: University of Maryland. August, 1966b)

————. *An Investigation and Development of the Cluster Concept as a Program in Vocational Education at the Secondary School Level, Final Report, Phase 1.* (College Park: University of Maryland. August, 1966c)

————. *Metal Forming and Fabrication Cluster—An Investigation and Development of the Cluster Concept as a Program in Vocational Education at the Secondary School Level.* (College Park: University of Maryland. August, 1966d)

Morris, R., and Murphy, R. "The Situs Dimension in Occupational Structure." *American Sociological Review.* XXIV, (April, 1969)

Oregon State Department of Education. *Oregon Statewide Study of Systematic Vocational and Educational Planning, Implementation and Evaluation* (Three Volumes). (Salem: Oregon State Department of Education. 1967)

Perkins, Edward A., and Byrd, F. Ross. *A Research Model for Identification of Task and Knowledge Clusters Associated With Performance of Major Types of Office Employees Work.* Final Report No. 5. (Pullman: Washington State University. December, 1966)

Rahmlow, Harold E., and Cavanagh, Catherine. *A Survey Instrument for Identifying Clusters of Knowledge and Competencies Associated With Performance of Child Work, Report No. 10.* (Pullman: Washington State University. December, 1966)

————, and Winchell, Leonard. *Mathematics Clusters in Selected Areas of Vocational Education, Report No. 8.* (Pullman: Washington State University. November, 1966)

————, et al. *A Survey Instrument for Identifying Clusters of Knowledge and Competencies Associated With Performance of Food Service Work, Report No. 9.* (Pullman: Washington State University. December, 1966)

Robinson, J.; Athanasiou, R.; and Head, K. *Measures of Occupational Attitudes and Occupational Characteristics.* (Ann Arbor: Survey Research Center, Institute for Social Research, The University of Michigan. 1969)

Roe, Anne. *The Psychology of Occupations.* (New York: John Wiley and Sons. 1956)

Schill, William J. *Curricula Content for Technical Education.* (Urbana: College of Education, University of Illinois. 1964)

Shelby, Gerald. "Cluster Concept Materials." (Carson City, Nevada: State Department of Education. 1971)

Smith, Robert G., Jr. *Controlling the Quality of Training.* HumRRO Technical Report 65-6. (Alexandria, Virginia: Human Resources Research Organization, The George Washington University. June, 1965)

————. *The Development of Training Objectives.* HumRRO Research Bulletin 11. (Alexandria, Virginia: Human Resources Research Organization, The George Washington University. June, 1964)

————. *The Engineering of Educational and Training Systems.* (Lexington, Massachusetts: D. C. Heath. 1971)

Super, Donald. *The Psychology of Careers.* (New York: Harper and Row. 1957)

Taylor, John E.; Montague, Ernest K.; and Michaels, Eugene R. *An Occupational Clustering System and Curriculum Implications for the Comprehensive Career Education Model.* HumRRO Technical Report 72-1. (Alexandria, Virginia: Human Resources Research Organization, The George Washington University. January, 1972)

U.S. Bureau of the Census. *1960 Census of Population, Alphabetical Index of Occupations and Industries* (Revised Edition).

U.S. Department of Health, Education and Welfare, and U.S. Department of Labor. *Vocational Education and Occupations.* July, 1969.

U.S. Department of Labor. *Dictionary of Occupational Titles, Third Edition, Vol. I, II.* 1965.

————. *Dictionary of Occupational Titles. Selected Characteristics of Occupations (Physical Demands, Working Conditions, Training Time).* Supplement. 1966.

————. *Dictionary of Occupational Titles. Selected Characteristics of Occupations by Worker Traits and Physical Strength.* Supplement. 1968.

————. *Occupational Employment Statistics, 1960-69.* Bulletin 1643. 1970.

————. *Occupational Manpower and Training Needs.* Bulletin 1971. 1971.

————. *Occupational Outlook Handbook.* 1971.

U.S. Office of Education. "Draft: Fifteen Occupational Clusters." Washington, D.C.: Division of Vocational and Technical Education, U.S. Office of Education, Department of Health, Education and Welfare. 1971.

KNOWLEDGE ABOUT WORK: A CAREER INFORMATION MODEL AND SYSTEM

Walter W. Adams

In differentiating between the growth of knowledge and more accumulation of data, Weiss (1966) contends that, "If one accepts this distinction, one readily perceives that this purported explosion is merely a glut of unassimilated data, rather than a spectacular breakthrough of deep insight and understanding." He defines knowledge as concepts, systems of thought and principles that, through understanding, reduce the mass of data and experiences to their common denominators. This distinction between information and knowledge has utility in analysis of the educational uses of occupational information or, more specifically, in the task of defining and evaluating the advantages and disadvantages associated with alternative methods of organizing information about work.

BACKGROUND AND RATIONALE

Industry, government, the military, civil service or fields of work like medicine have their own occupational hierarchies and grouping schemes used to define status, responsibility, authority, promotion or salary. Within education, occupations are frequently organized or grouped in some way for purposes of instruction, guidance, counseling or placement.

The importance of organizing occupational information has reached an unprecedented level for use within the total curriculum in career education. The new requirements associated with career education reveal the limitations and inappropriateness of most existing grouping systems.

The need for developing a comprehensive career clustering system for career education was recognized early by the United States Office of Education (Marland, 1972). Identifying occupational clustering as an essential element of a career education program, Swanson (1972) stresses the importance of adopting an "orderly system for comprehending the enormous number of occupations which may be examined in the process of accepting, rejecting, or otherwise considering an occupational choice."

The occupational world consists of more than 21,000 defined occupations, with many similar occupations having unique emphasis. To render it manageable and useful, information about these occupations must be reduced through grouping, clustering or some form of organization. In its final form, the information must be organized so it represents work as it occurs both in the community and society. It must also be developed so it will be appropriate to the developmental level of students at various grade levels.

Work in developing an occupational clustering system by Taylor, et al. (1972), reported in Chapter 10, is based on three criteria. A clustering system must (a) encompass most existing jobs, (b) be translatable into the design of an entire K-12 curriculum, and (c) show clear and specific advantages over other clustering systems.

In further work reported by Adams and Keilholtz (1972), three additional criteria are developed. These criteria specify that such an information system must (a) interface with existing occupational information resources, (b) be accessible by different users for a variety of educational purposes, and (c) possess substantive structure and uniform language for K-12 curriculum design purposes.

The need to interface with existing occupational information resources is based on the realization that it is not feasible to redesign the world of work in view of the extensive requirements for information about it. The goal is to bridge the gap between school and work. To do this will require maximizing interface with knowledge about work in our culture.

Occupational information must be accessible to a variety of users, such as teachers, curriculum developers and counselors, as well as to students for instruction, guidance, counseling, career exploration, career preparation and placement purposes. This requirement is based on recognition of the need to infuse a uniform and consistent use of career information into all aspects of the educational program in a planned and articulated way, an imperative in achieving continuous student growth.

The most crucial of the new criteria relates to the curriculum concept of structure. This consists of defining the content and determining how the content is to be structured in terms of the most basic elements of work.

CAREER INFORMATION

The term "career information" is used by Isaacson (1971) to emphasize expansion of the concept of occupational information to include educational and social information appropriate for vocational guidance. Further expansion of the concept is necessary for career education. Substantively, expansion includes relating curriculum subject matter or content knowledge to a knowledge base about work. Correspondingly, the scope of vocational guidance is also enlarged to parallel the more inclusive concept of career education. The definition for career information in career education accents the following important concepts:

1. Career information is essential to the conduct of career education.
2. Career information includes information about occupations,

educational development, career preparation and the labor market.

3. Curriculum subject matter or content knowledge is career information when related to preparation for or performance of occupational tasks.
4. Career development is facilitated by having information about educational and occupational requirements.
5. Career development is facilitated by having information about community, state and national labor market conditions.
6. Career development is facilitated by having information about economic conditions.
7. The meaning of educational and occupational experience is enriched through career information.
8. Career information is essential to the development of occupational and career competency.
9. Career information is essential to clarification of values, formulating goals and making career choices.

The definition of career information can be further delineated to express the interrelationships of its components—occupation, preparation, labor market and content knowledge. The basic element of the definition is occupational information. The new aspect is the recognition that the other elements of the definition help make occupational information relevant by enabling the student to relate his career plans and present educational experiences to anticipated educational and occupational opportunities. Information about occupations must be ordered in a fundamental way, to provide a base for integrating the other forms of information specified in the definition. This is a problem of structuring information about work and leads to the next step in the discussion.

CAREER INFORMATION— KNOWLEDGE ABOUT WORK

The problem of clustering career information is a problem of knowledge. The structure of knowledge in terms of "its connectedness and its derivations that make one idea follow another is the proper emphasis in education" (Bruner, 1962). Further, "the curriculum of a subject should be determined by the most fundamental understanding that can be achieved in the underlying principles that give structure to that subject" (Bruner, 1961). Determining structure, which consists of identifying the basic elements, concepts, or principles that give information about work meaning, becomes the logical starting point.

Approaching organization of career information as a knowledge problem leads directly to the task of analyzing the knowledge base.

Bloom, et al. (1956) provide a useful framework and helpful direction in this matter. Cognitive behavior is arranged within the Bloom Taxonomy in terms of increasing complexity. In this taxonomy, "knowledge" is considered to be the first in a hierarchy that is further subdivided into three levels. The lowest is "Knowledge of Specifics" (Bloom, et al., 1956). It describes the concern for the mass of specific job facts available apart from an acceptable organizational scheme. Resolution of the problem necessitates moving from the level of specific facts to higher levels of knowledge within the Taxonomy.

"Knowledge of Ways and Means of Dealing with Specifics" (Bloom, et al., 1956) describes knowledge organized into classes or categories. This is most descriptive of present efforts to organize or cluster information about occupations. Typical modes of organizing information include classes, sets, divisions, categories, arrangements and clusters developed for a given subject, purpose or problem. It is important to recognize that information organized at this level tends to relate to a specific area or discipline and is difficult to apply in other areas or expand for wider use. Schemes for organizing occupational information are typically geared to themes such as vocational interest, occupational information filing plans, subject matter, staffing arrangements or funding plans. Analysis of existing occupational clustering and grouping arrangements did not reveal any clustering scheme that fully met the information requirements of career education (Taylor, et al., 1972). Needed is a system to meet the information requirements of all components of career education in addition to providing a base for interface with the community in terms of employers and relationships with other institutions.

"Knowledge of the Universals and Abstractions in a Field" includes knowledge of theories and structures in the sense of identifying the body of principles and generalizations along with their interrelations to present a clear systematic view of a complex phenomenon, problem or field (Bloom, et al., 1956). Organization of career information at this level facilitates establishment of a comprehensive knowledge base for a career information system. The positive educational features that occur in structuring knowledge are succinctly stated:

> Viewed as strictly as possible from the position of a theory of learning, Bruner's structural emphasis may be summarized in the following three propositions:
> 1. Learning occurs when isolated elements of 'knowledge' are so organized, connected, or arranged as to allow them to take on meaning for the learner.
> 2. Further learning is facilitated by the perception of an organized, meaningful pattern into which new experiences may be integrated easily and quickly.
> 3. Self-discovery of the unifying or structural elements, the 'organizing ideas,' of any body of knowledge and the organization or reorganiza-

tion of these into larger patterns in order to discover larger meanings, serves as a powerful reward to the learner, reinforcing the present learning and motivating future efforts. (Beckner and Dumas, 1970)

THE STRUCTURE OF A
CAREER INFORMATION MODEL

The Career Information Model (CIM) described in this chapter represents an effort to develop an occupational clustering system. It is a composite of several clustering and occupational information systems that have either been adopted or modified to achieve a single integrated model. The multi-dimensional nature of CIM permits interface with other clustering approaches based upon similar concepts. CIM achieves maximum interface with existing sources of information about occupations, such as the *Occupational Outlook Handbook* (U.S. Department of Labor, 1972), the *Dictionary of Occupational Titles* (DOT) (U.S. Department of Labor, 1965), and local, state, and national labor market information. In addition, CIM provides for a logical flow of concepts about work expressed in elementary terms for the lower grades, to more complex and detailed concepts about work at the upper grade levels. The model provides potential for maximum use of career information by all the participants in the education process. The substantive structure of the system helps to insure proper sequence and articulation of curriculum unit content and guidance in terms of language and concepts about work. It also serves as a base for integrating efforts of the various components of career education program and coordinating community contacts as they relate to work.

The foundation for the CIM is the occupational definitions in the DOT, Volume I, *Definition of Titles* (U.S. Department of Labor, 1965). The DOT represents the most comprehensive and systematic organization of occupational information available. It is the legitimate base for a career information system, if knowledge about the entire scope of work found within our society is appropriate content for career education. The structure for organizing the base information for the CIM is derived from an analysis of the DOT, Volume II, *Occupational Classification* (U.S. Department of Labor, 1965).

The knowledge structure consists of the most fundamental statement of underlying principles that can be derived. This is analogous to classifying matter as basically animal, mineral or vegetable in the popular guessing game. Similarly, the concept *work* is considered to be reduceable to a structure of *product*, *process*, and *person*. Product includes *what* is done in terms of industry. Process refers to *how* work is done through tasks performed, and person describes *who* does the work. The latter includes the significant characteristics and traits of the worker, including such factors as interest, aptitude and educational development.

The occupational definitions in Volume I of the DOT serve as the information base and can be ordered or arranged in terms of each of the dimensions of the structure. This is possible because each definition includes information on the industry, tasks performed and characteristics of the worker. With the structure, one can start with a specific occupational title, find the definition, and follow it through the system to determine the relationship the occupation has to industry, tasks performed and worker traits. Alternately, one can start with information related to any dimension of the structure and trace it to the information base or either of the other dimensions.

The utility of CIM is exemplified in its adaptability. To illustrate, the process or occupation dimension of CIM includes information about tasks performed. As the tasks are identified, the skills and understandings required can easily be related to an external organization of information about educational preparation and training programs. Thus, CIM serves as an important link between information about work and the information requirements for career education. The linkage principle holds for many other types of external information as well. Among them are labor market demand, outlook and economics, a variety of human work characteristics, placement and follow-up information.

CIM is more than an occupational clustering system in the usual or popular sense; it is a structure of knowledge about work that serves to integrate a number of approaches to clustering; it is a multiple clustering system. As such, CIM possesses characteristics attributed to developmental structures (Piaget, 1970). Piaget's characteristics of structure include: *wholeness*—in the sense of embracing all relevant information; *transformation*—in being able to relate and reorder information about work meaningfully; and, *self-regulation*—in the sense of the structure having stability and direction for development.

The structure of knowledge about work is defined in the preceding manner. The initial criteria used by Taylor, et al. (1972) and the new requirements that emerged from analysis of their report are met in CIM. The decision to determine the structure of knowledge about work, instead of devising a special purpose clustering system, addresses squarely the mass of information available and the information requirements of career education. CIM provides a reasonable base upon which to develop career education programs and a framework to conduct required research activities.

DEFINITIONS OF MODEL COMPONENTS

The Career Information Base

The information base for CIM consists of the 21,741 occupations

defined in Volume I of the DOT. The occupational definitions con-
stituting the base possess two essential properties. The first is that
each definition is concise and includes: the occupational title, alternate
titles, DOT code number, industry identification, description of tasks
performed and indication of the worker characteristics. The second
property is that the information in the occupational definitions can
be organized into each of the three perspectives of the CIM structure: Product-Industry, Process-Occupation, and Person-Worker
Traits. (See Figure 1.)

Product Information-Industry. This perspective consists of grouping occupations in terms of the basic product or service provided. The
groups are called industries or clusters. Specific occupations are
arrayed vertically within the CIM cluster in terms of the variety of
occupations related to creating the product or service. The diagram
in Figure 2 illustrates the industry or cluster breakdown for each set
of grade levels.

Process Information-Occupations. This perspective involves organizing the occupations arrayed vertically by cluster or industry into
groups organized horizontally across the model. The resulting matrix
serves to identify specific occupations with their related occupational

COMPONENTS—THE CAREER INFORMATION MODEL

BASIC MODEL

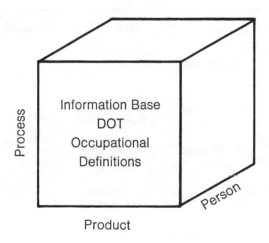

Figure 1

groups. The grade level organization of the horizontal occupational groups is as follows:

1. *Grades K-3*. Occupations in the Goods and Services clusters can be grouped horizontally by the basic tasks performed. Managers, leaders and policy makers can be grouped together while technicians and craftsmen or general workers and employees can be organized into separate groups based on the common or related tasks performed by the workers.

2. *Grades 4-6*. The five clusters used at grades 4-6 are divided into the nine Occupational Categories (first digit of DOT code number) of the DOT Occupational Group Arrangement.

3. *Grades 7-9*. The 12 clusters are divided into the 83 Occupational Divisions (first two digits of the DOT code number) of the DOT.

4. *Grades 10-12*. The 12 clusters may continue to be used or expanded to the 229 Industries in the DOT. In either case, the 83 Occupational Divisions may continue to be used or—in areas where greater specificity is required, such as guidance, placement or career preparation—the Occupational Groups (first three digits of the DOT code number) can be used. Use of the Occupational Groups provides the potential for dividing the vertical industries into a maximum of the 603 occupational groups or levels.

Person Information-Worker. The third, or depth dimension of

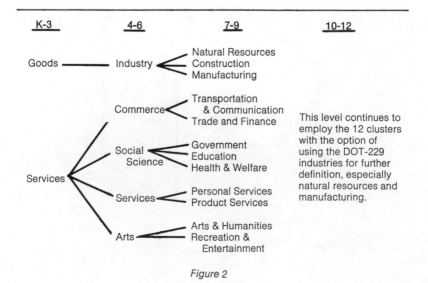

Figure 2

the CIM, relates to characteristics of the worker such as traits, aptitudes and vocational interests. The grade level arrangement of information on worker characteristics is as follows:

1. *Grades K-3.* Information about worker characteristics relates to the question, "What is the worker like?" Consideration of this question at grades K-3 would include a look at the worker in terms of personal, physical or educational factors related to performance of the basic occupational tasks.

2. *Grades 4-6.* The third dimension at grades 4-6 can be considered in terms of understanding the different levels of job functioning. The last of three digits of the DOT code number indicates the relationship an occupation has to different levels of significant functions with Data, People and Things (DPT). Learning about the different functions involved in work permits the student to assess occupational information in relation to his preferences for selected job functions. The levels of job functions are shown in Figure 3 (U.S. Department of Labor, 1965).

3. *Grades 7-9.* The person dimension of CIM can be approached at the career exploration level most effectively through the DOT Worker Trait Groups (WTG). This is an organization of Occupational Titles and definitions by worker traits. The WTGs represent occupations that are grouped together because of the similarity of their relationships to DPT and common trait requirements found in the WTG Qualifications Profile (QP). The QP is composed of

HIERARCHIES OF FUNCTIONS

	DATA (4th Digit)	PEOPLE (5th Digit)	THINGS (6th Digit)
	0 Synthesizing	0 Monitoring	0 Setting-up
Highest	1 Coordinating	1 Negotiating	1 Precision Working
	2 Analyzing	2 Instructing	2 Operating-Controlling
	3 Compiling	3 Supervising	3 Driving-Operating
	4 Computing	4 Diverting	4 Manipulating
	5 Copying	5 Persuading	5 Tending
	6 Comparing	6 Speaking-Signaling	6 Feeding-Offbearing
Lowest	7 No significant	7 Serving	7 Handling
	8 relationship	8 No significant relationship	8 No significant relationship

Figure 3

estimates and/or actual measures of the trait requirements (Crites, 1969). The requirements are expressed in terms of the level of the trait necessary for satisfactory or average performance of the major occupational tasks (U.S. Department of Labor, 1965). The QP includes estimates or measures of General Educational Development (GED), Specific Vocational Preparation (SVP), Aptitude, Interest, Temperament and Physical Demands. The most useful information will probably include DPT, interest and aptitude as they permit the student to assess the WTGs. The descriptions in the WTG include Work Performed, Worker Requirements, Clues for Relating Applicants and Requirements, and Training and Methods of Entry. In addition, specific Occupational Titles are found on the pages following each WTG description.

4. *Grades 10-12*. At the Career Preparation level, information of a more definitive nature is available within the Worker Trait Arrangement (WTA). As the student becomes more proficient in stating and describing what he has learned about himself in more precise terms, he can use this information in evaluating and determining career preparation options.

The diagram in Figure 4 illustrates CIM at grades 4-6 and shows how the dimensions of the model relate to each other in terms of the basic structure of knowledge about works. Graphic examples can also be developed for the other grade level ranges (K-3, 7-9 and 10-12). An important consideration is not whether the dimensions of CIM are orthogonally related as depicted in the cubistic model, but whether or not the dimensions constitute a valid structure of knowledge about work. If so, a means of organizing career information and giving it substantive meaning is provided.

THE CAREER INFORMATION SYSTEM

The focus of career education at the elementary school is on development of Career Awareness. Emphasis at the middle or junior high is Career Exploration, while at the higher grade levels attention is given to Career Preparation. At each of these levels the overriding objective of the program is to provide students with educational experiences related to this emphasis. The question becomes one of how to organize career information to support and improve achieving the objectives of career education.

Awareness aims at development of a broad base of general understanding about the world of work. This includes basic concepts and related vocabulary about work in terms of products, tasks and workers. Exploration focuses on extending the breadth of understanding about work and providing in-depth experiences, especially

CAREER INFORMATION MODEL
GRADES 4-6

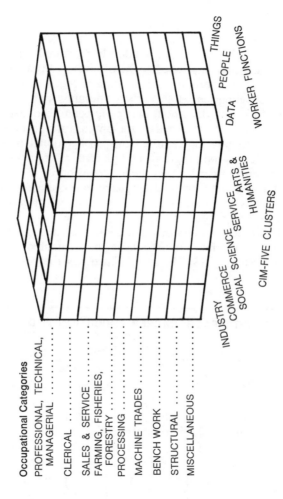

Occupational Categories

PROFESSIONAL, TECHNICAL,
MANAGERIAL ....

CLERICAL ....

SALES & SERVICE ....
FARMING, FISHERIES,
FORESTRY ....
PROCESSING ....

MACHINE TRADES ....

BENCH WORK ....

STRUCTURAL ....

MISCELLANEOUS ....

THINGS

PEOPLE

DATA

WORKER FUNCTIONS

ARTS &
SERVICE HUMANITIES
INDUSTRY
COMMERCE SOCIAL SCIENCE
SCIENCE

CIM-FIVE CLUSTERS

Figure 4

in those areas considered to be important by the student. Preparation is designed to provide students with opportunity to develop specific skills and understandings necessary for employment in an entry level occupation, or taking the next step of preparation related to their career goals.

Implied in the foregoing description of career education are extensive requirements for career information. These requirements are different for each level of the model. For example, information for awareness purposes is needed to help develop broad understanding about work; for exploration, information is required to help students interpret their experiences and relate emerging understandings about themselves to knowledge about occupations and broad areas of work; whereas information is needed at the preparation level about specific occupations, preparation requirements, instructional programs, postsecondary educational programs and placement opportunities.

It was discussed earlier that each dimension of the CIM could be developed using concepts and language appropriate to the different grades or levels of educational development. All three dimensions of the model are employed at each of these levels to insure balance in use of information about work. An additional step needs to be taken to establish a rationale for organizing the content of the Career Information System (CIS). Figure 5 illustrates the relationship of di-

INTERFACE: CAREER EDUCATION AND CIS

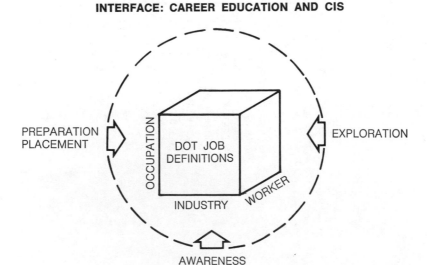

Figure 5

mensions of the CIM to selected curricular thrusts of career education —awareness, exploration and preparation. For awareness, the content can be organized by industry or clusters; for exploration, the content can be arranged by the Worker Trait Groups; and for preparation, it can be filed by the individual occupations.

The focus of career education at the elementary level is career awareness. The unique information requirements at this level are associated with developing breadth of understanding about the work, through an organized curricular approach. This requirement can be met through organizing career information by the industry dimension of CIM. CIS for grades K-3 and 4-6 is described as follows:

1. At grades K-3, the content of CIS is organized by Industry— Goods and Services. It consists of occupational briefs (11″ x 14″ cards) filed alphabetically within two clusters. Each card is labeled with the occupation and cluster titles. The front of the card has a large picture of the worker performing a basic job task(s) with a simplified occupational definition. The reverse side of the card has three sets of statements in large print, with key vocabulary words underlined. The statements provide information about the Industry, Tasks Performed and Worker Characteristics. It is expected that the K-3 CIS will have approximately 130 to 190 occupations that are representative of the world of work.

2. At grades 4-6, CIS is organized by industry using the five clusters. The content of CIS consists of a single page brief for each occupation. The briefs are color coded and organized alphabetically within each cluster. Each brief will have the occupational title, cluster identification and a sketch of the worker performing a major occupational task(s). The basic occupational information related to CIM structure is contained in descriptions of the related Industry, Tasks Performed and Worker Characteristics. In addition, related subject matter content, general preparation requirements and basic economics about the occupation will be included. It is anticipated that the grades 4-6 CIS will contain approximately 400 occupations.

Career education at the secondary level emphasizes the processes of exploration and preparation. Here CIS accounts for the fact that both exploration and preparation occur largely within the school and community environment. The content of CIS is, therefore, designed to be local in character to increase the potential of students for deeper understanding of these experiences. Given the objective, then, of providing locally oriented information through CIS, balance is maintained through maximizing interface with already existing information sources at the state and national level. The distinguishing feature of the CIS is to present the local information content of CIM in terms of structural knowledge about work. Interface of CIM with state and national information sources is contingent upon their common use of the DOT.

1. At grades 7-9, CIS content is organized by the worker dimension of CIM. This is accomplished using the Worker Trait Arrangement of the DOT. It enables students to assess information through understanding of such personal characteristics as aptitude, interest or by relating preference for worker functions to a wide range of occupations. The grade 7-9 CIS consists of guidelines for developing local career information, sample materials, filing and retrieval systems and recommendations for use of the system. Content of the system is in the form of occupational briefs. Each brief has the following file indexes: occupational title, DOT code number, Worker Trait Group title and number, and cluster identification. The content includes the job definition, industry description (what, where and why), occupation description (how) and worker description (who). In addition, related local information is included on employment factors, preparation requirements and alternatives, suggested exploration activities and state and national information sources. The total content of the system will be approximately 700 occupations, depending upon the occupational character of the community.

   The 7-9 CIS can be easily adapted for use with curricular based approaches to exploration. This is accomplished by sorting the content of the system into the 12 industry or cluster areas and using the DOT number or the alphabetical job title to order the content.

2. At grades 10-12, the content of CIS is organized by the occupational dimension of CIM. This organizational scheme interfaces with existing filing systems based on the DOT. Estimated content for the system is 1200-1400 occupations. This level of CIS will consist of guidelines for developing local information in hard copy form for manual use and in data base form for computer use.

3. A special file is being developed as an adjunct to the 10-12 CIS. This is the Placement Information System and supports operation of the placement program. It is designed to interface with the U.S. Employment Service Job Banking System.

4. A further extension of the 10-12 CIS is the Follow-up Information System. The data base concept of the CIS permits extension of the basic information structure and language to development of data collection and analysis procedures

necessary for monitoring progress and evaluating the over-all impact of career education on the career development of students after leaving school.

Efforts to identify and develop content for CIS have been carefully coordinated with the curriculum development process in the school-based Comprehensive Career Education Model (CCEM) described by Miller in Chapter 18. The occupation content for both K-3 and 4-6 CIS was selected by meeting one of the following criteria: first and most important, an occupation and related information had to be required by a curriculum unit; second, the occupation, if it was not directly covered in a curriculum unit, had to be representative of an area or level of work, as determined by CIM; or third, an occupa-tion, if it is indigenous to a particular community or geographical region, had to be representative of a major visible area of work. A final consideration in regard to content is to make provision for teachers and local curriculum developers to add new content to help them localize CIS and add support for infusing career education into other areas of the curriculum.

Knowledge about work, cast in appropriate language for each edu-cational level, is considered essential to career education. This knowl-edge together with knowledge of career and human development constitute the unique foundations for career education. Given exist-ing curriculum, they become the most basic resource for guiding the process of transforming American education.

SUMMARY

Attention has been called to the issue of whether to define oc-cupational clustering as essentially a problem of information or knowledge. The implications of defining occupational clustering as a problem of knowledge lead to consideration of special classification schemes and structuring as alternatives. In this chapter, preference has been given to structuring knowledge about work as the most practicable way of meeting the information requirements of a career education program. The concept of occupational information has been expanded to career information and a Career Information Model developed based upon a structure of knowledge about work. The developmental features of CCEM design were considered as they relate to CIM, and the resulting interface providing direction for de-velopment of a Career Information System. Aspects of CIS are presently in development, and implications for its continued develop-ment are inherent in the structure of knowledge about work and CIM.

REFERENCES

Adams, Walter W., and Keilholtz, Linda A. *Career Information System Model.*

(Columbus: The Center for Vocational and Technical Education, The Ohio State University. 1972)

Beckner, Weldon E., and Dumas, Wayne. *American Education Foundations and Superstructure.* (Scranton: International Textbook Co. 1970)

Bloom, Benjamin S., ed. *Taxonomy of Educational Objectives, The Classification of Educational Goals, Handbook I: Cognitive Domain.* (New York: David McKay Co., Inc. 1956)

Bruner, Jerome S. *The Process of Education.* (Cambridge: Harvard University Press. 1961)

————. *On Knowing.* (Cambridge: Harvard University Press. 1962)

Crites, John O. "The Foundations of Vocational Psychology." *Vocational Psychology: The Study of Vocational Behavior and Development.* (New York: McGraw-Hill Book Co. 1969)

Gorman, Anna M., and Clark, Joseph F., eds. *Sixth Annual National Vocational and Technical Education Seminar Proceedings.* (Columbus: The Center for Vocational and Technical Education, The Ohio State University. 1973)

Isaacson, Lee E. *Career Information in Counseling and Teaching* (Second Edition). (Boston: Allyn and Bacon Inc. 1971)

Marland, Sidney P., Jr. "Career Education: Every Student Headed for a Goal." *American Vocational Journal.* XLVII, March, 1972.

Piaget, Jean. *Structuralism.* (New York: Basic Books, Inc. 1970)

Swanson, Gordon I. "Career Education." *Career Education: Perspective and Promise.* Keith Goldhammer and Robert E. Taylor, eds. (Columbus: Charles E. Merrill Publishing Co. 1972)

Taylor, John E.; Montague, Ernest K.; and Michaels, Eugene C. *An Occupational Clustering System and Curriculum Implications for the Comprehensive Career Education Model.* (Monterey: Human Resources Research Corporation. 1972)

U.S. Department of Labor, Bureau of Labor Statistics. *Occupational Outlook Handbook.* 1971-72 Ed. 1972.

U.S. Department of Labor. *Dictionary of Occupational Titles.* 3rd ed. 2 Volumes. 1965.

Weiss, Paul A. "The Growth of Science." *The Knowledge Explosion.* S. J. Sweeney, ed. (New York: Farrar, Straus, and Giroux. 1966)

CAREER LADDERS AND LATTICES

Jean K. Kintgen

"Career ladder" is used to convey the idea of a mechanism that facilitates (not merely permits) vertical mobility in an occupational area. The basis of this mobility is generally the ability to perform at a higher level, and this ability is generally the result of learning, either formal or informal. "Career lattice" represents an extension of the career ladder concept which adds the horizontal dimension to career mobility. As generally conceived, a career lattice facilitates not only the individual's vertical movement within an occupational area but also his horizontal movement to another occupational area if he is inclined to alter his direction either on the basis of changing personal objectives, often resulting from developments in his individual life situation, or on the basis of changing conditions within the society. The foundations for this horizontal movement, as for the vertical movement, are some common areas of knowledges and skills.

PHILOSOPHY VS. TERMINOLGY

The terms "career ladder" and "career lattice" are well established in the occupational education vocabulary and, for want of alternative terms which are equally well understood, "ladder" and "lattice" will be utilized in this chapter. However, it seems appropriate to point out that perhaps educators should be searching for terms that would better express the underlying philosophy. What is wrong with the concept of a ladder? It certainly implies opportunity, but the observation has been made that the ladder concept almost *imposes* vertical movement—and probably more often implies rising to the top than just to the first rung. The purpose of a ladder (in the concrete sense) is to assist the individual to move vertically. If he does not do so he is not using the ladder in accordance with its purpose. If he advances only a rung, he is not making full use of the instrument. The same ideas might be applied to the concept of a lattice. One might conceive of a lattice as ladders placed side by side. Since the concept of a lattice also includes horizontal mobility, it places less emphasis upon vertical direction, but the implication is nevertheless present.

Advocates of the ladder and lattice philosophy would be quick to counter that these symbols should not imply the need for everyone to climb to the top. They would stress the importance of recognizing the dignity and worth of occupational roles at every level as well as the importance of providing opportunities for continuing vertical movement. Since such is the prevalent philosophy, perhaps the symbols and related vocabulary should change. It might be well to stop speaking about ladders, lattices, and levels and return to *terra firma* to talk about pathways and directions. Some possible pathways in the occupation of nursing, for example, might be described as follows: An individual might enter the educational path that provides preparation for service as a nurse aide. Having achieved this basic preparation, he might choose (for any number of reasons) to continue on the nurse aide path to serve with increasing skill, speed, love, self-assurance, job satisfaction, etc. Another individual might enter the nurse aide path and, having achieved this basic preparation, leave the nurse aide path where it intersects with the practical nurse path. In turn, he might leave the practical nurse path where it intersects with the technical nurse path and the technical nurse path where it intersects with the professional nurse path.

The imagery presented here is not proposed as an alternative to current terminology. Indeed it lacks the neatness of the ladder and lattice structures. The foregoing discussion is intended simply to call attention to the importance of the philosophy that is probably quite well accepted and to stimulate thinking about the possibility of utilizing terminology that would have positive rather than negative consequences for the implementation of that philosophy.

WHY CAREER LADDERS AND LATTICES?

Although there may be little disagreement about the philosophy of educational career ladders and lattices, once we have dealt with some negative connotations of the terminology it is the implementation of the philosophy that will mean an investment of energy. It is only reasonable, therefore, to ask the question: "Why is the career ladder concept so important?"

First, providing for career mobility means economy of training. Instead of the re-introduction of content to which the individual has been exposed, time may be devoted to the utilization of the content at increasingly higher levels: application, analysis, synthesis, evaluation, etc. Likewise, the individual can spend his time acquiring additional knowledge that is built upon the foundation of his previous knowledge.

A second reason for the importance of the career mobility concept is that the perception of pursuing a career leads to greater satisfaction on the part of the individual. Fine (1967: 1) compares the attitudes of two workers:

> Two men working side by side may be performing the same simple tasks, yet for one the activity is merely a job and for the other it is a step in a career ladder. The first feels "used," unvalued, disposable; the second feels involved, valued, committed. . . .
>
> . . . The first worker has no basis for feeling that what he happens to learn is part of an accumulating trade or craft knowledge on which he can build; the second worker believes that everything he learns, even

on a low functional level, may ultimately pay off since he is "learning the business."

Increased vocational satisfaction is tremendously important to the individual but should also have favorable effects upon production and/or service rendered.

Thirdly, the career ladder concept is important because of its appropriateness in approaching some of the vocational problems of the disadvantaged. Career ladder education implies interspersion of study with work experiences so that initial entrance into employment is earlier than it would be for the traditionally college prepared individual. This is in keeping with Gordon's (1968: 100) observation that the disadvantaged are motivated by the prospects of income production and social participation.

Career ladder education also implies the importance of short-range goals for which the disadvantaged learner tends to have a preference. He need not aspire to the top or second from the top rung on the ladder; there is evidence that success at endeavors of graded difficulty can raise the level of aspiration (Tuckman, 1967: 48). This basis for the career ladder need not be limited to the problems of the disadvantaged. Many kinds of life experiences can result in low levels of aspiration in capable individuals.

A fourth reason for the importance of the career ladder concept is its appropriateness to the needs of women. In the past, women have tended to choose shorter-term vocational preparation than men, doubtlessly because of a general tendency to "drop out" of the labor force for a time early in their employment careers. Yet when their family responsibilities decrease, many women establish or reestablish careers. Their participation in the labor force from that time forward continues over a considerable period. (A woman who enters the labor force at 35 and withdraws at 65 has a 30-year career!) Increasing numbers of women are following a different pattern of employment. They enter early and "drop out" only for brief periods for reasons of child-bearing and child-rearing. Investment in education would seem to be realistic and career ladders that can be ascended a rung at a time appear to be a feasible answer to them.

Finally, in answer to the question, "Why is the career ladder concept so important?" another question might be asked: "How well has education fared with traditional practices?" It has been quite common to "guide" students into vocational or college preparatory tracks just as it has been common to "guide" the prospective nursing student into the kind of educational program appropriate for him— one, two, three, or four year. All this has been accomplished with the view that enough is known in advance about the student to indicate the kind of program he should enter and that, having entered the prescribed program, he will be content with the outcomes. But such is not always the case—those prepared for college don't want to stay in college; the vocationally prepared want to enroll in higher education; practical nurses want to be registered nurses. Surely all of these phenomena cannot be counselors' mistakes. Many factors are operating: life situations change; increased maturity revises career plans in positive directions; occupational aspirations are raised; academic aptitude increased; achievement is improved through motivation and learning readiness. Traditional practices do not seem to be the answer.

APPROACHES TO CONSTRUCTING CAREER LADDERS

Approaches to constructing educational career ladders might be classified as follows:

1. Proficiency testing,
2. Supplementary educational programs, and
3. Provisions for career mobility built into educational programs.

Proficiency Testing

Proficiency testing is probably the best known approach, and the best known proficiency examination system is probably the New York State College Proficiency Examination Program (CPEP). The rationale for this program is clearly stated in the proposal that a committee composed of Marion Folsom, John Gardner, and Henry T. Heald presented to the Board of Regents:

> A large number of students are now doing college level work by independent study and in television courses, adult education courses, courses at industrial plants, and other courses outside regular college curriculums. One great difficulty with these courses is that they do not count uniformly, if at all, toward the achievement of a college degree. Yet, in many cases, the subject matter studied is equivalent to that offered in a course in a regular college or university curriculum.
>
> We can expect a great increase in the future in the number of students in educational activities other than full-time, day-student programs as the post-high school age population increases and the desire to do college work expands. Many of these students will be engaged in high-quality study, and we propose that a program be established by the Regents which would permit students to acquire regular college credit for their achievements without regular attendance at formal college classes (University of the State of New York and the State Department of Education, 1966: iii).

Occupational education areas such as accounting, engineering, graphics, and nursing are now well represented in the CPEP test offerings.

At this point in time, proficiency examinations are common practice at both the junior and senior college levels. However, important as proficiency testing may be in assisting the individual in career advancement, there is need to go beyond this measure. Consider the expertise, time, and expense entailed in developing proficiency examinations and add to these considerations the questionable reliability and validity levels of many such tests. Then consider the additional problem of cultural inequities. There are educators who insist upon a proficiency test for any student who wants credit for a course and has not taken it *in the institution in the form* in which it is currently offered. These educators insist that they want the credit conferred to be "respectable." However, they are frequently hard put to defend the quality of the tests they are using.

There are some possible variations of proficiency testing as usually conceived that could have merit in assisting individuals in their career advancement. Evans (1970) suggests that the ability to "do the job" is a criterion of knowledge and skill. Thus, if an individual's performance in a job is evaluated by his supervisors as satisfactory and if that job represents a certain level of achievement in a formal occupational education program, credit might be given in the program on this basis. Without a proficiency examination, the individual might be admitted to advanced courses in the program. The further test of proficiency would be ability to succeed in the higher level courses. Credit for the entering level of proficiency might even be withheld pending successful completion of the advanced courses.

Supplementary Educational Programs

The supplementary program offers a second approach to constructing an educational career ladder. In the kinds of situations in which jobs or roles have developed with no plan for career advancement, the result may be individuals who want to move up but find they are a "different breed." It is not feasible for them to put together bits of a higher level program to meet their needs. Educators have sometimes responded with the development of a supplementary program. A program is formulated or adapted to build upon the previous experience on the basis of the program developers' knowledge of the content of one educational program at a lower level or in another kind of setting, or, on the basis of knowledge of the content or experience gained in a setting other than an educational institution. The program developers' clear knowledge of students' previous learnings and clear-cut objectives with regard to the outcomes of the supplementary program are major keys to the success of this kind of program. One of the earliest efforts to construct a career ladder in nursing represents this approach. For some years, the Helene Field School of Nursing in New York City has offered a program that assists licensed practical nurses to advance to the registered nurse level (Feuer, 1967). The traditional one-year practical nurse program bears little resemblance to the first year of any of the types of conventional registered nurse programs so that the practical nurses for whom the supplementary program is designed are indeed a "different breed."

Built-in Provisions

A third approach to constructing an educational career ladder is to develop a system with built-in provisions for advancement from one educational level to another along with significant attainment in occupational proficiency at each level. A segment of education (a) prepares for occupational performance at a particular level, and (b) prepares a foundation for occupational education at the next level which builds upon the previous one(s). Such articulation should be possible between secondary and junior college levels, between junior college and senior college levels, and even between senior college and graduate levels.

An example of this approach to constructing a career ladder is the cooperative endeavor in the State of New York by the Board of Cooperative Educational Services in Nassau County and the Nassau Community College and Farmingdale Agricultural and Technical College to set up a distributive education program leading from senior high school to the community college with potential for articulation with the senior college (Modderno, 1971). Intended to open collegiate doors to minority students, the program includes a segment that provides for the development of knowledge and skills necessary for immediate employment of the high school graduate (training includes areas such as receiving, checking, cashiering, stock control, inventory practice). At the same time, it also serves as a foundation for the community college program that leads to employment in retail business management. Job opportunities for the community college graduate include department manager, floor manager, assistant buyer, executive trainee, section manager, assistant service manager, personnel trainee, and assistant to fashion coordinator. Many of the credits earned in the community college program, in turn, apply to baccalaureate programs.

In the area of nursing, educational programs that include segments not only to prepare for practice at specific levels but also to serve as foundations for education at the next level are gaining prominence. Practical nurse to technical nurse programs have been developed in community colleges in Iowa (Kerr, 1970: 3-11), at Long Beach City College in California (Drage, 1971: 1356-8), and at Columbus Technical Institute in Ohio (Oklahoma State Department of Vocational and Technical Education, 1971: 79-80). The State College of Arkansas in Conway offers a baccalaureate program in nursing and admits students who are interested in pursuing such a degree; however, career options are provided at various points in the total program. Candidates are prepared to practice as practical nurses after one year and as registered nurses after two years (Oklahoma State Department of Vocational and Technical Education, 1971: 62). Georgia State University at Atlanta (Lane, 1972) and the University of Nebraska at Omaha (Boyle, 1972) offer programs in which the first two-year segment leads to an associate degree and practice at the technical level, and the additional third and fourth year segment leads to a baccalaureate degree and practice at the professional level. It should be emphasized that the components of these nursing programs that provide preparation for practice at the various levels represent innovative approaches to educational preparation for these levels; they are not the traditional nursing programs joined together.

Interest in educational career ladders and lattices is also evident in the area of home economics. The rationale set forth in the report of a recent project of the American Home Economics Association would seem to lead in the direction of educational programs with built-in provisions for career advancement:

> . . . the home economics profession through research over some sixty years has developed a high level of science, technology, knowledge, and skill in the same areas of expertise as those needed in household service work . . .
>
> It is a generally accepted fact that different individuals have skill preferences and therefore do some tasks better than others. In view of the fact that there are indeed commonly recognized professional level jobs in preference skill areas as well as entry level jobs in most of them, it stands to reason that there are also intermediate jobs which would provide the rough framework for establishing a hierarchy or ladder in home economics through which the household worker might achieve further learning, lateral or vertical mobility (American Home Economics Association, 1972: 4-5).

CONSIDERATIONS FOR THE CURRICULUM DEVELOPER

Among educators involved in the three kinds of career ladder endeavors described above, those engaged in developing "from scratch" programs in which a segment of education both prepares the student for a certain level of practice and provides a foundation for occupational education at the next level are probably faced with the most serious problems.

One suggested system is to establish a hierarchy of tasks in terms of the levels of personnel currently performing the respective tasks and to base the curriculum on this hierarchy. For "Level I," the student would learn to do tasks A through F; for "Level II," G through L; for "Level III," M through S; for "Level IV," T through Z. But the answer is probably not this simple. The results of the UCLA Allied Health Professions Project indicated no significant differences in the frequencies with which approximately 60 percent of 306 nursing tasks were performed by nurse aides, licensed practical nurses, and registered nurses (Goldsmith, et al., 1970). Does this mean that if one were to plan a nurse aide through professional nurse sequence that a six-week nurse aide segment would constitute 60 percent of the four-year professional curriculum? Obviously this is not a legitimate conclusion.

Another system suggests constructing the basic levels of occupational curricula of manipulative skills on the premise that judgments and decision making are the province of the professional. This kind of reasoning seems to run counter to the philosophy that argues for career ladder curricula. Personnel at all levels make judgments and decisions. The knowledge upon which these judgments and decisions are based at the lower levels of practice provides a foundation for the acquisition of knowledge upon which more complex judgments and decisions are made at the upper levels. Indeed, if training at the lower levels were to be limited to the rote performance of manipulative skills, students capable of ascending the career ladder might quickly lose interest and withdraw from the program. Finally, this approach would seem to negate some basic concepts of career education. (The relationships between career education concepts and ladder and lattice concepts is discussed in the final section of this chapter.)

Gilpatrick (1972: 2-4), project director of the Health Services Mobility Study, offers criticism that relates to inappropriate emphasis upon tasks in curriculum development:

> There appears to be a tendency in the field of "paraprofessional" . . . training to confuse task performance and curriculum design. A number of projects have attempted to design curricula for new occupations or to develop programs for existing occupations with a view towards making *some* upward mobility possible for health services employees. These projects collect task data to determine what activities the curricula would have to prepare employees to do, but they then set about to design curricula which would teach students to perform the steps of the tasks, as the tasks are currently being done. That is, the curricula are designed to teach the actual procedures or steps of the tasks, and little more.
>
> The design of curricula based solely on teaching how to do the steps of tasks is a corruption of the possible uses of task analysis in curriculum design. The focus on teaching task procedures makes the curriculum content (and the student) obsolete as soon as technology changes and/or the procedures are changed. This leaves the performer with nontransferable knowledge.
>
> The focus on teaching task procedures does not lay the foundation of skills and knowledge needed to build upon if upward mobility is to be achieved through efficient design of job and curriculum ladders. The objective of job and educational ladders should be to carry the individual potentially through all the steps in a ladder from entry level to professional levels, even though they provide exit points along the way. . . .
>
> The difference in learning which separates the on-the-job trainer

performer ("first you do this and then you do that") from the performer trained in terms of organized knowledge ("you have to do certain kinds of things under certain kinds of circumstances") is that the first type of learning is *not* transferable, and the second *is* transferable. Transferability of learning means an investment of time and effort in learning something usable in more than one context: and this is the basis of mobility.

Simple task analysis and organization cannot provide an adequate basis for a career ladder curriculum. The tasks performed in an occupational area are a major key to the identification of required knowledge but it is probably the knowledge and the degree of understanding (comprehension, application, analysis, synthesis, evaluation, etc.) required that are the keys to developing curriculum levels to correspond with levels of practice in the occupational area. This is certainly not to say that performance on the job is less important than the knowledge of the worker; obviously, knowledge that is not applied in quality performance has no value in the employment situation. However, the fact remains that it is not the task itself but the related knowledge and the level of "knowing the knowledge" that are the determining factors in developing career ladder curricula; and the necessary related knowledge and level of knowing vary with the conditions under which a task is performed.

The appropriateness of a system for developing a career ladder curriculum is probably dependent upon the area in which the curriculum is being developed. One possible approach that has been demonstrated in part by the writer is outlined below:

1. On the basis of objectives in a total occupational area and the tasks performed in that area, identify a body of required knowledge. This body of knowledge may encompass several areas of study (e.g., mathematics, biology, psychology).
2. In each of the areas of study encompassed in the body of knowledge identified above, define some naturally progressive levels of curriculum content (two, four, seven—the number of levels is dependent upon the nature of the respective area).
3. Relate the curriculum levels defined above to levels of practice in the occupational area (e.g., relate curriculum level one to aide level practice).
4. Further define the levels of curriculum which have been related to levels of practice by attaching to each a level of understanding or a level of "knowing the knowledge" (e.g., comprehension, application, analysis, synthesis, evaluation).
5. Test the educational program which would result against the demands of the "real-world" employment situation and revise as necessary.

Educational programs developed in this way would not be the traditional programs linked together but rather new entities that "make sense" from the standpoint of the logic of the curriculum and its validity in terms of the demands of the employment situation. Likewise, although workers educated in these new programs should be able to move into existing jobs, they would probably have abilities that are somewhat different from those of their counterparts in the existing system and they would perform somewhat different roles. The new programs would probably affect the job structure in the particular occupational area, but, if the programs are valid, the quality and quantity of production and/or service rendered should be raised.

An Objection to Career Ladder Curricula

Possibly one of the strongest objections raised to developing a curriculum in which a segment of education both prepares for practice in the occupational area at a given level and serves as a foundation for occupational education at the next level, is that it will attract a heterogeneous body of students and they cannot be successfully taught in one group. There is no doubt that a program that provides for "spinning off" at a basic level, as well as progressing to the attainment of a high level of education, will involve a heterogeneous group in the lower levels. On the other hand, a program that provides just basic level education or one that admits only those interested in pursuing a high level of education will involve a fairly homogeneous group. There is probably also little doubt that a group that is fairly homogeneous in terms of academic ability is probably easier to teach than a heterogeneous one. However, educational technology has allowed for the individualization of instruction to the point that the teacher is probably better able than ever before to deal with heterogeneity. As technology continues to develop, and more is learned about individualized instruction, the feasibility of working with heterogeneous groups will continue to increase.

CAREER EDUCATION IMPLICATIONS

Career ladder and lattice concepts are certainly elements of the total career education philosophy. Well constructed career ladders will allow "flexibility for a youth to leave for experience and return to school for further education" and will help to "extend . . . time horizons from 'womb to tomb' " (Hoyt, et al., 1972: 5). Ladder and lattice concepts are obvious in the following statement regarding career education:

> . . . the school has the responsibility to stick with the youth until he has his feet firmly on the next step of his career ladder, help him get back on the ladder if his foot slips, and be available to help him onto

a new ladder at any point in the future that one proves to be too short or unsteady (Hoyt, et al., 1972: 6).

Probably the most exciting implications that the broad career education philosophy has for career ladder and lattice concepts lie in the emphasis that the career education philosophy places upon viewing education totally—from the kindergarten level through adult education and across areas of basic skills, general education, and vocational education. Proposed educational career ladders and lattices generally have dealt with senior high school and postsecondary education. The career education philosophy calls attention to the fact that this is not enough. The child should be aware of and then explore the extensive lattice of careers. Furthermore, his basic skills and general education should contribute to his vocational education and *vice versa*.

Reform may be necessary on the part of vocational educators. It has long been the practice of some to introduce "related technical information" (mathematics, science, etc.) at the high school level as something completely new, when actually the student was exposed to the same content some years earlier in his general education. The vocational educator's position has been that the student might have been exposed to it but never really learned it. The vocational teacher takes pride in having taught something that another teacher did not succeed in teaching. This achievement is commendable, but, in the context of career education, no longer enough. The vocational teacher who subscribes to career education concepts will broaden his perceptions and recognize that he has a part in coming to grips with the problem of the student's not learning the lesson at the earlier stage. Perhaps he can suggest—or even become involved in providing —some "hands on" experiences that will make the student's general education more meaningful.

If content that was taught in the fourth grade must be retaught in the eleventh grade in connection with vocational education, perhaps the presentation of general education content should be more gradual and interspersed with many more opportunities to "activate" the knowledge acquired through the processes of applying, analyzing, synthesizing, and evaluating, which are so much a part of effective vocational education. Some of these opportunities might be provided in the world of work. Early experiences in the world of work would also assist early school leavers whom career education advocates seek to serve.

There is need to conceive of educational career ladders and lattices as having their bases at the elementary school rather than the senior high or postsecondary level. Indeed, if one were to utilize the system of developing a career ladder curriculum outlined in the foregoing section, in step two the levels of curriculum content might be described in terms of school level, and in step three these levels might be related to levels of practice in the occupational area. For example, junior high level physiology might be related to aide level practice in the area of physical therapy.

The potential for the implementation of career education—and especially career ladder and lattice—philosophy is overwhelming and the prospect exciting. But such implementation will be hard work!

REFERENCES

American Home Economics Association. *Career Ladders and Lattices in Home Economics and Related Areas: Possibilities for Upgrading Household Employment.* (Washington, D.C.: American Home Economics Association. 1972)

Boyle, Rena E. "Articulation from Associate Degree through Masters." *Nursing Outlook.* XX, (October, 1972)

Drage, Martha O. "Core Courses and a Career Ladder." *American Journal of Nursing.* LXXI, (July, 1971)

Evans, Rupert N. Remarks at the University of Illinois Invitational National Conference for Health Occupations Education. New Orleans, Louisiana. 1970.

Feuer, Helen Denny. "Operation Salvage." *Nursing Outlook.* XX, (November, 1967)

Fine, Sidney A. *Guidelines for the Design of New Careers.* (Kalamazoo, Michigan: The W. E. Upjohn Institute for Employment Research. 1967)

Gilpatrick, Eleanor. *Suggestions for Job and Curriculum Ladders in Health Ambulatory Care: A Pilot Test of the Health Services Mobility Study Methodology.* HSMS Research Reports Four and Five. (New York: The Research Foundation, City University of New York. 1972)

Goldsmith, Katherine L., et al. *The UCLA Allied Health Professions Projects: A Study of Nursing Occupations.* Interim Report. (Los Angeles: University of California Division of Vocational Education. 1970)

Gordon, Edmund W. "Vocational-Technical Education for the Disadvantaged." Second Annual National Vocational-Technical Teacher Education Proceedings. (Columbus, Ohio: The Center for Vocational and Technical Education, The Ohio State University. 1968)

Hoyt, Kenneth B., et al. *Career Education: What It Is and How To Do It.* (Salt Lake City, Utah: Olympus Publishing Company. 1972)

Kerr, Elizabeth E. *An Overview of Health Occupations in Iowa.* (Iowa City, Iowa: Division of Health Affairs, University of Iowa. 1970)

Lane, Evangeline B. "The Associate Degree Program—A Step to the Baccalaureate Degree in Nursing?" Paper presented at the meeting of the National League for Nursing Council of Baccalaureate and Higher Degree Programs, New Orleans, Louisiana, March 22-4, 1972.

Modderno, Alexander S. "Articulated Programming Opens Collegiate Door to Minority Students." *American Vocational Journal.* XLVI, (October, 1971)

Oklahoma State Department of Vocational and Technical Education. *Career Development for Supportive Nursing Personnel.* (Washington, D.C.: Office of Education, U.S. Department of Health, Education, and Welfare. 1971)

Tuckman, Bruce W. "The Psychology of the Culturally Deprived." *American Vocational Journal.* XLII, (November, 1967)

University of the State of New York, and the State Department of Education. *The New York College Proficiency Examination Program.* (Albany, New York: University of the State of New York; State Department of Education. 1966)

PART THREE

facilitating processes and programs

*Personnel Development, Leadership,
Administration, Research and Development,
and Information Dissemination*

Certain processes and programs facilitate or undergird educational programs. If career education concepts are to be implemented, these processes and programs must adjust, adapt or change direction. The authors in Part Three have endeavored to explain how these processes and programs can facilitate the development and implementation of career education.

Keller maintains that implementation of career education requires changing people's value orientation, determining who needs development, determining program scope and focus, determining program outcomes, and designing a personnel development program. She makes specific recommendations for in-service training and pre-service preparation of teachers.

Wenrich reviews the significant research on leadership behavior in organizational environments with special emphasis on human relations and task oriented behavior. He outlines the characteristics of an effective leader and explains how a leader can help others accept career education as a common goal.

Proehl calls for a new leadership that can overcome resistance to change. He emphasizes the importance of the administrative tasks at the local level. He makes recommendations relative to the administrator, operation and structure, and staff.

Taylor and Ward believe that research and development provide a viable means of developing self-renewing educational programs that meet individual and societal needs. They identify several major clusters of variables deserving of priority attention by the research and development community—the efficacy of the career education concept, the evaluation of alternative delivery systems, technological and methodological applications, nurturing career education, and comprehensive program planning and evaluation.

White analyzes the characteristics of career education as an innovation and draws generalizations from the research literature on diffusion. He recommends guidelines for information dissemination to facilitate the development of career education programs.

PERSONNEL DEVELOPMENT FOR CAREER EDUCATION

Louise J. Keller

Inherent in career education is the means for revitalizing educational experiences for learners, educators, and possibly all citizens of a community who become involved in a community-based system of education. Career education is a challenge for all levels of education to redirect educational efforts toward significant social and economic roles in life in order to make these experiences more purposeful and personal to the individual learner.

This part of the 1973 AVA yearbook is concerned with certain processes and programs needed to implement career education at all levels of education. It is most appropriate that a chapter be included that deals with personnel development, as it is people who implement programs.

IMPLEMENTATION CONCERNS

Any attempt to implement career education eventually requires individuals to cope with problems related to (a) changing people's value orientation, (b) determining what personnel need in-service education, (c) determining the scope and focus of career education, (d) identifying desired outcomes for career education, and (e) designing a comprehensive personnel development program that is continuous and directed to these concerns.

Changing people's value orientation is a critical variable to the success of career education. People change programs, but traditionally "education is considered 'the knowledge business,' not the business of capacitating human beings so that they can live contributing, participating, self-fulfilled lives" (Goldhammer, 1972). It has always been contended that educational goals and objectives are affected by the society for which they exist and by the social and economic realities prevailing in that society. One such reality is that individuals spend most of their adult lives in an activity called *work*. The history of education reflects that we have yet to accept this fact. Through the years, various sets of goals have been delineated to give new directions to curriculum designers; for example, the "seven cardinal principles of education," and the "ten imperative needs of youth." Yet the curriculum of today remains essentially a subject-centered, college-preparatory type of curriculum with little attention given to extending skills, knowledge, and personal attitudes into an application mode of learning. As new courses and programs have been developed through the years, educators have tended to separate these into three domains: academic, vocational, and general.

Career Education

Knowledge has been identified, classified, and departmentalized. This phenomenon has permeated the entire educational system. The education of teachers for this type of curriculum organization has also been departmentalized. The interrelationships of learning with the realities of life, such as work, are often not perceived by teachers to be important.

The quest for relevancy in education, the stress on accountability, and the assertion that a more humanistic educational process is needed have catenated to form a new educational thrust labeled as career education. A current leading concept is that not only development for one's career roles in life is a responsibility of all educational enterprises, but, also, it is career roles that may well serve as mechanisms for making existing subject matter more interesting and understandable for youth and adults.

To move from a subject-matter orientation to a student-centered orientation focused on a learner's present and future career roles requires a new value orientation on the part of those who direct the teaching-learning processes as well as a change in value orientation for those who support the educational enterprise efforts in a community. When an educational system accepts career education, that system is declaring that learning experiences will be more relevant to the needs of all learners if these experiences are built around a career development theme. This kind of commitment is not totally understood, nor are the educational personnel often willing to change just because the local school board has announced its acceptance of career education as a viable goal.

Determining what personnel need in-service education is another major implementation concern. Schaefer and Ward's (1972) model for a comprehensive state personnel development system in vocational education has merit for this consideration of career education. For example, in an analysis of personnel needs for career education one must look at the entire spectrum required to effectively design, implement, maintain, extend, and improve careers curricula. The primary target group includes:

1. Personnel for the functional roles involving—
   Instruction
   Administration/Supervision/Coordination
   Guidance
   Research and Development
   Curriculum/Instructional Materials Development
   Youth/Adult Leadership Development.

2. Personnel for differentiated responsibilities within the functional roles from the paraprofessional through the post-doctorate preparation level.

3. Personnel employed within both public and private local/ area educational agencies, state departments of education, universities, federal educational agencies, industry and business, and others. In addition, and not to be ignored, are—
    (a) lay members of educational policy-making and advisory groups such as legislators and members of boards, advisory committees, councils, and commissions; and,
    (b) non-educational public agency personnel who relate closely to education, such as employment security, rehabilitation personnel.

A secondary target group that will eventually be listed with those noted here will be the new educational partners—voluntary personnel for both in-school and out-of-school assistance together with a new group of non-school remunerated personnel to serve in various coordination roles.

Little attention has been given to the area of personnel development for volunteers in education. The education of volunteers should be considered as part of the in-service training program for career education. Listed here are some of the roles that could be assumed by volunteers after participating in a program of in-service training, as identified by Keller (1972a):

Career counselor assistants,
Career discussion leaders and listeners,
Resource and activity supervisors,
Neighborhood home-school coordinators,
Referral agency school-home coordinators,
Business and industrial tour guides,
Role players,
Work simulation supervisors,
Career cluster aides,
Basic education tutors,
Special education task-development helpers,
On-the-job training supervisors,
Work-sampling consultants,
Career cluster coordinators,
Preapprenticeship sponsors,
Advisory committee and task force committee members.

Strategies that bring segments of the community together through personnel development can well be the fusing element badly needed in many communities.

Those seeking the answer to the question of who should be involved in personnel development for career education should read

Coleman's (1972) article. He asserts that the schools should concentrate on a "new goal" that "must be to integrate the young into functional community roles that move them into adulthood." Achieving this goal will require fundamental changes in our present society. Coleman makes the following observations and recommendations.

> Practices currently barring young people from productive activity in many areas—such as minimum wage laws and union-imposed barriers against the young—must be relaxed. The school must be integrated with service organizations, business, industry, and home. Since the school's function will no longer be to protect the child from society but rather to move him into it, the school must be integrated with these other organizations of society and not insulated from them.

Coleman foresees the time when we will modify the work place to incorporate the young. Thus, the idea of full-time school followed by full-time work "would be replaced by a continuing mix that begins at an early age and runs through adulthood."

Career education will call for a more comprehensive *community plan* than a school plan for education. Any definition of personnel development must include ancillary and adjunct personnel who can bridge the gaps between schools, homes, industries, businesses, labor unions, organizations, and agencies. New community-based remunerative jobs may well be the positions that coordinate educational experiences outside the school walls. There are some individuals who believe that we should not attempt to build additional facilities for vocational education but rather should place vocational and basic education teachers within business and industry. Some schools are beginning to experiment with "clearing houses" for job development, job placement, work-study coordination, and training plan development and supervision. Occupational training is becoming more and more a community function. Tax write-offs for businesses could provide the incentive necessary to expand these efforts. We have yet to understand the real impact career education could have on the educational system of this country.

Determining the scope and focus of career education is one of the major impediments to implementation and sooner or later emerges in any philosophical discussion. There are those who argue that career education is concerned only with development for roles within the world of work. Career education's developmental stages are awareness, exploration, preparation (vocational and professional), and finally, job placement. It is this emphasis on the work role that has led many educators and the lay public to view vocational education and career education as synonymous. There is a second group of individuals who view career education as a unifying theme that encompasses all the goals of the school, therefore serving as a catalyst for integrating and correlating isolated goals and subject matter. This latter group is able to take this stand because it views career education as having a much broader scope. In addition to the work role, advocates of this concept also include those other roles in life such as the avocational/leisure role, the citizenship role, and the social role as related to home and community.

The interpretation of the word "career" is considered by the first group to mean one's productive/service role as a wage earner, while the second group prefers to interpret a career to be the combination of all one's roles. This rather unsophisticated explanation of a fundamental philosophical issue facing many educators who attempt to design and implement career education clearly illuminates the need for establishing a philosophical base of understanding among all educational personnel before moving dramatically into curriculum restructuring. These philosophical differences cannot be ignored in any plan for personnel development. Perhaps the unifying strategy is to accept the premise that a "careers curriculum" should concern all the basic roles in life; but, at any given time in one's human development, the educational enterprise will need to stress one or more roles over another. The work role may well be the major focus for many youngsters. This kind of philosophical discussion on the part of educators will lead them to an awareness that individualized program planning is needed.

Thus, the scope and focus of career development become important concerns in any discussion related to career education.

Identifying desired outcomes for career education has not received much attention in the educational literature, nor have the processes or mechanisms for producing these desired outcomes been delineated. Those working with a personnel development program often find it necessary during the orientation stage to provide the participant with some concrete examples that are both content and process oriented in order for the participant to better perceive his role in career education. To date, there has been little dissemination of curriculum and instruction information from the national exemplary school-based model project. It is important that these materials and processes not be released until they have been properly validated in various classroom situations. However, any cursory examination of the literature will reveal a number of goals that have been identified by various school districts.

A critical examination of the instructional or school goals identified by Keller (1972a) and grouped as to levels of education may serve as discussion topics as well as clues to the kinds of student outcomes to be expected, and the processes/mechanisms needed for producing such desired outcomes.

Elementary School Goals

Encourage development of work habits and realistic attitudes toward occupations and other career roles.

Identify those broad career development concepts that will serve as criteria for guiding future curricular and instructional activities.

Identify and integrate occupational cluster information with basic educational skills.

Involve children in self-discovery activities.

Introduce problem-solving and decision-making skills.

Provide elementary pupils with the opportunity for rendering services.

Provide the opportunity for students to interact with selected community work models.

Establish an advisory committee for occupational awareness, citizenship awareness, community and home awareness.

Junior High School Goals

Orient students to (1) society and work, (2) occupational information, (3) self-knowledge, (4) career planning, and (5) occupational training.

Assist students to acquire a level of competency in the basic technologies (Altman, 1966).

Expose students to a wide range of occupations through "cluster" explorations.

Involve students in human development experiences related to (1) physical development, (2) interpersonal relationships, (3) esthetics.

Provide for "hands-on" experiences in simulated work environments as well as personal identification with role models from the community.

Organize a career development center for diagnostic, prescriptive, and discretionary learning experiences.

Strengthen career guidance activities.

Provide appropriate occupational preparation for students who have decided to leave school prior to completing junior high school.

Establish cluster advisory committees and select module sponsors.

Provide for youth participation in career development activities through work sampling activities within the community, career clubs, employer buddy system.

Senior High School Goals

Improve student performance in basic subject areas by unifying and focusing these around career development themes to make the subject matter more meaningful and relevant.

Expand the occupational programs in order to provide every student with intensive preparation in a selected occupational cluster or in a specific occupation in preparation for job entry and/or further education.

Expand guidance and counseling services and work-study programs to prepare for employment and for further education.

Expand "cooperative" education.

Provide for job development and job placement services.

Provide for placement for all students upon leaving school in (1) a job, (2) a postsecondary occupational education program, or (3) a four-year program.

Develop an instructional-learning system based on competency levels that permit ease of entrance, ease of exit, ease of return.

Provide for continuous follow-through of all dropouts and graduates and use the information for program revisions.

Provide a coordinated advisory system.

Postsecondary and Adult Education Goals

Provide for the community at large a career development program which includes guidance, counseling, referral services, instructional programs based on manpower and human needs, job development and placement services, and educational renewal activities.

Provide for a community-based system of education which utilizes existing facilities and manpower personnel to assist in the career development needs of people.

Develop a cadre of volunteers for school-based, community-based, and home-based career development activities.

Diffuse throughout the community the concept that education is a continuous process which can have a recreative or renewal effect on those who pursue a career development plan.

Designing a comprehensive personnel development program that supports many of the notions presented here will require educational personnel to enter into a program for change: in attitudes, in instructional foci, in organizational structure, in learning environments, in administration/management practices, and in funding practices. Schaefer and Ward (1972) stated emphatically that:

The personnel development system within our profession has been measured and found inadequate. There is neither the quantity nor quality of personnel needed to move forward the vocational components of the educational system. Qualified administrators, teachers, and ancillary personnel are in short supply.

This could easily be applied to career education, of which vocational education is an integral part. Designing a personnel development system must first involve the process of effecting change.

Before focusing attention on the process of effecting change, it seems appropriate at this time to issue a few words of caution. In designing and implementing a comprehensive personnel development system, regardless of the level of education, the responsibility for planning should not be carried by a few individuals. There has been a tendency to assign the task to a small group of administrators or to a nearby college or university. Another pitfall occurs when a local school system purchases all the available world-of-work media and creates a resource center without orienting teachers to the utilization of materials. The material seldom becomes an integral part of the instructional program. Some schools claim to have a personnel development program for career education when one evening a week their teachers are enrolled in an extension class. This class often becomes the "alpha and omega" experience unless there is extensive follow-through to the classrooms. It is also hoped that schools will not make the greatest mistake of all—that of confusing career development education with vocational education, thus establishing a dual-track system: academic education and career education.

When a local school system is seriously interested in career education, one of its first tasks will be to design a plan for personnel development. It is important that those who plan and those who participate understand the process of effecting change.

THE PROCESS OF EFFECTING CHANGE

Those who wish to implement career education will need to become immersed in the process of effecting change. The educator's knowledge of planned change is still a blend of experience and intuition, with a large dash of folklore, to which there is slowly being added a body of scientific literature (McClelland, 1968). The process of change as practiced still remains an art form. Through our experiences with career education exemplary projects, a number of simple propositions about planned change have evolved:

Proposition No. 1. Career education will not be accepted on its own merits. Regardless of the dissemination of information on career education, people will not accept the philosophical and theoretical concepts of career education without becoming personally involved in discovery experiences and having internalized these concepts of career development and made them a part of their own value system.

Proposition No. 2. The development of personnel needed for implementing, maintaining, and improving career education requires money, time, and continuous effort. Speaking metaphorically, these three requirements are also needed when a community plants flowers and shrubs in its city parks. Career education, to grow and survive, will need the wisdom of a landscape architect; gardeners willing to take bold new steps to unearth the hidden talents of personnel and discover new processes which enrich the learning experiences of youth and adults; the devotion of caretakers to safeguard the developmental growth stages of career education; and, a financial commitment to support adequately the total operations.

Proposition No. 3. There is no orderly diffusion process an educational enterprise should follow to transport the elements of career education from an experimental mode to a system-wide adoption. Several guidelines exist which suggest processes for implementing career education and explicitly detail plans for personnel development; for example, the guides by Hoyt, et al. (1972); and, the guide by Keller (1972a).

Proposition No. 4. The implementation of success will notably lie in the acceptance of philosophical and theoretical concepts by those who are recognized as engineers of change. These may be building administrators, teachers who have been innovative in the past and still have credibility with existing faculty, and recognized community leaders who have demonstrated their influence on education decisions.

Proposition No. 5. A key element in any plan for development and implementation is time. It will take considerable time for all facilitators of education to move from their present value orientation to a new set of constructs. The development and installation of a curriculum which focuses on career development will require an internal adaptation to a significantly different set of commitments. A massive change is too much to expect of a school system its first year. A more reasonable expectation for the first year would be to effect changes which involve all personnel in curriculum development activities through a developmental mode that prescribes some "minimal" efforts for the purpose of initiating the change process.

Proposition No. 6. Besides personal attitudes which need to be changed, the other major factor which inhibits or accelerates change is the organization or structure of curriculum. That which impedes progress is a program structure which does not permit ease of learner entrance, exit, return; nor does it allow for interventions such as (a) linkage of one subject matter field with another, or (b) utilization of volunteers, lay advisors, or outside environments for learning, perhaps under the supervision of community helpers. That which accelerates change is the "modulization" of content and learning experiences to permit small units of instruction to be (a) integrated or correlated with other subject matter, (b) prescribed for some learners and become discretionary experiences for others, (c) individualized into learning/experiencing blocks of time, (d) purposefully directed to a specific type of career role, (e) purposefully linked with other modules/units to strengthen the entire teaching-learning experience. The structure and organization of curriculum and instructional practices together with the preconceived notions as to what makes a person educated are major constraints which must be overcome through a personnel development program.

The value of these propositions may become more obvious as one examines the process of effecting change through "in-service training" and "pre-service preparation," two possible mechanisms for producing the desired outcomes of personnel development for career education.

In-service training of personnel for career education must be concerned with a planned, sequential program. Where one begins will depend upon what stage of development the personnel have reached. No attempt will be made in this chapter to outline a detailed in-service training procedure. Rather, several important elements will be noted. For example, there are many skills needed by educators. Keller (1972a) has identified the following skills that could be developed through in-service training:

Assessing the needs of learners and the community,

Formulating objectives for career education,

Structuring curriculum and instruction around an occupational cluster system,

Securing and utilizing community resources,

Analyzing clusters to determine learning modules/elements for individualizing education,

Integrating and correlating subject matter,

Designing student personnel services,

Evaluating and measuring achievement,

Selecting, collecting, and disseminating career education materials and media,

Articulating curriculum and instruction vertically and horizontally,

Counseling for occupational preparation,

Managing things, data, and ideas,

Placing students, once competency levels have been reached,

Involving volunteer helpers in the educational process.

These skill requirements do not represent an all-encompassing list; considerable attention needs to be given to any one of the above items.

It should be evident that no curriculum innovation has been more dependent on a developmental system than has career education. In analyzing the scope of the innovation, Reinhart (1972) identified nine tasks. Each must be considered for a comprehensive in-service program.

1. Relate the philosophical and theoretical concepts to the desired outcomes and mechanisms for producing outcomes.

2. Interface the various components—for example, curriculum guidance, in-service training, community relations, and evaluation.

3. Develop supporting information systems, such as pupil data system, career information system, community resource system, and placement and follow-up system.

4. Articulate the relationship between instructional levels and educational institutions.
5. Develop program units and instructional methodology.
6. Coordinate programs designed to generate institutional and community acceptance.
7. Develop formative and summative evaluation and feedback.
8. Select and set goals and establish priorities.
9. Manage the allocation of resources and time.

Much can be written about the strategies and tactics for implementing career education through personnel development. Most schools begin in-service training with extensive orientation sessions for school board members, administrators, teachers/counselors, and the lay public.

In-service training for vocational educators does not imply that as an identifiable group of educators they should be provided with a separate in-service training program, but this group does have specific in-service training needs for service in a career education environment. In the initial stages of designing and implementing various components of personnel development programs, vocational educators must take part in any discussion whether it is focused on elementary education or higher education. The rationale for this is rather simple. The quantity and quality of future vocational education programs may well depend upon the curriculum development and instructional practices in the lower grades and in the higher education personnel development programs. Just as the academic and general educators have been reluctant to recognize the importance of a career curriculum that may focus considerable attention on the work roles of people, so are the vocational educators reluctant to examine their own value orientation as it relates to the sharing of school-community resources and to accepting general principles for (a) guidance and counseling, (b) job development and job placement, (c) advisory committees, (d) team teaching, (e) volunteer and paraprofessional personnel utilization, and (f) curriculum development and instructional practices. Vocational educators have the opportunity to extend and expand their involvement in career education through new role relationships and through new and expanding training offerings. In-service training becomes essential. One of the major tasks will be to confront honestly the problems and issues and seek alternatives for solving the concerns that are bound to creep into the developmental activities.

Pre-service preparation of teachers will also need to provide a process for effecting change. Institutions that are serious about the preparation of personnel for career education will be equally concerned about their own program design and operations for profes-

sional development. Some of the program design features that char-
acterize career education K-12 are implicit criteria for evaluating
teacher preparation program designs and operations; for example:

Program designs and operations are non-traditional.

Students have an opportunity to become aware of, explore, and
prepare for multiple job opportunities.

Subject matter is integrated and correlated to provide an interdisciplinary experience that is more understandable and relevant
for many learners.

Human development services such as career guidance, counseling, directed part-time occupational experience, and follow-up
services in the field for early school leavers and graduates enhance and support the total educational enterprise.

Adjunct community helpers and paraprofessional personnel are
utilized.

Professional teachers are involved in new coordinating roles and
role relationships.

Curricula are performance based.

Any plan for supporting career development concepts and career
education in higher education will need to explicate its commitment
in four distinct ways: (a) a philosophical commitment through mission and goal statements, (b) a commitment to personnel development for differentiated roles in teaching, (c) an instructional program
commitment to career education, and (d) a commitment to on-
campus and field services (Keller, 1972b).

Other than two conferences held in Columbus, Ohio, and sponsored by The Center for Vocational and Technical Education at The
Ohio State University—one for deans of colleges of education and
the other a meeting for key educators from colleges of education—
little has been done to design and install a comprehensive personnel
development program for teacher-educators. More conferences of
this kind are vital to the survival of career education.

Graduates entering school systems that have implemented career
education programs are required to integrate, correlate, and differentiate subject matter. Academic and general education teachers often
find it difficult to relate content and process to occupational environments. On the other hand, vocational teachers find it equally difficult
to blend their activities with academic education components and
even to communicate with other vocational instructional areas.
Strategies for exposing students to and involving them with other
subject areas and blending educational experiences with career development concepts should be high on the priority list for pre-service
education and for the in-service education of teacher-educators.
Career guidance, counseling, and placement skills are needed by all

teachers. Child development concepts need to be understood. All future teachers should be exposed to the world of work.

Work observations and experiences seem to be highly desirable for all teachers and guidance personnel and should be an integral part of the pre-service education program. For some teachers, work experience becomes a "point of view" that is transferable; for others, certain rigorous, technical, occupational experiences are necessary. Any process for effecting change in higher education institutions that prepare future teachers will need to be concerned with helping the future or present teacher relate subject matter of his specific discipline to the career roles of people.

The process of effecting change in pre-service education will require institutions to:

Establish a comprehensive in-service training program for their own faculty.

Develop a framework and organizational strategy for implementing career development within their own programmatic operations.

Became aware of and sensitive to the actual needs and concerns of local communities.

Provide assistance to state educational agencies and local school units to develop viable strategies for career development diffusion. A viable strategy must recognize an enlarged organizational structure that encourages cooperative development.

Support local school efforts through pre-service and in-service education, research and development activities, and with field services.

Develop new communication and partnership systems that will help initiate as well as sustain the career education thrust.

SUMMARY

This chapter is concerned with certain processes and programs needed to implement career education at all levels of education. The implementation of career education must be concerned with problems related to (a) changing individuals' value orientation, (b) determining what personnel are to be included in a comprehensive personnel development program, (c) determining the scope and focus of career education, (d) identifying desired career education outcomes, and (e) designing a personnel development program for effecting change. A process of effecting change is one of establishing and implementing a personnel development plan through in-service and pre-service education. Implicit in any personnel development plan are the facts that: (a) people change programs; (b) planning for change depends largely on cooperative activities effectively organized; (c) career education requires restructuring of curriculum and instruction; (d) career education requires a thorough needs assessment including an assessment of community needs, needs of learners, and needs of the educational personnel; (e) in-service training begins with extensive orientation sessions; and (f) pre-service education reform will be necessary to maintain and support local educational efforts.

Career education will only be as effective as the personnel who design, implement, maintain, and improve its administrative and programmatic components are effective. A number of states have mounted leadership development programs for career education, and special appropriations have been allocated for this purpose. The Education Professions Development Act (EPDA) has provided the impetus needed to develop comprehensive state systems for personnel development, but there is a need for more dynamic state leadership.

The successful implementation of career education depends in large measure on the quality of leadership at the state and local levels. The real challenge is to think through the possibilities of career education for all youth and adults in a community and to initiate a long-range, developmental system that exemplifies concern for maximizing the potentialities of people in order that they may live productive and rewarding lives.

REFERENCES

Altman, James W. *Research on General Vocational Capabilities* (Skills and Knowledges). (Pittsburgh: Institute for Performance Technology, American Institute for Research. 1966)

Coleman, James S. "The Children Have Outgrown the Schools." *Psychology Today,* V (February, 1972)

Goldhammer, Keith. "Roles of Schools and Colleges of Education in Career Education." A paper presented at the National Conference on Career Education for Deans of Colleges of Education, Columbus, Ohio, April, 1972.

Hoyt, Kenneth B., et al. *Career Education—What It Is and How To Do It.* (Salt Lake City, Utah: Olympus Publishing Company. 1972)

Keller, Louise J. *Career Education In-Service Training Guide.* (Morristown, New Jersey: General Learning Corporation. 1972a)

————. "Preservice Preparation of Teachers for Career Education." A paper presented to the Sixth Annual National Vocational-Technical Education Seminar, Columbus, Ohio, October, 1972b.

McClelland, William A. "The Process of Effecting Change." A Presidential Address delivered before the Division of Military Psychology of the American Psychological Association, San Francisco, California, September, 1968.

Reinhart, Bruce. "Nature and Characteristics of Emerging Career Education Curriculum." A paper presented at the National Conference on Career Education for Deans of Colleges of Education, Columbus, Ohio, April, 1972.

Schaefer, Carl J., and Ward, Darrell L. "A Model for a Comprehensive State Personnel Development System in Vocational Education." A staff paper for The 1971 National Leadership Development Seminar for State Directors of Vocational Education, Columbus, Ohio, July, 1972.

PROFESSIONAL LEADERSHIP FOR CAREER EDUCATION

Ralph C. Wenrich

Anyone reviewing the literature on leadership is soon impressed by the amount of it. Leadership has been studied in the abstract by the social scientists, but the subject has also been of great concern to researchers and practitioners interested in leadership as it relates to organizational effectiveness.

The author believes that successful educational programs and institutions have one major attribute that sets them apart from less successful programs and institutions; it is effective leadership. This is a basic resource that is unfortunately in short supply in most educational institutions. What can we do to identify and to nurture the leadership talent that we have in our schools?

LEADERSHIP DEFINED

Webster defines a leader as "a person or animal that goes before to guide or show the way, or one who precedes or directs in some action, opinion or movement." Ordway Tead, author of a book titled *The Art of Leadership* says, "Leadership is the activity of influencing people to cooperate towards some goal which they come to find desirable."

A review of research done by psychologists and sociologists on leadership suggests that neither discipline alone can adequately explain leadership. That is, both the individual dimensions of leadership (psychological) and the group or organizational dimensions of leadership (sociological) must be considered together. Most of the recent studies of leadership do indeed consider both the individual and the organizational dimensions and the interaction between the two. Gibb (1954) recognized the complexity of the concept when he stated:

> Any comprehensive theory of leadership must incorporate and integrate all of the variables which are now known to be involved, namely (1) the personality of the leader, (2) the followers with their attitudes, needs, and problems, (3) the group itself both as regards to (a) structure of inter-personal relations, and (b) syntality characteristics, (4) the situation as determined by physical setting, nature of task, etc. Furthermore, any satisfactory theory must recognize that it will not be these variables *per se* which enter into the leadership relation, but that it is the perception of the leader by himself and by others and the shared perception by leaders and others of the group and the situation with which we have to deal.

What appears to be one of the more useful approaches to research on leadership is a series of studies focusing upon leadership *behavior* in organizational environments.

Leadership Behavior

Many of the studies of leadership behavior have resulted from and are based upon the work of the Personnel Research Board at The Ohio State University. A study by Halpin (1960) of school superintendents and another by Everson (1959) of high school principals have revealed that effective or desirable leadership behavior was characterized by high scores on two dimensions of leader behavior that were designated "initiating structure" and "consideration." Initiating structure was defined as the leader's behavior in delineating the relationships between himself and the members of his work group, and in establishing clear organizational goals, communication channels and procedures for accomplishing group tasks. Consideration was defined as the leader's behavior indicative of friendship, mutual trust, respect and warmth in the relationships between the leader and group members.

The Survey Research Center at The University of Michigan has also been involved in studies dealing with organizational leadership; even though this research was done in work organizations other than schools, it may be equally applicable to schools. Cartwright and Zander (1960) have pointed out that most group objectives may be accomplished under the two headings of "goal achievement behaviors" and "group maintenance behaviors." The kinds of leadership behavior directed toward goal achievement describe one who (a) initiates action, (b) keeps members' attention on the goal, (c) clarifies the issue, (d) develops a procedural plan, (e) evaluates the quality of work done, and (f) makes expert information available. The types of leadership behavior that exemplify group maintenance include one who: (a) keeps interpersonal relations pleasant, (b) arbitrates disputes, (c) provides encouragement, (d) gives the minority a chance to be heard, (e) stimulates self-direction, and (f) increases the interdependence among members.

While Halpin and Everson did their research in the school setting and Cartwright and Zander did their research with small nonformal groups, it is interesting to note the similarity in their findings.

Katz and Kahn (1966), also at The University of Michigan, identify two major modes of behavior among supervisors in business and industry. They claim that some supervisors are *production-oriented* while others are *employee-oriented*. Employee-oriented supervisors focus primarily on employee motivation, satisfaction of employee needs, and the building of employee morale. Production-oriented supervisors, on the other hand, emphasize increased efficiency, greater production, and institutional goal attainment.

The studies done at The Ohio State University reveal that initiating structure and consideration were separate and distinct dimensions.

The fact that a person is high in one dimension does not necessarily mean that he will be high or low in the other. The behavior of a leader can be described as any mix of both dimensions. To show this relationship, the study plotted leader behavior on two separate axes rather than on a single continuum. Four quadrants were used to show various combinations of initiating structure (task-oriented behavior) and consideration (human-relations oriented behavior). Figure 1 illustrates these relationships.

Blake and Mouton (1964) have popularized the concepts that have grown out of the Ohio and Michigan studies in their "managerial grid." In this graphic presentation, Figure 2, the horizontal axis scales concern for production, while the vertical axis scales concern for people. Production becomes more important to the leader as his rating advances on the horizontal scale, while people become more important to the leader as his rating progresses on the vertical axis. In other words, a leader with a rating of nine on the horizonal axis has a maximum concern for production, while a leader with a rating of nine on the vertical axis has a maximum concern for people.

Implicit in most of this research is the idea that the most effective leader is the person who is high on both dimensions of leadership behavior that have been identified in the Ohio and Michigan studies—initiating structure (goal achievement) and consideration (group maintenance). But other researchers, most notably Likert (1967), suggest that the ideal and most productive leader behavior, for industry at least, is employee-centered, or what Likert would call participatory. Likert developed the principle of supportive relationships that provides a formula for obtaining the full potential of every major motive that can be harnessed in a work situation. He stated the principle as follows:

> The leadership and other processes of the organization must be such as to insure a maximum probability that in all interactions and all relationships with the organization, each member will, in the light of his background, values, and expectations view the experience as supportive and one which builds and maintains his sense of personal worth and importance.

The relationship between the superior and subordinate should be one that is supportive and ego-building. To the extent that the superior's behavior is ego-building rather than ego-deflating, his behavior would have a positive effect on organizational performance. But the superior's behavior must be perceived as supportive by his subordinates as viewed in the light of the subordinates' values, background and expectations. The subordinates' perception, rather than that of the superordinate, determines whether or not a particular experience is indeed supportive.

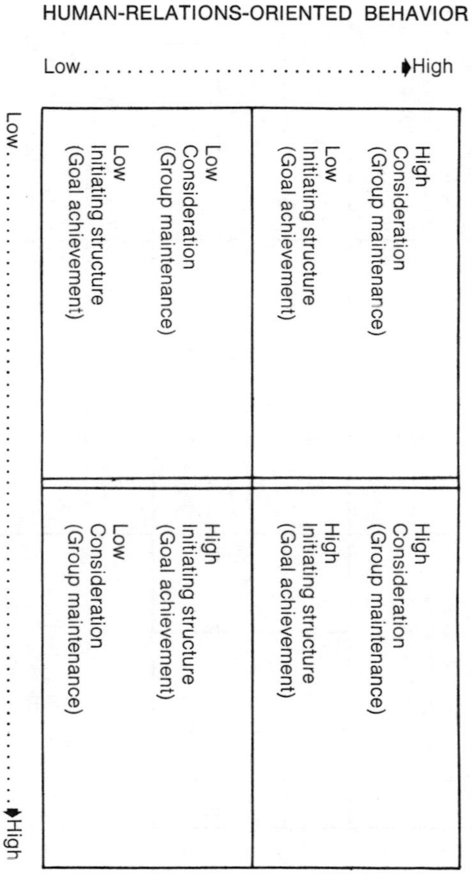

HUMAN-RELATIONS-ORIENTED BEHAVIOR

Low............................▶High

High Consideration (Group maintenance) Low Initiating structure (Goal achievement)	High Consideration (Group maintenance) High Initiating structure (Goal achievement)
Low Consideration (Group maintenance) Low Initiating structure (Goal achievement)	High Initiating structure (Goal achievement) Low Consideration (Group maintenance)

TASK-ORIENTED BEHAVIOR

Low...............................▶High

Figure 1

THE MANAGERIAL GRID

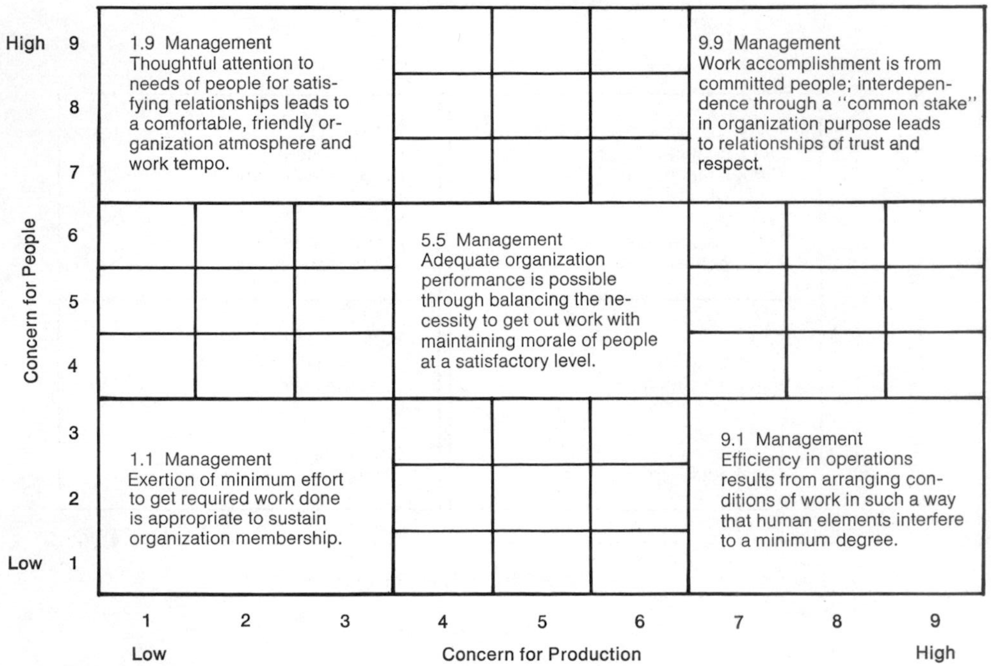

Concern for People (vertical axis, High 9 → Low 1)
Concern for Production (horizontal axis, Low 1 → High 9)

1.9 Management
Thoughtful attention to needs of people for satisfying relationships leads to a comfortable, friendly organization atmosphere and work tempo.

9.9 Management
Work accomplishment is from committed people; interdependence through a "common stake" in organization purpose leads to relationships of trust and respect.

5.5 Management
Adequate organization performance is possible through balancing the necessity to get out work with maintaining morale of people at a satisfactory level.

1.1 Management
Exertion of minimum effort to get required work done is appropriate to sustain organization membership.

9.1 Management
Efficiency in operations results from arranging conditions of work in such a way that human elements interfere to a minimum degree.

Source: Blake, Robert, and Mouton, Jane. *The Managerial Grid.* Houston, Texas: Gulf Publishing Co., 1964.

Figure 2

The Likert (1967) research also provides a rationale for the concept of team or group decision making and supervision. In the traditional organization, the interaction is on a one-to-one basis between the superordinate and the subordinate, but in Likert's "System Four" type of management, the interaction and decision making relies heavily on group process. This concept is illustrated in Figure 3.

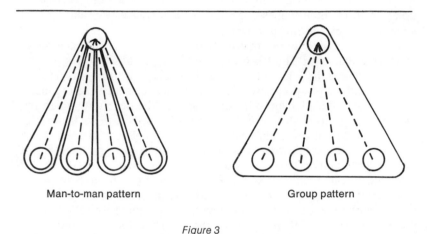

Man-to-man pattern   Group pattern

Figure 3

Bowers and Seashore (1966) defined leadership behavior in terms of four dimensions: (a) *Support* is behavior that enhances someone else's feeling of personal worth and importance; (b) *Interaction facilitation* is behavior that encourages members of the group to close, mutually satisfying relationships; (c) *Goal emphasis* is behavior that stimulates an enthusiasm for meeting the group's goals or achieving excellent performance; (d) *Work facilitation* is behavior which helps goal attainment by such activities as scheduling, coordinating, planning, and by providing resources such as tools, materials and technical knowledge. Bowers and Seashore found that these four dimensions of leadership that were developed initially for the description of formal leaders, appear to be equally applicable to the description of leadership by group members. They also discovered that group members do engage in behavior that can be described as leadership and the total quality of peer leadership is at least as great as the total quality of supervisory leadership.

Leadership and Organizational Effectiveness

Fiedler (1967) has studied leadership in the organizational context in relation to organizational effectiveness. He defines leadership as a problem of "influencing and controlling others" and leadership effectiveness must therefore be measured on the basis of the performance of the leader's group. He takes the position that different situations require different leadership; that is, the same leadership style or the same leader behavior will not be effective in all situations. He accepts the two major modes of behavior identified by leadership research that may be characterized by such terms as (a) "task oriented" or "initiating structure," and (b) "people-oriented" or "consideration." Both of these modes of leader behavior have been effective in some situations and not in others.

Fiedler identifies three major situational factors that determine whether a leader will find it easy or difficult to influence his group: (a) the degree to which the group accepts and trusts its leader; (b) the leader's position power, that is the power which the organization rests in the leadership position; and, (c) the degree to which the task of the group is structured or unstructured. But these factors by themselves do not determine group performance. Just as there is no one style of leadership that is effective for all groups, so there is not one type of situation that makes an effective group.

According to Fiedler, liked leaders do not, on the average, perform more effectively than do disliked leaders; and powerful leaders do not perform better than leaders with low position power. Effective group performance, then, requires the matching of leadership style with the appropriate situation. Fiedler has worked out a system for classifying situations as to how much influence the situation provides the leader and then matching the situation with the style of leadership required. Fiedler and others who have worked with this Contingency Model of Leadership Effectiveness have concluded that the effectiveness of the leader depends on the favorable attitude of the group as well as on his own particular style of leadership. For example, task-oriented leaders perform best in extremely favorable and extremely unfavorable situations, while the human-relations oriented leaders perform best in the intermediate situations.

The training of persons for leadership roles can be effective "only if it teaches the individual to diagnose the situation correctly and then either modify his leadership style to fit the situation or modify the situation to fit his leadership style" (Fiedler, 1967).

Leadership and Power

One of the characteristics of leadership in managerial or supervisory roles is that leaders exercise power. Power is generally defined as the capacity to influence the behavior of others. It is important to differentiate between *position* power and *personal* power. The mere fact that an individual occupies an official position in a work organization may at the same time give him certain authority or power. An individual might also have power because of his personal influence over the behavior of others. Therefore, one individual who is able to induce another individual to do a certain job, because of his position in the organization, is considered to have position power; while an individual who derives his power from his followers is considered to have personal power.

Obviously many individuals have both position and personal power. Position power tends to be delegated down through the organization, while personal power is generated upward from below through follower acceptance. The effective leader will tend to influence the group through the use of his personal power. He will use the power and authority of his official position most judiciously.

Leadership and Administration

Although most of the research described here was concerned with leadership behavior in administrative or management roles, it should not be assumed that there is a one-to-one relationship between leadership and administration. In any large formal organization, such as a school or school system, a person might hold an administrative position but exercise little or no leadership. Conversely, not all leaders in school organizations are in administrative and/or supervisory positions. To exercise leadership one need not hold a position of authority in the administrative or supervisory hierarchy of the school. In fact, anyone occupying a role in the school or school system in which he has some responsibility for managing the environment also has the opportunity to exercise leadership in that position. Not the least of these roles is that of teacher.

The vocational teacher of the future must organize and direct the learning environment and use the educational technology. He must play the role of manager of the instructional unit for which he is responsible, whether it be in a shop, laboratory, or classroom. He must be able to create and maintain a learning environment in which youth and adults can develop the competencies needed for employment. In this respect, the teacher must have many of the same leadership skills and competencies needed by administrators and supervisors.

Although our concern here is primarily with persons in administrative and supervisory roles, the basic concepts are equally applicable to a wide range of functionaries needed in the management of career education, including teachers (instructional managers), counselors, department heads, supervisors, coordinators, directors, principals, superintendents, and deans.

To be a leader, a person must have the capacity to "live ahead" of his colleagues and his institution; to interpret his institution's needs to the public and the public's needs to his institution; and, to conceive and implement strategies for effecting changes required by his institution in order to fulfill its purpose. The leader in administrative roles tends to have a stimulating, prodding and sometimes even disruptive influence. He tends to emphasize creative planning, initiative and future-facing boldness.

The effective leader tends to have the following characteristics:

1. He helps others to accept common goals. The leader must himself be enthusiastic about what he is doing and bring other members of the group to accept "the cause."

2. He initiates productive action in group situations. He realizes that he is effective to the extent that he can influence the behavior of others, but perhaps more important, he *initiates* the action. That is, he provides an atmosphere or set of conditions in which things will happen. He motivates the group to act and then makes available to them the resources necessary to get things done.

3. He establishes clear plans and work procedures. Once a goal has been accepted and action has been decided upon, the leader must chart the course and set the ground rules.

4. He maintains warm relationships with members of the group. While the leader must be goal-oriented, he must also be people-oriented. He can hope to accomplish the goals only through the active and constructive involvement of the members of the group.

5. He obtains the commitment and cooperation from those with whom he works. He does this through persuasion rather than through threat or force (such as using the authority of his official position). He also realizes that he must have the cooperation of groups outside the school; the schools cannot do the job alone.

6. He effects change and builds structures for the achievement of meaningful purposes. He is basically an innovator and should be a student of how change is achieved. He must be careful, however, not to encourage change solely for the sake of change.

THE NEED FOR LEADERSHIP IN CAREER EDUCATION

Anyone who has read other chapters in this yearbook will be impressed by the breadth and scope of career education. It starts in early childhood and never ends. Therefore, all levels of education— elementary, secondary, community college, college, and adult—must be involved. Career education is not confined to any one subject matter area; any subject that has any relevance at all to careers should also make its contribution to career education. Career education is just as tall and as broad as education itself; the total education enterprise must be permeated with the notion that all who go through our public education system will ultimately find themselves in a career (except those physically or emotionally disabled), and that the public school system should help the learner find and prepare for a career in which he can achieve maximum self-realization and self-fulfillment, and in which he can make his contribution to the welfare of society. This is obviously a task that requires all the leadership that can be mustered.

With the right kind of leadership and with the task that lies ahead, educators could go a long way toward eliminating the dichotomy that has traditionally existed between general and vocational education. In career education, there exists a goal or purpose of education that can only be achieved through the combined efforts of both the general educator and the vocational educator.

Leadership for career education must come from all types of persons in the schools. Teachers, counselors, supervisors, and administrators must have a commitment to the concept and then through their own individual roles provide whatever leadership they can. To be sure, if career education is to be implemented in spirit as well as in fact, it will be done informally as well as formally; that is, by persons in non-supervisory positions as well as by persons in such positions. It will be done by teachers and counselors who have a professional commitment to do whatever needs to be done to serve the best interests and needs of children, youth, and adults. It will not happen simply because administrators or others in authority positions mandate it. Career education requires a total professional staff commitment. Having recognized career education as an important goal of public education, this author does not doubt that the necessary leadership is present and will emerge.

A New Type of Leadership Needed

A research report prepared by the National Conference Board (1972), titled *Some Innovations in the Training of Educational Leaders,* states that the educational system during the past decade has been in a state of "pervasive and continuous turmoil at all levels." The board states that at the elementary level it has been the parents who have pressed for change; at the secondary level, it has been both students and parents; and, at the postsecondary and higher education level, it has been the students alone. They attribute much of this dissatisfaction with the educational system to the fact that educational leaders "have not demonstrated the ability to cope effectively with the newly surfacing problems."

One of the major shortcomings that the report identifies is the failure of the educational system to prepare youth for the world of work; particular attention is given to the high dropout rate of high schools and colleges. These conditions, they say, have:

> given rise to the approach of making information on careers and the world of work a central focus in elementary and secondary education. Some have argued with eloquence, and often persuasively, that much of the curriculum could be organized around this focus. Only in this way can education become 'relevant' to many passing through our educational system. *To pursue this approach constructively also requires a new type of leadership both in general education and in vocational and technical education.* (Italics added.)

If career education is to become a central and dominating theme of public education, and if it is to permeate the total curriculum, a new breed of educational leaders is indeed needed—especially in administrative roles. Persons who can serve in the role of change agent and who have the leadership capability to help teachers, counselors, and others in the education enterprise are needed to define new goals for public education, goals that are consistent with the needs of the individual and society. Such leadership will also require technical competence to design new and better ways to achieve these goals and to do it in an organizational climate that will bring maximum satisfaction and personal fulfillment to both the teacher and the learner.

ADMINISTRATIVE LEADERSHIP DEVELOPMENT FOR CAREER EDUCATION

Although we have recognized that leadership is needed on all levels and that it indeed exists among all categories of professional personnel in the education enterprise, our attention is now directed toward the leadership and development of persons in administrative roles in public education. We will consider first the need for in-service programs of leadership development and then conclude the chapter by taking a brief look at pre-service leadership development programs.

In-service Leadership Development

Anyone in the business of occupational education, whether on the high school, community college, college, or university level, knows that the rapid rate of change in our society makes it imperative for most workers to continue their education and training throughout their active careers in order to remain viable in the labor force. While this condition exists in nearly all occupations, it is especially true for the professions. It has been said that any practitioner in such professions as engineering and medicine who has not done something more than read his professional journals within the past five years is probably guilty of malpractice in his field.

Many school administrators—including superintendents, secondary school principals, community college presidents, and vocational-technical education administrators—have not engaged in any formal in-service training program since they acquired their last degree. But this may be attributable to the fact that there have not been enough appropriate opportunities provided. Simply to return to the university for some additional course work is not automatically beneficial. However, many institutions engaged in the preparation of school administrators are now providing short, intensive conferences and workshops on specific problems or challenges to which school administrators should respond.

The author has worked with the University of Michigan in planning a "retreat" for school of education faculty members interested in occupational education *and* those involved in administration and supervision. Persons holding leadership positions in organizations of school administrators in the state, such as elementary school principals, secondary school principals, community college deans and presidents, school superintendents, vocational administrators, and others will be invited to participate. This program is being designed to help school administrators understand career education and how it might be implemented at various levels. Many higher education institutions interested in the in-service training of local school administrators will undoubtedly undertake similar programs.

The in-service training of local administrators can also be accomplished through the professional associations in which administrators hold membership. An example of this is the National Academy for School Executives operated by The American Association of School Administrators which provides in-service programs for school superintendents. The National Association of Secondary School Principals, The National Council of Local Administrators, and other similar groups should be encouraged and helped to plan and operate in-service programs for their members. Similarly, state associations of administrators should be encouraged and helped to plan in-service career education progams for their members. Vocational education leadership can assist these various national and state organizations of administrators to organize and stage career education conferences and workshops. There must also exist a genuine interest and concern and complete and full involvement on the part of general school administrators as well as vocational administrators.

The research report of the National Conference Board (1972) identifies a number of recent innovative programs for the training of school administrators. A program that has been particularly attractive to persons who are principals is The Ohio State University "Mid-Career Program for Practicing Administrators." The program operates for two quarters with an option given a student of continuing for one more quarter. It is designed to assist these educators in solving some of today's changing problems. It is conceivable that principals participating in this program who are concerned with curricular problems might give attention to career education and other problems associated with the preparation of employment-bound youth for the world of work.

The University of Michigan Leadership Development Program in the Administration of Vocational and Technical Education has been in operation since 1964 (National Conference Board, 1972). This is an in-service training program for teachers, coordinators, and supervisors, many of whom are in minor administrative roles. It is designed to prepare them for more responsible leadership positions. Other state universities are operating similar programs for the training of leadership personnel in vocational education.

Pre-service Leadership Development

If any significant impact is to be made in regard to career education, it will come, as discussed, through the efforts of those professional personnel already in the schools, some of whom are now in administrative positions. It will also come through the efforts of others preparing for such positions through formal degree programs at teacher education institutions that train school administrators. Therefore, every effort should be made to build into these formal programs learning experiences that will enable the graduates to implement the career education concept when, and as, they move into administrative posts. Personnel in teacher education institutions—including vocational and practical arts teachers, counselors, and others knowledgeable about career education and its role in public education—should take steps to have these learning experiences and instruction incorporated into graduate degree programs.

SUMMARY

Leadership implies change and the leader is the "change agent." The implementation of career education makes it mandatory that there be some fundamental changes made in public education so as to turn the schools around and focus the primary attention on preparing children, youth, and adults for careers on all levels.

The leadership to do this must be prepared to help others to accept career education as a common goal. The leader must be able to initiate action in group situations. He must be able to establish clear plans and work procedures to accomplish the goals of career education. In this total process, he must maintain warm relationships with members of his work group. The leader must be able to obtain commitment and cooperation from those with whom he works; he must do this through persuasion rather than through threat or force. He must also have the cooperation of groups outside the school because the schools cannot do the job alone. He is basically an innovator, and should be a student of how change is achieved.

Public education in the United States must adapt to the changing conditions and needs of society. If career education is to serve children, youth, and adults, and at the same time the society in which they live, then the goals and priorities of public education must be re-examined and modified to determine appropriate goals to initiate the necessary action, to establish clear plans and procedures, and then to help others work cooperatively toward the achievement of these goals. This is the challenge for the leader in career education. The leader can be expected to succeed only if he knows how to work with people both within his own group and in other groups whose cooperation is essential.

REFERENCES

Blake, Robert, and Mouton, Jane. *The Management Grid.* (Houston, Texas: Gulf Publishing Company, 1964)

Bowers, D. G., and Seashore, S. E. "Predicting Organizational Effectiveness With a Four-Factor Theory of Leadership." Paper read at International Congress of Applied Psychology, Ljubljana, Yugoslavia, August, 1964. *Administrative Science Quarterly.* II, (1966)

Cartwright, Darwin, and Zander, Alvin, eds. *Group Dynamics: Research and Theory.* (Evanston, Illinois: Row, Peterson and Company. 1960)

Everson, Warren L. "Leadership Behavior of High School Principals." *National Association of Secondary School Principals Bulletin.* NASSP, National Education Association, XLIII, (September, 1959)

Fiedler, Fred E. *A Theory of Leadership Effectiveness.* (New York: McGraw-Hill Book Company. 1967)

Gibb, Cecil A. "Leadership." *Handbook of Social Psychology.* ed. Gardner Lindzey, (Cambridge, Massachusetts: Addison Wesley Publishing Company. 1954)

Halpin, Andrew W. *The Leadership Behavior of School Superintendents.* (Chicago: Midwest Administration Center, University of Chicago. 1960)

Katz, Daniel, and Kahn, Robert L. *The Social Psychology of Organizations.* (New York: Wiley. 1966)

Likert, Rensis. *The Human Organization.* (New York: McGraw-Hill Book Company. 1967)

The National Conference Board, Inc. *Some Innovations in the Training of Educational Leaders.* (New York: The National Conference Board, Inc. 1972)

Sergiovanni, Thomas J., and Starrett, Robert J. *Emerging Patterns of Supervision: Human Perspectives.* (New York: McGraw-Hill Book Company. 1971)

Tead, Ordway. *The Art of Leadership.* (New York: McGraw-Hill Book Company. 1935)

Wenrich, Ralph C. "Professional Development and Leadership Roles." *Contemporary Concepts in Vocational Education.* First Yearbook of the American Vocational Association. ed. Gordon Law, (Washington, D.C.: American Vocational Association, 1971)

ADMINISTERING CAREER EDUCATION

Carl W. Proehl

Wanted: A new administrative leadership for education!

The task of administration in any field of endeavor is necessarily a difficult one. It is, and has been, no less so in the field of public education. Now there has emerged a new approach, already far above the horizon, already more than merely a concept, which promises to challenge educational administrators at all levels beyond their most reasonable expectations and, in many cases, beyond their present capabilities. Finally, due primarily to the dogged insistence of Sidney P. Marland, Jr., a meaningful, productive relationship between academic and vocational education has been initiated. We know it as *career education.* To make it work effectively requires a new administrative leadership with the moral courage and ability to bring about the necessary adaptations, adjustments and changes explicit in its demands and specifications.

It is interesting and significant to note that an analysis of career education reveals that some of its component parts, such as vocational education and the basic and elemental idea of career development, have withstood biting criticism, rebuke and nonsupport from many quarters for almost a century. Despite this, these basic components themselves have effected what many have long recognized to be so vital to the nation's citizens: the need to make learning truly meaningful and significant for them. This is the central thrust of career education.

The effort to make learning meaningful and significant would certainly appear to find no opponents and, yet, the central function of career education—the fusion of the academic and the vocational—is immediately attacked on the grounds that it is "anti-intellectual" as well as "anti-cultural" and that it threatens academic excellence.

Even if career education were so oriented, it would nevertheless be more positively effective than the present academically-oriented curriculum that has not met the needs of 80 percent of today's youth. Some would discredit this promising new venture. Even so, reports from across the nation indicate that its initial implementation is well underway and that it is meeting with great success. Despite the efforts to discredit, career education will not "disappear" or silently "go away" as did some of its less effective predecessors. The social and political forces that have produced career education as a reaction to the present educational approach, and the recognition by many of what it can do *for* people, will not permit it to disappear.

These factors, coupled with the fact that some of the components of career education have already withstood severe opposition, leads one to assume that its further growth is assured. To a large and representative segment of the population, to many legislators, businessmen, parents, youth, teachers and school administrators, to other professional and lay people, the time for more aggressive positive action with *forward* movement is now.

A disenchanted citizenry has recognized in career education the factor of "humanization" that requires reaching out and providing for the individual educational needs of all students. Many of the present educational barriers and obstacles are recognized as nothing more than man-made and self-imposed. The alternatives are clear; without removal of educational barriers, there will result educational failure beyond a reasonable level of tolerance.

THE NEW LEADERSHIP

Career education can be a reality for all, for it is already more than a concept for many. Forward looking schools and school systems are beyond the point of "conceptualization" and well into the practicality of implementation. What is needed now is a *new leadership* across the nation in every state and territory, and from the federal level to the individual school and classroom. A "crash program" and forced implementation are not suggested, but neither can a "next generation" approach be considered acceptable. Already in evidence, the new leadership must come forward in greater numbers, more boldly, with broader, deeper commitments and a willingness to effect educational change. The new leadership must modify the present approach to managing education so that change can indeed take place.

Much has been said and written about the concept and the realities of leadership. The new leadership must, at a minimum, provide three basic elements if conditions are to allow change in education to take place. This developmental process is highly pertinent to the matter of administering career education for, without these elements and thus the requisite change, there can be no significantly accelerated forward movement in career education. By means of effective *communication,* the new leadership must bring a broad representation of people in every community to total *involvement* in the development and implementation of career education and lead them to full *commitment* in active support of its further growth.

The task of generating this new leadership has been, and will continue to be, difficult, much more difficult in the days ahead than in the past. In the initial days of career education there were many who were ready, many who from their own experience and long-held philosophy, saw an opportunity in the concept of career education.

There yet remain those who, for a variety of reasons, must be convinced that neither the American economy nor its social order can afford to ignore the educational needs of so many people. The continued emergence and development of this new leadership is now, and will remain, the single most important and difficult aspect of successfully administering career education. This is so, irrespective of the structural level concerned, federal, state, or local; or the educational level involved, kindergarten through the university.

Although the emphasis on administering career education in this chapter is placed upon the local level, it is at the state level—with the superintendent or commissioner of education and the state board of education—that the initial responsibility for action and the effort for continuing support must lie. It is at this level, and in concert with the legislature, that initiating policy must be molded and priorities established. At the state level, the first thrusts of administrative leadership must bring about a coordinated effort, with full involvement, not only of all elements of the department of education but of all other segments of state government that impinge upon the well-being and the educational needs of the citizen. This in no way minimizes the significance and the urgency of the administrative leadership role at the local level. However, without leadership and sound administrative practices at the state level, little activity of effective, long-term significance is likely to develop. Given effective state (and federal) leadership and support and framed within sound but flexible administrative practices, the focal point of program initiation, development and implementation shifts to the administrative leadership at the local level. Assuming continued state and federal support, it is at this level that the program becomes a reality or falls by the wayside.

RESISTANCE TO CHANGE

The matter of initiating action is of paramount concern to the administrative leadership at any level of operation. Because of its far-reaching implications for the entire educational family, and the broad involvement of the community, career education poses a problem of unprecedented magnitude in moving it through initiation to implementation. Generating and maintaining the long-range, in depth, logistic support is no less a challenge to administration. To set the wheels in motion demands acceptance and willingness to *change* on the part of many who may have a system of "built-in resistors." Frequently, the degree of resistance to innovation and change on the part of educators is in direct proportion to their station on the "educational ladder," extending from the elementary through the university levels. There appears to be a progressively increasing resistance to the support of career education and an increasing reluctance to disturb the *status quo* the higher the station on the "educational ladder."

Primary factors regarding such resistance to change are: (a) the fear of change because it can be disruptive and may impinge unfavorably on one's capabilities, knowledge and strengths; and, (b) plain reluctance to change, because to do so means additional effort and work, to leave things as they are is acceptably comfortable and undisturbing. Beyond that, the vested interests in methodology, techniques and curricula far removed from needed individualization build and maintain a strong resistance to change.

There are also those secondary and collegiate level educators who are so deeply steeped in academic traditionalism that they are unwilling to concede the need for change even though years of the general and academic curricula have spelled nothing but disaster for millions of American youth. One might well wonder whether the concern for self-preservation isn't the dominant force in the continued effort to maintain a college education as the *sine qua non* of a successful life for all.

Resistance to change could also be a direct result of inadequate communication between those seeking support and those to be reached. Similarly, other factors in the leadership capability and technique must be examined as potential causes for resistance to change. Whatever the reason, whatever the bias or motivation, it is essential that the administrator be able to identify the nature of resistance, to analyze it properly and to apply appropriate behavior and attitude modifiers if he expects to move the program forward.

LOCAL LEVEL RESPONSIBILITY

The central focus of administering career education lies at the local school district level. While it is self-evident that a positive state-local relationship must exist, and that through effective leadership state level influence (beyond the purely regulatory elements) can and must be effected, the very nature of local autonomy places the burden on the local administration. Local administration includes all those persons who have the assigned responsibility and authority to direct or influence the actions of subordinates in the local educational structure. Such direction and influence must be a coordinated total involvement if career education is to succeed in any given local situation.

The administrative structure of a local school system, although varying from district to district, has a number of distinct levels from superintendent to the administration of the individual school. Each level has its respective depth and breadth of direct involvement and its degree of relevance to the ultimate implementation of career education. All must possess or develop a realistic understanding of all elements of education, not just that administrative entity for which it is immediately responsible. Thus, administrative responsibilities for career education carry beyond those ascribed only to the local district and demand an effective articulation with postsecondary and collegiate elements. Career education cannot be managed in fragments, by individual grades, schools or levels, if it is to serve its intended purpose; it must be articulated by administration at and between all levels of education.

The individual and collective tasks of successfully operating career education are many, but of all of them, the problems and demands involved in administering the program are unquestionably the most critical and significant. This in no way minimizes the importance of the individual classroom, the difficulty and the problems experienced there, or the effort expended at the level of implementation, for this is "where it happens." If the full, coordinated efforts of teachers are not forthcoming, a program cannot exist. It is only to say that without administrative leadership and effort, the program cannot and will not permeate the total structure. To be sure, some innovative and forward looking teachers will, as they always have, carry out great new things in the classroom, but a widespread total effect will not take place without administrative encouragement.

CHANGE IN PRACTICES

Any major restructuring or "remodeling" of the educational effort calls for a much broader change in practices at all levels of education than is at first realized. Inherent in the *new leadership,* the *need for change* and the *centralization of responsibility,* requisites for the full and successful implementation of career education, are a multitude of modifications and positive approaches that must be effected.

The nature and purpose of career education demand new approaches, adaptations, adjustments or changes that impinge upon administration, staff, students, community, organizational and administrative structure and practices, curriculum, methodology and fiscal capability and accountability. There are others, to be sure. Whatever their nature or their number, each one focuses directly or indirectly on the administration of career education. The nature of some of these modifications and approaches is examined here. They have been identified through the observation and evaluation of a number of exemplary programs, career education programs, and reports of early efforts to develop and implement such programs. Although it is recognized that required modifications and approaches generally have an impact on more than one element involved in career education, those more specifically identified here are grouped under three principal elements: (a) the administrator, (b) the operation and structure, and (c) the staff. The interrelated and overlapping impact in certain instances will be apparent.

The Administrator

It has been said that the job of the administrator is a lonely one. If so, it may be a significant reason for the troubled state of education today, for an effective program cannot be administered solely from the confines of an office without direct involvement. Career education cannot and will not emerge from the solitude of the administrator's office. Career education must be nurtured by communication, by involvement and by commitment. All of these require personal interaction and confrontations with people.

Administration must make change possible. Administrative leadership must provide the conditions so that which needs to be done can and will be done. To this end, the administrator must assume full responsibility for opening the lines of communication with staff at all levels, with students, parents and the community, and for keeping these lines open. Without meaningful two-way communication, there can be no effective leadership. There is no other single educational principle more broadly acknowledged and loudly acclaimed and, at the same time, flagrantly disregarded than the significance of effective communication. Innumerable are the cases of educational leaders whose removal was prompted by a failure to communicate.

The administrator must prepare the way for his staff; he must be a provider of human and material resources and the protagonist who applies administrative pressures to dispel inertia. He must understand and react positively to the frustrations of his staff; he must be a facilitator, an expeditor, and one who provides a climate conducive to coordinated efforts at planning, development and implementation. The administrator who would successfully administer career education must be imaginative. All of these qualities and capabilities, and more, have been demonstrated by successful administrators in the past. Given similar continuing conditions, they would be expected to carry on in the same manner. But the future will make even greater demands: Greater effort, commitment and expertise in all of these are requisites of the success of career education.

Today's job of dealing with people is an in depth operation of much greater complexity. The task of dealing with the "now" generation, its attitudes and demands, the vast changes in curricula and learning in face of the knowledge explosion, demand a greater expertise. If one is to proceed with an effective approach, administration must effect a comprehensive in-service training program for itself.

Career Education

Such a program will require the broad involvement and full assistance of universities, the community, business and industry. In such a program, the administrator must develop new techniques in interpersonal relations and group dynamics. He must become an expert in bringing together individuals and groups for the effective deployment of their individual and collective skills toward serving a common purpose. New approaches to community-wide comprehensive planning for career education and the techniques for community involvement must be developed. Briefly stated, the administrator must be assisted in developing a new management capability, one that will permit him to manage more effectively the human and material resources in his charge.

Two significant aspects of school administration bear notation. The first is in the area of involvement. Far too frequently, administrators divorce themselves from the intricacies and details of planning and relegate this important matter to subordinates. This is especially critical at the local level. The principal must be actively and personally involved in this process if the effort is to be successful. This is an adjustment that many administrators will find difficult to make. The second adjustment lies in the area of communication. It is not unlikely that public disenchantment with education, reflected through widespread criticism and "no" votes on bond issues, could have been avoided to a great extent with an effective public information program. This is another important aspect of communication where inadequate effort toward implementation has been made. There is evidence that a well-informed public whose advice is sought understands educational problems and is more likely to rally to education's support and rescue.

The Operation and Structure

The implications for change imposed by career education upon the operation and structure of the educational system are no less demanding than the constraints already placed upon the administrator. If career education is to humanize education's approach to people through individualization, if it is to fuse the academic and the vocational, if it is to be truly accountable, if it is to eliminate the dropout, then new operational techniques and a restructuring of the system are in order. These, too, are the responsibility of the administrator.

Although it is difficult to set forth needed changes or adjustments in rank order, it is clearly evident that the establishment of role and purpose is a matter of initial priority. From here, the goals and objectives of the system and of the individual school centers will develop. Under career education concepts, the role and purpose of the school will be vastly different than under the present configuration.

Whatever the role and purpose, they must be explicitly set forth in each instance if goals and objectives, the role of the staff, and the place of the student are to be clearly established. The newly defined role and purpose of the school or system will reflect and embody a new philosophy and a new set of values that must carry over into goals and objectives. The development of the latter will result in greater specificity in a broadened demand for behavioral objectives and the measurement of learning by proficiency and performance rather than by time and subjective judgment.

Performance-based assessment of student accomplishment and achievements prompts other changes and innovations in the conduct of education. The need for providing and maintaining flexibility throughout the operation and structure is of paramount importance. This calls for flexibility of movement on the part of students into and out of programs as well as into and out of the system if it is in the best interest of the student. The design of the system must be such that will prepare a student for successful entrance into a career at whatever level he may choose to leave the educational system. Such exit from the system may be into a profession at the end of college, into technical work at the end of a postsecondary program, into skilled work upon graduation from high school, or into an unskilled or semiskilled job if he leaves prior to graduation from high school. Effective planning and a diversity of programs must provide beginning skills at the junior high school level for some students in the event that they exit from the program at that point.

Assessment by performance requires flexibility in scheduling classes and activities for students without the rigidity and conformance of established patterns of time and sequence. If performance-based assessment is to be effective, greater flexibility is necessary for the active involvement of students in planning and program evaluation. Student opinion and judgment can have a positive and constructive effect on the student's behalf as well as on the school and program. Occupational competency tests used at strategic intervals and at different levels will provide credit for what students have already mastered and avoid unnecessary duplication of instruction. It follows that greater flexibility will be necessary in what we now know as graduation requirements. Certainly, performance assessment cannot find compatability with the time-honored unit completion requirement.

Progression on the basis of performance and the accompanying flexibility will activate much of the individualization of instruction and will promote individual growth over which educators have long expressed deep concern. In spite of this concern, programs and techniques, even when available, have not materialized in great enough numbers or gained adequate acceptance. Extensive work in the development of materials and methods for individualized instruction must be done through programming and simulation, as well as in the improvement of instructional techniques for dealing with students on an individual basis.

The demands of time and energy placed upon the school staff through greater flexibility, assessment by performance and individualization will necessitate major revisions and changes in the staffing pattern of individual schools and whole systems. Teachers alone cannot carry the instructional load and related responsibilities envisioned under career education. Support personnel at the professional, para-professional and non-professional levels are necessary to assist in the great diversity of activities and responsibilities at all program levels. The greatly expanded utilization of resources in such a program alone will require additional staff assistance as well as the involvement of community personnel. Many of these people from the community will need to be brought into the staffing pattern on varying bases because of their unique and expert contributions in special areas of the educational programs.

A serious adjustment that will need to be made concerns the reallocation of financial resources in order to provide adequate facilities and equipment for instruction in the vocational areas from the level of exploratory experiences through the skill development areas. Under career education, the expansion of vocational offerings to permit involvement by all students will require enormous expenditures. One of administration's major concerns and efforts will lie with its continued efforts at providing an adequate financial base for career education. This, in turn, will require a massive and continuing public information program for the purpose of reaching the voter, and will necessitate a significant reordering of priorities at the national, state and local levels.

The Staff

Few of the administrator's problems challenge him more or cause him greater concern than the responsibilities and demands placed upon him by his staff. It is generally recognized and accepted that the instructional staff of a system forms the backbone of the educational program. Equally as well established, but too frequently ignored or misunderstood, is the fact that the staff, especially the classroom teachers, constitute the most sensitive, fragile and potentially volatile elements in the educational system. This is not an indictment, rather it is a recognition of the continued daily pressures under which they operate. It is intended to emphasize the urgency of an intelligent and realistic approach to staff involvement in the process of developing a career education program. The staff will need help and consideration to bear the pressures of change and adjustment. More than ever before, the administrator must demonstrate a genuine personal and professional interest in his staff.

A recognition of all of these administrative responsibilities in the leadership role of the administrator does not minimize the responsibility inherent in the respective roles of the staff itself, either at the administrative, supervisory or instructional level. The staff must be willing to face the issues and problems prompted by the career education movement with an open mind; the staff must recognize both the need for greater flexibility and the need for a change in attitudes. Staff members must be willing to recognize theirs as a changing role and must assist in effecting needed changes. Without acceptance of this responsibility, career education cannot emerge significantly and education will again have defaulted.

One of the most urgent responsibilities in the administration of career education is the need to overcome negative attitude among many teachers, supervisors and administrative staff concerning the significance of work, and thus the need for occupational education, in the life of the individual. Unfortunately, too many educators have the attitude that occupational training is irrelevant and that an academic approach is the only preparation for life. Still others are indifferent to the issue or reluctant to become involved in making a change. Until these attitudes are dispelled, effective progress in planning career education will be hampered.

Administration must be sensitive to the varying needs of staff members as they examine the need for greater flexibility in the learning process and as they effect a change in their own roles. The individual teacher's approach to planning, his continued involvement in it, and his approach to dealing with students to effect greater individualization must all become a part of the pattern of adjustments. Teachers will need to learn more about careers and counseling and the world outside of education than most of them now know if they are to work effectively with tomorrow's students. The opportunity must be given for extensive in-service training. They must be encouraged to experiment, to innovate, and to examine the results of their work at first hand.

Administration must accept the staff into the "inner circle" by permitting greater involvement and participation. Staff members, and especially teachers, need to be involved more fully in decision making and need to be given more responsibility than before. Positive efforts must be made to assure all staff members that they are necessary partners in the undertaking. Only in this way can administration be reasonably certain that status is not threatened, that morale is maintained and, hopefully, that any sensitivity is directed only to the urgency of the job and getting it underway.

All of these involvements have one big factor in common. Their resolution, development or modification will take *time*. For the staff there is already too little time. Administration at all levels must come to grips with this problem realistically and quickly. Beyond the matter of providing additional support personnel, two other approaches are suggested: (a) 12-month contracts be established for teachers to give them the necessary time to fulfill their responsibilities in effecting a changing role, and for purposes of expanding the opportunity for year-round school; and, (b) provision be made for adequate compensation when the required work load of the staff carries beyond the regular school day. These are considerations whose potential has been overlooked too long; they could be powerful motivators in initiating and maintaining forward motion.

SUMMARY

There are no easy solutions in administering the complexities of career education. New competencies, high level financial support and extensive human involvement will be demanded. At the very center of this complex stands the administrator. Even after he has gathered all of the newly-found competencies, the material and human resources, his qualifications may still be lacking. Beyond all of these, he needs the faculty for skillfully blending patience and perseverance.

RESEARCH AND DEVELOPMENT PROGRAMS FOR CAREER EDUCATION

Robert E. Taylor and Darrell L. Ward

Research and development is a means of developing valid and reliable educational programs to meet individual and societal needs. Continuous, adequately supported research and development at local, state and national levels provide a means for organizational self-renewal. Research and development self-renewal mechanisms make provisions for identifying, studying, developing, testing, and disseminating new and improved techniques and procedures. Operating in consort with the broader lay community, the educational profession can maintain viable and relevant educational programs through the use of research and development results. Unfortunately, educational research and development has been considerably underfunded, as compared to aerospace, medical, and industrial research. The need for its support should be readily apparent.

This chapter is designed to provide an overview of the current status of research and development in career education, to identify some of the broad clusters of research and development needs, and to set forth some examples of needed research and development.

THE CAREER EDUCATION CONCEPT

Career education has probably gained more attention from educators, politicians, and the general public than any other educational innovation of the past decade. In contrast to other educational innovations, career education focuses more directly on ultimate educational outcomes. It focuses primarily on the capacitation of students (ends) and, secondarily, on the many variables that impinge on the delivery (means) of these educational outcomes. This focus upon ultimate educational outcomes is in contrast to an innovation such as differentiated staffing. Such an innovation is non-substantive in nature and does not directly affect the ultimate educational outcomes, but presumably improves the efficiency and effectiveness of the delivery system. Because of career education's direct focus on educational outcomes through the capacitation of individuals for all life roles, it predictably will focus debate concerning the values and purposes of education. Career education effort will be the center of philosophical and ideological discussions for some time.

Former Assistant Secretary for HEW Sidney Marland and other educational leaders at the federal level may have wisely resisted precise definition of career education. Such reticence has probably been a good political strategy, recognizing the dynamics of federal, state, and local relationships in education, and it has facilitated wide-ranging debate and varied conceptualization. However, it has not contributed to the scientific development of the concept. Researchers and practitioners concerned with the evolution of career education programs have defined and developed concepts in accordance with their own perceptions of the needs. A variety of definitive statements and characteristics have been derived, as can be seen in Chapter One.

The closest that federal leadership has come to defining career education was when Marland (1972:2) said "Career education is essentially an instructional strategy aimed at improving educational outcomes by relating all teaching and all learning activities to the concept of career development."

Goldhammer (1972:165) has expressed the following views concerning the career education concept:

> It would be deluding to think of the careers curriculum as a panacea for all our educational ills in this century. It would also be deluding simply to reject the concept without carefully assessing its potential. If fully developed into an operating conceptualization of the curriculum, it has the potential for providing the flexible curriculum, adaptable to the needs for each youngster, and directed toward realistic goals, which conditions in our society require. It turns the emphasis of the curriculum away from purely academic goals, and it redirects the knowledge mission of the school away from the purely integrative and more toward the applicative dimensions. Knowledge is not an end in itself but a means to ends, a tool used by human beings and human society to achieve definite ends. The schools will still fail to meet all the needs of every child at times, but hopefully it will meet a much larger range of needs of more children than is presently the case.

Career education is considered to be *systemic*—an integrated and cumulative series of experiences designed to help each student achieve increased skill in the performance of all his life roles—economic, civic, cultural, moral and aesthetic.

In addition, career education introduces a new sense of purpose into education. It serves as the new paradigm for education by focusing on individual career development. Career education recognizes the centrality of careers in shaping students' lives in that careers determine or limit where students work, live, who their associates are, and affect other dimensions that are significant in defining a life style. Career education should not be viewed as another add-on. It is not incremental or cross sectional. It represents an infusion throughout the curriculum, and calls for restructuring and reorienting of the total educational program. Career education, then, should be viewed as lifelong and pervasive, permeating the entire school program and even extending beyond it. Knowledge is viewed as applicative, not descriptive. It is designed for all students.

Career education is a systematic attempt to *increase* the career options available to individuals and to facilitate more rational and valid career planning and preparation. Through a wide range of school and community-based resources, young people's career horizons should be broadened. Their self-awareness should be enhanced. Career choice and preparation need to be explicit and not accidental, fortuitous or circumstantial. Such can happen only through an increased understanding of self, career options, and the implications of selecting a certain life style. In the largest sense, and in harmony with developmental theory, career education could be viewed at five general levels:

1. Pre-school through grade six,
2. Middle grades often extending to grade 10,
3. Grades 10 through 12,
4. Postsecondary,
5. Continuing education.

Career education is not a radically new idea on the American educational scene. Rather, it is an evolutionary concept with many historical antecedents. Philosophical bases can be traced back to the 1800s in statements of educational goals, legislation, and fragmented developmental efforts. (See Part One, *The Foundations for Career Education.*) However, career education is not a mere repackaging of existing educational programs under a new title. It is the best of existing educational practice synthesized to optimize individual career development. Career education promises educational outcomes long awaited by the American public.

THEORETICAL BASES

Career development theory has provided the major organizing construct for career education. (See Chapter Six by Drier.) While no single theory is adequate, several have been advanced that, when combined, explain much about the attitudes, knowledge, and skills that facilitate or inhibit career development. Budke (1971) has treated these and related theories in a thorough fashion in his recent *Review and Synthesis of Information on Occupational Exploration.* The many theories of how occupational choice occurs have been classified as trait-factors theories, sociological theories, personality theories, and developmental theories. (See Chapter Four by Herr and Swails.)

Advocates seem to focus most heavily on the developmental or self-concept approach as the appropriate guide for the development of career education. This approach implies a series of compromise choices and adjustments as young people pass through the occupational decision-making periods of fantasy, tentative, and realistic choice (Ginzberg, 1951). The developmental approach to career choices is a logical and systematic process that can be incorporated into a comprehensive educational program. This approach is reflected in the school-based career education model by the use of awareness, orientation, exploration, and preparation stages of program emphasis. It has been assumed that the individual may control his occupational choice when provided with occupational information and experiences upon which to base decisions. This assumption and others surrounding the theoretical bases for career education require continued, rigorous research.

RESEARCH AND DEVELOPMENT PRIORITIES

Too much of the current development in career education is based upon "face validity" and liberal extrapolations from existing theories. This dynamic and pervasive concept of education will require rigorous and extensive research and development to establish an empirical base to guide future actions.

Though not the theoretical construct for long-term programmatic research and development, it is possible to identify several variables that need to be examined. These variables seem to group into the following clusters: (a) the efficacy of the career education concept (i.e., its summative evaluation as a new paradigm for education), (b) the evaluation of alternative delivery systems, (c) technological and methodological applications to career education, (d) nurturement of career education, and (e) comprehensive program planning and evaluation.

The priorities cited are suggestive and designed to stimulate thinking about the range of research and development efforts that should be undertaken.

Efficacy of the Career Education Concept

In contrast to many other educational innovations and approaches, career education has received strong support from educational, political, business, and industrial leaders in terms of its purposes, goals, and underlying values. However, in the full development and implementation of the approach, it is essential that the efficacy of the concept be substantiated through rigorous research. It is recognized that if career education is to sustain high interest and support and be adopted by educational systems across the nation, its outcomes must be compatible with the needs and desires of society. Evidence about experience-based learning and occupational experiences must be reviewed. Do the outcomes differ quantitatively and/or qualitatively? What different types of experiences lead to different outcomes for different students in different contexts? What are the desires of the

American public for education? Recent research and writings concerning these and other related questions need to be reviewed. More sophisticated needs assessment techniques should be perfected.

Coleman (1972) feels that youth have been excluded from the "educational mainstream" in their society. The major transitions that have occurred in the family setting, the workplace, and the school, have placed youth more on the fringes of society, outside the important institutions denying them essential experiences. Schooling, according to Coleman, cannot be regarded as a synonymous term for education, since the majority of the educational skills learned by a young person occur outside the school walls. Coleman cites several skills that should be learned in the educational system before age 18:

1. Intellectual skills, the kinds of things that schooling at its best teaches.
2. Skills of some occupation that may be filled by a secondary school graduate, so that every eighteen-year old would be accredited in some occupation, whether he continued in school or not.
3. Decision-making skills: that is, those skills of making decisions in complex situations where consequences follow from the decisions.
4. General physical and mechanical skills: skills that allow the young person to deal with physical and mechanical problems he will confront outside work, in the home or elsewhere.
5. Bureaucratic and organizational skills: how to cope with a bureaucratic organization, as an employee, a customer, a client, a manager, or an entrepreneur.
6. Skills in the care of dependent persons: skills in caring for children, old persons, and sick persons.
7. Emergency skills: how to act in an emergency or unfamiliar situation, in sufficient time to deal with the emergency.
8. Verbal communication skills in argumentation and debate.

According to the Fourth Gallup Poll of Public Attitudes Toward Education, the ultimate consumer of education, the American public, is ready and anxious for the implementation of the career education concept (Gallup, 1972). The study sample included a total of 1,614 adults, which according to Gallup described a modified probability sample of the nation. Interviewing was conducted in every area of the country and in all types of communities during April 1972.

A high percentage of public response supported four basic educational goals that have direct relevance to, and provide strong support for, career education as it is presently conceptualized: (a) to get better jobs, (b) to get along better with people at all levels of society, (c) to make more money—achieve financial success, and (d) to attain self-satisfaction. The results of Gallup's poll seem to indicate that Americans are highly practical people who firmly believe that education is the road to success in life. There is a need for further explication and replication of this and similar studies.

A recent *Time* essay posed a basic question concerning whether basic attitudes toward work have gone out of style:

> There is considerable evidence that they have not. After all, more than 90% of all men in the country between the ages of 20 and 54 are either employed or actively seeking work—about the same percentage as 25 years ago. Over the past two decades, the percentage of married women who work has risen from 2 to 42%. Hard-driving executives drive as hard as they ever did. Even welfare recipients embrace the work ethic. In a recent study of 4,000 recipients and non-recipients by Social Psychologist Leonard Goodwin, those on welfare said given a chance, they were just as willing to work as those not on welfare (Morrison, 1972:96).

A study for The Center for Vocational and Technical Education was specifically designed to identify attitudes toward career education (Brickell and Aslanian, 1972). The Institute limited its study to the six cities (Hackensack, New Jersey; Atlanta, Georgia; Pontiac, Michigan; Mesa, Arizona; Jefferson County, Colorado; and Los Angeles, California) in which the Comprehensive Career Education Model (CCEM) is currently being tested. Approximately 3,000 pupils in grades four to six, 3,000 pupils in grades seven to 12, 4,000 staff members, and 3,000 parents were asked to respond to a series of attitudinal statements pertaining to career education.

The study revealed that no one city has a monopoly on positive attitudes toward career education. People at all six sites agree not only that career education is desirable, but they also agree point-by-point and feature-by-feature on that desirability.

What is perhaps of even greater interest is that there are only negligible differences in teacher attitudes among the six cities. Correlation for school staffs ranges from .93 between Atlanta and Mesa to .98 between Jefferson County and Mesa. This has significance when planning content for in-service training programs.

It is equally clear that parents in these six cities positively agree in their attitudes toward career education. Correlations for parents range from .80 between Los Angeles and Mesa to .99 between Jefferson County and Mesa. This implies that community information and community involvement programs can be developed in a common design for use by all six cities. It also suggests that a concept that is invented and used successfully in one city will probably work in the other five. The ultimate success of career education as the new paradigm for education will depend on whether it can meet the career development needs of the general population, as well as diverse sub-populations, and still maintain harmony with societal requirements.

The efficacy of the career education concept must be examined as it relates to different geographical, socioeconomic, and cultural contexts. Career development needs of students in El Paso may not necessarily be congruent with those persisting in Detroit. How viable a motivative and catalytic force, then, is the career development concept as the central curricular approach to all of education? Will its effectiveness vary significantly among subgroups? What is the feasibility of fulfilling leisure and other noneconomic type individual goals through a career-oriented educational program?

Existing knowledge concerning how human growth factors affect learning abilities needs to be examined and used to further refine and perfect career education approaches. Is a threat posed to an individual's creative ability by subjecting him to various elements of careers and career planning at certain ages? Can 65-year olds be prepared for a more productive life?

Diagnostic, systematic and continuous needs assessment in all educational settings will be required if career education is to be successful in delivering according to public demands.

Evaluation of Alternative Delivery Systems

If career education is to meet individual and societal needs, then a wide range of alternative "delivery systems" should be developed, tested and refined. In accomplishing this, we should not blindly accept existing structures and constraints.

The most extensive alternative delivery systems under development and testing currently are the National Institute of Education career education models described more fully elsewhere. (See Part Four, *Conceptual and Operational Models.*) It is especially important that we closely examine the consequences of each of the models.

1. *School-based model.* The school-based model has the basic aim that eventually the entire school program from the early grades through high school, community college, and university shall offer career-related learning opportunities for *all* students, including hands-on experience in fields of interest to the learner. The Center for Vocational and Technical Education at The Ohio State University is funded for pilot projects in six school districts involving over 85,000 students and more than 3,600 teachers. The Center, in cooperation with the six districts, is developing coherent and readily transportable organization and curriculum designs (See Chapter 18 by Miller).

2. *Employer-based model.* The employer-based model is a program for youngsters 13 to 18 years of age. Students will graduate from programs run by business and industry in which they will receive both academic and realistic occupational preparation. Students will be given credit for this

experience so they will either "graduate" from the employer-run facility or will return to school with full credit. The employer-educator will receive reimbursement for costs incurred. The model, being jointly developed by four research organizations, is serving 25 to 100 students at each of four pilot sites now in their first year (See Chapter 19 by Banathy).

3. *Home/community model.* The home/community model is designed to encourage citizens of all ages to take advantage of career-renewal resources in their areas. Heavy reliance on educational technology is implicit in this model. The Educational Development Center of Newton, Massachusetts, is working in Providence, Rhode Island, to develop ways in which use of the media and neighborhood counseling can mesh with community needs and facilities. Major attention is being given to the use of audio-visual cassettes used individually at home for this model (See Chapter 20 by Guilfoy and Brudney).

4. *Rural/residential model.* The rural/residential model serves residents of six western states and is run by the Mountain Plains Education and Economic Development Program. This model is in operation at a pilot center established at a former Air Force base near Glasgow, Montana. It operates under the theory that entire disadvantaged rural families can experience lasting improvement in their economic and social conditions through intensive exposure not only to career preparation for the male head of the household, but to all the competencies and understandings that are required of a family today—for the wife, the ability to run the house, be an effective mother, budget and buy intelligently; for the children, elementary and secondary education in the career mode, as well as contributions to the family well-being that they are expected to make. The center has a capacity for 200 families and 110 are presently there and involved in the program. When they leave they will be assisted in job placement by the counselor who originally selected them for the center. This is a high-risk program seeking family renewal, based on the assumption that homes have much to do with the effectiveness of the children in them.

Basic questions need to be raised concerning these and other evolving career education delivery systems in terms of the efficiency and effectiveness with which they provide career education. The most fundamental question evolves around, "Are the student outcomes consistent with individual and societal needs and the promise of career education?" Other basic questions for which valid and reliable answers must be sought include:

1. What useable and useful products are being produced? (Outputs)
    a. What kinds of transportable products will the model produce?
    b. For whom (student, teacher, others) are these products intended?
    c. What impact or change may be expected to result from the use of these products?
    d. What is the rationale for developing these particular products?
    e. How were the products evaluated?
    f. What kinds of "non-transportable" benefits will be derived from the project?
    g. How are these non-transportable benefits being evaluated?

2. What will be the results of the models' operation? (Student Outcomes)
    a. To what portion of the student population are the outputs relevant?
    b. Are outputs available to meet the needs of the total student population, i.e., culturally disadvantaged, handicapped, etc.?
    c. Do the outputs provide learning experiences that capacitate individuals for their multiple life roles?
    d. Are there sufficient diagnostic techniques, procedures, and materials to support individualized programming and development?
    e. Are key intervention points identified and exploited to determine the appropriate intervention point for students with differing rates of development?

3. What are the operational considerations for the delivery system?
    a. What are the comparative start up and maintenance costs of the alternative systems?
    b. Does the system permit partial or incremental opportunities?
    c. What are the relative (across the models) cost-benefit ratios?
    d. Are installation procedures and materials provided?
    e. Are adequate evaluative procedures and materials available?

In addition, fundamental design and implementation problems

have arisen during the development of the four national models. These problems must be given immediate attention by educational researchers. For example, a number of fundamental problems have been confronted by contractors of the employer-based model, including:

1. Business and industry are not equipped to educate, they are not academicians.
2. Employers do not wish to cause a rift between business and education.
3. Business and industry feel that young people are undisciplined and uninterested, and furthermore, it may be too early for them to choose a career.
4. Employers question their involvement because educators are being paid to do the job.
5. Employers are in business to make a profit and this program offers them no economic advantage.
6. Labor unions feel that the program may be counterproductive to their apprenticeship programs.
7. There are legal implications involved in employing students below a certain age and paying students in a training situation (Miller, 1972: 11).

The four national models should not be viewed from the standpoint of being the only alternatives but should be examined in terms of other variations, modifications and crossovers, which could be effected to evolve even more creative, imaginative and effective approaches for the delivery of career education.

Technological and Methodological Applications

There are an infinite number of "non-substantive" variations in career education that should be tested and that may alter the efficiency and effectiveness of achieving desired outcomes. For example, current demands for accountability of expenditures in terms of student outcomes implies a need for improving the efficiency of learning. More sensitive instrumentation will be needed to determine the full range of *benefits* growing out of experiential and action-based approaches. Ways to accommodate differing learning styles in alternative delivery systems must be found.

Forecasts for education need to be carefully reviewed and incorporated into planning efforts. One group cited the following scenario for 1985:

Twenty-five percent of all high schools will base promotions and graduation on the attainment of measurable skills, abandoning the Carnegie unit system of credits; 50% of all public schools will be operating year-round; three-fourths of a student's time will be spent in independent or individualized instruction in 50% of the nation's high schools; and high school students will spend more than one-third of their learning time outside of school. The group also agreed that by 1985 half of all school districts will utilize differentiated staffing,

75% will open school to 3 and 4 year olds, and 30% will have replaced the principal's decision-making role with policy-making bodies of teachers ("Futurists . . .," 1972: 97).

The relevancy of current developments to future student clientele will depend largely on the degree to which these and other educational innovations can be incorporated into existing school systems. The primary research and development effort should be directed toward identifying and designing new strategies to help planners.

Nurturing of Career Education

The successful nurturing of career education programs will depend heavily on the ability of local, state, and national leaders to deal with specific problems and needs. Research and development should be aimed toward dealing with the following problems and needs:

1. Determining the knowledge and beliefs of key community groups concerning career education.
2. Determining the readiness of the educational staff to provide leadership in career education.
3. Exploiting the knowledge base that supports career education.
4. Conducting demonstration programs.
5. Securing policy group action and establishing long-range program goals for career education.
6. Initiating staff development programs.
7. Assessing congruence of current programs to career education goals.
8. Involving the community in developing career education.
9. Assessing alternative delivery systems.
10. Establishing instructional materials development teams.
11. Reviewing manpower projections.
12. Expanding cooperative education.
13. Extending career education to adults.
14. Initiating an active community information program.
15. Establishing career education advisory councils.
16. Operating a job placement service.
17. Maintaining an effective evaluation capacity.

There are many unresolved issues and unanswered questions that require research and development efforts if career education is to be nurtured. With respect to resources needed to install it, educators must find ways to realign priorities within educational budgets. Ways must be found to establish a better interface and integration of career education concepts in every phase and level of the total educational setting. Ways also must be found to integrate occupational preparation within the total career education concept.

Several operational questions need to be answered. What are the most appropriate approaches to orienting teachers, administrators, and communities to emerging career education programs? What new educative roles and relationships emerge from the implementation of this concept? What procedures are needed to articulate career education between elementary, secondary, postsecondary and continuing education? It is essential that we study adaptive versus adoptive behavior, along with the related problems associated with aiding the profession in becoming more intelligent consumers of research and development products and/or services.

Comprehensive Program Planning and Evaluation

Rigorous and thorough evaluation and planning procedures to assure effective and efficient delivery of career education goals must be perfected. Never have educational planners promised more nor has the public expected more. Career education has arrived at an opportune time. It is less expensive and more socially justifiable than corrective remedial programs. However, the public, Congress and others will demand greater accountability. A comprehensive plan will take some of the speculation out of career education's destiny. Explicit and detailed guidelines need to be developed.

As one views the several elements of education, considers needs and recognizes economic constraints, one is led to recommend some form of state master planning. In the past, states delegated planning responsibilities to local communities. The resultant programs offered were often too parochial and did not meet statewide needs. Little attention has been given to job placement, and student follow-up, or to program revision based upon occupational needs assessment, manpower forecasting and student job performance. To think about population mobility, the specialization needed in some dimensions of training programs, the comparative costs, and the competition for funds leads to the need to place more emphasis on statewide master plans. How does career education relate to current educational programs? How do educators adequately provide for all phases and dimensions of a complete system for the delivery of career education? How do they effectively utilize the unique capacities of the several elements of the educational enterprise? What means are there to involve effectively all dimensions of education?

Evaluation, including job placement and student follow-up, needs to be included in the organizational and administrative structure of career education. It must be internalized—not imposed, sporadic and isolated. Evaluation results (information for decision making) are tools for program planning and development. Evaluation should not be viewed as a ritualistic kind of activity, but a means to generate information needed to make decisions.

Evaluators have consistently been concerned with effectiveness and efficiency. There is currently an emphasis throughout government on economic efficiency, program budget analysis, cost benefit analysis, and cost-effectiveness studies. There is also a new implication for education in terms of national evaluation. To some degree, in the various states, new kinds of questions are being asked. They concern not whether what is being done is good or of some value, but whether if it is the *best* way to use available funds. Is what is being done the *best* alternative for individuals and society? What are the alternative economic returns? What are the benefits from various types of investments?

One key to the outcome evaluation of any educational program will be accurate and complete student data files. Accurate student needs assessment and manpower forecasting must be directly linked to the articulation of educational systems at local, state and federal levels with other educational and educationally related institutions and agencies.

The need for an accurate "audit track" on all students as they move in and out of school is critical. A continual comprehensive transitional record allows both educators and employers to assess effectively individual student needs and capabilities. Such records should be diagnostic, analytic and prescriptive. A typical record set might specify several of the following elements: academic preparation, work experience annotations, employment and other follow-up, and educational and/or employment recommendations of school personnel.

The scholastic transcript as the sole credential for entry into advanced educational pursuits or employment is no longer viable. Comprehensive student data files are needed by employers and counselors as a tool for proper placement and advancement of individuals.

Student data files and manpower forecasts should enable institutions to place students appropriately on the next step of their career ladder, be it a job, further education, or other special services. Continued follow-up of students, both for their benefit and for feedback to the educative process, will be feasible and essential.

In planning and evaluation, educators must look at more than what they presently serve. There are many unmet needs. Continual systematic needs assessments should give rise to new program developments.

SUMMARY

Recognizing that career education is gaining momentum and receiving visibility, educators need to confront the many issues and questions posed by this major innovation. Research and development must be maintained as a priority so that it can more effectively help the educational community capacitate all individuals for their multiple life roles.

REFERENCES

Brickell, Henry M., and Aslanian, Carol B. *Attitudes Toward Career Education.* A Report of an Initial Study of Pupil, Staff, and Parent Opinions in Atlanta, Hackensack, Jefferson County, Los Angeles, Mesa, and Pontiac. (New York: The Institute for Educational Development. February 15, 1972)

Budke, Wesley E. *Review and Synthesis of Information of Occupational Exploration.* Information Series No. 34. (Columbus, Ohio: The Center for Vocational and Technical Education, The Ohio State University. June, 1971)

Coleman, James A. "How Do The Young Become Adults." *Review of Educational Research.* XLII, (Fall, 1972)

"Futurists Forecast Education for 1985." *Education U.S.A.* XCVII, (January 9, 1973)

Gallup, George H. "Fourth Annual Gallup Poll of Public Attitudes Toward Education." *Phi Delta Kappan.* Vol. LIV, (September, 1972)

Ginzberg, Eli, et al. *Occupational Choice: An Approach to a General Theory.* (New York: Columbia University Press. 1951)

Goldhammer, Keith. "A Careers Curriculum." *Career Education: Perspective and Promise.* ed. Keith Goldhammer and Robert E. Taylor. (Columbus, Ohio: Charles E. Merrill Publishing Company. 1972)

Holland, John L. *The Psychology of Vocational Choice.* (Waltham, Massachusetts: Blaisdell Publishing Company. 1966)

Marland, S. P. "Meeting Our Enemies: Career Education and the Humanities." Paper presented at the Conference on English Education sponsored by the National Council of Teachers of English, Minneapolis, Minnesota, November 24, 1972.

Miller, A. J. "A Synthesis of Research in Progress on the National Career Education Models." Paper presented at the Fifth Annual National Leadership Development Seminar for State Directors of Vocational Education, Columbus, Ohio, September 21, 1972.

Morrison, Donald M. "Is the Work Ethic Going Out of Style?" *Time.* C, (October 30, 1972)

INFORMATION DISSEMINATION TO FACILITATE THE DEVELOPMENT OF CAREER EDUCATION PROGRAMS

Glenn White

The purpose of this chapter is to discuss selected generalizations and principles from the area of communications research, and to explore the implications of these generalizations and principles for disseminating information in order to facilitate the development of career education programs. The specific focus of the chapter will be on two aspects of the general communications model: (a) the relationship between the characteristics of innovations and their rate of adoption, and (b) the effects of differential use of communication channels at various stages of the innovation-decision process.

Researchers and writers in the communications field have produced a tremendous amount of information under such headings as diffusion, dissemination, knowledge utilization, and information transfer. Basically, this research has concerned the issues and problems encountered in moving the results of research and development to an implementation or operational stage. The slow pace of diffusing new educational practices is discussed by Miles (1964) and others.

Although this research activity has involved a variety of subject areas, research designs, geographical locations, and types of populations, there are some basic generalizations and principles that are relevant for disseminating information to facilitate the development of career education programs. As dissemination strategies are developed, efforts will be more productive if these generalizations and principles are considered.

Procedural guidelines will be discussed here in order to help information disseminators. Farr (1969) points out that acquaintance with the practical considerations involved in utilizing educational knowledge is relatively low among knowledge producers. The linking or intermediary role is the province of the information dissemination specialist. Havelock (1967) uses the term "linker" to identify this individual. In addition to having the job of devising ways and means of translating research and development information into a variety of different "packages" for a diverse clientele, the dissemination specialist, or linker, must also overcome any apathetic or suspicious feelings towards research often generated by this group.

Havelock (1967) has identified two major problems common to knowledge linkers. He refers to these as *overload* and *marginality*. Overload problems include difficulties encountered in dealing with the massive amount of educational knowledge available. Such could present retrieval problems. Also, once the information has been retrieved, it must be sorted and packaged a number of different ways for a diverse and complex user clientele.

Marginality refers to the linker's "middleman" position. He is usually not the source of the knowledge, nor is he usually a member of the client group that will utilize the information. While marginality is inherent in the role of the linker, Farr (1969) points out that it can be construed as an advantage as well as a disadvantage. The impartial "no-axe-to-grind" middleman is able to attain an acceptable level of credibility.

Before moving to the specific focus of this chapter, it will be helpful to get an overview of a general communications model as a general framework. Also to be discussed are some of the characteristics of career education used in discussing generalizations about the characteristics of innovations and how they influence the role of adoption.

A GENERAL COMMUNICATIONS MODEL

Although many writers in the field of communications research employ different labels, there is general agreement in their descriptions and operational definitions of the process involved in moving the results of research and development to user groups in particular social systems. Rogers and Shoemaker (1971) list the crucial elements in diffusion as an *innovation communicated* through *channels over time* among the members of a *social system*. They point out that these four elements differ only in nomenclature from the essential elements of most general communications models. The elements are defined in the following paragraphs.

The Innovation

An innovation is an idea, practice, or object perceived as new by an individual. It may have two components: (a) an idea component, and (b) an object component. All innovations must have the ideation component, but many do not have the physical referent. Several characteristics of innovations, as sensed by the receivers, contribute to their different rate of adoption.

Communication Channels

Communication is the process by which messages are transmitted from a source to a receiver. A communication channel is the means by which the message gets from the source to the receiver.

Over Time

Time is an important consideration in the process of diffusion. The time dimension is involved in (a) the innovation-decision process by which an individual passes from first knowledge of the innovation through its adoption or rejection, (b) the innovativeness of the individual, that is, the relative earliness-lateness with which an individual adopts an innovation when compared with other members of his social system, and (c) the innovation's rate of adoption in a social system.

Among Members of a Social System

A social system is defined as a collection of units functionally differentiated and engaged in joint problem solving with respect to a common goal. The members or units of a social system may be individuals, informal groups, complex organizations, or subsystems.

CHARACTERISTICS OF CAREER EDUCATION

Since definitions for career education are discussed in Chapter One, it will be sufficient for the purposes of this section to summarize the characteristics of the concept.

In summing up descriptions of career education, Herr (1972) suggests that the term can mean at least the following:

1. An effort to diminish the separateness of academic and vocational education.
2. An area of concern which has some operational implications for every educational level or grade from kindergarten through graduate school.
3. A process of insuring that every person exiting from the formal education structure has job employability skills of some type.
4. A direct response to the importance of facilitating individual choice-making so that occupational preparation and the acquisition of basic academic skills can be coordinated with developing individual preference.
5. A way of increasing the relevance or meaningfulness of education for greater numbers of students than is currently true.
6. A design to make education an open system in that school leavers, school dropouts, and adults can reaffiliate with it when their personal circumstances or job requirements make this feasible.
7. A structure whose desired outcomes necessitate cooperation among all elements of education as well as among the school, industry, and community.
8. An enterprise which requires new technologies and materials of education (i.e., individualized programming, simulations).

9. A form of education which is designed for all students.

Pratzner (1972) summarizes the concept as:

an emerging construct and mechanism for achieving (a) a better balance between two essential roles performed by the educational system, (b) a better synthesis of general and specialized education, and (c) a more appropriate distinction between vocational and college programs.

Hoyt, et al. (1972) list the following points as key concepts in career education:

1. Preparation for successful working careers shall be a key objective of all education.
2. Every teacher in every course will emphasize the contribution that subject matter can make to a successful career.
3. "Hands-on" occupationally oriented experiences will be utilized as a method of teaching and motivating the learning of abstract academic content.
4. Preparation for careers will be recognized as the mutual importance of work attitudes, human relations skills, orientation to the nature of the workaday world, exposure to alternative career choices, and the acquisition of actual job skills.
5. Learning will not be reserved for the classroom, but learning environments for career education will also be identified in the home, the community, and employing establishments.
6. It will begin in early childhood and continue through the regular school years, allowing the flexibility for a youth to leave for experience and return to school for further education.
7. Career education is a basic and pervasive approach to all education, but it in no way conflicts with other legitimate education objectives such as citizenship, culture, family responsibility, and basic education.
8. The schools cannot shed responsibility for the individual just because he has been handed a diploma or has dropped out. While it may not perform the actual placement function, the school has the responsibility to stick with the youth until he has his feet firmly on the next step of his career ladder.

The foregoing summaries of career education point out that implementation of the concept will require a radical restructuring of the whole curriculum, a tremendous amount of training and retraining of staff in both cognitive and affective areas, extreme flexibility in scheduling both during the school day and throughout the school year, and massive financial support for curriculum materials and resources.

The concept of career education is not entirely new. There are historical and philosophical antecedents for much of it. Goldhammer and Taylor (1972) list three major sources that have made substantial contributions to the conceptual framework. These three sources are: (a) statements of the major goals of education enunciated by various groups such as The Commission on Reorganization of Secondary Education, The Educational Policies Commission of the National Education Association, (b) educational legislation reflecting society's collective intentions in this area (this includes such legislation as the Morrill Act, the Smith-Hughes Act, and the Vocational Act of 1963 and its 1968 Amendments) and (c) the accumulation of research findings concerning individual development. In summarizing the historical, philosophical, and conceptual antecedents, Herr (1972) lists five points:

1. Virtually every concept which is presently embodied in career education has been advocated at some point in American education. This is not to suggest that such concepts have either been operationalized or tested in practice. Nevertheless, philosophical support for the major elements of career education has historical construct, if not evaluative, validity.

2. Most of the elements of career education have their roots in the early efforts to embody industrial education and, somewhat later, vocational guidance in the public schools. Both vocational education and vocational guidance were direct responses to the needs for distribution, classification, and preparation of manpower occasioned by the rising industrial character of the U.S. in the late 1880s and 90s as well as the first two decades of the twentieth century.

3. Advocacy of vocational education and vocational guidance has largely been precipitated by economic and industrial needs rather than personal or individual needs, although there have been social reform and social welfare threads running through advocacy of these services. It is apparent that at the present time, as was true in the last decade, this situation has largely reversed with individual needs being considered the major base from which educational programming must begin.

4. Until approximately 1960, concern for the vocational needs of individuals was reflected principally in providing different categories of vocational training. To a high degree, the categories of vocational training were defined by occupational or industrial needs or, in some cases, inertia. Thus, persons needed to be fitted to programs rather than programs fitted to persons. Since 1960, however, increased attention has been focused on the needs of special groups of persons—i.e., the disadvantaged, the handicapped, the academically retarded—as well as the affective dimensions of employability as reflected in terms such as vocational identity, vocational maturity, and vocational decision-making.

5. Although there were antecedents in life adjustment and progressive education positions prior to 1960, since then increased emphasis has been focused on the prevocational elements of decision-making and preparation to be found in the elementary, middle or junior high school educational levels.

CHARACTERISTICS OF
CAREER EDUCATION AS AN INNOVATION

Are characteristics of career education more likely to facilitate or impede the acceptance and implementation of the concept? This issue can be explored within the framework of innovations derived from past research and writings. Rogers and Shoemaker (1971) list five characteristics of innovations. Each of the five is somewhat empirically interrelated with the other four, but they are conceptually distinct. They are: (a) relative advantage, (b) compatibility, (c) complexity, (d) "trialability," and (e) observability.

Relative Advantage

Relative advantage is the degree to which an innovation is perceived as being better than the idea it supersedes. The degree of relative advantage may be social or economic. The generalization is: *The relative advantage of a new idea, as perceived by members of a social system, is positively related to its rate of adoption.*

Career education has a relative advantage in that it has appeared on the education scene at a time when there is evidence of dissatisfaction with the existing system. It provides an attractive alternative for educational reform. Hoyt, et al. (1972) state:

> . . . among the reasons for believing that career education is a concept whose time has come are that: (a) it has emerged at a moment when dissatisfaction with educational practices and outcomes are at a peak, and (b) it promises to attack and improve some of the apparent sources of that dissatisfaction.

> . . . a useful exploration of the demand for educational reform must identify the reasons for that dissatisfaction, test their reality, and assess their relationship to what career education reasonably can be expected to offer.

They further indicate that most of the dissatisfaction directed toward education is in reality frustration with social ills for which the schools bear little fault, or can make, only modest contributions.

Although career education may be perceived as an attractive alternative for reform, if the expectations are too high or unrealistic, this relative advantage is likely to be short-lived.

Economic incentives may be used to speed the adoption rate of innovations. Former U.S. Commissioner of Education Sidney P. Marland, Jr. has indicated that career education is a top priority in the U.S. Office of Education. To date, most of the funds that have been allocated to career education have been vocational. If additional U.S. Office of Education funds are made available to support local programs or develop materials for career education, the rate of adoption is likely to be increased considerably.

Compatibility

Compatibility is the degree to which an innovation is perceived as consistent with existing values, past experiences, and needs of the receivers. An idea that is not compatible with the salient characteristics of a social system will not be adopted as rapidly as an idea that is compatible. Compatibility ensures greater security and less risk to the receiver and makes the new idea more meaningful to him. An innovation may be compatible with sociocultural values and beliefs, with previously introduced ideas, or with client needs.

The generalization is: *The compatibility of a new idea, as perceived by members of a social system, is positively related to its rate of adoption.*

The concept of career education has several positive characteristics in terms of compatibility. The values underlying the concept are closely related to the values existing in society. The historical and philosophical antecedents provide some validity for the compatibility of career education with previously introduced ideas. To the extent that endorsement of the concept by a wide variety of professional and lay groups indicates that it will fill the need for a different approach to education, career education can certainly be considered compatible. These endorsements have been for the *concept* of career education. When it is operationally defined in terms of programs and activities, such endorsements may begin to dwindle.

Complexity

Complexity is the degree to which an innovation is perceived as relatively difficult to understand and use. Any new idea may be classified on the complexity-simplicity continuum. The generalization is: *The complexity of an innovation, as perceived by members of a social system, is negatively related to its rate of adoption.*

An integrated career education program is an extremely complex concept to make operational. Some of the realities of implementation are not apparent in many of the descriptions. As pointed out previously, implementation of a career education program will require a restructuring of the whole curriculum, intensive training and retraining of staff, extreme flexibility in scheduling, and massive amounts of financial support for curriculum materials and resources. It will also call for the type of cooperation between the schools and outside agencies that will, in most cases, be greater than ever before.

"Trialability"

Trialability is the degree to which an innovation may be experimented with on a limited basis. New ideas that can be tried on the installment plan will generally be adopted more rapidly than innovations that are not divisible. An innovation that is "trialable" is less risky for the adopter. It might be noted that this characteristic was previously referred to by Rogers (1962) as "divisibility." Rogers and Shoemaker (1971) now feel that trialability implies a broader meaning, including the notion of psychological trial. The generalization is: *The trialability of an innovation, as perceived by members of a social system, is positively related to its rate of adoption.*

There are some components and activities of career education that can be implemented on an installment basis; but, this cannot be done without some planning to show how these components and activities fit into the total sequence. For example, a career exploration program at the junior high level should be built upon a comprehensive career awareness program at the elementary school level.

The career awareness program could be implemented without implementing the career exploration program. However, to maintain the sequence of the program, when the career awareness program ends for the first group of students the career exploration program should be ready for implementation. Outside of financial considerations, the need for the trialability of career education activities is more important for those who adopt the innovation relatively early. Later adopters will assume less risk in implementing complete programs or larger segments.

Observability

Observability is the degree to which the results of an innovation are visible to others. The results of some ideas are easily observed and communicated to others, whereas some innovations are difficult to describe. It might also be noted that Rogers (1962) previously referred to this characteristic as "communicability." Rogers and Shoemaker (1971) feel that *observability* is a more precise term. The generalization is: *The observability of an innovation, as perceived by members of a social system, is positively related to its rate of adoption.*

The observability of career education is limited at the present time by the fact that it is more a symbolic innovation than a material innovation. Once an ample supply and variety of materials have been developed and activities have been implemented, observable characteristics of the concept will be greatly increased.

Summary

It appears that most of the characteristics of career education are positive in terms of possible influence on the rate of adoption. The following summary statements are derived from the foregoing discussion.

    1. Career education has a relative advantage in that (a) it is an

attractive alternative for educational reform, and (b) economic incentives in the form of financial support at a national level are likely to be available.

2. The concept is compatible with (a) current values, (b) previously introduced ideas, and (c) current needs of a variety of lay and professional groups.
3. The complex nature of the concept at an operational level is likely to be the biggest drawback or negative characteristic in the rate of adoption.
4. The fact that the trialability aspects of the concept must be looked at in terms of a total program is likely, in many cases, to be ignored. This may result in many career education activities being tacked onto existing traditional programs with little thought given to what kinds of activities go before or come after.
5. At the present time, it is relatively easy to describe the concept in general terms. However, when we move to describing what career education looks like at an operational level, it becomes much more difficult to communicate. This situation should improve when an ample supply of materials and tested activities are available and implemented.

DIFFERENTIAL USE OF
COMMUNICATION CHANNELS

Innovation-Decision Process

Before discussing differential use of communication channels, it will be helpful to describe the *innovation-decision process*. Rogers and Shoemaker (1971) define this as the mental process through which an individual passes from first knowledge of an innovation to a decision to adopt or reject and to confirmation of this decision. This model replaces the "adoption process" model used by Rogers in his earlier edition. The "adoption process" was postulated by a committee of rural sociologists in 1965 as consisting of five stages: (a) awareness, (b) interest, (c) evaluation, (d) trial, and (e) adoption. The revision of the model has been made in light of criticisms and recent empirical evidence.

The present conceptualization of the innovation-decision model consists of four stages:

1. *Knowledge.* The individual is exposed to the innovation's existence and gains some understanding of how it functions.
2. *Persuasion.* The individual forms a favorable or unfavorable attitude toward the innovation.
3. *Decision.* The individual engages in activities that lead to a choice to adopt or reject the innovation.

4. *Confirmation.* The individual seeks reinforcement for the innovation-decision he has made, but he may reverse his previous decision if exposed to conflicting messages about the innovation.

There are other variables such as personality characteristics (e.g., general attitude toward change), social characteristics (e.g., "localite" or cosmopolite), perceived need for the innovation, and certain social system variables that affect the individual's innovation decision.

Communication Channels

Research evidence indicates that certain channels are more effective than others for disseminating information at certain stages of the innovative-decision process. Communication channels are classified as either interpersonal or mass media in nature. Mass media channels include radio, television, film, newspapers, magazines, newsletters, institutional publications, etc. Mass media can reach large audiences rapidly and spread information. Interpersonal channels are those that involve a face-to-face exchange between two or more individuals. Interpersonal channels can permit a two-way exchange of ideas, and persuade individuals to form or change attitudes.

Rogers and Shoemaker (1971) present several generalizations regarding differential use of communication channels. The first generalization is: *Mass media channels are relatively more important at the knowledge stage, and interpersonal channels are relatively more important at the persuasion stage in the innovation-decision process.*

Copp, et al. (1958) point out that certain information sources reach large audiences with the most recent technological advances because they have become institutionalized as disseminators of information. This would be true for state level organizations such as departments of education, and federal level organizations (e.g., U.S. Office of Education) and vocational centers (e.g., The Center for Vocational and Technical Education). Although information should be packaged for specific types of audiences, at the knowledge stage it still will be written at a general "awareness" level and be nonspecific as to local areas. Once the client knows about an innovation, he usually needs a more interpersonal source for specific information and exchange of ideas as he forms favorable or unfavorable attitudes toward the innovation.

The second generalization about communication channels is: *Cosmopolite channels are relatively more important at the knowledge stage, and "localite" channels are relatively more important at the persuasion stage in the innovation-decision process.* Cosmopolite communication channels are those from outside the social system; other channels of information about new ideas come from sources inside the social system. Rogers and Shoemaker (1971) point out that interpersonal channels may be local or cosmopolite. Mass media channels are almost always cosmopolite.

The third generalization is: *Mass media channels are relatively more important than interpersonal channels for earlier adopters than for later adopters*. Initial information about new innovations has to come from sources outside of the system since no one inside the system has had any experience with the innovation. This is not so important for later adopters because information about the innovation begins to accumulate and is available from interpersonal sources inside of the system.

The fourth generalization is: *Cosmopolite channels are relatively more important than "localite" channels for earlier adopters than for later adopters*. Innovations usually come from external sources; early adopters are more likely to look to these outside sources. Early adopters then become interpersonal and "localite" channels for the later adopters.

GUIDELINES FOR INFORMATION DISSEMINATION

The guidelines listed in this section are derived from the foregoing discussion about the characteristics of career education and their influence on the rate of adoption, and the differential use of communication channels at various stages of the innovation-decision process.

1. Establish contacts with a variety of sources of new information and developments in career education. This will enable you to make your clients aware of new materials relatively early.
2. Acquire a variety of materials and documents including (a) the results of experimental and action research, (b) descriptions of exemplary programs, (c) descriptive literature about available products, and (d) curriculum guides, lesson plans, units, etc.
3. Establish ways of letting your clients know what is available. This can be done through pamphlets, brochures, publications of professional associations and state agencies.
4. Contact different target groups to determine their information needs. This will be extremely helpful in developing derived products and packages from basic materials and documents.
5. Develop a pool of human resources to call upon for face-to-face interaction when more detailed information about career education is needed.
6. Disseminate information about possible funding sources for career education activities.

7. Since career education is still largely at the conceptual stage, emphasis should be placed on documents and materials that will aid in translating the concepts into operational programs.

CONCLUSION

The results of research activity in the field of communications have shown the importance of having a systematic approach to disseminating information. There are many variables that influence the rate at which an innovation is adopted. These include characteristics about the innovation, the individual clients or client group, and the environment in which these individuals operate.

This chapter has focused on only two aspects of the general problem: (a) characteristics of career education as an innovation, and (b) differential use of communication channels at various stages of the innovation-decision process. Information dissemination activities in career education should provide an excellent opportunity to gather additional empirical evidence about present generalizations and principles in the area of dissemination.

REFERENCES

Copp, James; Sill, Maurice; and Brown, Emory. "The Function of Information Sources in the Form Practice Adoption Process." *Rural Sociology.* XXIII (1958)

Farr, Richard S. *Knowledge Linkers and the Flow of Educational Information.* An Occasional Paper from ERIC at Stanford. (Stanford, California: ERIC Clearinghouse on Educational Media, Stanford University. 1969)

Goldhammer, Keith, and Taylor, Robert E., eds. *Career Education: Perspective and Promise.* (Columbus, Ohio: Charles E. Merrill Publishing Co. 1972)

Havelock, Ronald G. *Dissemination and Translation Roles in Education and Other Fields, A Comparative Analysis.* (Ann Arbor, Michigan: Center for Research on Utilization of Scientific Knowledge, University of Michigan. 1967)

Herr, Edwin L. *Review and Synthesis of Foundations for Career Education.* Information Series No. 61. (Columbus, Ohio: The Center for Vocational and Technical Education, The Ohio State University. 1972)

Hoyt, Kenneth B., et al. *Career Education: What It Is and How to Do It.* (Salt Lake City, Utah: Olympus Publishing Company. 1972)

Miles, Matthew B., ed. *Innovation in Education.* (New York: Bureau of Publications, Teachers College, Columbia University. 1964)

Pratzner, Frank C. "Career Education." *Career Education: Perspective and Promise.* eds. Keith Goldhammer and Robert E. Taylor, (Columbus, Ohio: Charles E. Merrill Publishing Co. 1972)

Rogers, Everett M. *Diffusion of Innovations.* (New York: The Free Press of Glencoe, Inc. 1962)

Rogers, Everett M., and Shoemaker, Floyd F. *Communication of Innovations.* (New York: The Free Press. 1971)

conceptual and operational models

*School-based Model, Employer-based Model,
Community and Home-based Model,
Statewide Implementation, and Local
Implementation*

Conceptual and operational models for career education are being developed at national, state and local levels. In mid-1971, the National Center for Educational Research and Development in the U.S. Office of Education funded the development of the school-based, employer-based, community and home-based, and residential career education models. When formed in mid-1972, the National Institute of Education assumed sponsorship of the national models. Efforts to develop three of these models are described in Part Four. The Bureau of Adult, Vocational and Technical Education, now the Bureau of Occupational and Adult Education, in the U.S. Office of Education facilitated the development of career education models in the states through Part C of Public Law 90-576. Local exemplary programs are also being developed through Part D of the same legislation. Some of these activities are alluded to in Part Four.

Miller reasons that the most practical alternative for providing career education is in a school-based program and explains how the comprehensive career education model was developed by The Center for Vocational and Technical Education at The Ohio State University. Included are project strategies, career education tenets, program goals, model structure and components, and priorities for the future.

Banathy explains how the Far West Laboratory for Educational Research and Development conceptualized the employer-based model. He identifies problems to be solved, outcomes to be attained, organizing concepts, and program characteristics.

Guilfoy and Brudney outline the focus, outcomes, curriculum, target populations, target institutions, limitations, and outreach of the community and home-based career education model under development by the Educational Development Center.

Clary describes the nature of the planning and promotion for state-wide implementation of career education programs. He stresses the importance of obtaining the commitment of the state board of education, assigning priority, involving the total state agency, planning by an interdisciplinary task force, developing a state plan, and other specific steps.

Olson emphasizes the importance of effective decision making by local educational leaders in implementing career education. He suggests critical external examination of goals, internal examination of alternatives, and evaluation of effectiveness. He outlines a management model and elaborates on its components.

THE SCHOOL-BASED COMPREHENSIVE CAREER EDUCATION MODEL

Aaron J. Miller

A historical concern of some parents and most students relates to the relevance of public education. Although teaching techniques and educational hardware may periodically change, it seems that American public education has been unable to develop a system that has the potential for fulfilling the needs of the overwhelming majority of students. That is, a system that will not only allow but assist the overwhelming majority of students to become fully capacitated, self-motivated, self-fulfilled contributing members of society.

If one considers the various roles in life for which students must be prepared, these roles could be classified as the economic or worker role, the family role, the sociopolitical role, the leisure-time role, and the aesthetic role. Goldhammer (1972) relates these roles to one's careers in life that are concurrently pursued. He identifies these roles or careers as:

1. a producer of goods or a renderer of services,
2. a member of a family group,
3. a participant in the social and political life of society,
4. a participant in avocational pursuits, and
5. a participant in the regulatory functions involved in aesthetic, moral and religious concerns.

Public schools in America have tried to address most of these life roles or career needs. However, the role or career need for which preparation traditionally has been least effective has been the economic role or the career that relates to one's production of goods or rendering of services. This does not imply that some schools do not provide vocational training programs that prepare a few students for gainful employment, but rather that few schools provide a program that allows a student to choose rationally an economic life role based upon personal interests and aspirations and then enables him to pursue an educational program that leads to those career goals. Until the total curriculum of the school can become oriented to the career needs and aspirations of the student, there is little chance that the majority of either students or patrons will view school programs as being relevant to their needs.

There are a number of alternatives to the present educational system that might provide the relevance necessary to prepare students for productive careers of their choice. One alternative would be to utilize the business, industry, or professional community as a training agency. Such a choice would reject the existing school system as the vehicle for specific career skill preparation. Another alternative would be to create parallel educational systems devoted to the pragmatic needs of career development. The student could then shuttle back and forth between the two educational systems. Such an alternative would be duplicative, expensive, and further entrench the multiple-track system. A third, and more practical, alternative would be to utilize the existing educational system with its available resources and investments to create more relevant educational programs.

At the beginning of the 1970-71 school year, there were more than 17,000 operating school districts in the United States, with a total combined annual expenditure of more than $44 billion (U. S. Office of Education, 1970). It is highly unlikely that taxpayers would be eager to duplicate existing investments to create duplicate systems. Therefore, the most logical approach to delivering a relevant educational program, based upon the total career needs of the individual, is through the existing school system; or, a "school-based" career education program.

INITIAL PLANNING FOR THE SCHOOL-BASED COMPREHENSIVE CAREER EDUCATION MODEL

Initial planning for a school-based comprehensive career education model was begun in early 1971 as a cooperative effort of the National Center for Educational Research and Development, and the Bureau of Adult, Vocational and Technical Education of the U. S. Office of Education (USOE). This early planning called for the establishment of four independently developed experimental career education models that could be evaluated in terms of their potential impact on the career development of youth. These model programs were to be developed jointly with schools, employers, communities, and families.

In June 1971, The Center for Vocational and Technical Education was awarded a grant by USOE to be the prime contractor in development of the School-Based Comprehensive Career Education Model (CCEM). The objectives of the proposed program were to develop, test, and install a comprehensive career education system in several local education agencies (LEA's) by restructuring their existing educational programs around career education objectives.

The Capstone Concept

During the several years prior to 1971, a number of school districts throughout the United States had developed and installed career education programs. However, these programs varied greatly in quality and comprehensiveness. It was the belief of CCEM planners in the early phases of the project that there must be several local school districts with rather complete career education programs. It was reasoned that, if these several districts (LEA's) could be identified, they could be assisted by a prime contractor to complete the development of their local models. The prime contractor could then provide technical expertise and resources to "capstone" the ongoing local effort to produce a comprehensive career education program. These school districts could then serve as national demonstration sites. Furthermore, the materials and support systems generated by and for these LEA's could become components of a validated and transportable CCEM for use in other school districts.

During the summer of 1971, USOE selected several "capstone" sites for the development of CCEM. More than 50 sites were nominated and screened for consideration and 13 sites were visited before the final selection of six sites. These were: (a) Atlanta, Georgia, (b) Hackensack, New Jersey, (c) Jefferson County, Colorado, (d) Los Angeles, California, (e) Mesa, Arizona, and (f) Pontiac, Michigan.

The rationale for selecting six sites, rather than the two initially planned, was that a greater number of sites could provide greater generalizability for developed products, increase the number of students exposed to career education, and provide more LEA talent for the project. On the other hand, the amount of support per site would be greatly reduced and consensus among the LEA's on a uniform program would be more difficult.

While one can only speculate about the optimum number of participating partners or LEA's in a project of this type, the decision to expand the number of participating sites from two to six was the most important single factor in influencing the later scope of work and in shaping future project decisions for CCEM.

A Refined Project Strategy

Shortly after the selection of the six LEA sites, it became apparent that the "capstone" strategy was *not* feasible for the following reasons: (a) the career education materials in place in the six districts were tailored to the unique needs of those districts and had little chance of adoption at other sites, (b) the materials existent at the sites generally had not been validated or tested in any rigorous evaluative context, and (c) there was no consensus among the sites as to the meaning of "career education." Therefore, it was necessary to abandon the "capstone" process for a refined strategy that would require the following sequence of events:

1. Agreement on a conceptual definition of career education that could be operationalized,
2. Identification and evaluation of career education curriculum materials or systems, either in place at the six LEA's or available "on the shelf" elsewhere, that could be integrated into a total program,

3. Assembly, modification and testing of these materials and strategies in actual classroom settings, and
4. Revision of materials and strategies based upon evaluation data.

Concurrent with these steps was the necessity of providing staff training, support systems, and evaluation.

Tenets of Career Education

Based upon a coalescing of the expectations for career education by numerous authors in the growing body of related literature, it is possible to identify certain basic principles or tenets that are fundamental in the design of CCEM. The tenets upon which the School-Based Comprehensive Career Education Model is based follow (Miller, 1972):

1. Career education is a comprehensive educational program focused on careers. It begins with the entry of the child into a formal school program and continues into the adult years.
2. Career education involves all students regardless of their postsecondary plans.
3. Career education involves the entire school program and unites the schools, communities, and employers in a cooperative educational venture.
4. Career education infuses the school program rather than provides a program of discrete career education curriculum "blocks."
5. Career education provides the student with information and experiences representing the entire world of work.
6. Career education supports the student from initial career awareness, to career exploration, career direction setting, career preparation and career placement; and, provides for placement and follow-up including reeducation if desired.
7. Career education is not a synonym for vocational education; but vocational education is an integral and important part of a total career education system.

With these principles as parameters it is now possible to further define a career education program in more specific operational terms.

Developing Career Education Program Goals

In an effort to define operationally career education, the CCEM staff worked with consultants and LEA practitioners in identifying a set of eight components or elements that could define the content of career education. These elements were identified by examining and integrating reliable theories in the field of vocational education, guidance, curriculum development, and human growth. The eight elements are (a) career awareness, (b) self-awareness, (c) appreciations and attitudes, (d) decision-making skills, (e) economic awareness, (f) skill awareness and beginning competence, (g) employability skills, and (h) educational awareness. When placed graphically against the 13 grade levels, K-12, the eight elements constitute a matrix with 104 blocks or cells (eight elements x 13 grades) that can be filled with specific sets of learning experiences or goals.

The next major step was to identify specific outcomes or realistic learning goals for each element that a student could reasonably be expected to achieve upon completion of 13 grade levels. This matrix of elements and their associated outcomes is displayed in Figure 1.

Upon completion of the general matrix, teams composed of educators, psychologists and sociologists proceeded to develop general program goals and objectives for each element by grade level. After iterations, a refined document resulted that provided an operational definition for a career education system (Center for Vocational and Technical Education, 1972).

STRUCTURING A
CAREER EDUCATION MODEL

Career development activities, via the eight education themes (Figure 1), should be *infused* throughout the curriculum in a *comprehensive* model. Career education goals may be achieved during the teaching of reading skills, language arts, mathematics, and virtually every traditional educational discipline. Infusion of career educational goals into the curriculum positively influences the academic learning and strengthens the learning context by adding the relevance of meaningful examples to the student's ultimate occupational, career and life goals.

Some career education goals are appropriate for all grade levels and for most all educational disciplines. For example, the goals associated with the matrix elements of self-awareness, which leads to career identity, are appropriate at all grade levels in a variety of discipline settings. The same can be said for the elements for career awareness, appreciations, and attitudes, and economic awareness.

Some career education goals are appropriately addressed at the middle and high school years. An example would be the development of employability skills that lead to career placement. For some students, these skills would lead to placement in an occupation upon leaving high school. For others, placement in an occupation, consistent with one's career goals, would be deferred until after postsecondary education—if this was within the student's overall career plans. A schematic of the system that could achieve these career education goals is shown in Figure 2. In this schematic, activities that relate most directly to career awareness begin in elementary school years. This does not mean, however, that these activities do not continue into the upper level grades.

	K-3	4-6	7-8	9-10	11-12	TERMINAL CHARACTERISTICS
CAREER AWARENESS						CAREER IDENTITY
SELF AWARENESS						SELF IDENTITY
APPRECIATIONS ATTITUDES						SELF-SOCIAL FULFILLMENT
DECISION MAKING SKILLS						CAREER DECISIONS
ECONOMIC AWARENESS						ECONOMIC UNDERSTANDINGS
TOOL AND PROCESS APPLICATIONS						EMPLOYMENT SKILLS
EMPLOYABILITY SKILLS						CAREER PLACEMENT
EDUCATIONAL AWARENESS						EDUCATIONAL IDENTITY

ELEMENTS OF CAREER EDUCATION

MATRIX

Figure 1

**COMPREHENSIVE CAREER
EDUCATION MODEL**

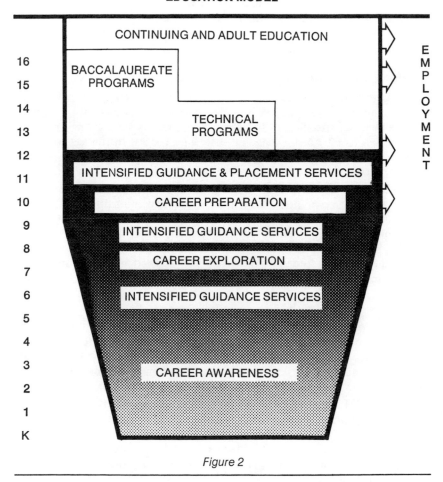

Figure 2

Activities that allow students to explore various career activities related to their specific interests can take place in the middle school years. These activities can include field trips, actual work experience, and relevant learning activities that take place as part of the school curriculum.

In the high school years, the student is capable of making certain career direction-setting decisions based upon his interests, aptitudes, and knowledge of various careers and how they relate to his career goals and aspirations. Through career counseling activities, he is able to select the educational options that will provide him with employment skills for a job upon high school graduation, or prepare him for the postsecondary educational experience consistent with his career plans. However, every graduate will have acquired a minimum set of skills that will enable him to be employed at some entry level position upon high school graduation.

Critical Guidance Points

Career guidance is an integral part of CCEM. Each career education curriculum unit has career guidance implications. Guidance implications must be specified in the teacher's materials so that they can be addressed as part of the ongoing teaching process. In this respect, the classroom teacher is serving the guidance function contained within the curriculum.

There are certain times throughout the K-12 program that are critical guidance points. These are the times of transition for the student from elementary to junior high school, junior high to senior high school, senior high school to employment or senior high to postsecondary education. These are specific times when student data must be analyzed and students counseled and assisted in translating their aptitudes, interests, and aspirations into educational plans.

Vocational Preparation

Vocational preparation serves a crucial role and is an integral part of career education. It is through vocational education programs that employment skills can be delivered. Furthermore, the linking of specific employment skill activities to academic subject matter can reinforce the relevance of all subject matter.

In CCEM, most students will have completed a series of occupational exploration experiences by the end of the ninth grade. These experiences can be arranged and taught through a series of career clusters. Upon completion of these exploration experiences, the student will be able to make certain career direction-setting decisions in grades 10, 11 and 12.

In high school, the student will have many opportunities to build upon his career interests. These might include a vocational preparation program in grades 10, 11 or 12 for in depth preparation for employment after high school, or as preparation for a postsecondary technical institute or vocational school. Another option might be to select college preparatory courses appropriate to chosen career goals. However, every student choosing to prepare for a program of higher education (rather than in depth vocational preparation) should have at least one of a variety of short-duration, accelerated employability skill programs.

This variety of programs allows the student to select a program consistent with his career goals. These might range from one hour per day for as little as two weeks to several hours per day for several months. Every exiting student should possess some minimum employability skill, regardless of his ultimate career goals. Furthermore, a career education system should provide not only the educational mechanism for training, but also the system for appropriate placement of every exiting student.

COMPONENTS OF AN OPERATIONAL
CAREER EDUCATION MODEL

If CCEM curriculum is to have maximum potential for transportability and adoption in other school districts, it must be packaged for the maximum convenience of the adopter. Most school districts are faced with already overcrowded curricula and shortened school days. To propose that career education be installed as a separate unit is unrealistic. A realistic alternative is the "infusion" strategy that revises existing curricula so that career education concepts to achieve career education goals are included. At the same time, basic substantive learning goals in the discipline for which the curriculum materials were originally designed may be met. In CCEM, the infusion strategy has been used whenever possible.

In a standardized format, curriculum units can be pilot tested, refined, field tested, and transported to other settings with some control of quality. In CCEM, both a standardized format and guidelines for curriculum unit revision or development have been designed. These guidelines and formats specify the following components of a career education unit:

1. A teacher guide that specifies:
   a. the rationale for the unit,
   b. intended use of the unit by suggested grade level, subject areas, time, grouping, and special considerations,
   c. goals and performance objectives.
2. Teaching procedures that contain:
   a. learning activities,
   b. resources,
   c. performance evaluation.
3. Teaching materials.
4. Evaluation procedures.
5. Specifications for in-service training of the teacher or other person implementing the unit.

During the 1972-73 school year, more than 100 career education curriculum units were developed and field tested in the six cooperating local education agencies. The units will be refined, based upon the field test. These units will vary in length, up to 20 classroom hours, and will be designed to achieve specific goals in the career education matrix.

Student Support Services

Included in the broad area of student support services are the three specific components of guidance, placement and support systems.

Guidance. Within the framework of career education, guidance fulfills the important role of linking career development and educational theory. Within CCEM, the specific aspects of the counselor's role, which are essential to the delivery of career development experiences, are being identified. To achieve this, a matrix of guidance goals is being developed that relates desirable outcomes of career education through guidance to the matrix of goals to be achieved through curriculum interventions. With such a goals classification schema, specific career guidance packages or modules can be developed for use by either the counselor or classroom teacher.

As part of the total guidance program, student aptitude and interest assessment packages that will be useful at the junior high school level are being developed. These packages will support specific guidance curriculum units designed for classroom use at grades seven to nine.

Placement. The placement component of the CCEM is concerned with the transition of each student from high school to the next appropriate work or educational setting. It is anticipated that many students will develop the competencies necessary to taking the next step in their career development, whether it involves the decision to enter an area of employment relating to their vocational preparation or the decision to pursue some form of continuing education. A direct placement service must be provided to assist students requiring such in identifying and selecting careers and then adjusting to them.

An initial aspect of CCEM placement program includes developing the capability to identify and assess the characteristics of the individuals and selected groups of students in relation to their career goals. This data is to be considered in relation to collected data that describes continuing educational preparation and employment requirements. The resulting analysis will provide direction for placement programs.

The placement program is an extension of the CCEM guidance program and has a direct working relationship with the vocational preparation programs of CCEM. Furthermore, it is integrally related to the program of support systems, career placement information systems, and a student follow-up information system. Another feature is that it must have a direct relationship to the community in terms of educational and occupational requirements and opportunities.

Such a placement program is in the final phases of conceptualization and was pilot tested during the 1972-73 school year.

Support Systems. The function of a support system is to gather, analyze, store and disseminate information required for the effective delivery and management of the career education process. It is intended that all students participating in the career education process be provided with the information required to achieve their career goals.

A support system component also is essential because of demand for information needed to implement career education programs. This includes occupational information, pupil records, pupil progress reporting, program evaluation, student follow-up and placement and college admission requirements.

The understanding and utilization of these data have generally been associated with the school counselor's preparation and role. In view of the increased demand for such information, it is anticipated that special provision must be made for collecting and formatting these data. Otherwise, the already overextended school counselor will become overly involved in data collection, leaving less time for direct interaction with students.

A support systems program will establish the necessary information base about work and have a uniform set of language for inclusion in curriculum units, guidance units and the job placement program. Further, it will establish a student follow-up information system that will serve as a means of evaluating changeable base line data for CCEM, and will provide a data base for making decisions concerning program modification. The support system will also develop a pupil data conceptualization for the model with descriptors, data requirements and reports necessary to record performance, monitor progress and manage resources relative to group and individual career development and education.

At the present time, the support systems component of CCEM is developing and field testing a career information system for grades K-6. It is further testing a follow-up system that relates student plans upon graduation with the student's actual accomplishments or choices.

Professional Support Services

Professional support services activities in CCEM include staff development and community involvement.

Staff Development. High quality curriculum materials are important to the development and installation of an educational innovation. However, of equal importance is a qualified and well-prepared teaching staff that will use the materials.

In CCEM, materials and accompanying instructions have been developed for the in-service training of school personnel at five different levels. These are:

Level 1: A general orientation to career education concepts. This level is for all school personnel. It serves to define career education and identify the difference between the ongoing educational system and the career education system. It answers the questions, "What is career education?" and "Why should we adopt this new system?"

Level 2: An orientation to the specific program for that school. Such orientation is for all teachers, administrators and personnel who will have some contact with the new career education curriculum units or support systems. It provides an overview of the total "set" of new units and systems that will be installed.

Level 3: A specific orientation program for teachers of curriculum units. This level of training is designed to provide teachers with a thorough familiarization with the goals, outcomes and content of the units or support system activities for which they will be responsible. In addition, teachers become familiar with the units that precede and follow so that they understand the "systemic" importance of their own unit. At this level of activity, academic departments such as mathematics and English will receive an orientation to the group of units that are delivered or infused into their disciplines.

Level 4: Unit of specific training for teachers. This training level provides an opportunity for teachers to indicate specific areas of in-service training needed by them in order to teach their curriculum units. This is accomplished through a check sheet arrangement that lists areas of: (a) subject matter content, (b) teaching methods, and (c) resource materials. These lists are coded to specific portions of the curriculum unit and allow teachers to assess their own in-service training needs.

Level 5: Specific skill training. This level of in-service training provides specific instruction in areas where the teacher feels additional skills are needed. These are self-instructional modules keyed to expressed needs as indicated on the check list at Level 4.

This five level in-service staff development program is presently being tested in the six cooperating LEA's. The materials and procedures will be refined based upon the field test data. It is recognized that most school districts cannot afford a massive in-service program for their professional staff prior to adopting an educational innovation. At best, most districts can afford a few hours of in-service training per person at LEA expense. However, by providing a wide variety of tested materials for a five level program as described, adopting districts may choose from a variety of materials that may suit their unique installation needs.

Community Involvement. If career education is to endure as a continuing priority in a school system, it must be supported by the local community or communities. The purpose of the community involvement component of CCEM is to develop and maintain community involvement and support. CCEM's present direction is to develop guidelines for the involvement of three groups at the local level. These groups are: (a) local business and industry, (b) minority groups, and (c) parent groups. These guidelines will identify the various goals and objectives for the involvement of communities with recommended strategies for achieving the goals.

It is recognized that there are many important groups other than the three previously listed. However, because of limited resources, programs for all important community groups cannot be developed concurrently in the CCEM project.

Evaluation. CCEM evaluation efforts may be divided into two units; one devoted to internal evaluation and the other to external evaluation.

Internal evaluation is responsible for the implementation of formative evaluation procedures, that is, the development of testing procedures and instruments for assessing the effectiveness of both the curriculum materials and the supporting services of the project. Because of the massive evaluation requirements and limited resources, the majority of the present internal evaluation effort is being devoted to the formative evaluation of curriculum units, that is, developing the instrumentation and procedures for gathering data on the quality of curriculum units. These data can be analyzed and used for revision of curriculum materials.

External evaluation has been concerned with CCEM summative evaluation, or the "impact" that CCEM has upon students, school personnel, and community. This includes the assessment of attitudinal changes toward career education on the part of these three groups (Brickell and Aslanian, 1972). In this particular research and development project, summative evaluation has been contracted to an external organization to assure valid and unbiased evaluation.

TESTING THE MODEL

Field testing of the curriculum units will be followed by revision and refinement. They will then be released for dissemination and adoption by other school districts. Concurrently, supporting components for staff development and evaluation will be field tested, revised, and made available.

Also undergoing concurrent development and initial pilot test are the guidance, placement and support systems components. These will be field tested during the following school year. Upon refinement, they will be ready for dissemination.

PRIORITIES FOR THE FUTURE

Probably the greatest number of materials generated by the current thrust relate to the elementary school. One reason for this is that elementary school classrooms are generally self-contained and present fewer problems in installation of new curriculum materials. Also, students in the elementary school generally are in educational programs at each grade level, thus reducing the problems generated by student selection of educational options at higher grade levels.

While career education program activities are extremely important at the elementary school level, it must be remembered that the program goals at this level are designed to capacitate the student to make realistic career related choices at junior and senior high school levels. A future priority of career education must relate to expanding and improving program content at the junior and senior high school level.

Another priority must relate to the mid-career adult. Probably no other single group is in greater need of career education programs and services than adults in the 30-50 year age bracket. During this age period, many adults wish to make career changes that are congruent with changing personal goals and aspirations. In the few instances where career guidance and counseling services are available, there is no mechanism for providing educational opportunities at a reasonable cost. Therefore, solving the unique retraining problems of the mid-career adult is an especially challenging priority for future efforts.

REFERENCES

Brickell, Henry M., and Aslanian, Carol B. *Attitudes Toward Career Education.* A Report of an Initial Study of Pupil, Staff, and Parent Opinions in Atlanta, Hackensack, Jefferson County, Los Angeles, Mesa, and Pontiac. (Columbus: The Center for Vocational and Technical Education, The Ohio State University. February, 1972)

Center for Vocational and Technical Education, The. *Developmental Program Goals for the Comprehensive Career Education Model.* Preliminary Edition. (Columbus: The Ohio State University. August, 1972)

Goldhammer, Keith. "A Careers Curriculum." *Career Education Perspective and Promise.* eds. Keith Goldhammer and Robert E. Taylor. (Columbus, Ohio: Charles E. Merrill Publishing Company. 1972)

Miller, Aaron J. "Career Education Tenets." Proceedings of the Sixth Annual National Vocational and Technical Teacher Education Seminar, The Center for Vocational and Technical Education, The Ohio State University, Columbus, Ohio, 1972.

U. S. Office of Education. *Statistics of Public Elementary and Secondary Schools.* (Washington, D.C.: Office of Education, U. S. Department of Health, Education and Welfare. Fall, 1970)

EMPLOYER-BASED
CAREER EDUCATION MODEL

Bela H. Banathy

The Far West Laboratory for Educational Research and Development has a contractual arrangement with the National Institute of Education to study and test the feasibility of the Employer-Based Career Education (EBCE) Model.

The initial analysis indicated a need for four phases of involvement: (a) an exploratory analysis of the notion of EBCE, (b) in depth feasibility studies in the various key areas of EBCE, (c) some advanced design work, and (d) pilot testing.

During phase one, five questions were asked:

1. Why career education in general, and why EBCE in particular?
2. What issues, problems, and needs should EBCE address?
3. What are desired outcomes of EBCE?
4. Given outcomes, what might EBCE look like (an initial image)?
5. What are the issues and areas one should explore and study in assessing the feasibility of EBCE?

In response to the last question, some 25 areas were identified that indicated a requirement for in depth study and analysis and these areas were then explored. Seven of the areas related to input studies and another six to the curriculum model. Eight studies focused on support systems and interface studies, and the rest on identification of research and development requirements and work. Advanced design work was accomplished in the first part of 1972, and pilot experimentation began in the fall of 1973.

The intent of this chapter is to: (a) provide a definition of career and career education, (b) identify some key parameters of EBCE, (c) identify problems that career education may address, (d) formulate some outcomes, (e) define the organizing concepts, and (f) define key characteristics of the EBCE model.

A DEFINITION OF CAREER
AND CAREER EDUCATION

The term career has many definitions according to Webster, ranging from career as solely "an occupation or profession" to career as "one's progress through life." A broad definition of career that addresses the individual's total life—that is, his occupational, his social and personal concerns—will be implemented here.

Career encompasses the selection of and advancement in a meaningful vocation within the world of work, the selection and pursuit of fulfilling avocational and leisure activities, and satisfying participation in the social and political processes of society.

Career education for the employer based model is conceived as education for one's progress through life. It is the aggregate of involvements by which an individual acquires and develops knowledge, attitudes, and skills to engage in meaningful vocational, avocational, leisure, social and personal pursuits. Career education enables the individual student to assess realistically and develop his own interests and potentials in view of the opportunities offered and constraints imposed by society.

There are two important educational implications of the notion of career:

1. *Career is unique to a given individual.* The prevailing practice of schooling today is to provide a generalized curriculum derived from stated educational goals. Attempts made to adjust curriculum to the individual learner, at best, cope only with differences in learning rate. Curriculum content, its context, and method of presentation are identical. On the other hand, as applied to education, the unique notion of career will lead us to design curriculum around each and every individual learner.

2. *Career is future oriented.* Education today is past oriented. The schools provide for education in the past tense. The student is focused backward in coping with parts of the "accumulated knowledge." The content and context of education are taken from the past; its method of mass instruction has been designed to cope with the requirements of the industrial revolution a century ago. Probably the most exciting dimension of designing a new educational alternative is the challenge to provide education in the future tense.

Early formulations of the EBCE concept have provided some key parameters of the EBCE model. Essentially, these are as follows:

1. EBCE is to be a comprehensive program of education melding the positive aspects of the existing school curriculum—academic, vocational and general.
2. The program should meet the individual learning needs of students.
3. EBCE will present a viable open-enrollment alternative to traditional schooling (but not a replacement).
4. The target population is a cross section of youth from age 13 to 18.
5. EBCE will significantly and directly involve "employers" in the education of young people.
6. It will provide students with multiple work/learning experiences.
7. A unique feature of the program is that the major portion of

students' learning experiences will take place in real-life, non-school settings.

PROBLEMS TO BE ADDRESSED
BY CAREER EDUCATION

The study group's analysis indicated five problem areas related to outcomes, relevance, responsiveness, discontinuity, and separation of educational domains.

Inadequacy of Outcomes

An important criterion of formal education's ability to meet societal needs is the employability of its graduates. The failure of young people to obtain employment upon termination of formal education is one of the fundamental problems facing education and society.

While some of the factors contributing to high unemployment rates among young people are beyond the control of the educational system, the system can address some of the problems that inhibit these job seekers. Five areas of concern related to outcomes are identified here:

1. *Lack of experience and lack of job skills.* The kinds of work experiences that are available to most teen-agers cannot be included in a resume of job qualifications. Newspaper routes and gardening, etc., are not considered "real" work. These experiences are not assumed to endow the teen-ager with the kinds of attitudes and behaviors considered by employers to be appropriate to employees.

2. *Lack of learning skills.* This is the area where the schools' contribution to the employability of their students is most pertinent. It is found that public schools are unable to retain a significant proportion of their students until graduation.

3. *Lack of occupational awareness.* Schools today do not prepare youth to make an intelligent choice of the kind of occupation they wish to pursue. As a result, industry has inherited an increasing problem of turnover and high training expense.

4. *Lack of sociopolitical participation.* Another aspect of the inadequacy of the present formal system of education is the failure to prepare students for the part they might play in the social and political areas of life.

5. *Lack of preparation for continuing personal development.* A final aspect of major inadequacy of output is failure to prepare students for the time when personal development will be their own responsibility rather than that of the home or school.

Relevance

Formal education does not adequately relate what goes on in the classroom to what happens to the student outside of school. The school does not directly address the real, immediate needs of adolescents: identity, purpose, value system development, peer-group relating, decision making, and so forth.

Responsiveness

To survive, a system needs to respond to the changing requirements of its environment. Present-day schooling appears to be responding neither to student needs nor to societal needs.

Other aspects of responsiveness are accountability and cost-effectiveness. The current system of formal education has difficulty in accounting for its performance. Emphasis has been upon the acceptance of students into the institutions of higher learning as a measure of school performance.

Discontinuity

EBCE's analysis revealed that a paramount problem is the discontinuity between formal education on the one hand, and occupational participation, sociopolitical activities and personal development on the other. The existing educational system does not adequately prepare individuals for these other spheres of human activity.

Students cannot be expected to possess the innate ability to communicate with, relate to, be tolerant of, and work effectively with diverse types of people. They must be provided the opportunity, through exposure to a wide variety of real-life situations, to develop the skills of social interaction. Students cannot be expected to become self-sufficient, self-directed, responsible individuals unless, again, they are exposed to real-life situations that enable them to develop a level of personal competence.

Furthermore, students cannot be expected to make wise decisions about their lives, life styles and futures in general, unless they are provided an opportunity to learn about the requirements and consequences of available alternatives, to develop the skills of decision making and to accept responsibility for directing their own lives.

The Separation of Educational Domains

Another key problem is the separation of educational domains into academic training, vocational training and general education, and the division of those domains into subject matters. What is required, in essence, is an educational system that adequately restructures the separate domains of academic training, vocational preparation and general education, melding the positive aspects of each into a viable alternative to traditional education. Such a system would strive to provide each student with a means to select and pursue a life path that would support his aspirations and abilities. Every student would have the opportunity to develop the kinds of knowledge, understanding and skills needed to live in a complex society. Such a model of education can be considered career education—education for life.

OUTCOMES TO BE ATTAINED

Given the problem that career education might address, the EBCE staff has formulated expectations of outcomes at two levels. At a broader level, they defined a set of EBCE goals and also stated educational goals relevant to the learner.

The broader goals of EBCE are:

1. To provide an alternative to the existing general education and vocational programs for young people and adults who wish to achieve comprehensive career education;
2. To increase the relevance between education, the world of work, and life in general by adopting career competence as the central theme of the individual's experience within the educational system;
3. To integrate existing programs of general, academic and vocational education into a new educational experience;
4. To broaden the base of participation in education by involving the community, public and business sectors more directly and significantly in the process of preparing students for responsible careers within the community and especially within the world of work; and,
5. To broaden the base of student participation in the educational process by involving students in decision making.

Career education aims to develop in the learner:

1. *Self-awareness.* Each student needs to acquire knowledge and understanding of himself—his goals, abilities, interests and values—so that he is able to realistically plan and pursue his own life path.
2. *Self-sufficiency.* Each student needs to develop the knowledge and skills necessary for: proper physical maintenance (health and hygiene); effective management of personal finances and other resources; accepting responsibility for and functioning effectively in selected familial roles; and, selecting and pursuing goals of personal development or fulfillment. The student needs to develop an ability to gather information, analyze it critically, and make his own judgments and decisions based upon available information.
3. *Social skills.* Each student needs to acquire the skills required to communicate effectively with other persons, to develop understanding and tolerance of individual and group differences and values, and to work cooperatively and effectively with others in group endeavors.

4. *Basic cognitive skills.* Each student should develop skills of logical analysis as well as the ability to read, write and compute. These skills are essential to personal development, continued education or successful employment.

5. *Career/life skills.* Each student must be exposed to a broad range of occupational, avocational and leisure activities, so that he has the information and experience necessary to make rational career choices involving all of these realms of endeavor. Each individual needs to possess some minimal skills representative of vocational/avocational areas of interest to him as bases for further growth and development in his chosen pursuits.

6. *Skills and employability.* Each student should be helped to develop the basic skills essential to seeking, and acquiring, employment so that he may compete more effectively for available employment opportunities.

KEY ORGANIZING CONCEPTS OF THE MODEL

While existing schooling is built around classes of students, the *EBCE model is to be designed around the individual learner.* Today, educators select instructional programs and, at best, they try to individualize them.

The content and the context of instruction is the same; its mode of presentation might be different in order to accommodate the individual. The EBCE model leads one to design individual education in which not only the mode but also the content and the context of the experience are tailor-made to fit the individual. The model provides for the integration of the personal, social and intellectual development of the individual within the context of vocational, avocational and leisure pursuits (See Figure 1).

Another key organizing concept of the EBCE model is that *learning is never context-free;* it is provided within the functional context of real-life situations. Life situations are vocational/avocational/leisure and other involvements that the learner may pursue and which, in an important way, provide situational frameworks for his learning experience. These situations are the functional contexts in which learning takes place relevant to the four competence domains (cognitive, social, personal and vocational/avocational/leisure). Life situations are here and now rather than something in the distant future for which one needs to be prepared. The notion is that the best way to prepare for the future is to help the individual to acquire competencies that enable him to perform successfully in present life situations.

The educational experience projected in the EBCE is *performance-based.* The student will not be required to undergo an experience if

CAREER EDUCATION: A CURRICULUM MODEL

SELECTED CAREER/LIFE COMPETENCIES

Vocational/Avocational/Leisure

- Information/orientation about all viable careers/activities (vocational/avocational/leisure)
- Exploration of various career clusters (self-selected)
- Representative skills attained in self-selected areas
- Skills and attitudes of employability
- Entry level skills acquired in one or more vocations/avocations

Within the functional context of

PERSONAL COMPETENCE

- Information/Knowledge base for decision making
- Self-sufficiency in maintaining life, health, property
- Acquisition of sense of own uniqueness
  - knowledge of self
  - positive self-image
  - knowledge of life styles
  - own life style
- Habit of self-actualization

Interactive

Within the functional context of

REPRESENTATIVE CAREER/LIFE SITUATIONS

Multiple Vocational/Avocational/Leisure/Personal/Activities
(Individual & Group Activities)

e.g. work experience
public service
community action
recreation
entertainment
personal development

Interactive

Within the functional context of

COGNITIVE COMPETENCE

Cognitive skills and cognitive heuristics

- Communication skills (verbal, reading and writing)
- Quantitative skills
- Skills of problem solving/decision making
- Skills of logic

Within the functional context of

SOCIAL COMPETENCE

Skills and attitudes relevant to effective group membership leadership behaviors, such as:

- Get and give information
- Get to know—and know how to use—the resources of the group
- Evaluate
- Plan and make decisions
- Know the characteristics of members of the group
- Keep the group agreeable to members
- Control and correct
- Counsel
- Represent the group
- Set example
- Share leadership

Interactive

Figure 1

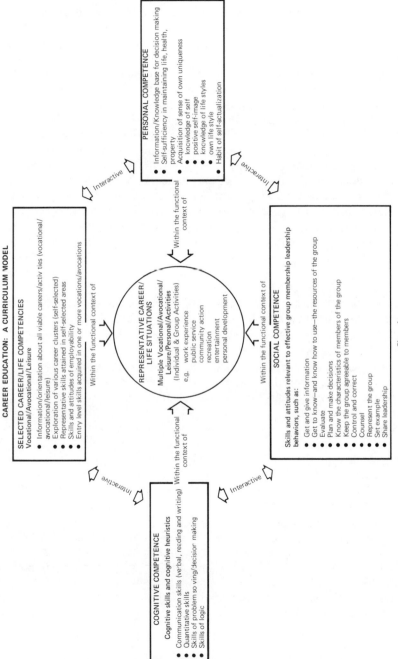

he already demonstrates competence; he will be allowed to move on whenever he has acquired the desired skill or knowledge.

Another set of concepts relates to the involvement of *the learner*. Learning-focused refers to the placement of emphasis on the learning task rather than the teaching task. Arrangements are made in the learner's environment to enhance his mastery of the learning task. Learner-active describes a process in which the individual is actively and intensively involved in learning experiences, and a staff and the learner are involved in creating learning environments to facilitate the success of the learner. A learner-directed program is: self-paced (learning not bound by time period); self-selected (learner selects own content); self-initiated (learner initiates own involvement); and, self-evaluated and self-adjusting. All in all, the learner progressively assumes a higher degree of responsibility for his own learning.

The resource boundaries of the conventional school are set around the physical plant with only occasional excursions allowed beyond the boundaries of the plant. A student of a typical high school can legitimately spend all his school time within the physical boundaries of the school. In the EBCE model no such boundaries exist. *The resources available to the learner are those of the larger community.* New territories for learning are to be identified and developed, and new learning environments can be created by which to facilitate the attainment of learning tasks.

Employers are people or organizations who employ other people in profit-making, governmental, and other not-for-profit enterprises. They include large industrial firms; small businesses, like a family hardware store; government or quasi-government operations, like the postal service; and public, nonprofit agencies, like the American Red Cross.

Whether a given career education model is employer-based, school-based, or other-based depends primarily on who sets policy and has fiscal control. *EBCE is employer-based* in that employers as a group will play a dominant role in deciding on educational goals and in mobilizing and allocating resources to achieve those goals.

The governance of schooling today is usually in the hands of a single agency, the school board. *The governance of the employer-based model is conceptualized as a partnership of a variety of interests and involvements.* Public and private employers, community agencies, the education sector, parents and students constitute a new alliance and would share power in establishing and governing this new type of educational involvement.

KEY CHARACTERISTICS OF THE PROGRAM

A set of characteristics has evolved and is considered the most salient aspect of the program.

The Concept of "Experience" and the Notion of "Experience Trail"

The concept of "experience" has two major characteristics, one related to learning as the content of the experience, the other to *the context* in which the experience takes place—the vehicle of learning. *"Experience"* is a learning opportunity provided in the context of life; it is a definable unit of potential learning, presented in a functional context of vocational, avocational or leisure involvement. A sequence of purposeful experiences brought together and organized into a situational scheme becomes an *"experience trail."* The concept of experience and the notion of experience trail are core aspects because they organize the model.

Education is to be designed around the *individual learner,* whereas existing schooling is built around *classes of students.* To date, the schools have selected instructional programs and, at best, individualized them. The EBCE model leads us to design experience trails that are always individualized. Although others may even go along with him for quite a length, a given trail is always designed with and for the individual learner. If the notion of the experience trail is implemented, the learner always knows: (a) what trail he is following, (b) why, (c) where it leads, (d) how far he has gone at any given time, and (e) what he has to do to make further progress along the trail.

A Modular, Flexible Curriculum

An experience trail is made up of a set of definable units of potential learning experiences, presented within a functional/situational context. Learning units can be organized in various configurations and presented in a variety of contexts. Thus, the notion of the experience trail calls for a modular approach to curriculum organization. A module is a unit of learning that the learner must master in order to acquire a specified competence or have an experience or involvement judged to be of value. The main task of design is to define learning modules in the four domains—cognitive, social, personal, vocational/avocational/leisure; exemplify their relevance to the various situational contexts; describe the modules in such a way as to allow the learner an efficient survey of available modules; identify resources that the learner can use in mastering the modules; and, build these elements into a system of arrangement that will facilitate the learner's mastery of the module.

Variety of Social Settings

Depending on the nature of the desired outcomes, various social settings might facilitate the learner's experiences.

1. Often the student will be *on his own*—studying, working,

pursuing an avocational/leisure interest, or just contemplating and planning.

2. *Conferences with individuals* in the student's environment will facilitate planning, decision making and the exchange of ideas.

3. *Working in a team* through designed experiences will enable youngsters to acquire competences needed for effective group leadership/membership and will provide group identification and social support.

4. *Tutorial settings* will facilitate learning.

5. *Small-group settings,* seminars, discussion groups, etc., will serve the same purpose.

6. *Large-group meetings* may be suitable for receiving information and watching staged presentations.

The Team Approach

Because of its design, traditional schooling fails to provide significant opportunities to learn how one can be an effective member/ leader of groups. In contrast, the EBCE model provides for structured and purposeful social involvement as a vehicle for developing social competence. Small groups of four to eight people would be formed to constitute peer teams.

The team would make it possible to develop the skills and attitudes needed for successful membership/leadership performance in groups and enhance the application of these skills in appropriate situations and real-life contexts. Furthermore, it provides a means of identification (with the group) and social support (by the group) and serves as a resource for peer instruction and guidance. It also may become a work/production unit.

The Staff: A Learner-support Team

The staff is perceived as the learner-support team constituted of various kinds of people working for or with the learner or available to him. For example:

1. *Designers* set up learning modules and sample experience trails, correlate experience trails with competence domains, and select, adapt or develop materials required for the mastery of learning modules and the implementation of planned experience trails.

2. *Coordinators* work with students as they plan their experience trails and monitor their progress, assist students as they make adjustments in their program, and help them to cope with their personal concerns and problems.

3. *Resource persons* assist the student in coping with his learning task and help him locate and make use of resources required to provide for specific experiences.

4. *Territory developers* explore and map territories for learning/ work/avocational/leisure experiences, develop territories for the learner's use, and maintain territories to ensure their continued utility and effectiveness.
5. *Managers* manage the interaction of all those involved in the program, provide for the resources required for the maintenance of the system, and interact with the larger system in which the program operates.

Territories of Learning

Territories that offer a basis for various experiences may include sites for vocational or avocational exploration and involvement, sites for reisure involvement, the home and neighborhood (personal, social and other life skills development), other sites selected to pursue special interests and self-development, and finally, the learning resource information and arrangement center that is considered to be the "home base" for the learner.

Territories need to be mapped out in detail and information about these should be provided to the learner. A territory has to be developed by preparing those who operate in the territory to be helpful to the learner. Furthermore, territories have to be maintained by a frequent assessment of learner-territory relationship, and by making adjustments if needed.

SUMMARY

In this chapter, the author has briefly reported the intent of the EBCE model staff in designing and testing a career education model and described the organizing concepts that guided their design work and some of the key characteristics that may define the program.

THE HOME/COMMUNITY-BASED CAREER EDUCATION MODEL

Vivian M. Guilfoy and Juliet F. Brudney

The home/community-based career education model under development by the Education Development Center (EDC) has as its central concern expanding and improving the options of home-based adults for employment in the future. It proposes to test the effectiveness of particular strategies, services, materials and institutional changes in achieving this goal. The central focus has been to determine the primary choice of program components and the objectives for each, the plans to evaluate these components and the research design. An additional criterion for selection was the potential of the strategies, services and materials for dissemination among the target population and for adaptation by education and training institutions. To enhance this potential, cost considerations have been paramount.

The strategies to be developed and tested concern:

1. Arousing interest in the target population in seeking career education.
2. Delivering new services to those individuals seeking career education.
3. Achieving certain changes within the target institutions.

The multi-media materials to be developed and tested are intended to convey certain career-related concepts and self-help skills to the target population and the target institutions. The services to be developed and tested are designed to assist individuals within the target population to arrive at and implement decisions on career focus and career training. The research and evaluation activities are designed to provide on-going improvement to the program strategies, materials and services as well as to document the model's efforts.

Proposed Outcomes

The model's six program components seek to produce one or more of the outcomes, listed below, among the target population and target institutions.

Among the Target Population:

1. Knowledge about expanding career areas and their educational and skill requirements,
2. Skills in assessing career interests and preparatory needs,
3. Knowledge about local preparatory and supportive resources that relate to career interests and preparatory needs,
4. Selection of a career focus,

5. Planning an educational and/or training effort to prepare for that career,
6. Initiation of a career-preparatory effort.

Among the Target Institutions (and for adult part-time students):

7. New or expanded career counseling services,
8. Additional part-time program slots that provide educational or technical training for expanding career areas,
9. New part-time program slots with credit, which provide supervised field-placement at work-sites in private industry, public agencies or volunteer organizations.

Career Education Curriculum

EDC views career education from two general perspectives: one deals with education about careers and with decision making on career focus and preparation; the other perspective deals with the educational and technical training requisite for the career. The strategies, materials and services of the model relate to both perspectives, focusing on the former with the target population and on the latter with the target institutions.

The project's interventions (strategies, materials, services) are based upon a collection of information, research findings and concepts about: (a) careers, (b) the target populations, and (c) the target institutions that EDC has been acquiring and analyzing since June 1971. This collection is called the model's Career Education Curriculum. The Career Education Curriculum will shift and expand as new materials and ideas from outside the locality and from project experiences and research are incorporated. The basic factors are not apt to change and are presented briefly here, as the frame of reference for the program components, and for the evaluation and research proposed.

1. *Career Opportunities.* Occupational and professional fields differ in respect to their opportunities for entrance and advancement. Labor market analysts identify those that are projected to expand in number of job openings, locally and nationally, during the next five to 10 years; and, the nature of their advancement opportunities from entry level to semi-skilled and skilled positions, pay scales, etc.

2. *The Target Population.* Most home-based adults are cut off from sources of information about the labor market and preparation for it and from well-informed sources of assistance with decision making on career choice and career preparation. Many have the desire and the potential to improve their career options, but lacking self-confidence and relevant information they will enter the labor market without sufficient skills to move forward.

3. *The Target Institutions.* Many existing institutions in urban areas offer educational and/or technical programs that prepare adults for

expanding careers. Most of their students are not home-based. Most of their programs are specialized, and there are few linkages among them. Learning experiences are largely limited to the classroom.

The Target Population

The model has selected for its target population home-based adults defined with respect to age, current employment, educational status and residence. The criteria are outlined here:

1. *Age*—16 and older,
2. *Employment Status*—not working full-time and not actively seeking work,
3. *Educational Status*—not studying full-time,
4. *Residence*—not institutionalized.

According to estimates from the 1970 census, the model's Year One pilot area of Providence County and Warwick, Rhode Island, contains approximately 134,000 persons who meet these criteria. There are 195,000 in the State of Rhode Island (Rhode Island Department of Employment Security, 1972) and 47,000,000, nationally meeting the same requirements.

Despite differences in age and outlook, the young people, housewives and older adults who comprise the target population share certain career-related characteristics. First, many will be entering the labor market at some future date, particularly younger men and women. Currently in Rhode Island, approximately 45 percent of the women over 16 are working (Rhode Island Development Council, 1972). According to some estimates, by 1980 seven out of ten women in the United States in the young and middle-aged categories will be employed. Furthermore, older adults have established pressure groups seeking to eliminate age as a hiring factor.

Secondly, many home-based persons, according to research and site investigations undertaken by EDC during 1971-72, are not familiar with labor market conditions and have not thought through their own career potential and focus. Those with middle-to-low socioeconomic characteristics (income, education, occupational history) regard career as synonymous with profession (doctor, lawyer, social worker) and, consequently, beyond their capacity because of the length and costs of training. If they have any occupational plans, they concern unskilled jobs in factories, sales or offices. The project has selected for priority focus those home-based adults with a high school education or less, and previous employment, if any, in unskilled or semi-skilled categories. They are identified as the "core group" among the target population.

The rationale for this focus concerns relative need and relative benefits for the core group as compared with the better educated and/or more experienced target group numbers. As to need, the core group's access to interventions other than the project's is far more limited. College-educated women and young men, for example, are apt to have friends and relatives in more varied and more skilled career areas and are, therefore, more knowledgeable about career opportunities and career preparation. Members of this group can also obtain career information and assistance from their colleges. They are financially able to purchase private counseling. They are exposed to and can purchase and comprehend a greater variety of multi-media materials than non-college men and women. For the core group, then, the interventions that the model proposes may represent the only source of information and guidance.

Because of the greater need, the core group can also gain proportionately more in earning potential than can the better educated group, if the strategies, services and materials that the Project proposes prove effective. Most core group members would presently qualify only for those low-wage occupations that offer little opportunity for advancement. Recent findings from the U.S. Census Bureau's Employment Survey (CES), designed by the Bureau of Labor Statistics, document the problems of the low-skilled, undereducated worker. These individuals are not the welfare population. They are the underemployed, and number 13,000,000 in the 51 cities surveyed (U.S. Bureau of the Census, 1971a, b, c). A national Manpower Administration study on women in the labor force found that only those with specific vocational or professional skills earn above minimum levels. The study also reports that women who reenter the labor market do so at *lower* occupational levels than when they left (Marshall, 1972). In Rhode Island, according to reports from the State Division of Employment Security and the 1970 U.S. Census, the average earnings of female workers is $2,392 a year, as compared with average male earnings of $6,062. Information on young male dropouts parallels these findings.

The Target Institutions

Research by EDC in the pilot locality, as well as in other small cities, revealed that many educational institutions offer a wide range of educational and skill-training programs. A substantial number of these programs (courses) relate to the requirements for expanding career fields and are available on a part-time basis. These include adult basic education, high school equivalency, continuing education at junior colleges and colleges, vocational and technical training. Sponsors are public, private non-profit, and proprietary. Thus far, 76 institutions offering a total of 381 individual programs on a part-time basis, have been identified in the pilot area, Providence County and Warwick. Most programs (courses) are on an educational level at which the core group can be admitted. Many cost less than $150.00

and require attendance of only three to six hours per week, important features for home-based adults whose financial constraints and home responsibilities make full-time study difficult.

Despite these ease-of-access characteristics, existing training and educational resources are also characterized by certain barriers to home-based students.

1. *The Division Between Educational and Technical Offerings.* Few institutions contain *both* the educational and training programs that the core group is apt to need. Although most employment opportunities above the unskilled level require both basic education and vocational-technical skills, adult education institutions often focus on one or the other of these areas. Thus, those that offer vocational-technical training usually provide little in basic education. Conversely, institutions that offer basic education generally do not provide vocational-technical training. The student who attempts technical training with insufficient skills in reading and/or math is severely handicapped and may not be able to master the technical skills, as manpower programs of the 1960s demonstrated all too frequently. On the other hand, students in adult basic education programs and evening high schools drop out at alarmingly high rates. Studies have found that many adult basic education (ABE) dropouts see no connection between their ABE classes and their career interests and needs and, therefore, no point in continuing.

2. *Full-time Requirements.* Some institutions, especially those in technical and higher education, offer programs that are highly relevant to careers, but only students who are enrolled full-time are permitted to take the course, e.g., nursing schools. Home-based (and other) adults face severe restraints in utilizing full-time programs because of other demands on their time, such as child care or part-time employment that they either cannot afford to ignore or do not wish to.

3. *The Absence of Work-based Learning Experiences.* Most part-time programs take place within the educational institution. Although efforts are made to inject career realities through shop sessions, speakers from business and industry, films about different careers, etc., there are few opportunities to investigate work-sites firsthand except through the work-study program. Work-study is essentially income-producing rather than a planned learning experience. There is no question as to its importance to the student, but in many cases it does not add to his career-related skills to any significant degree. Opportunities for learning experiences at actual work-sites are especially needed by the home-based core group. Many have been out of the labor market for years (women), or have never really entered it (young men and women), or are exploring a new career focus (older men). As we have pointed out earlier, this group's access to career

information from friends and relatives who are working is limited severely by the nature of the peer group's occupations.

Limitations of the Model

Although the project proposed can produce significant gains for the home-based population, all educational and self-help efforts such as the project's are dependent upon and substantially affected by external factors. If, for example, the nation and/or a locality is suffering from widespread unemployment and a stagnant or deteriorating economy, career education graduates will face severe problems. Even in a reasonably healthy labor market, the individual may confront discriminatory employment practices, poor quality job-finding services, and restrictive upgrading opportunities at the work-site.

An equally significant external barrier is the absence of any mechanism for obtaining and relating data on future labor force supply to data on future labor market opportunities. Although forecasts of labor market opportunities, e.g., expanding career areas, are reasonably accurate, matching data on training resources and trainees in the pipeline are virtually nonexistent. Consequently, today's short-supply skill may become tomorrow's glut.

The six program components of the model constitute a multi-faceted design with a central focus and a framework of common concepts.

Each component looks to the others for information about and access to the target group. Each gains considerable strength from the other's input. During the four year research and development period, the design will remain intact. But each component has been deliberately formulated to permit separation from the others, component modification resulting from research and development, and adaptation by others of its strategies, services or approaches to printed and audiovisual materials. Considerable testing and evaluation of the materials and services are planned prior to dissemination. Irrespective of which components or strategies or services could be adapted by others, one aspect of the model seems to be essential to the proper utilization of such materials or services. This aspect is the development, or possession, of considerable information on local and national career opportunities and on local preparatory and supportive resources.

A brief description of each of the six components follows.

Outreach

Outreach is the project's effort to involve target population adults in the project and its services. The effectiveness of each of six strategies for making contact with the core group will be tested in terms of the responses elicited. These responses are, in order of preference: (a) a call to the counseling service, (b) a visit to the resource center, (c) an increase in career education awareness.

Outreach is essentially promotional and, consequently, faces a number of barriers because of the product (career education), the audience, and each of the channels to that audience—mass media (television, radio, newspapers), and more personal access routes (telephone canvass, public locations, organizations).

For example, although almost all residents of the pilot area own television sets and view them for several hours each day, the outreach programs may be misunderstood as an invitation to job placement. Telephone canvasses may be a better strategy for explaining the project, but if many of those who are called are not home-based, the effort can be extremely costly in terms of results.

By the end of Program Year One, the plan is to determine the relative merits of each strategy in terms of costs and the number and kinds of responses. This determination is a primary input for the planning of Year Two.

Counseling

The counseling component proposes to develop and test a new service—information-guidance-referral to individual members of the target population, and especially the core group. The service format is designed to encourage and enable clients to help themselves in achieving the outcomes established by the model. Literature searches and field investigations since 1971 disclose that the service being tested is new (Ginzberg, 1971). Programs that currently provide career-related assistance to home-based individuals are either job-placement agencies or restricted, tacitly or openly, to particular groups such as welfare clients, veterans, college-trained women, etc.

The service is to be rooted in a strong information base. It offers facts and figures on a wide range of career opportunities and local preparatory and supportive resources within the context of self-development counseling. The counselor's ability to find the relevant environmental data and to communicate and relate them to the client is essential. Certain aspects of other program components, e.g., resource center and printed materials, are intended to help the counselor facilitate self-assessment and self-help.

In addition to developing and testing the service format, the model is concerned with designing a service that is highly accessible, especially to the core target group, at a cost that is considerably lower than the current fees charged by private counseling agencies.

Because of the practical and psychological constraints that the target population, and especially the core group, face in dealing with outside agencies, the accessible format selected for testing is telephone-based. Other than personal visits, the telephone is the only two-way communication system now available between service agency and home-based. There have been a number of successful efforts to counsel via telephone but none, as yet determined, that calls for the kind of sustained self-help relationship with clients that the project's service intends to test.

In order to reduce costs, a category for counselors has been designed—the associate-professional. The service will use these personnel under professional supervision. The telephone format itself has cost-saving potential in comparison with the usual system of appointments at set intervals. Aside from no-shows, a cost-drain not present in telephone delivery, the amount of counseling time required at any particular point in a self-help format is unpredictable. Frequent short contacts appear to be required to exchange particular pieces of information. Occasionally, longer sessions may be needed for synthesis and decision making.

Because telephone counseling does not permit clients to meet together and gain reinforcement from others like themselves who face similar problems, the model is also testing a group counseling format. By collecting data on costs as well as outcomes, findings at the end of Year One will determine relative emphasis between telephone and group delivery during Year Two.

The Resource Center

The resource center is designed to locate, organize and disseminate multi-media materials on career education concepts and issues from sources throughout the country and from project-generated findings and products. Dissemination targets include the home-based population, career-preparatory institutions and project staff. The center is the primary source for building and classifying the project's curriculum. Its contents include catalogues and guides on schools and supportive resources; several hundred books and periodicals; 500 microfiche; pamphlets, clippings, and audio-visual materials; descriptions and abstracts of 30 computer searches.

Despite this extensive and varied collection, many of the materials are designed for professionals or for those with high-level reading comprehension skills. The easier-to-read materials are usually written for junior and senior high school students and are quite inappropriate, in tone and content, for adults.

The center staff will, consequently, construct special modules of materials that will convey relevant components of career education. Existing materials will be organized, synthesized and, when necessary, translated into simpler or more appropriate form. These modules are intended for dissemination to institutions and organizations on a loan or purchase basis. Six modules should be completed in Year One and at least an equal number in Year Two.

A workshop format, built around module themes, and used with groups of core clients, will be tested as a method for increasing their self-help skills.

Institutional Development

The institutional development component has designed and will test strategies for achieving one or more specific changes within private, public and proprietary career-preparatory resources. The changes concern new counseling services, additional part-time program slots, and supervised field placement at work-sites.

Efforts are to be concentrated on a small number of institutions selected by objective criteria from the set of career-preparatory resources in the target area. Assistance to be offered to this sample calls for planning and development funds and technical assistance from the project to the institution in exchange for their agreement to seek and obtain the necessary approvals, space and personnel for the proposed changes.

Printed Materials

The products to be designed and tested by the print component staff are intended to be disseminated outside the target area to permit replication, adaptation or utilization of one or more of the model's components. One aspect of the model, namely data on expanding local and national career opportunities and on local educational, training and supportive resources, is prerequisite for effective utilization of any other component. These data must be acquired and/or developed and synthesized into a locally useful form. Consequently, the key printed product will be a "how-to" manual on the design and production of such a data base, including descriptors, methodologies, costs and staffing requirements.

During Year One, the project's data base will be developed further and utilized. The research and evaluation findings resulting from these experiences provide a primary input for the production of such a manual during Year Two. Additional "how-to" manuals based on the experiences and findings from other program components are to be produced in Years Two, Three and Four.

Analysis of the core group underscores its need for the kind of concrete information contained in the data base. In an attempt to produce, for dissemination, printed materials that respond to this need, two prototypes will be designed and tested during Years One and Two. One concerns several individual information kits, each on a career field that is expanding both in Rhode Island and nationally. Generic problems in career planning, choice and preparation will be related to the locality data that is to be in the form of inexpensive-to-print removable inserts. Other localities, using the data-base "how-to" manual can adapt these inserts. The second prototype is designed for core group adults who have not yet made a career choice. It will present the wide range of possibilities in a cross-referenced catalogue.

Audio-visual Materials

The audio-visual component will:

1. Produce, test and disseminate audio-visual materials to interest the home-based in opportunities offered by expanding careers and their educational and technical skill prerequisites.

2. Produce audio-visual documents on project strategies and services that will interest leaders in adult education, counseling, and planning, and in the adaptation of these strategies and services.

The *TV Specials* are designed for commercial television to arouse interest in career and career preparation among mass audiences. They will consist of videotaped or filmed segments that evolve through a process of testing, selecting and lacing together a number of self-contained, five-minute modules. Each module presents, in human terms, the generic concepts of the curriculum—expanding career areas, selecting a career focus, rearranging personal responsibilities, dealing with institutions. In producing these modules, the audio-visual staff will draw upon the rich reality-based information about careers, career interests and needs of the home-based available from the other components. Products will encourage viewer participation and interest through test-taking devices, genuine role models, and humorous formats used to present facts and problems.

The Career Development Film Series, scheduled for Year Two, is designed to engender sustained self-help among core group clients. The series will address, in depth, the same generic issues covered by the tv specials in a step-by-step treatment of the career development process. It will be made available to adult basic education classes, vocational schools, or other institutional settings through educational tv outlets. Guides for group utilization will be provided.

For project documentation efforts, a task force will set priorities during Year One in terms of strategies and service formats to be filmed or videotaped during Year Two. Production of 10 to 20 minute videotapes of counselor training, information modules construction and utilization, development of field placement sites, etc., is expected then. In Year Three, these will be edited for distribution to educational institutions, counseling agencies and libraries as back-up illustrations to the various "how-to" manuals described in the print component.

Based on test findings in Years One and Two, the products will be marketed in Years Three and Four to commercial and public tv and other institutional outlets. During Year Three, additions may be made to the tv series so that it could be adapted for large urban audiences.

RESEARCH AND EVALUATION

During Year One, the project will be testing the services, strategies and materials summarized earlier. The research and evaluation plan must be somewhat open-ended, adaptable and able to incorporate the shifts that the action part of the project takes. However, priorities must also be established from the outset for data gathering, analysis and assessment. These need not exhaust the capabilities of the design to supply information and to provide an opportunity to learn.

In establishing research and evaluation priorities, and the design for their implementation, targets that are not only significant but also achievable within the limits of the budget have been sought. Also, measures of outcome, impact and effectiveness that are appropriate to the short-range nature of the project have been considered.

The project's meaning of research is one of a deliberate and systematic inquiry into an issue related to the project where the primary objective is to add to the specific and the general body of knowledge and understanding. An example is the research proposed during Year One on the home-based universe. Formative evaluation will be conducted to enhance the efficiency and effectiveness of these activities, based on what is learned from operational experiences. Summative evaluation will be conducted to enhance the overall outcomes of the project, such as the net effects on clients who engage in career preparation, and the net effects on career preparatory programs and services of local institutions.

The research and evaluative findings are intended for four audiences—the project staff who will use them to adapt and tune more finely their own activities; public administrators who must assess the project's components to determine the merits of adopting; the academic and research communities concerned with economic and social circumstances related to home-based persons; and, the general public, a large portion of which is, indeed, the home-based.

A primary objective for Year One is to put in place a data collection and processing system that will produce comprehensive and reliable data in keeping with the desired data formats. The system will collect and process for the project:

1. The career-related information (i.e., local and national expanding career fields, preparatory and supportive local resources) needed by adult clients of widely differing backgrounds.
2. The evaluative and substantive information needed by units of the project as they refine and extend their activities.
3. The cost information on project activities needed by managers of the project to estimate the cost-effectiveness of the project.

A second major objective is to analyze the data for purposes of formative evaluation. During the first year, the cross-tabulations will, of necessity, take into account a comparatively limited number of variables, since the client population will be increasing gradually. The formative evaluation plan focuses on the outreach and counseling components and uses two time frames for analysis:

1. Short-term to provide periodic feedback to the project staff regarding the consequences of their activities as they test alternative strategies. For example, feedback will be provided to outreach concerning the number of respondents who have contacted counseling because of a radio spot last week, or a newspaper article yesterday, etc.

2. Longer-term to provide analytic findings in the final months of Year One to guide design formulations for Year Two, e.g., the outreach strategies that are most apt to reach young people; the counseling format that is most apt to optimize career development progress for core group clients.

Research on the Target Population

1. A Comparative Study

Knowledge about the target population universe has been limited until recently because particular 1970 census subsets of data on general population characteristics of special relevance to the project were not available. These data are now coming through. The Rhode Island and national data on home-based groups will be collected and analyzed in terms of family characteristics, educational and occupational background, ethnic and religious descriptors, etc. Corresponding data will be collected on the respondent population and on a dropout subgroup among them in order to identify similarities and differences between and among these groups.

2. Dropout Study

In addition to collecting data on the income, education, occupational history, etc., of dropouts for the comparative study just described, a special study on dropouts is also planned to provide insights for revising, updating and more finely tuning the project's services. For the most part, these issues are addressed through the formative evaluation of each of the components. But there are some additional pieces, the "falling-in-the-crack" issues, that are not covered there:

1. Why do the home-based drop out of the career development progression?

2. When, and under what circumstances, can the dropouts' interest in the project and/or career education, in general, be revived?

3. Should the dropouts' interest in the project be revived?

3. *Descriptive Case Studies*

To enhance the value of the two studies just described, the project will also develop longitudinal descriptive profiles on home-based respondents to illustrate combinations of variables that occur over time and their effects on involvement in the career education process. One hundred cases from the project's clientele will be selected, stratified by age/sex/core/non-core and, then, by length and stage of counseling.

These three studies have been summarized and will be conducted in an order of increasing specificity. The first two are primarily concerned with the development of profiles of the various populations with whom the project interacts. To enhance the value of these profiles, the third study will help prepare case studies on representative home-based respondents to illustrate the combinations of life-experience variables that can affect involvement in the education process.

Research and Evaluation of the Career Education Curriculum

The model's services and multi-media products are rooted in a body of information and concepts that could be termed its Career Education Curriculum. Everything the project does stems from this, so, naturally, there are many issues concerning the nature of this curriculum that will call for research and development during the lifetime of the project.

For the most part, this research and development will be conducted as part of the project's operations. There are, however, two additional parts of the curriculum requiring special research and evaluative efforts: (a) The determination of expanding career opportunities locally and nationally, and (b) An evaluation of the effectiveness, thoroughness and usability of the data formats for the inventories of educational and training resources and of supportive services.

Formative Evaluation of Project Services

In addition, each project component will be evaluated in terms of its effectiveness in delivering services and products. This includes evaluation of alternative forms of outreach; client progress in the career development process and the various counseling strategies; utilization and quality of resource center materials and services; work with selected institutions that deliver career education; and, pre-testing of the model's permanent products.

REFERENCES

Ginzberg, Eli. *Career Guidance: Who Needs It, Who Provides It, Who Can Improve It.* (New York: McGraw-Hill. 1971)

Marshall, Patricia. "Women at Work." *Manpower.* IV, (June, 1972)

Rhode Island Department of Employment Security. *Rhode Island Industry and Occupational Projections to 1975.* (Providence, Rhode Island: Rhode Island Department of Employment Security. July, 1972)

Rhode Island Development Council. *The Rhode Island Economy: Summary and Trends.* (Providence, Rhode Island: Rhode Island Development Council. 1972)

U.S. Bureau of the Census. *Census of Population 1970—General Population Characteristics.* Final Report PC (1)—B41 Rhode Island. (Washington, D.C.: U.S. Bureau of the Census. 1971a)

————. *Census of Population—General Social and Economic Characteristics.* Final Report PC (1)—C41 Rhode Island. (Washington, D.C.: U.S. Bureau of the Census. 1972b)

————. *Census of Population and Housing 1970—Census Tracts.* Final Report PHC (1)—166 Providence-Pawtucket-Warwick, Rhode Island-Massachusetts SMA. (Washington, D.C.: U.S. Bureau of the Census. 1972c)

STATEWIDE EFFORT TO IMPLEMENT CAREER EDUCATION

Joseph R. Clary

If career education is to make a strong impact within a reasonable time period on a state's educational program, it is essential that a statewide effort be made to implement the concept at the highest educational levels. The effort should be planned, directed and evaluated.

In early 1973, statewide efforts to implement career education still were generally limited to the planning and organizing stages. Pilot and exemplary efforts in career education programs in individual local education agencies were going on in most states. Local programs are receiving exposure in reports and presentations, and descriptions of the many elements of these programs underway deserve your attention. Real *statewide* thrusts in career education might be described as "nearing the launching pad."

This chapter will emphasize the nature of the planning and promotion for statewide efforts for the implementation of career education programs. Some states are already organizing leadership efforts, seeking legislation and funding and planning for evaluation. Examples of these will be described.

PLANNING EFFORTS

In nearly every state educational agency in the United States, major planning efforts for career education were a top priority for 1972 and early 1973. These planning efforts were launched through policy statements and resolutions of state boards of education and/or through the leadership of the chief state school officer. Planning groups generally ranged in size from 5 to 25 persons and were organized as interdisciplinary task forces from the various segments of each state education agency. Membership on the task forces usually represented most of the major divisions in the agency.

The work of the task forces was characterized by: (a) intense study of three to six months, (b) a compilation of career education materials from throughout the country, (c) the use of consultants who were knowledgeable about the concept and who had been involved in or observed pilot or exemplary efforts, (d) visits by individual members or small groups of task force members to observe pilot programs in action or to confer with local and state education officials about the concept, and (e) a written task force report submitted to the state education agency and the state board of education. The final reports proposed direction for that state.

The task force reports dealt with such issues as: definition, assumptions, major goals, major components (curriculum design, professional development, community involvement, teaching materials, equipment and facilities, and evaluation) necessary to implement the goals, roles of the state education agency in implementing career education, and guidelines for implementing career education in local school administrative units.

In *Alabama,* the Career Education Committee working on a state plan was comprised of personnel from each of the five divisions of the State Department of Education, in recognition of the fact that career education is a major goal for all divisions and all levels of the State Department of Education.

The State Advisory Council on Public Elementary and Secondary Education in *Arkansas* selected career education as one of its six priority areas of concern and assigned a Career Education Task Force to present a status report prior to submitting legislative recommendations to the General Assembly.

The Career Education Task Force in *California* has developed a "Career Education Operation Plan" for that state and "working document" guides for the implementation of the concepts of career education. The guides will undergo revision after being tried in local schools. Titles of the guides are: "Early Childhood Education— Pre K;" "Early Childhood Education—Kindergarten;" "Attitude Development—Grade 1;" "Educational Awareness—Grade 2;" "Economic Awareness—Grade 3;" "Career Exploration—Grade 4;" "Career Planning and Decision-Making Skill Development—Grade 5;" "Career Orientation—Junior High;" "Adult Education—Career Exploration;" "Counselor Module;" "Vocational Education Module;" and, "Administrator's Activity Package for Career Education Implementation."

The Career Education Task Force in *Colorado* was composed of representatives from all levels of education, and it also included a base from business, industry, labor, government, and representative community interests. The viewpoints of various minority groups were obtained through varying components both from school personnel and the individuals in supporting agencies.

The target date for implementing career education in every grade in the *Delaware* public schools is September 1976. In the master plan for Delaware Career Education, the State Board of Education declared five priorities: (a) to seek increased state appropriations, (b) to allocate funds for additional career guidance and placement counselors, (c) to expand vocational youth organizations, (d) to develop mobile career counseling centers, and (e) to retrain teachers. A task force has been at work since May 1970 to develop procedures for a comprehensive approach toward statewide implementation.

The State Task Force on Career Education in *Florida,* with membership from each division of the Department of Education, was charged to:

1. Formulate and adapt a written department-wide position on career education in Florida;
2. Assign appropriate responsibilities for career education to each division of the department;
3. Establish a practical procedure for inter-divisional coordination of career education efforts; and,
4. Prepare appropriate information to inform adequately the staff in institutions and school districts, the legislators, and the public.

The *Iowa* Department of Public Instruction has identified the responsibility for the planning, development and implementation for career education in the Area School and Career Education Branch of the agency. The planning function has been initiated by staff in the Career Education Division through modification and revision of the State Plan for Vocational Education now identified as the State Plan for Career Education. In 1970, the modification and redirection was facilitated by involvement of people from various educational backgrounds and training from throughout the state of Iowa. Continued inputs at yearly public hearings, plus results from exemplary and demonstration projects and participation of personnel from local educational agencies have helped interpret the career education concept.

A "Career Education Five-Year Action Plan" has been adopted by the State Board of Education in *Maryland*.

For the purpose of planning for career education, Career Education Planning Districts have been designed in the state of *Michigan*. The 49 districts encompass each K-12 district, intermediate district, area center and community college in the state. The purpose of these planning districts is to increase the local planning efforts in career education in terms of a better articulation among local representatives.

In the *Nebraska* State Department of Education (1972) an interdepartmental Career Education Task Force was organized to serve as a vanguard for career education within the department. As the Task Force analyzed and evaluated the many facets of career education, the decision was made to formulate a position paper on career education that would offer a basis for the development of additional materials and for assistance to facilitate the establishment of career education programs in the schools of Nebraska. The position paper examined the general concept, a rationale, some basic concepts of career education, and components of a career education program. They developed 14 guidelines for implementation to serve as a guide to administrators planning to initiate career education. They are:

1. Organize a career education advisory committee;

2. Promote an understanding, within the advisory committee, of career education;
3. Establish goals and objectives for a local career education program;
4. Build a basic model for a career education program;
5. Analyze the present curriculum to identify elements of career education currently underway;
6. Develop a career education curriculum plan which will expand or build upon desirable career education elements already included in the instructional program;
7. Identify any modifications needed in materials, equipment, facilities, or personnel;
8. Determine what components can be implemented immediately. Establish a time line for implementation of the entire program;
9. Order any materials and equipment needed;
10. Conduct in-service training for the entire school staff and community persons who will assist with the program;
11. Implement the program;
12. Build in an evaluation process;
13. Provide follow-up assistance for teachers;
14. Make any needed revisions.

The *New Hampshire* Department of Education formed a State Planning Committee for Career Education composed of members of all divisions of the Department of Education. Its task was to determine what the state plan would be like in format, scope and content; what tasks must be undertaken; and, the necessary strategies for accomplishing these tasks.

In July of 1972, the *North Carolina* State Board of Education appointed a Task Force on Career Education. The group was composed of 25 members of the state education agency, which is comprised of the department of public instruction, the department of community colleges, and the controller's office. Also included on the Task Force was the executive director of the State Advisory Council on Vocational Education. The Task Force was charged with the responsibility of developing a comprehensive state plan for a program of career education in the public schools of North Carolina from kindergarten through grade 12. The plan was to focus attention on:

1. A definition of career education;
2. The major objectives of a program in career education for North Carolina;
3. Specific roles to be assumed by the various areas and divisions of the state education agency in implementing the program in North Carolina;

4. Identification of the components of the program at various levels in the public schools;
5. Procedures for reorganizing the curriculum and school structure to make the career education concept a part of the total school program;
6. Identification of state and community resources so as to make the program broader than just the school program;
7. Involvement of educators, parents, people in business and industry, etc.;
8. Presentation of the plan to the State Board of Education.

Once the planning efforts have been accepted and adopted by appropriate policy making bodies and statewide implementation agreed upon, state level management of career education becomes a key factor to successful statewide implementation.

Bottoms (1972) in *Georgia* emphasized the importance of state level management for career education:

> The concept of career education cannot materialize, however, unless its implementation is established as a priority by the state board of education.
>
> Priority status for any program is reached when funds are allocated; when personnel is assigned; when necessary regulations and standards pertaining to teacher certification, facilities, textbook adaptation, etc., are changed; when staffing patterns are arranged for the several units in the state department of education to plan together; and when the program becomes a major objective of the several sources of discretionary funds available to the state board of education.
>
> Firm commitment to career education from top management will provide the visibility, stimulus, and status necessary for local and state leaders to see it as a priority.

Bottoms has also suggested a cycle pattern of functions for state level management of career education, shown in Figure 1.

In *Ohio,* the responsibility for planning for career education was delegated by the Department of Education to the Division of Vocational Education. A task force broadly representative of the staff of the Department of Education was organized to spearhead their state's efforts.

The *Texas* Education Agency has developed a series of objectives for implementing career education in that state. It has also developed and published "A Tentative Framework for Developing Comprehensive K-12 Career Education."

Education personnel in the state of *Washington* are working on a five-year plan for career education. It will define career education and spell out some goals and objectives that are to provide guidance in the statewide implementation efforts.

Two invitational workshops were held in *West Virginia* to develop a state guide for career education. The purpose of the state guide was

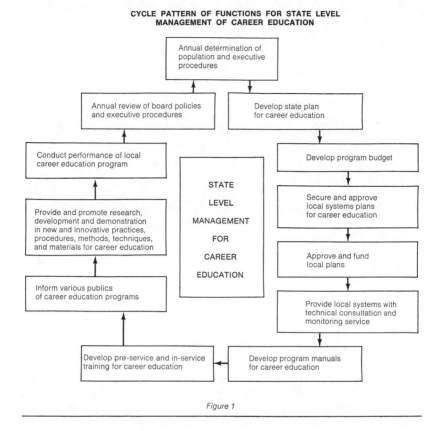

CYCLE PATTERN OF FUNCTIONS FOR STATE LEVEL
MANAGEMENT OF CAREER EDUCATION

Annual determination of
population and executive
procedures

Annual review of board policies
and executive procedures

Develop state plan
for career education

Conduct performance of local
career education program

STATE
LEVEL
MANAGEMENT
FOR
CAREER
EDUCATION

Develop program budget

Provide and promote research,
development and demonstration
in new and innovative practices,
procedures, methods, techniques,
and materials for career education

Secure and approve
local systems plans
for career education

Inform various publics
of career education programs

Approve and fund
local plans

Provide local systems with
technical consultation and
monitoring service

Develop pre-service and in-service
training for career education

Develop program manuals
for career education

Figure 1

to assist local educational agencies in the development of career education programs.

The *Wisconsin* State Department of Public Instruction began its planning efforts in 1970 with the appointment of a State Study Committee for Career Development. The membership of this committee consisted of school counselors, counselor educators, local vocational education coordinators, administrators, and consultants from the State Department of Public Instruction.

PROMOTION

Statewide promotion of career education has taken a number of forms. Governors' conferences, state education agency conferences, in-service workshops, the publication and dissemination of task force reports and state plans, the development of curriculum materials, the efforts of the news media, professional journals, speakers bureaus, multi-media programs and education exhibits are representative of the various types of promotional efforts for career education.

Governors' conferences on career education were held in a number of states during 1972. An invitational conference on career education held in Hot Springs, *Arkansas,* September 21 and 22, 1972, was attended by approximately 275 participants representing business, industry and education. In *Vermont,* promotional activities for career education began with a governors' conference. This was followed by five regional conferences in the state. Governors' conferences were also held in *New Hampshire* and *Tennessee.*

A "Governor's Lay Conference in Career Education" was held in *Maryland,* May 1972. In June, the Maryland State Department of Education Professional Conference had as its theme "Career Education." Regional conferences are also being held. Releases to the news media are constantly being made. A slide-tape presentation of the state's activity in career education is being prepared.

In *Florida,* a statewide conference was held for selected business-men, educators, legislators, and representatives of governmental and proprietary agencies, organizations and institutions to inform them of the concepts, ideas and proposed outcomes of career education programs. Following this, district and county conferences were held for the purpose of acquainting the decision makers with the concepts and proposed programs in career education.

Other states have held statewide conferences on career education to make people aware of the concept. These states include: *South Dakota, Delaware, Florida, Michigan, Ohio, Alaska, Oklahoma* and *Indiana.* Some states have promoted the concept of career education through a series of statewide in-service workshops. These include the states of *Washington, Delaware,* and *Colorado.*

In a proposal to establish a *Nevada* Department of Education Career Education Steering Committee, the following goals were included in a strategy for dissemination and implementation:

1. A large scale program to inform and "sell" the public;
2. Technical assistance in school districts and individual schools required in understanding career education, relating it to current practice, and devising specific curriculum plans that adapt the concept to the local setting;
3. Developing curriculum and career education instructional materials, manuals, etc.;
4. Programs of in-service training for department personnel. They must become experts;
5. Methodological programs of in-service and pre-service training to be designed and initiated by the department in co-operation with school districts and the universities;

6. Setting priorities in allocating federal funds for effort in career education;
7. Collecting information and disseminating it among participating schools;
8. Evaluation.

The *Arizona* Department of Education has developed several slide presentations for viewing by groups and organizations around that state. A brochure, "Career Education in Arizona," has been printed and distributed. Numerous feature stories have appeared in the local newspapers. A career education television series is being produced for airing on local educational stations.

The *North Carolina* State Department of Public Instruction has developed a slide-tape presentation to assist in promoting the concept of career education throughout North Carolina.

ORGANIZATION

The organization of statewide career education efforts begins with the designation of one or more persons within the state education agency to provide leadership for these efforts. A major role for this person or group is that of coordinating the efforts and expertise of personnel within the state agency.

The State Superintendent of Education in *Louisiana* named an assistant superintendent for career education who is to develop and coordinate all activities related to career education. A career education consultant, directly responsible to the Office of the Commissioner of Education, has been designated in *New Hampshire.*

The organization designated for statewide administration of career education in *Ohio* is the Division of Vocational Education with assistant directors of that division responsible for the K-10 development.

In *Texas,* the assistant commissioner for regional services was assigned the responsibility for implementing career education. By the summer of 1973, a minimum of five school districts in each regional education service center should have developed specific plans for the implementation of career education in their schools.

The *Vermont* State Department of Education has organized teams to work with local districts in the following areas: (a) department leadership training; (b) resource materials; (c) budget processes; (d) local leadership training; (e) educational television; (f) inquiries, meetings, presentations; (g) in-service and implementation; and, (h) evaluation and service.

In the state of *Washington,* three people have been identified as career education specialists. Their titles are: supervisor of career education, state board for community colleges; career education specialist for the coordinating council for occupational education; and, the state supervisor of career education for the superintendent of public instruction.

A coordinator of career education was designated in *Wyoming* and other members of the Instructional Services Division of the Department of Education will serve as consultants to local districts to assist them in planning and implementing programs in career development.

Other states in which a person has been designated to coordinate statewide efforts in career education include *Montana, Missouri, Colorado,* and *Wisconsin.*

State Advisory Groups

In the state of *Washington,* a State Advisory Committee for Career Education has been organized. The *Pennsylvania* Department of Education has a career education advisory committee that has developed a definition for career education, established goals and objectives, and established a state plan for career education.

Other Techniques

In *Alabama,* the State Board of Education has adopted resolutions to extend the Course of Study Committee to include three persons representing career education. The Board has also approved adding a representative to the State Textbook Committee to represent career education. Thus, most state educational agencies have begun to "gear up" for statewide efforts to implement career education.

LEGISLATION

Few states have enacted legislation dealing with career education or appropriated funds specifically for it. However, the need for such legislation is being studied.

Arizona has made a substantial commitment to career education. In 1971, the Arizona Legislature, first in the nation to enact specific legislation with a major appropriation for career education, set aside 1.9 million dollars.

On June 29, 1971, House Resolution 11.65, Session of 1971, authorized the Speaker of the House of Representatives of the General Assembly of *Pennsylvania* to appoint a committee of 11 members of the House to "explore the concept of career education." The committee, headed by Representative Roland Greenfield, was directed "to ascertain what changes are necessary to make this area of education more relevant and (to) make recommendations to correct the present situation. . . ." The Committee was also directed to "report its findings together with recommendations for appropriate legislation as soon as possible." The House committee, in conducting its hearings, in the taking of testimony, and in conducting studies, concerned itself with the following questions:

1. What is the present situation in education which calls for correction?
2. What is meant by "career education?"
3. What recommendations should it make in order "to make this area of education more relevant . . . and to correct the present situation?"

Representative Roland Greenfield's education committee held a series of hearings across the commonwealth to enable any interested person or group of persons to speak on the topic of career education. House Bill 2574 was the result of his committee deliberations. This bill died in committee during the December 1972 legislative session. However, there are plans to resurrect it.

A comprehensive Career Education Bill will be introduced in the forthcoming session of the *Michigan* Legislature to include such items as a mandate for local occupational advisory committees, a State Career Education Advisory Council, career education planning districts, youth job placement services, the requirements for career education in each school district, and professional development pertaining to career education.

A resolution supporting career education will be introduced in the next session of the *Montana* State Legislature.

In 1963, through the efforts of interested members of the *North Carolina* State Legislature, an act, known as the Clark-Long bill, established funds for instituting in the public schools of North Carolina, a program of "Comprehensive and Diversified Vocational Education." One part of this program developed into a course called "Introduction to Vocational Education." The course was concerned with providing occupational information for ninth grade boys and girls as a basis for making better and more appropriate decisions concerning their vocational futures and determining the educational requirements and opportunities associated with these decisions. In 1969, under the leadership of former Governor Robert W. Scott, three million dollars was appropriated by the General Assembly for the purpose of developing a career exploration program for the middle grades of the public school system.

FUNDING

To the present time most of the funding for statewide career education planning and pilot efforts has come from federal vocational education monies. As states begin to implement truly statewide efforts, many have indicated that there will be a continued use of vocational education monies. However, these are to be supplemented with redirected state appropriations, additional appropriations from state legislatures, the use of educational funds from federal appropriations other than those available for vocational education, foundation funds, and other sources still to be identified.

In 1971, the *Arizona* Legislature appropriated 1.9 million dollars for career education. In the current fiscal year, the state appropriation for career education is 3.8 million dollars. The money largely has been directed to fund career education projects around the state—experimental projects at the K-12 grade levels that are exploring various ways of implementing career education concepts.

The state of *Delaware* has received a grant for $345,000 to start designing a model system for effectively integrating academic and vocational education. Efforts are being made for Delaware to become a model state for career education.

In *Florida,* the 1973 session of the State Legislature will be requested to appropriate 5.6 million dollars to establish a career education program in each of the 67 school districts of Florida. Regular state sources of funding may also be used. A reallocation of existing resources may be used to achieve career education objectives.

The *Louisiana* State Legislature appropriated one million dollars in its 1972 regular session to implement career education programs. The funds are to be utilized for purposes of providing resources for implementing new thrusts in educational programs designed with objectives directed toward the development of occupational awareness activities, career orientation and meaningful exploration experiences, job preparation programs, placement opportunities, and retraining and/or upgrading instructional efforts.

The General Assembly in *Missouri* is being asked to appropriate funds to assist local educational agencies in the development of their concepts of career education. A budget request for statewide implementation of career education is also being made in the state of *Washington.*

Present funding of programs in *Wisconsin* includes funds from ESEA Title III, from the Vocational Education Act, and from local school budgets.

EVALUATION

Evaluation efforts, to date, have centered around the evaluating of exemplary programs. Most state departments of education are assisting local education agencies to develop evaluation procedures for career education exemplary programs. It is expected that these will provide a nucleus for statewide evaluation efforts.

The *North Carolina* Career Education Task Force discussed a general framework for evaluation:

> Evaluation by school personnel is concerned with finding what is done in the school with students and how change may be brought about to

help them realize their potentials as completely as possible. The evaluation process should be guided by the objectives for learners as outlined in a comprehensive curriculum plan. The evaluation of the sum total of the learners' progress can be directly related to the school's progress in planning and accreditation.

With a career education emphasis in the curriculum, a variety of techniques of evaluation must be used to determine its effectiveness. In essence this evaluation is evaluation of the entire curriculum. We have traditionally used formal tests, usually of a standardized and written nature, as the main instrument of evaluation. More and more we must include other forms of evaluation, including use of interviews, anecdotal records, experience diaries, check lists, and other forms of informal tests. Even with informal tests, however, there must be a common format and uniformity of application. Teachers, in particular, need to know a great deal about evaluation and how to use specific evaluative techniques.

There is a need to go beyond measuring of information learned and skills acquired. There is concern with the kinds of habits and attitudes children are forming. The question of concepts, thinking ability, interests, appreciations, and personal adjustment must be considered. Additionally, the extent to which the student is using and applying knowledge and skills must be evaluated.

Finally, we must remember that the *primary* purpose of evaluation is the improvement of teaching and learning (North Carolina Department of Public Instruction, 1973).

SUMMARY

Statewide efforts to implement career education appear to incorporate one or more of the following elements:

1. Commitment by state board of education;
2. Recognition of career education as a major priority;
3. Involvement by total educational agency;
4. Planning coordinated through an interdisciplinary task force;
5. Development of a state plan (or master plan) for career education. The state plans (or task force reports) deal with such issues as: definition, assumptions, major goals, major components necessary to implement the goals (curriculum design, professional development, community involvement, teaching materials, equipment and facilities, and evaluation), roles of the state agency in implementing career education, and guidelines for implementing career education in local school administrative units;
6. Promotional efforts for career education on a massive statewide basis. These included such things as governors' conferences, regional conferences, statewide in-service workshops, newspaper features, radio and television programs, and brochures;
7. Designation of specific responsibility for leadership and coordination of career education efforts. In some states responsibility for this has been assigned to a single individual, in

other states to a committee, and in others to a division within the state agency;

8. Legislation being sought to give legal status to career education activities at all levels;

9. Funding for career education from new and additional appropriations from state legislatures, federal funds, redirection of current funds, and/or allocations of existing resources;

10. Evaluation plans written into state plans for career education.

REFERENCES

Bottoms, Gene. "State Level Management for Career Education." *American Vocational Journal.* XLII, (March, 1972)

Nebraska State Department of Education. "Career Education: A Position Paper." (Lincoln, Nebraska: Nebraska State Department of Education. 1972)

North Carolina Department of Public Instruction. "Career Education: A Report of the North Carolina Career Education Task Force." (Raleigh, North Carolina: North Carolina Department of Public Instruction. 1973)

IMPLEMENTATION OF
CAREER EDUCATION IN
A LOCAL EDUCATION AGENCY

Jerry C. Olson

It is inevitable that general and vocational education be combined by local education agencies, though cautiously, to face the demands placed on individual students in the 70s. Career education marries the functional components relative to students, personnel, resources, facilities and programs. It exists as a catalyst to prod, steer and encourage early initiative. More importantly, disbelievers in the marriage and rigid humanist proponents may become tolerant, if not supportive, of educational efforts that teach someone to become "a mechanic" as well as how to become "a person."

The fact that the career education movement has been sponsored by the Commissioner of Education's office and endorsed by President Nixon does not guarantee success. Educational leaders must "make it happen." Leadership should be utilized wherever it can be found to produce resounding success stories. The development of model components that can be put together in different configurations by others is essential. The problem obviously involves deep-seated principles. Therefore, practical solutions that have implications for the "total educational process" in local education agencies must be provided.

The overriding implication for public education goes beyond implementing better school career programs and services. In fact, it charges the public education sector to find better ways of insuring that career programs and services are more productive, and that results are observable. To accomplish this large task along with the myriad of other responsibilities directed toward the public schools, the author suggests the following three steps:

1. A critical outside examination of the career goals and expectations for the public schools.
2. A critical inside examination about what exists, what has to be done, and creative alternatives for producing change.
3. An on-going evaluation that responds to the goals, and measures the effectiveness of the approaches.

Several comments about items 1 and 3 will allow the major theme of this presentation to be placed into perspective. First, outside critics of the public school system generally perceive the schools as nonproductive because they (a) provide too rigid a curriculum; (b) impose a set of values; or, (c) operate as a social regime. Positive direction and the use of goal-setting techniques by spirited non-professionals can launch a new era of rising expectations for career education. Parent/student groups have certain expectations for schools. They can have a great influence on what is taught in schools. It is essential that they be better informed. They sometimes fail to understand the place of school in the real world. Too often, they are looking for simple solutions rather than a range of viable alternatives.

Educators must become alert to the standards that the business/industry community is applying to schools. The standards must be explicitly stated and understood by those outside and inside education for progressive change to occur.

Second, continuous evaluation and upgrading techniques are essential in career education. Inappropriate and irrelevant programs and services are not only unproductive, they also discourage the expenditure of the time and energy needed to develop sound career goals. Any irrationality prevalent in today's career education programs and services must be overcome by the work of insightful and knowledgeable people who establish goals, set priorities (program and monetary), and constantly evaluate results. Poor, inefficient and nonproductive programs and services in career education cannot and will not be tolerated by the new generation of local school administrators.

A CRITICAL EXAMINATION FROM INSIDE

Far too many educators have been taught to accommodate themselves to the existing profession, not to improve it. A critical process and product evaluation must be consciously and consistently applied in education. To effect this approach in career education, educators must have requisite skills and knowledge relating to the field as well as an understanding of the overall objectives. The educator must become more self-critical and, therefore, more concerned with the improvement of his own performance.

The internal communication networks required to eliminate fragmentation and duplication will also assist in ordering priorities and in placing the responsibilities for career education. More importantly, the human element must pervade education. Students' feelings, anxieties and self-expectations precede concern about their career and career preparations. These elements must be dealt with by educators who set out to help others fulfill career expectations through educational programs.

Program reform seldom holds enduring promise if new policies are developed and imposed in detail only by top management or outsiders. The reform program in a local education agency must be developed from within. Leadership cannot be conferred by directive, it can only be earned by competence. There are many who argue that large institutions such as education cannot reform. It is suggested here that it must because the alternatives are unacceptable. The author is convinced that professional educators are prepared to take an exhaustive and objective look at themselves and their institutions. Local education agencies are in the best position to arrive at a comprehensive modernization program, utilizing career education as a catalyst. A reform program developed from within, utilizing the task force method, would be more readily acceptable to the professional establishment.

A COMPILATION OF IDEAS

There are two factors that should contribute to the success of program reform from within. First, there already exists a compilation of ideas and recommendations for reform on which a local education agency task force can draw. These are available from a series of imaginative studies—still largely unacted upon—performed by innovators, program designers and university curriculum/research personnel. Practical programs that identify components relevant to the requirements of local schools are needed.

Second, there appears to be a significant change in the attitude of professionals in the field. This change is symbolized by new efforts to individualize teacher-counseling methods, such as: individual counseling systems, career information retrieval systems, computerized scheduling, teacher-advisory programs, student social-environment programs, demonstration-unit models, individually prescribed instruction, simulation and gaming techniques, programmed learning, integrated instructional systems, automated library systems, information retrieval systems, computer-assisted instruction, closed circuit T.V. instruction, multi-media instruction, and individual study carrels.

There is a call for reform and administrators are being asked to look at themselves and their institutions with a new objectivity. This does not mean disparagement. Objectivity recognizes that many educational institutions are often slow to adapt to change, especially in the dimensions of relevant education for all students. Traditional educational programs have allowed practitioners to define their role narrowly and rely heavily on sensitivity and intuition acquired through personal experience. With the reentry of progressive humanistic approaches and the rapid growth of educational technology, traditional education has come to an end. Such advances have not only added to the agenda of education, but they have the capacity to change the character of the educational profession.

American education is at the crossroads of decision; a unified and coherent national policy in career education must be forthcoming. The danger exists that educational promises will be discordant and resulting programs at cross purposes. To prevent this, national program efforts in career education must take the lead in formulating and executing exemplary undertakings in local education agencies.

ADMINISTRATIVE REFORM

In spite of outstanding achievements by individual administrative practitioners at all levels, administrative performance has sometimes been disappointing. A principal cause appears to be weak management capability. Because of the diversity, complexity and demands of today's educational system, effective coordination calls for a wide range of management skills and management tools. The traditional reliance on experience and intuition is no longer sufficient. Administrators have never entirely succeeded in overcoming the strong pressures for conformity without a dulling of creativity. Often they have been guilty of excessive caution and tended to defend established policy and programs. Administrators have not always been able to surmount adequately the spirit of parochialism that has tended to isolate the local education agency. These factors have all contributed to the weakness in management capability that must become the principal item for administrative reform. Education in the 70s requires a new breed of educational manager equipped with up-to-date techniques and backed by a system organized on modern management principles.

IMPROVED ADMINISTRATIVE PLANNING ROLES

An important step in equipping the system to improve career education coordination is to give operational managers a greater capacity to relate resources to the objectives of the instructional programs. A clear identification of the goals and priorities is essential to establish a sounder basis for decision making, the allocation of funds, and the resolution of issues. Procedures for more systematic identification of educational goals and determining priorities among these goals must be devised. Policy objectives flowing from a needs assessment must be followed by plans and policies that respond to these objectives.

If decisions are to be made with greater awareness of the established policy and goals, a process of needs assessment, administrative planning functions and decision making must be greatly strengthened. A strong planning function that looks beyond the present preoccupation with day-to-day issues is essential to system-wide administrators. Educational decisions must not be the result of a series of piecemeal tactical decisions forced by the pressure of events. Problems must be considered before they become emergencies with responses being made on a crisis basis.

STRENGTHENED DECISION MAKING

Administrators need a stronger capacity to identify and analyze the key issues of education and to determine the relative degree of urgency and importance among these issues. They also need to strengthen their procedures for considering alternative courses of action. Another important requirement is to establish procedures for linking policy analysis to resource management to insure that resources (personnel and money) are allocated in accordance with policy requirements. Education's most serious weakness could well be its inability to link resource allocation to policy analysis.

The decision-making process would be strengthened with an improved evaluation capacity permitting the follow-up of policy decisions to determine how effectively they have been carried out. This would also allow a continuous reexamination of decisions in the light of changing circumstances to determine whether decisions are still appropriate or whether they need to be modified.

ADMINISTRATIVE SPECIALIZATION

To reform the educational system, administrative responsibilities center on the performance of three specific roles—developing, administering and facilitating. The principle of functional specialization as applied to career counseling, assignment practices and management development is essential to increase managerial effectiveness. It is clear that this is an age of specialization and educational administration can no longer escape the consequences. Each of the three management personnel functions as described in a local educational administrators management model (system management personnel—within the school system; operational management personnel—within the school; program management personnel—within the classroom) serve developing, administering and facilitating roles. (See Figure 1.)

The model is based on the premise that three general managerial functions (to develop, to administrate, to facilitate) are performed "within the system," "within the school," and "within the classroom." However, different responsibilities are performed by personnel designated under the three groupings. Personnel "within the system" include the superintendent, assistant superintendents and central office staff responsible for educational programs across the system. Personnel "within the school" are typically principals responsible for the management of a school building. Personnel "within the classroom" represent a composite of people directly responsible for programs impacting on students. The latter is comprised of a new configuration of program staff including professional teachers, paraprofessionals and student service persons such as counselors, social workers, mental health workers and medical personnel. The process and responsibilities for each are different and each must be clearly defined and evaluation criteria established to insure a more responsive performance. By defining functions and responsibilities and assigning potential management leaders to varied positions over a period of time, educational leaders should soon witness fewer "unidimensional" school managers. See Figure 2 for an indication of the personnel responsibilities required to effect an educational reform system. The interrelationship of developing, administering and facilitating roles is graphically depicted in Figure 3.

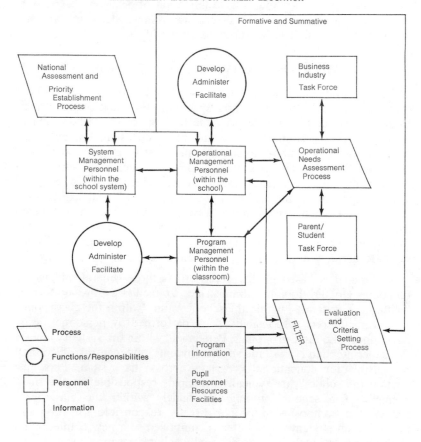

**A LOCAL EDUCATIONAL ADMINISTRATORS
MANAGEMENT MODEL FOR CAREER EDUCATION**

Figure 1

PERSONNEL RESPONSIBILITIES TO IMPACT AN EDUCATIONAL REFORM SYSTEM IN CAREER EDUCATION

	System Management Personnel (Within the School System)	Operational Management Personnel (Within the School)	Program Management Personnel (Within the Classroom)
DEVELOP	**Leadership Role** Include dynamic people who are responsible for the grand design, mission and the great plan calling for a change and progress, through a chain-like sequence of relevant and integrated events that serve as stepping stones. They have the capability to change the character and direction of the organization by initiating activities born of imagination and a sense of mission.	Communicate with system management personnel regarding changes in objectives, strategies or priorities as a result of an analysis and evaluation of program and service conduct in the system. Utilize "the plan" to be implemented adapt operational procedures that will facilitate the production of end results.	Suggest overall priorities, strategies or objective changes and new plans to operational management personnel. Develop activities and new plans to emerge in the process of solving specific problems, ascertaining causes and searching for alternative solutions.
ADMINISTER	Delegate a sizable amount of responsibility to operational personnel, but measure the program details against priority, sequence and timing of steps established in the developmental steps. Also utilize community resources as a check and balance to measure the effectiveness of the administration of programs and services.	**Leadership Role** Efficient people execute change warranted by the situation and appropriateness to the organization. They operate in terms of responding to active needs by working through community channels that can be handled by immediate adjustments in the program design, allocation of resources via the assignment, training and development of staff.	Report the details and results of the hourly and daily schedule to operational management personnel, suggests changes in staffing, allocation of resources, and facilities that would enhance the program.
FACILITATE	Delegate a majority of th s responsibility to program management personnel who perform the major task of facilitating program and services that impact on students. Motivate, measure global results and recommend corrective actions that will enhance the facilitation process.	Coordinate the program and service components that impact on individual students and fulfill the goals of the task. Evaluate the organizational structure in light of individual personalities and their ability to work together effectively and efficiently to serve students. Adjust resources and procedures when conclusions and judgments call for change in policies.	**Leadership Role** Purposeful people work with others to bring programs and services directly to students. They exhibit an ability to make major innovations in bringing program and service delivery by assuming responsibility beyond their discipline. They take risks by breaking from tradition and seeing a broader or higher purpose to which the educational system, and they personally, may become devoted. That is, they provide relevant and integrated programs that serve the individual needs of each student on an hour-to-hour, day-to-day basis.

Figure 2

**PERSONNEL RESPONSIBILITIES AND RELATIONSHIP
TO IMPACT AN EDUCATIONAL REFORM SYSTEM**

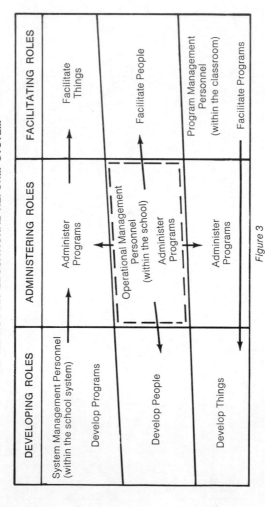

Figure 3

A MANAGEMENT MODEL

Coupling these roles with the concepts illustrated in Figure 1, the responsibilities are described in following sections.

Developing Objectives

System management personnel within the school system will establish exemplary career education programs and test innovative methods at all levels of the system through (a) identifying community needs and requests; (b) surveying the current labor market; and (c) surveying the current facilities, program offerings, enrollment patterns and instructional methods of the school district.

Administering Objectives

Operational management personnel within the school will "operationalize" the development of career education programs and facilities in line with technological change both in education and in the labor market by defining and outlining supervisory and administrative direction, control and evaluation for program implementation. Identification of systematic procedures for determining financial status and related operational services will be made by maintaining inventory of all educational material, physical facilities and program participation comprising the program. Operational management personnel reevaluate the purpose, structure and functioning to meet stated goals. The manager may replace old objectives with new, may reorganize the structure, or may create new positions to meet the challenge of these recent events. The main responsibility is to facilitate the development of the student.

Facilitating Objectives

Program management personnel within the classroom will coordinate all career education programs, activities and services, and organize an instructional system to provide individualized programs and services for all students, grades K-12. Instructional resources, facilities and program personnel will be managed in such a way that effective results are produced. The identification and interpretation of duties that can be carried on by program managers utilizing various techniques to discharge responsibilities and evaluate effectiveness will be continually made.

A close examination of responsibilities reveals "interfunctional" relationships particularly in the area of utilizing broad managerial skills. These are clearly "core skills" of management leadership (such as, the ability to negotiate, to observe facts and situations clearly and to report them precisely and concisely, and to adapt readily to new situations) that must be exhibited in the performance of any functional leader. Educational managers should have and continue to develop the following personal qualities and core skills:

1. *Leading*

   Communicate precisely, concisely and promptly both orally and in writing.

   Inspire confidence and respect.

   Delegate and coordinate.

   Encourage performance.

   Organize the work and set priorities.

   Exercise authority.

2. *Observing*

   Observe and perceive facts and situations.

   Select the relevant.

   Analyze and synthesize.

   Identify, plan and direct the use of resources needed to achieve policy goals.

3. *Negotiating*

   Perceive human motivation.

   Persuade and develop agreement.

   Anticipate.

   Apply critical intelligence to issues on which one is not expert.

4. *Adapting*

   Respond to unfamiliar situations (cultures and values).

   Accept discipline.

   Weigh diverse considerations in many areas.

Through experience in operating in various roles, the career education manager must remain flexible as he performs responsibilities relating to the school system, the school and the classroom. All concerned with implementing career education should be kept constantly attuned to the need for change by leading a wide variety of problem-oriented groups.

Often, system management personnel within the school system find themselves engaged in both staff and line functions. The purpose of the model is to define specific functions and responsibilities and establish an organizational rationale that supports the concepts of career education in the system, in the schools and in the classroom.

One of the important aspects of this model is that it allows personnel functioning in all three areas to engage in program planning and creative innovation, as well as perform overall administrative and facilitation duties. It also allows for the analysis, collection and synthesis of data for research purposes. Too many administrators spend the majority of their time reacting to crisis situations. Such behavior prevents the fulfillment of the myriad of responsibilities that must be assumed in effectively executing program responsibilities.

Many important issues could be resolved through utilization of the proposed model and organization chart. Briefly, they might be stated as follows:

1. Time could be spent in the development of new programs.
2. Research could be undertaken for the analysis and modification of existing programs.
3. Information concerning career education could be communicated to the disadvantaged community, the community-at-large, the industrial community, the department of public instruction, other school districts in the state and school districts throughout the United States.
4. The model would allow for concentrated and innovative communication with industry, in order to ascertain the relevancy of the current educational program and relatedness to major labor demands and projected labor demands. In this manner, programs may be added, modified or, in some cases, deleted.

LOOKING AHEAD

It is imperative that functions and responsibilities be identified at the start if career education is to be successful in any school district. The statements of philosophy and rationale for career education are becoming clear, but the task ahead is to implement the philosophy and to sensitize those concerned at the professional and nonprofessional levels with the problems that must be attacked and overcome. For example, a great many management problems will surface when placing any one of the following programs or activities into operation:

1. Exploratory programs.
2. Diagnostic and pre-vocational experiences.
3. Occupational information and counseling programs.
4. Health programs.
5. Post-graduate programs of all types.
6. Utilization of existing vocational-technical facilities in different time sequences.
7. Expansion of skill-centered activities for the hard-core unemployed and underemployed.
8. Extensive work in occupation analysis, job clusters and spin-off levels of placement.
9. Modification of cooperative work experience programs and creation of new ones.
10. Implementation and management of modularized time periods.
11. Definition of the role and composition of advisory committees.

12. Implementation of new instructional teaching methods.

INFORMATION SYSTEM

It is clear that a carefully planned information system, which has as its basic task the communication of activities relating to career education, is necessary. Most public information sections are engaged in sending information out but it is often not understood, misinterpreted, or has little meaning to the receiver. Continuous follow-up and reinforcement activities are essential to true communication activities.

The system will require not only a system for dispersing information, but also a system for data collection. The system must send people on policy-making levels to various sectors of the community in order to communicate the activities, as well as to accumulate data for program modification and development. Some major area considerations would be information exchanges with:

1. Business/industry community.
2. Parent/student community.
3. Other divisions of the school district.
4. Counselors within the school district.
5. Individual school principals and school administrators.
6. Academic instructors.
7. Supervisors in other divisions.
8. Board of education members.
9. Department of public instruction.
10. Federal agencies in education and labor.
11. Other school districts in the state.
12. School districts in major urban centers.

CHANGES IN APPROACH

In all too many cases, instructors continue to teach in the same manner they were teaching 20 years ago, although program developments are in diametric opposition to these ways of teaching and of viewing people. There must be a synthesis of program and curriculum development in order to bring about the marriage of developmental concepts and curriculum modification.

The body of knowledge presented in each discipline, on an individual subject schedule basis, must be identified by function. This enables individual student programs to be prescribed by crossing discipline lines. Because of the functions to be taught and competencies of teachers, the traditional use of year-long courses is no longer possible in all cases and approval is needed for subjects that are shorter than a year in duration. It is no longer necessary to label a student "general," "academic," or "vocational," or likewise, "business," "trade and industry," or "home economics." A single diploma for the entire school system with an accompanying document showing the competencies and achievement for each student, regardless of his interest and abilities, can become a communications vehicle in its own right.

Hopefully, this model will allow management personnel in a local education agency to gain perspective, establish priorities, improve techniques and ultimately achieve a greater satisfaction from implementing career education. In addition, it is hoped that those educators presently in administrative roles will maintain an interested but critical attitude, and conscientiously point out, to their students and community, changes and accomplishments made through career education. Educators must each be able to answer the basic questions: (a) What can I expect myself to do in implementing career education? (b) What management processes can I use to organize career education programs within the system, within the school, and within the classroom? and, (c) What techniques can I use to evaluate the effectiveness of career education programs?

Essentially, facilitating teams assigned to schools would have responsibility for interfacing programs and students. Through the utilization of this method, program management personnel could be used more efficiently, as their realm of responsibility would rest primarily in the program implementation areas. Others would be able to devote more energy to program development and administrative functions. It is felt that this would free facilitators to work more closely on instructional techniques with teachers, and on program organization with principals. They would also have an opportunity to undertake an in depth analysis of ongoing programs, and to assist in developing programs.

Placing many of these components together, the goals of implementing career education programs in any district may be "capstoned" as follows:

1. Institute, for all students in the district, a career education program that considers the interests and demands of all communities affecting educational programming.

2. Design and implement career education programs that prepare and enable all individuals to assimilate the mobile patterns of work and technology operating in the economic and social communities of today.

3. Develop educational facilities that are "responsive" to the dynamic technologies inherent in the business/industrial community as well as the educational community.

PROGRAM INFORMATION DATA CHAIN MODEL

A budget expenditure accounting report system is essential to determine systematically the costs for implementing career education. (See Figure 4.) The most essential elements in the information chain are contained in facts, in each data cell, that allow: (a) problems to be anticipated; (b) pertinent questions to be asked; and (c) informational data from various cells to be combined to answer specific programming changes essential for implementing a career education program. The magnitude of collecting essential facts to determine program implementation costs and to make pertinent decisions at critical points in school systems with thousands of students requires the use of computer resources. It is essential that the ingredients and facts needed to make decisions regarding programming be identified. They would allow development of a system for collecting raw data to be used in formulating usable data in the various data cells.

In addition to examining the chain of information to determine costs and make program decisions, additional implementation process costs must also be considered. The activities and costs fall into three major categories of communication, adaptation and overhead costs. The process and costs of communications center on the task of conducting a communication analysis, and performing internal, external and inter-communication efforts. Adaptation contains a series of uncertain costs regarding the achievement of goals. The costs are uncertain because the variables introduced in achieving stated goals are dependent on individual viewpoints and value systems that lead to negotiations, the search for alternatives and the process of organizational learning.

Costs incurred in the implementation process may be viewed as overhead. Out of necessity, many presently operational systems (purchasing, inventorying, accounting, personnel) will require alterations or complete overhaul. These are classified as "red tape costs" even though in the long run such procedures may actually reduce unnecessary delaying steps. Featherbedding costs will likely occur and must become a budgeted item to provide funds to accommodate the misfits in the new program. Ideally, all personnel would be able to adapt to the new goals and divert their energies toward reaching new career education objectives. Realistically, varying degrees of acceptance from personnel must be anticipated. Critical positions must be covered with "sold" personnel, with nonsupporters placed in positions where the system can devote both time, effort and dollars into changing actions, attitudes and behavior.

Organizational slack refers to costs that will be incurred in the process of continually examining problems and infusing new operational ideas into the system to attack the problems. It will be essen-

PROGRAM INFORMATION
DATA CHAIN MODEL IDENTIFYING COSTS TO IMPLEMENT $$$$
CAREER EDUCATION

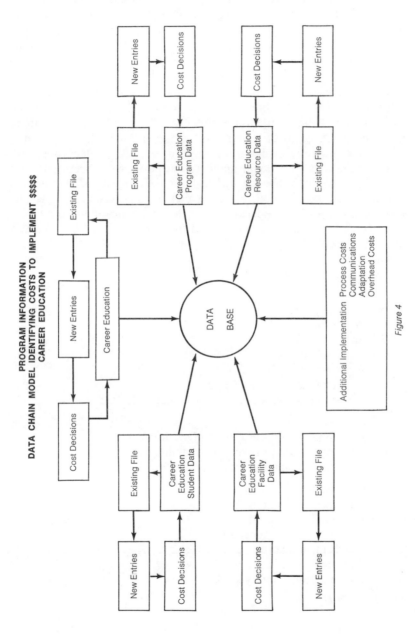

Figure 4

tial for certain employees to devote a considerable amount of their time and efforts into "dreaming" activities that provide alternatives at the operational level. These costs, which include examining research data and assessing program facts, will strengthen the efforts toward goals but will entail costs that may or may not be budgeted in the present operation of the local education agency.

The data base, as defined in the data chain chart, must contain information and facts about students, personnel, resources, facilities and programs. Program information from each cell will be infused into the filter process of evaluation and criteria setting. Both formative and summative evaluations, in turn, are distributed to system management and operational management personnel. (See Figure 1.) Each local education agency will have an existing file of information that provides factual input for each cell. In all likelihood, new and additional entries will be needed in each local education agency. The completeness of each existing file and the number of new entries will mean that costs will vary considerably from district to district. Following are a list of variables by data cell that illustrate by examples.

Student Data
Full name
Date of birth
Age
Sex
Nationality
Place of residence
Name of parent or guardian
Name and address of the school where enrolled

Personnel Data
Personnel within the system (Developers)
Personnel within the school (Administrators)
Personnel within the school room (Facilitators)

Resource Data
Technical assistance
Information processing
Information management
Needs identification
Research
Organization stability

Facility Data
Building
Equipment
Maintenance
Space modification

Program Data
    Curriculum
    Supplemental teaching materials
    Supplemental learning materials
    Supplemental supportive materials

A computerized system for collecting "data base" facts to be utilized in decision making appears to be the most efficient, accurate mechanism in any large local education agency. The system should be designed to help personnel do their jobs better; not eliminate jobs, or the people in them. While it is true that jobs may be altered somewhat in their content, most will still be necessary. People are absolutely essential in all components of the model for managing the implementation of career education programs. The utilization of career education as a vehicle for renewing efforts that combine what educators know about children, learning, the climate of learning and the characteristics that foster good teaching must center on people and on the management of a delivery system.

In conclusion, the proposed model for career education is based on identifying responsibilities that personnel involved in the process are to perform. Decisions that influence effectiveness are made daily by personnel functioning "within the system," "within the school" and "within the classroom." If each is to be accountable for his decisions, he must know what he is to do; have some idea of how to begin the task; and, then adapt, adjust, and alter plans to "free" individual learners. Developers, who function from a system-wide base, provide the leadership that can make public service technology work and do so by facing their challenge and by concentrating on people. Decisions that directly affect the student must be made by facilitators who work closely with him and know him best. Administrators are the personnel who expand and contract to provide a learning environment designed to further learning for each individual student.

Perhaps the key lies in viewing the educational enterprise as a person. Research studies reveal that all work and no play makes one dull indeed. Well-rounded individuals, people who live life more towards the hilt, are those who manage to combine a rewarding work life with a self-actualized and a vibrant nonwork existence. Perhaps, career education is an attempt for education to find self-fulfillment as an institution. All the ingredients of a successful marriage have always existed in the public school system. The marked trend toward activism and the study of the world that surrounds man, dictate that a response be forthcoming in both quality and quantity through involvement by many professional "decision makers" within the system.

perspectives on career education

Elementary Schools, Secondary Schools, Area Vocational Schools, Rural Schools, Urban Schools, Postsecondary Institutions, Colleges and Universities, Teachers, Counselors, and Organized Labor

In the final analysis, career education will succeed or fail in institutional settings because of those who conduct the educational programs. Many practitioner roles and educational levels are represented in Part Five, a compendium of important perspectives.

Topougis, career education director in an urban school system, explains how the elementary school must concentrate on developing student self-awareness and occupational awareness.

Dixon, a city high school principal, stresses the importance of a team effort by teachers, counselors, and administrators to effect a comprehensive career education program in the secondary school.

Fitch, an area vocational school superintendent, delineates the unique role of the area vocational school in providing individuals with opportunities for occupational preparation.

Hardin, a school district superintendent, describes how a rural community has begun to implement career education.

Gillie, a professor, proposes a career education program for postsecondary institutions that provides a common core followed by job placement and concurrent skill development.

Fite, a university president, traces the history of career education in colleges and universities, describes articulation between secondary schools and higher education, and identifies the concerns of college faculty members faced with emphasis on career education. In addition to explaining how higher education can contribute to individual career development, he emphasizes the responsibility of higher education to prepare personnel for a role in career education as a teacher, counselor, or administrator.

Robinson, a high school cooperative office education coordinator, presents her own and others' views on career education. She makes an appeal for a concerted effort to implement career education.

Richins, a counselor, cites the need for improvement in guidance programs and development of the counselor's role. He suggests that career education can provide the setting for needed changes.

Tuma presents the perspective of workers and their leaders who are saying, "We want a good education for ourselves as well as our children, so that we can make a living in a job we like, or even go on to more schooling." He explains how organized labor, if accepted into partnership with education, can offer positive benefits to the educational program.

CAREER EDUCATION AT THE ELEMENTARY LEVEL

Nicholas J. Topougis

The confused, unrealistic understanding that many secondary pupils display concerning their career choices often may be attributed to the lack of attention to career development at the elementary level. To introduce career planning concepts early and to reinforce them continually is a natural approach. Most theories of vocational choice stress occupational decision making as a developmental process —not a single decision, but a series of decisions made over a period of years. Therefore, career development is an on-going process that extends from infancy through adulthood. It provides a spiral of insights and experiences growing in complexity at each level. Furthermore, the process takes place whether or not the individual is provided with help. Leaving such an important life choice to chance invites confusion, misinformation and dissatisfaction.

The schools of today have vastly different roles than they did a generation ago. Basically, this is a result of the changing world in which we live. Today when individuals enter the world of work, there is a probability that they will change jobs at least three times before reaching their late 20s, and by 40, their earlier jobs may have been completely eliminated. Today's potential employee is faced with thousands of jobs, each requiring certain training, personal qualifications or experiences. To find the occupation for which one is best suited, an exploratory survey of most of the possibilities must be made.

A planned elementary program of career development can provide the student with the base for making realistic and satisfying occupational choices.

At an elementary guidance conference in Dayton, Ohio, regarding the importance of career planning at the elementary level, Nelson (1968) stated the following reasons for career education:

1. To help children develop a personal sense of present and future worth,
2. To help children develop a feeling of place in their society,
3. To help children see how adults achieve the place they have,
4. To help children see the value and significance of all honest work,
5. To help children develop enthusiasm about the whole prospect of work as a way of life,
6. To help provide a model of the working male or female and their attitudes toward work for pupils who experience the real or psychological absence of such,

7. To help children understand that life extends through several interrelated and interdependent phases.

These reasons inspired the early development of career education in the Akron Public Schools. Additional reasons for providing career planning at the elementary level will be mentioned later in this chapter.

The author's experiences have led him to conclude that there are three basic approaches to career programming. Various project sites operate under one of the following approaches as identified by Quaranta (1971), or a combination of all three:

1. Unit level—site personnel employing the unit approach conduct career activities as a separate process from the on-going curriculum, i.e., activities are by the teachers during a specific daily, weekly, or monthly time block.
2. Guidance unit level—this approach is similar to the unit level described above. However, a guidance specialist assists teachers by tools and techniques available to him in helping students to develop greater career awareness.
3. Integrated level—this is the most widely utilized approach. At sites practicing this method, career activities are incorporated throughout the entire curriculum. Besides the usual concepts of subject matter, work concepts are included and receive equal attention. Even though work activities may extend beyond the environment of the classroom they continue to relate to the curriculum.

Presently, there is a paucity of research to indicate the most effective level in career planning. Drawing from the author's experience, it appears that any one or a combination of these approaches can be utilized. However, if an impact is to be made on present curriculum so that career concepts play an essential part, the integrated approach must be primary with other levels playing supporting roles.

Although approaches differ from one program to another, career education goals at the elementary level have much in common. The goal similarities are:

1. To develop pupils' attitudes about the personal and social significance of work;
2. To develop in each pupil self-awareness along with occupational awareness;
3. To increase pupils' awareness of the school program and how it relates to the world of work; and,
4. To develop in each pupil a sense of industry and the subsequent personal rewards gained from accomplishing a task.

While a number of federal, state and local model elementary programs provide for the specifics of occupational orientation and exploration, others concentrate upon developing thorough and sound wholesome attitudes about work. They leave the more detailed inquiry into occupational descriptions, educational requirements, etc., to the junior and senior high school levels.

MODEL FOR CAREER EDUCATION

New ideas require new blueprints. Consequently, it is necessary to first design a career education model for individual programs before the process can even begin. In order to provide an example of a model and a program that can grow from it, the author will utilize his own involvement in career education in the state of Ohio and the Akron Public Schools. There are many parallels between Ohio's model and the others throughout the country.

The Ohio model has a horizontal dimension and a vertical continuum (McCormick and Wigtail, 1971). The horizontal component represents a developmental element related to the academic and work world that will contribute to a total development program. The vertical continuum is divided into three levels, representing the educational stages through which a child progresses in completing his education. For optimum effectiveness, appropriate materials and resources must be generated for each cell and component mentioned. (See Figure 1.)

By working vertically across the seven developmental elements at any given grade level, it is possible to determine the interrelationship that exists in the content of each of the elements. While several of the horizontal elements may be quite related, others may be remotely related. However, there should be a basic relationship between all stages of development.

Ohio's Career Development Continuum, shown here, contains five separate time spans and their corresponding goals. The first three have been developed and are presently operational, as well as vocational education in the eleventh and twelfth grades. The focus of this paper will be the kindergarten to sixth grade span and its goal, career motivation.

OHIO'S CAREER DEVELOPMENT CONTINUUM

Kindergarten—sixth grade .... Career Motivation

Seventh—eighth grade .... Career Orientation

Ninth—tenth grade .... Career Exploration

Eleventh—twelfth grade .... Vocational Education
Pre-professional careers

Postsecondary .... Technical Education
Adult Education
Higher Education

OHIO CAREER DEVELOPMENT FRAMEWORK

	Individual and Environment	World of Work	Self	Education & Training	Economics	Employability & Work Adj.	Vocational Decision Making
Elementary School							
Junior High or Middle School							
Senior High School							

Figure 1

Considerations other than those apparent in a model, must also be incorporated in effective career planning at the elementary level. They are:

1. Career concepts must be integrated within the entire school instructional program and have a strong curriculum base.
2. The program must include all students and teachers at every level.
3. The program must include provisions for in-service training for educators as well as community members.

OBJECTIVES FOR
ELEMENTARY CAREER EDUCATION

The first objective for the elementary program is to assist students in developing a positive self-concept. This is accomplished through a series of experience-centered activities to give students a chance to succeed. By completing simple tasks, each child develops a sense of accomplishment and a sense of respect for himself and the work he can do. Through effective developmental guidance activities, self-concept and career development can be significantly related.

Providing each child with the understanding and experiences that will assist him to increase his knowledge of the world of work and develop a more realistic view of it is the second objective. Through the process of utilizing vicarious, experiential and simulated activities in and out of the classroom, a child begins to understand that everyone works and that all work is important.

The third objective is to develop a positive attitude toward work in each child. The child learns that work means accepting responsibilities for the completion of a task. He must develop an understanding that more complex work requires more complex skills. The child can be assisted in seeing the importance of school work in the development of skills necessary for increasing successful experiences. By illustrating that all work is composed of data, people and things in varying degrees, the child will find it easier to understand work that he sees in and outside the classroom. The curriculum can then be related to the child in those terms.

Developing the concept that individuals are interdependent upon other individuals is the fourth objective. This can be demonstrated by a variety of methods. For example, a production line project can demonstrate how one individual contributes to a whole project. Field observations give teachers many opportunities to relate the interdependency factor outside the classroom.

The elementary program (K-6) should emphasize that every healthy individual is at work at something (Ohio State Department of Education, 1972). Work means accepting responsibilities that require certain tasks to be completed. By becoming aware of his responsibilities at home and at school, and by appreciating the personal meaning that comes from these responsibilities, the child develops work motivation. Upon leaving the elementary school, he should be ready for an orientation to work as "jobs," and for subsequent work exploration translated into occupational endeavors.

The nature of work for a child must be clearly defined. A child's entrance into school begins his contact with a broader environment than he has had previously (Quaranta, 1971). School requires him to deal with a sense of industriousness and initiates his first real work experiences. He becomes aware of, engages in and competes in demanding activities. At this point, the degree to which the child develops this sense of industriousness, awareness and motivation determines the degree to which he participates in the work around him. An effective career education program maximizes the development of these factors.

From kindergarten level through the first two grades, the class and the home comprise the work setting. In these levels and settings, many opportunities are available for increasing awareness and appreciation of the work of others and for motivating participation in work activities.

In grades three and four, the child expands his awareness to include the community around him as well as home and school. At this time, he becomes aware of forces such as cooperation, competition, power and contact, and finds meaning within them. At grades five and six, the world of work expands to an even greater awareness of the community and beyond, to society and the world.

Enhancing the natural progression of work motivation from kindergarten through the sixth grade, as outlined here, is the very *raison d'etre* of career education at the elementary level. This progression has given to the fifth and sixth grades the background against which the introduction of jobs or occupations can be made.

In summary, career development goals in kindergarten through sixth grade consist of developing: (a) an awareness of the world of work in the form of school, home and community tasks; (b) an appreciation for work as a meaningful activity; and (c) a motivation for work. Thus, the elementary school provides important foundational awareness and motivation for becoming involved in the greater dimensions of career development.

Designing an elementary career education program that will provide for sequential career activities is a thoughtful and extensive process. Many questions need to be answered. A key one is, "Are revisions of the present elementary curriculum necessary, and if so, who, how and what is involved in bringing about revisions?" Many educators are stating that career education demands a change in curriculum.

If the proper foundation has been laid in the planning stages of career development and procedures for continuous improvement are provided, curriculum growth and change will inevitably occur. Suggestions will be field tested, evaluated, formally accepted and finally adopted. Obviously since traditional patterns of education are deeply rooted, this process will occur only after an extended period of time.

One of the first considerations in adopting a career education program at the elementary level is staff. Responsibility must be assigned to individuals who possess the ability, ingenuity and creativity to work, communicate and coordinate with the following program components: (a) administrative personnel, (b) teachers, (c) counselors, (d) the local community and (e) parents. Provisions must be made for in-service training that will provide the total school staff with adequate knowledge, techniques and the tools necessary for effective programming.

ELEMENTARY GRADES CAREER EDUCATION PROGRAM COMPONENTS

Administrative Component

The management factor involved in the conduct of the program should include the following linkages:

1. The project director should be in the curriculum division and have a direct line of action to personnel responsible for financing, curriculum development, guidance, vocational education, as well as having immediate contact with the superintendent of schools.
2. The project director must insure that coordination and communication is constant with the central office and local school administrative staffs in order to:
   a. Determine administrative system for career education,
   b. Assist in the design of implementation strategies,
   c. Review and approve curriculum innovations,
   d. Obtain commitment from the board of education,
   e. Endorse the necessary curriculum changes,
   f. Incorporate the career education philosophy into the total school philosophy, and
   g. Assist in the establishment of steering and advisory committees.

Teacher Component

The classroom teacher is the key to an effective elementary career development program. The elementary teacher assumes the responsibility for the total child. This is unlike the secondary school where several educators become involved in the process with the single child. Thus, it is vital that the teacher in the elementary school becomes aware of the goals, objectives, concepts and strategies of the career program. The classroom teacher should be involved in the developmental as well as the operational phase of programming. He must feel that he has a part in developing the strategies and activities that are fused into the total program. As a team working with one another and the elementary curriculum specialist, teachers can:

1. Analyze the present school curriculum in the elementary grades in order to determine how suitable materials and career concepts can be integrated and related to the subject matter in line with the program goals and concepts.

2. Develop classroom activities wherein this infusion takes place. This procedure is limited only by the ingenuity of the personnel involved. Cooperative planning by teachers at various grade levels will aid in correlating the sequential steps of the career program.

3. Analyze and select suitable career materials that will supplement classroom activities. Many textbooks, novels, biographies, pamphlets, films, filmstrips, work and value kits, which are suitable for classroom assignment, have been developed.

4. Select suitable projects that will provide students with real life experience-centered activities in observing the panorama of the world of work. Listed here are samples of the many projects that can be utilized.
   a. Schedule and conduct field observations in which emphasis is placed on the workers, and the tasks they perform and the interdependency of one to another.
   b. Study work tasks of family members.
   c. Prepare a work or task chart, relating to the skills of the subject matter being taught.
   d. Invite community workers and parents to visit classrooms and relate the work tasks they perform.
   e. Write short stories on selected topics that have work connotations.
   f. Design bulletin boards related to work performed at home, school and in the community.
   g. Role play various tasks performed by a variety of workers.
   h. Utilize illustrations related to the world of work.
   i. Play a variety of career games that can be utilized as motivators.

j. Utilize supplemental career material such as films, film-strips, etc., scrapbooks, crossword puzzles and puppets that can be used as motivators.

Teachers must become involved and assume responsibilities for revising the elementary curriculum in order that it may incorporate world of work concepts. This can be approached in the following manner:

1. Through in-service training, teachers can gain an awareness of the philosophy, developmental concepts, goals, objectives and basic strategies for program implementation.

2. They must then begin to develop and incorporate their own concepts and procedures into the classroom structure. These procedures must be collected, analyzed and evaluated as to their effectiveness in reaching the developmental and behavioral objectives already determined.

3. As a result of this collection, analysis and evaluation, these procedures should be utilized in the development of curriculum guides. These guides will identify clearly curriculum concepts, objectives, activities, resources and performance statements that will further assist staff in program implementation for each grade level and subject area. (This phase has been completed in the Akron Public Schools for grades K-6 and soon will be available for further field test.)

Guidance Component

The focus of guidance at the elementary level should be on the development, integration and coordination of guidance services into the total educational program.

Many experts suggest that self-concept and career development are significantly related and both are developmental in nature. Both processes begin early in life. Therefore, in order to set the stage for a balanced and effective elementary career developmental program, developmental guidance must be an integral part of that program. Children need the assistance in both the process of career development and in the building of a positive self-concept.

The major emphasis in a well-rounded career guidance program is in the classroom guidance activities that are conducted by the teacher, preferably with the assistance of an elementary guidance specialist.

Keeping in mind the importance of primary years for the development of a child's attitudes, values and involvement with the educational process, several group guidance techniques and programs can be used effectively. *Developing Understanding of Self and Others* is a guidance kit utilized with children in the first and second grades (Dinkmeyer, 1970). It assists each student to gain greater awareness of himself as well as other individuals. The activities promoting this include stories, problem situations, role playing and puppetry. The learning experiences provided by this kit have definite implications for career motivation. The kit enables teachers and counselors to help children mature in terms of knowledge about self and environment. As individuals grow, this knowledge, when integrated with their career activities, can lead to relevant behavior toward the world of work.

Strategies developed by Raths, et al. (1966) provide staff with methods to assist children in gaining a greater understanding of their values. Because values are a part of living, they operate in a complex circumstance and are related to an individual's self-concept and his perception of the world of work. Through a series of workshops conducted since 1969, a number of teachers in the Akron Public Schools have been trained to utilize this concept on a regular basis.

Bruck's (1969) study on group guidance is another attempt at humanizing education. It is designed for use with students in grades four through six. Presently, the program is being piloted in selected elementary schools with the primary focus being on life as the child faces it. It aims to aid the student in coping with frustrations and emotional blocks that can prevent educational, vocational and emotional growth.

Classroom discussions developed as a result of Glasser's (1969) suggestions can be used effectively by counselors or teachers. These classroom meetings are nonjudgmental discussions related to what is important and relevant to the student.

In addition to the mentioned classroom activities, many commercially prepared materials such as "Our Value Series," Westinghouse Learning Corporation, "Junior Guidance Series," by Science Research Associates and "Seeing Ourselves and the People Around Us," by American Guidance Service, can be effectively employed and integrated with the career development concept.

Community Component

Involving the local business, industrial and professional community in the planning, developmental, implementation and evaluation phases of career programs is absolutely essential.

In the planning and developmental stages of any career program, a cross-fertilization of ideas and concepts must be obtained from the local community in relationship to their needs. Community commitment to the program must be realized if it is to attain its objectives.

In order to generate public and private interest and concern in the planning, development and implementation of a career education program, informational publications can be disseminated; talks with local business, service and professional organizations can take place; and, selection of an advisory committee composed of representatives from the various businesses and institutions in the local community can be made. The advisory group can be of great assistance in:

1. Identifying problems and concerns at the elementary level.
2. Obtaining reaction to program efforts.
3. Providing recommendations relative to the community's educational needs.
4. Soliciting and encouraging contributions of time, personnel, materials and equipment from business including the professions, local government, parents, service organizations, etc.
5. Providing suggestions and advice relative to curriculum that will assist teachers in planning their career activities.
6. Providing strong community support.

The need to utilize community resources is quite evident. Without the community resources, the classroom is in many ways limited in providing a learning environment that maximizes the workings, the human interaction and the role and impact of technology on the present and future society.

Field observations that are integrated into the subject and the career developmental area being emphasized can aid greatly in making abstract concepts more realistic. Prior planning on the part of the teacher in cooperation with hosts will assure that a maximum learning experience will be provided for the elementary student at an observation site. Certainly, the experience being sought in such an observation must be related to the emotional and educational maturity of the pupil, as well as the concept being developed by the teachers for the student.

Parent Component

The child's initial self-concept is related to the importance that parents and other members of the family have placed on his uniqueness. Even later, parents have a greater influence on the child's self-concept, emotional and social outlook on life, and career planning than any other one element. Because of this factor, parents must become involved and play a vital role in career programming.

From the beginning, parents can share their ideas and thoughts with educators as to what they regard to be important in assisting their children in career planning. Parents can share thoughts on such topics as:

1. Understanding children's interest and aptitudes.
2. Motivating children in obtaining higher level of educational achievements.
3. Vocational education programs designed to meet the occupational needs of the community and the child.

Not only can parents be utilized in a reading, sharing and advisory capacity, but their contribution as resource people in career activities can assist students to gain a greater awareness of just how important and vital parents are to the total economic structure.

SUMMARY

In order for students to prepare themselves for the estimated 50 years of their working life, development of work concepts must begin in the elementary grades. At the elementary level, career education must concentrate its efforts on developing self-awareness as well as occupational awareness. Awareness at this level is interpreted as the process of creating a greater sense of industriousness and respect for all work with the intention of providing the foundation for becoming further involved in career development at the secondary level.

A meaningful career development program must include the input and cooperation of the total educational system as well as the local community and parents. Administrative support and commitment are essential, although the key implementors are the classroom teachers. Although a number of approaches can be utilized in program operation, career activities incorporated in the entire curriculum are most suitable.

In order to obtain an effective career program, a guidance component is essential inasmuch as self-concept and career development are significantly related. In addition, strong community and parent support and involvement are necessary at all stages of development.

To change education in order that it will accept and implement to its fullest the career theme will require a great deal of time. Whether this time becomes available or whether career education becomes another fad, along with other good concepts introduced into the educational structure and later forgotten, is yet to be determined.

REFERENCES

Bruck, Charlotte M. *Discovery Through Guidance, Group Guidance for Elementary Schools.* (St. Paul, Minnesota: Bruce Publishing Company. 1969)

Dinkmeyer, D. *Developing Understanding Self and Others.* Guidance Kit. (Circle Pines, Minnesota: American Guidance Service Incorporated. 1970)

Glasser, William. *Schools Without Failure.* (New York: Harper and Row. 1969)

McCormick, Roger D., and Wigtail, James V. "Guidelines for Planning, Implementing and Evaluating Career Development Programs, K-12." Unpublished Report. Columbus: Ohio State Department of Education. 1971.

Nelson, Richard C. "Opening New Vistas to Children Through Career Education." A Report of the Eighth Annual All Ohio Elementary School Guidance Conference, Dayton, Ohio, November 1, 1968.

Ohio State Department of Education. *World of Work Career Motivation.* Curriculum Guide for Grades K-6. Ohio's Career Continuum Program. (Columbus: Division of Vocational Education, Ohio State Department of Education. 1972)

Quaranta, Joseph. "Implementing Career Development Programs in the Elementary School." Unpublished Report. Columbus: Ohio State Department of Education. 1971.

Raths, Louis E.; Harmin, Merrill; and Simon, Sidney D. *Values and Teaching: Working with Values in the Classroom.* (Columbus, Ohio: Charles E. Merrill Publishing Co. 1966)

CAREER EDUCATION IN THE
SECONDARY SCHOOL

Curtis Dixon

According to the U.S. Department of Labor, 80 percent of the nation's jobs are currently being handled by employees having less than a baccalaureate degree. Yet, for many years, secondary schools have been so strongly college-oriented that most of their planning and effort have been directed toward an academic program that has tended to deemphasize, if not ignore, many alternative and equally worthy options. Recently, however, educators have begun to speak of "a curriculum for every student" rather than selected curricula to which students are assigned. This emphasis on the individual—the very basis of career education—must, of necessity, produce many new demands for reevaluation and change of traditionally accepted professional roles in the classroom and in the community as a whole.

In the past, teachers and counselors have employed a single strategy that has often forced decisions of vocational choice on students who were not developmentally ready for them. The concept of career development is a broadening of the older idea of simply matching individual characteristics with occupational requirements. It strives to draw attention to the processes through which vocationally relevant behavior is developed and expressed. Career development programs provide students with occupational information so that they may make appropriate and enlightened career choices based on knowledge of general mental, physical and aptitudinal requirements, and on specific preparations necessary for entry into their fields of interest. The educator's role in this process is not to evaluate the material for the student, but to suggest possible choices and to help him face reality in selecting career goals. Such selection requires close attention to and knowledge of the student's own individuality, and a close cooperation between teacher and student and among educators themselves.

It is likely that comprehensive career education programs can best be accomplished by leadership teams composed of vocational educators, counselors and academic teachers who, in close cooperation with business and industry, can invest their separate talents in a program based on this concept of career development. Both vocational educators and counselors have unique contributions to make in promoting career development—the vocational educator's leadership potential lies in his knowledge of the world of work; the counselor's in his understanding of human behavior. However, the effective exercise of these potentials requires a fundamental change in the manner in which these two specialists are to function—specifically, the placement of greater emphasis on their consultative roles.

The counselor is urged to get out of his office and to become increasingly involved with the students and their activities in order to know each student as a total person rather than simply seeing him as he is revealed through test scores and grade reports. The vocational educator is urged to utilize his talents by working closely with teachers and staff in promoting the students' self-development, bridging the gap between vocational and general education, and increasing the relevancy of the school experience as a whole.

Similarly, the classroom teacher in this learner-centered situation must emerge from behind his podium and become a facilitator who works with learners as they become active participants in the educational environment. He must strive to assist students in determining their own educational needs. He must become a source rather than a dispenser of knowledge, a diagnostician of learning difficulties rather than a disciplinarian, and a teacher of self-evaluation rather than an educator. In short, the teacher needs to develop a genuine interest in and knowledge of each and every one of his students, in order that he may counsel them wisely and effectively concerning whatever educational, social, personal or occupational problems they may experience.

Comprehensive career education also requires that the teacher be both willing and able to integrate vocational, college preparatory and general education instead of dividing these into separate compartments. This, of course, will require a considerable change in attitude and practice on the part of those academic teachers who see little educational value in anything outside their own classrooms. Educators must avoid the rigid and disjointed curricular structure that has, in the past, forced many students into hasty and virtually irrevocable career decisions. This has contributed greatly to the widespread student feeling that their secondary school experience bears little, if any, relationship to the real world of work. It is absolutely essential that such "closed classroom" attitudes be abolished.

Teachers must strive to instill in their students a feeling of continuity between academic subject matter and personal career goals. Through continuous and extensive involvement with businessmen, industrial leaders and parents, and through careful classroom planning and inter-team cooperation, educators must coordinate these areas in order to realize a truly individualized and relevant program of career education.

No longer can the teacher who merely possesses the ability to "educate" his students in his own subject area be considered successful. No longer is that counselor successful who works with students only within the confines of his own office. Comprehensive career education demands much more than mere competence from those whom it involves. Educators working within the framework of the leadership team must be willing and able to move beyond the professional lines that have traditionally separated the administrator from the counselor and the academic teacher from the vocational educator. This is not to suggest that such specialties should not exist, but rather that they should be made to serve the total educational process. Members of the team should endeavor, regardless of their titles or training, to broaden the scope of their educational activities.

The classroom teacher must possess all the qualities of a good administrator as well as those of a good counselor as he schedules activities, keeps records, conducts interviews and becomes involved with his students in the many different situations that are a part of the total career development program. Similarly, the counselor and the administrator must become even more closely involved with student activities on all levels—observing, participating and working alongside teachers and learners to create a total involvement of all members of the educational community.

In their efforts to involve all members of their community in the career education process, team members must strive to inform parents and business leaders as to the objectives and methods of the career development concept. They must endeavor to dispel the false notion, still held by many, that career education is simply job training intended only for those students who "can't make the grade" in the academic programs; and they must seek to extend the field of career education out from the classroom and into the homes and business establishments within the community. Only through extensive efforts in the area of public and community relations and subsequent involvement of community members can the career education team truly integrate the community and the classroom.

Career education helps create a school climate that encourages the staff to take an interest and pride in assisting each student in shaping his career life. In addition, a new basis for educational accountability results from implementation of career education. Public education could be held accountable for insuring that each individual chooses, prepares, enters and progresses in activities furthering his career life. Schools would have a new reason for being— not only to help the individual make the initial entrance into the world of work, but to progress in his career.

Finally, in reviewing the many implications of the career development concept of career education, no single ability becomes more obvious as being absolutely essential for each and every member of the career education team than does that special ability to work effectively and congenially in a group situation. Career education requires extensive coordination, cooperation and sharing by all team members; and all team members must realize that a true concern for the individual members of the group is of vital importance not only within the team itself, but also in the classroom. Knowledge of the group process is essential in attaining a classroom climate that is conducive to self-examination and group involvement. The characteristics of openness and cohesiveness in a small group are of considerable importance in the attainment of the affective objectives requisite to career development—the exploration of self in relation to the world of work.

CAREER EDUCATION IN THE AREA VOCATIONAL-TECHNICAL SCHOOL

Jonah L. Fitch

Career Education. Is it a real solution to some of today's educational problems or merely an addition to ever-increasing educational terminology?

The concept of career education—as advanced on May 4, 1971, by Sidney P. Marland, Jr., then U.S. Commissioner of Education—is more than an addition. It is a refreshing consolidation of many historical education concepts.

The career education concept is not necessarily new as a whole but is a refined articulation of educational concepts dating back at least as far as the Greek and Roman civilizations. Career education encompasses fragments from both of these renowned cultures. The Grecian concept of the cultured student, harmoniously enriched in mind, body and spirit was complemented by the utilitarian and practical spirit of the Romans. The concept of career education today is a culmination of many of the ancient, but persistent, ideas that have flowed, altered to be sure, into our modern times.

The pursuit of knowledge has been with us since the beginning of recorded history and many times throughout our history has become a shell of its former self. Many worthy concepts, innovative in their day, were only glimpses of what has since become commonplace. Today, it behooves administrators and educators to try to focus attention toward the implications that career education holds for ensuing generations of students.

DEVELOPMENT IN THE UNITED STATES

Many of the outstanding educators and events in our current century have played vital roles in sowing and nourishing the seed for the fruition of career education. These include: (a) John Dewey's distaste for the conventional school, (b) the Progressive movement, and (c) the tremendous wave of criticism that followed the orbiting of the first satellite by the Russians in 1957.

As a result of pervading uneasiness and, at times, disintegrating illusions about the *status quo* of our educational system, a fresh and sharply critical eye has been focused on the American school. Many of the criticisms that have been directed at our system of education have, in turn, been studied, disputed and discounted; the outcome of such critical studies and evaluations has been a thrust toward improvement. Today, probably more than at any previous time, our schools are within close reach of their goals and serve as a viable manifestation of the great hopes and dreams of educational reformers throughout the centuries.

As education in America has evolved, so has the philosophy that every individual in this country deserves the opportunity to pursue learning experiences, within organized education, that will enable him to earn a livelihood and live comfortably within modern society. This does not preclude the fact that many individuals across the country will never profit by any efforts in formal education due to lack of ambition, as well as psychological and moral characteristics.

Career education infers the premise that meaningful educational opportunities should be made available to all individuals who have the time, energy and ambition to profit from them. Not only should meaningful education be made available, but it should be relevant to an era of progress unparalleled in history.

CAREER EDUCATION TODAY

In our modern society of soaring technological advances and astounding rapidity of social change, an individual and his family are required to maintain an economic posture that will enable them to compete. One of the goals of career education is the provision of knowledge and experiences that enhance adaptability to available jobs. The term "career education" implies the implementation of an educational program to develop the whole individual.

While attempting to interpret career education, administrators must be extremely mindful of the importance of the basic learning skills offered historically by academic education. Basic to almost any worthwhile practical skill is the ability to read with interpretation, to communicate both in written and oral form, and to be proficient to an acceptable degree in mathematics. To satisfy the needs of the nation, the concept of career education must be all-encompassing, including every phase of formal education through which an individual progresses.

Unless education is placed at the learning level of the individual and is geographically accessible to him, no meaningful results can come from any form of formal education. One of the goals of career education is to guide the student in the development of a plan, which is suitable to him as an individual, for a continuous process of learning. Thus, within the broad concept of career education, the area vocational-technical schools bridge a gap in the total educational system.

ROLE OF
AREA VOCATIONAL-TECHNICAL SCHOOLS

The word "delivery," which is seldom used in educational circles, is the key to the total concept of career education. The area vocational-technical schools stand in a near optimum position to deliver educational opportunity, specific knowledge, and skills salable and usable within the locale. The fact that the area vocational-technical schools are unencumbered with numerous extracurricular activities enables the staff and students to concentrate their efforts on teaching and learning. These schools are unique in that, in order to survive, they have to forge ahead with new ideas, techniques and skills. The area vocational-technical schools must stay abreast, and if possible ahead, of the technological development of industry and business, or they will sink rapidly into oblivion.

Too often in the history of American education, educators have tended to get into a comfortable rut and become calloused to new methods, ideas and concepts. Many educators are like the farmer who kept driving his wagon in the same tracks across a muddy field until the ruts deepened and hardened so that he could neither get out nor go forward.

The term "area vocational-technical school" implies certain conditions, such as:

1. Careful planning results in the institution being located in such a place as to insure accessibility to the students it is designed to serve. In some states, area vocational-technical schools are geographically located so that every citizen resides within commuting distance of an institution.

2. Existing employment opportunities vary according to locale. This makes it imperative that the program of instruction and curriculum content are designed to train individuals for available jobs within the geographical area being served.

3. A variety of course offerings is essential with varying levels of instruction emphasized to insure that training is within the potential learning level of most individuals who possess ambition and adequate personal drive to pursue training.

4. Flexible admission policies make it possible to enroll the individual who has an occupational objective (his previous educational accomplishments notwithstanding).

5. Flexibility must be assured by planning and changing course offerings, content or direction in order to keep abreast of technological change.

6. Individual needs are paramount, and teaching methods must include individualized instruction in order to allow the individual to progress at his optimum rate. In presenting a description of the term "career education," Bice (1972) indicates, "Career education . . . *does* emphasize individualized instruction." Since their inception, the area vocational-tech-

nical schools have strongly emphasized the importance of individualized instruction and have found that it is vital to individual progress.

Area vocational-technical schools in Tennessee have organized their course content in accordance with job descriptions outlined in the *Dictionary of Occupational Titles* (U.S. Department of Labor, 1965) and the U.S. Office of Education classification code.

A certificate of accomplishment is issued for all courses offered by the Tennessee area vocational-technical schools, and for units set up by themselves. The certificate indicates the highest title in the area of training that the individual is capable of performing as described by the USOE and DOT codes. Those who complete a full preparatory course are given a diploma. These certificates and diplomas are issued according to the highest level of accomplishment by the student rather than being based on a time factor.

This method and procedures are used to identify positively within the course offerings (a) the course content, (b) individual training needs, and (c) proficiency levels achieved by the student. This is also a good means of communicating to the prospective employer what an individual is capable of doing.

The relative newness of area vocational-technical schools gives opportunity for experimentation (trial and error), research and evaluation. Continuing evaluation is necessary in any educational system. In the area vocational-technical schools, the fact that the student goes to work immediately after graduation makes it much easier to evaluate accurately the program. The area vocational-technical school has the opportunity of follow-up evaluations within six months of the student's departure from the classroom, while general education is deprived of this opportunity for a much longer period.

The career education concept makes it necessary for all school administrators to evaluate carefully each program to determine if the desired goals are being met. If career education is to work to advantage, each phase of the entire program, from kindergarten through the highest level of education, must be carefully planned and fitted into the total system, thus eliminating duplication and lack of continuity. Goals, which are subject to change, must be scrutinized constantly. Consequently, administrators must focus their attention on the implication for the future of career education within the broad spectrum of education, *per se*.

IMPLICATIONS OF CAREER EDUCATION

What are the implications of career education as pondered by an administrator? One implication, if career education comes into its own, is that the current dichotomy between the academic and vocational aspects of education will disappear. Even the descriptive terms, such as vocational education, college preparatory, etc., will be passé, and the avant-garde of educational circles will substitute, through planned and studied endeavor, the term "career education." This is not to say that career education will replace traditional schools; however, an attempt will be made to place the academic program and the vocational program in proper perspective as components of the larger scope of career education. Different types of learning will be integrated in an organized and meaningful way. This career education movement must be recognized as a total educational concept for everyone throughout life. The cliché "education from the cradle to the grave" may aptly describe the belief, as advocated by career education promulgators, that our educational institutions should be open, and opportunities available, to all individuals throughout life.

Another implication, as seen through the eyes of an administrator, is that an irrelevant general education, as such, will be uprooted by programs designed with individual goals in mind. As a result, the vast number of secondary students who are now enrolled in general education and who could become unskilled graduates will be guided into suitable programs, appropriate to their interests and aptitudes.

An ever-increasing cooperative working relationship among the secondary schools, the area vocational-technical schools and higher education will result from the current interest developing in career education. When various educational groups work together effectively toward solving the problems created by implementation of a new program, the groups tend to become more solidified. There is a sense of sharing and more consideration of needs common to all groups and facilities. In order for career education to have the opportunity to find its true place as a movement designed toward improvement of our nation's educational system, support must come from *all* levels of education.

Also, a continuing development of liaison between the school program and the industrial world will be necessary if career education is to succeed. The area vocational-technical schools are in a prime position to develop and enhance closer relationships with industry.

Because of the impressive array of personages who are already displaying intense interest and energy toward meeting the challenge of educational reform with emphasis on the development of a vigorous innovative program of career education, the implications are that a strong thrust for the new program will be forthcoming in the ensuing years. The movement is now experiencing the embryo stage —many improvements are indeed forthcoming.

LOOKING AHEAD

Some of the results from attention directed toward the relatively new concept of career education are for the prophets, not the historians, to identify. The implications for future generations are countless. Much of the value will depend upon the extent of dissemination of information, careful study and forethought prior to implementation of the program in any particular school system.

First, administrators need to update themselves on the concept of career education and then attempt to develop an awareness among others concerning adjustments in the curriculum, etc., that will necessarily be an outgrowth of the implementation of this concept. An understanding by all educators is essential to the successful outcome of such a program.

Also, parents and other interested lay people need to be informed about what the schools are attempting to do. No doubt, as the need becomes apparent, many innovative programs will be developed, from kindergarten upward, that will provide the individual student with a much wider range of information and experience relative to his aptitudes and interests.

One can further expect that an increase in the development of pertinent instructional materials concerning career education will be in evidence during the next few years, resulting in part from an upsurge in courses for instructional personnel being made available at colleges and universities. Some of the means by which this new information could be disseminated in the school system include: distribution of materials to administrators, teachers, curriculum supervisors, and other interested persons; visual or media presentations that would serve to explain the goals of career education; and, workshops in which administrators, teaching personnel and interested citizens would be actively involved.

As the favorable aspects become apparent and enthusiasm builds for the concept, a warning should be interjected against any delusion that the panacea for all the social and educational ills of the nation can be found in the relatively new career education. Its potential is great; but in order to realize optimum benefits, the proposed program should be carefully studied, thoroughly planned and strengthened through step-by-step implementation.

One of the most reliable of American reasons for doing anything is that "it works." Surely, the future holds the answer to the question of career education; certainly, it is off to an impressive beginning. According to Hoyt, et al. (1972), "Few concepts introduced into the policy circles of American education have ever been met with such instant acclaim as career education." If, after the program has been carefully and fully implemented, one can evaluate it and say, "it works," then the term "career education" will be more than a mere addition to educational terminology.

REFERENCES

Bice, Garry R. "Career Education: An Overview." Paper presented at the Building for Career Education Conference, The University of Tennessee, College of Education, School Planning Laboratory, April 19-21, 1972.

Hoyt, Kenneth B., et al. *Career Education: What It Is and How To Do It.* Salt Lake City, Utah: Olympus Publishing Co. 1972.

U.S. Department of Labor. *Dictionary of Occupational Titles.* 3rd ed. 2 Volumes. 1965.

WE'RE INTO CAREER EDUCATION

Dallas Hardin

Washington County, Tennessee, is into career education, as common parlance would have it. It came suddenly, like a clap of thunder from the neighboring Smoky Mountains.

We were not ready and yet we were. A substantial expansion of vocational programs, with the assistance of a grant from the Appalachian Regional Commission, was just being implemented. Exciting new programs such as automotive mechanics and cosmetology were being equipped and offered for the first time in two new consolidated high schools, each serving about 1300 students.

Two elementary schools were nearing completion and would serve grades one through four in two central areas of the county. The open-space concept was a feature of the new buildings. Satellite feeding was being introduced in half of the elementary schools. Renovation of older schools was high on the community interest list. Therefore, acceptance of the career education concept came naturally.

Lacking an educational phenomenon that would lead a student to success as surely as the gypsy moth to its mate, we welcomed the new concept. Career education would follow through with the 300 percent expansion in vocational course offerings and with Head Start, special education, and other enrichment efforts already underway.

The system took pride in praise from officials of the state department of education hierarchy who complimented Washington County on having made a great deal of recent progress. Career education seemed a natural for the future.

Agriculturally oriented critics might be inclined to say that this was another case of sheep scrambling with alacrity to follow the leader. After all, hasn't everyone been told that similar past educational ideas have been as readily accepted and yet have failed? They have failed, we are told, to produce a product uniformly acceptable in the personnel rooms. Similarly, past ideas have failed to produce individuals so oriented to a career as to be productive and to achieve satisfaction from their work.

Consolation can be drawn from Hoyt (1972) in his contention that the need for career education is brought on by a "social crisis, not just a school crisis"—a crisis in which the classic Protestant Work Ethic is threatened, if not rejected.

CAREER EDUCATION FOR STUDENTS

The delineations of educational theory upon which the career education concept is based are impressive (See Chapter 4 by Herr). Similarly impressive is the massive congressional fund-giving challenge—raise the gross national product (GNP) by improving entry-level workers. To succeed with career education will raise the GNP by funneling job-ready workers into the national economy! The responsibility is mind-boggling.

We have tried to keep our feet on the ground and our heads out of the clouds. Actually, ours is more a sort of gut reaction of experienced school teachers than it is a development of logical planning based on established educational theory.

Sufficient local satisfaction will be gained from some small, recognizable improvement in the ability of students leaving the Washington County school system. Other more sophisticated school systems can assault the GNP.

True, the foundations of career education have been around for a long time (See Chapter 2 by Barlow). In fact, teachers in our own system have been making effective individual applications of career concepts in their instruction for years. It isn't simply that a great idea has just filtered out to the hinterlands. It may be that career education, like the Wankel engine, has finally reached a point in time when it can be acceptably marketed. What has been welcomed in Washington County is the total package so wrapped and delivered that it can be the goal of a total school system.

Will career education help to impress upon the student mind the difference between education and compulsory school attendance? Will it help to make education a gradual transition into work? These are current concerns in Washington County. Accomplishments in neighboring Knoxville and other places are interesting and encouraging.

PROGRAM CHANGE BASED ON TENETS

Tennessee does not abhor change, it just likes time to think about it. Being true Tennesseeans, we have not gone hogwild into drastic program alterations, but we are doing a lot of thinking. Immediate changes have been improvements on existing practice rather than a revolutionary shake-up. Some changes have been based on new programs, some on new ways of looking at the old. Ever in our minds is a longer range plan.

Basic tenets have been established to guide changes as they are implemented:

1. Programs should permit optimal use of physical facilities.
2. Modifications should strive for greater flexibility, individualization of instruction, and broadening of programs in any way that will more effectively serve student needs.

3. Means and approaches should be devised for increasing student self-responsibility for career preparation.
4. Efforts should be made to remove stigma or status from courses and programs. The real individual goal shall be preparation for a satisfying career in which the student recognizes interest and capability. (The new vocabulary substitutes career-exploratory, career-entry, and career-academe for the stigma and status terms vocational and college preparatory.)
5. Guidance should emphasize preparation rather than problem-solving.
6. Student evaluation should assess progress on individual career goals realistically, including demonstration of work attitudes that will be contributing to later productivity.
7. Assistance should be offered to dropouts, stop-outs and graduates in areas of job placement and/or continued career preparation.

The result has been a five-pronged program involving the following:

1. Restructuring of vocational programs to provide career-exploratory and career-entry phases.
2. Instituting short-term, career-exploratory classes in seventh and eighth grades.
3. Organizing a career education awareness project system-wide.
4. Offering evening classes to those who would return to school for general or specific instruction.
5. Creating a placement service for students going directly from high school to employment.

Experimental restructuring of high school vocational courses, with the blessing of the state commissioner of education under whose aegis county systems operate in Tennessee, has been enthusiastically received by students and teachers. Course restructuring is the major program adjustment for career education.

CAREER EXPLORATION AND ENTRY-LEVEL PREPARATION

The basic Washington County career education plan recognizes the virtue of the prescribed prevocational exploratory training on a rotational basis. The plan reaches out to broaden this in order to serve more students in a more extensive way in career exploration. It also awards serious career-entry students with the same amount of credit for time invested as is granted to students in other courses. This does not interfere with acquisition of state-required credits for graduation.

Courses in automotive mechanics, drafting, electricity and welding have been scheduled so as to provide exploratory as well as career-entry facets. The pattern can be illustrated with automotive mechanics as an example.

The automotive mechanics departments offer exploratory courses (Automotive Mechanics I) to sophomores. These courses meet for one hour a day for one semester and yield one-half credit. New groups of students enroll for the second semester. Career-entry courses for juniors (Automotive Mechanics II) meet two hours a day for a full year and yield two credits. Advanced career-entry courses for seniors (Automotive Mechanics III) meet for three hours a day and yield three credits. A summary of the courses involved in this sequence is shown in Table 1.

COURSE	CREDITS
Automotive Mechanics I (sophomores)	½
Automotive Mechanics II (juniors)	2
Automotive Mechanics III (seniors)	3
Building Trades I (juniors)	3
Building Trades II (seniors)	3
Cosmetology I (sophomores)	3
Cosmetology II (juniors)	3
Cosmetology III (seniors)	3
Drafting I (sophomores)	½
Drafting II (juniors)	2
Drafting III (seniors)	3
Electricity I (sophomores)	½
Electricity II (juniors)	2
Electricity III (seniors)	3
Welding I (sophomores)	½
Welding II (juniors)	2
Welding III (seniors)	3

Table 1

In addition, there are high school exploratory courses in small engines, home electricity, wood shop and metal shop. Some of these are open to freshmen.

Seventh and eighth grade students are receiving limited exposure to hands-on experiences related to traditional vocational instruction. Home economics, business education and industrial arts units have been added to the curriculum. Small groups rotate over the three areas, receiving a few weeks of instruction in each until all students have had some exposure. Acquisition of skills is of no consequence in these classes. Students simply explore for interest and aptitude.

Other courses on all grade levels, outside the vocational area, have been oriented to career exploration. Courses stress career consciousness through a county-wide career education awareness program.

CAREER AWARENESS

An additional thrust, the career education awareness program, was devised in the fall of 1972 to bring about an involvement of students, teachers and administrators as quickly as possible. Descriptive and illustrative material had been prepared and distributed in the spring of 1972 and at in-service meetings at the beginning of the 1972-73 school year. A plan for participation seemed advisable.

Specific guidelines were prepared by the central office to unify planning of emphases to be carried out during the year by the staff of each school. These provided little more than a statement of procedure and definition of the scope of the proposed project. Aware that teachers, administrators, guidance personnel, students, parents and the community were all to be involved during the year, each school presented a written *modus operandi*.

System-wide meetings for the evaluation of the efforts were conducted in May, 1973, with staff, students, board of education members and the county advisory committee. Hopefully, some productive results will be evident. Perhaps some input for our long-range plan will be forthcoming from the evaluation.

PLACEMENT

One of the most promising additions to the programs has been the placement service. New in 1972, its results are encouragingly productive. Full ramifications are yet to be utilized.

Placement personnel spend considerable time in group and individual student conferences with seniors. They consider what employers are looking for in an employee, and also effective approaches to job application and interview. They serve as resource people in classes and make program appearances in community group meetings. The placement coordinators (who, by graduation time, have first-hand knowledge of the interests, attitudes, aptitudes and job capabilities of each student) assist students in job searching.

This job placement function has been recognizably successful. Time limitation has prevented much service in part-time job search, but nearly 200 students utilized the service for full-time job procurement upon high school graduation. Some students were helped in locating summer jobs.

A comprehensive career education approach in which students may stop-out for work and drop-in for advancement will dictate future development in the area of adult education. Continuing education never has been extensively offered or locally funded in the Washington County system. Expansion of evening programs is not being undertaken in vocational departments.

MEETING LOCAL NEEDS

The career education program, as outlined, is designed to meet the practical situation in a small school system (8,000 students, K-12) in which a 46 percent dropout rate in grades one through 12 prevails. Less than 20 percent of 1972's graduating classes went on to advanced schooling, although nearly 50 percent of high school students indicated pre-graduation intent to continue formal education. The stated goal of a typical senior class is basically homemaking or office work for the girls and assorted kinds of unskilled or semi-skilled work for the boys. More than half of the boys report indecision as to occupational intentions. Three categories, "industrial and kindred workers," "homemakers" and "unemployed," constituted the choices of half of a class of 1972 graduates. Less than one-fifth are pursuing postsecondary education.

With career education effectively sold, the program may prove that some of the dropouts actually represent symptoms of educational failure rather than student problems. Experience may show whether courses reoriented to recognizably practical purposes have greater student acceptance. No one likes to admit failure, but a new approach that alleviates failure of this kind would surely be welcome.

EMPLOYERS CITE PAST SHORTCOMINGS

A survey of business and manufacturing employers indicates five areas of deficiency in the work force that is the product of Washington County schools or of the other several schools in the tri-city area of Bristol, Johnson City and Kingsport. Employers feel that schools could help supply better employees by working on:
1. Basic communication and mathematics skills,
2. Practical human relations skills,
3. Vocational training appropriate to the needs of the area,
4. A sufficiently close working relationship between the schools and the business-industrial community, and
5. Establishing serious purpose and work habits on the part of future employees.

Vocational programs instituted since the survey partially answer the third listed deficiency. At least a part of items one, two and five must be attributable to the societal crisis described by Hoyt (1972). The career education sales pitch may, hopefully, have some influence on future workers through greater acceptance of school courses re-oriented to visibly practical purposes. It would be nice to believe that greater acceptance could bring about a resurgence of the work ethic. Placement service contacts possess special potential for correcting the fourth item listed.

CONCLUSION

All of this may lead one to conclude that Washington County's career education effort is a sort of scatter gun approach based on an inordinate quantity of hope. It is easy to sigh, "the normal curve," and take a defeatist attitude for ourselves and for our cause.

But, are not school people possessed of eternal faith and hope—faith that all people, from whatever part of the normal curve they come, may be inspired to a career of worth and personal satisfaction; and, of hope that the particular efforts employed can accomplish the task.

Perhaps career education efforts in Washington County schools can help demonstrate that work is still the way to advancement; that meaningful education is not really such a bore, but actually a profitable effort-investment in a future of satisfaction.

REFERENCE

Hoyt, Kenneth B. "The Case for Career Education," address delivered at the Governor's Career Education Conference, Nashville, Tennessee, December 14, 1972.

THE POSTSECONDARY INSTITUTION'S ROLE IN CAREER EDUCATION

Angelo C. Gillie, Sr.

The theoretical concept of career education and several ways it can be implemented are described in earlier chapters and also in other publications (see Goldhammer and Taylor, 1972). Therefore, this author elects not to belabor the fine points contained within the concepts of career education. It is sufficient, for the viewpoints presented in this chapter, that career education be considered a concept that encompasses the entire framework of American education. In conjunction with this position, an individual's career is meant to include all of his life experiences. One critical part of career education is vocational education, which includes those aspects of a person's education that most directly relate to occupational preparation. Having established vocational education within this context, we can proceed into examining the most important roles of postsecondary institutions—vocational preparation, but in a new manner.

DEFINITION AND DESCRIPTION OF POSTSECONDARY INSTITUTIONS

We need to clearly indicate what schools are considered to be postsecondary in this presentation. There are several generic types, specifically public community colleges, private two-year colleges, proprietary schools, area vocational schools, and less than baccalaureate degree programs in senior colleges and universities.

There are aspects that these institutions have in common. First, their students are either secondary school graduates or persons more than 17 years of age. Second, their graduates are awarded certificates, diplomas or degrees, depending upon the "rigor" of the program and the philosophy of the school. Third, the programs are generally conducted at higher cognitive levels than customarily found in secondary school vocational curriculums. Fourth, the major orientation of the program is focused upon occupations, although considerable variations are found as to the degree of specialization. Fifth, the overwhelming majority of schools prepare individuals for occupations *first,* then assist them in finding jobs *later.*

SHORTCOMINGS OF PRESENT DAY POSTSECONDARY PROGRAM MODES

This chapter focuses on two major shortcomings of present day postsecondary program modes. First, there is a serious deficiency in coordination among the many institutional types and, in some places, even among those of the same type. The second drawback is the philosophy of preparing for a job *before* having a job. The contention here is that this approach should be reversed, particularly in view of the great possibility that an individual may be receiving the *wrong* specialized training. It is important to stress that no objection is being made to high specialization. On the contrary, specialization to an even greater extent than is now the case in many places seems to be in order. But, such skill development should not be provided until the student has accepted a specific job. An alternative addressed to these two shortcomings is the basis for this discussion.

AN ALTERNATIVE: A CAREER EDUCATION PROGRAM FOR POSTSECONDARY INSTITUTIONS

The vocational aspects of individual needs can be listed as follows: (a) every person who wants to work should be provided with skills to do so; (b) it is well known that a job provides social and economic status to an individual; (c) no matter how far down the occupational ladder a person may be, he needs to believe that he has a chance to improve both his earnings and status; (d) every person needs and deserves a maximum number of employment opportunities; and, (e) in order to make wise choices about occupational decisions, everyone needs sound, up-to-date knowledge concerning the world of work. Any good postsecondary career education model would address itself to these five needs in the vocational aspects of the program.

In addition to the five needs, another reason for establishing a new model is the clear-cut trend toward more cognitive jobs and increased frequency in job changing (U.S. Department of Labor, 1971). The most significant change in the nation's occupational structure has been a shift toward white collar jobs (Lerner, 1970), particularly in the human service occupations. It has been stated in several places that the average 20-year-old in the work force today will change jobs four to six times during his lifetime (U.S. Office of Education, 1969). These factors have obvious critical implications for adults in vocational education. In the proposed model, a broad type of occupational education is offered up to the point where the student would no longer benefit from such type of instruction. This point would be identified through careful, frequent counseling and testing. When a student reaches this point in his development, he would be placed on the job. The specific skills required would be indicated by the employer. At this time, the student would return to a "skill center" environment for the acquisition of those skills needed for that job. As can be seen, the last part of an individual's occupational program would be a *topping-off* process and would serve to meet immediate skill needs of the graduate. This approach simultaneously provides the student with a solid foundation in a middle-level occupational area and training for a specific job in that occupational group. An added advantage is that workers who have a good basic preparation can later be referred back to the skill center for acquisition of additional skills. This approach meets the five personal occupational related needs stated here.

Who should receive this kind of occupational preparation? Assuming that not more than 20 percent of the working population can become professionals (Lerner, 1970), it seems logical that a large fraction of the remaining 80 percent should obtain this type of education. Included in this latter group are both younger and older elements in the population. The younger persons would consist of:

1. High school dropouts (presently about 20 percent of students who enter high school);
2. High school graduates who are not expected to go beyond high school immediately after graduation (50 percent of high school graduates). The high school dropouts and graduates who don't go on to college make up 60 percent of the students that enter high school (Lerner, 1970).
3. About 70 percent of entering college freshman who are not going to become professionals. In other words, high school dropouts and about 85 percent of high school graduates should receive this variety of postsecondary career education.

In addition, older groups that would benefit from the proposed occupational education model would include persons in need of upgrading or updating their skills, and/or complete retraining for new jobs. With a labor force of more than 80,000,000 (U.S. Department of Labor, 1971), the need for these kinds of occupational services is obviously a great one.

The two-year model has a student input that consists of the two components just described. (See Figure 1.) It would be a truly "open door" school, with provisions for admission into one of the several core curriculums (three multi-level occupational cores are displayed in Figure 1). The term "open door" means that all persons will be admitted, but the program in which an individual is placed would be the one deemed best suited to his potentialities and interests. An integral part of admissions would be the counseling process that would synthesize interviews, test results and other records. Furthermore, a careful assessment of the individual's multiple assets would be made. All of these would be used in predicting the broad occupational areas in which an individual would most likely succeed. Heavy reliance upon counseling and testing would require a large admissions team.

Another input for the model would be related to the skill center where specific skill development, upgrading and updating would take

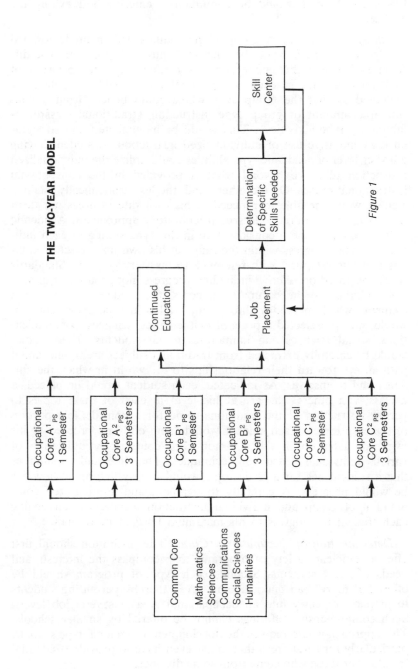

THE TWO-YEAR MODEL

Common Core

Mathematics
Sciences
Communications
Social Sciences
Humanities

Occupational Core A^1 PS 1 Semester

Occupational Core A^2 PS 3 Semesters

Occupational Core B^1 PS 1 Semester

Occupational Core B^2 PS 3 Semesters

Occupational Core C^1 PS 1 Semester

Occupational Core C^2 PS 3 Semesters

Continued Education

Job Placement

Determination of Specific Skills Needed

Skill Center

Figure 1

place. Job holders would be continuously entering and exiting the skill center.

Student Placement. A group of individuals with a predetermined spectrum of abilities would be counseled into each program. The differences between the upper and lower ranges of the spectrum of individual abilities in each occupational core would be sufficiently delimited so that the group as a whole could benefit from a considerable amount of group type instruction (traditional classroom-laboratory type activities). This would be augumented and strengthened by intensive use of individualized instruction. A student having a higher level of academic type abilities could utilize the individualized instruction to move beyond what is provided in the conventional instructional modes. On the other hand, the less academically inclined student would be able to proceed at his own rate in areas not dealt with in the conventional classroom-laboratory approaches. Academic failure would not be a consideration in this type setting as each individual would progress within the range of his own unique set of abilities and interests, and with reference to his starting point. Standards would be based on *relative* individual progress, not group averages.

In addition to the occupational cores, the model has a common element, which pervades throughout, called the common core. It would offer preselected aspects of mathematics, sciences, communications, social sciences and humanities to all students. These topics would be carefully extracted from traditional subject areas and taught with an eye toward their relationships to the world in which the students find themselves. As indicated, each student would be placed in a class with others who are at his level in each of these topics to permit instruction of the traditional type for a considerable portion of the core topics. Each student would "spin-off" and proceed at his own rate later on in the common core courses, by utilization of various individual instruction techniques. The time and capabilities that a student has for a given topic would largely determine how far he would progress. A carefully thought out and administered combination of group and individual instruction techniques can enable each student to progress to his maximum level of performance.

Determination of Occupational Cores. The institution should first offer a sufficient variety of programs to encompass the interests and needs of most students. Second, each type of program should be offered at more than one academic level, thereby permitting students to prepare for entry into an occupational area at several job levels. Such comprehensive offerings cannot be offered by smaller schools. This approach would require the development of regional type schools, particularly for rural areas that might even have to provide residential facilities for those who come from some distance.

The suburban and urban schools would be better able to provide a rich variety of occupational cores. Ideally, such an institution would have a population base of at least 100,000 from which to draw enrollments. The smaller schools should provide a minimum of three dual level occupational cores, one in each of the areas of health-related, social-related, and manufacturing-related occupations. The larger institutions would likely splinter any one or more of these three into more specific cores.

It needs to be emphasized that the treatment of information and subject matter in the occupational core would be done in a cognitive and broad manner with no specialization toward particular jobs. The basic rationale for keeping away from specialization at this point is that each student would thereby have maximum flexibility in terms of future job selection, reserving his specific skill training for the skill center.

Because of the great amount of individual instruction demanded, a complete array of teacher aides should be integrated into the system.

Evaluation. Evaluation should be built into the overall program at the beginning. It should be primarily based on the measurement of behavioral outcomes that were carefully laid down before the program started. In addition to establishing these objectives, strategies for achieving them must be developed. Methods for ascertaining the extent to which the objectives were achieved and what problems were encountered in the process should be devised prior to starting the program. Long-term evaluation strategies (including follow-up studies) must also be established, so that the effectiveness of the program over the long haul can be reviewed and assessed, and used to determine where the program should be modified or discontinued.

The Skill Center. When the student has reached his cognitive limits, he is connected with a specific job acceptable to him. Once the student has a job, the occupational guesswork is done away with since he now knows where he will work and his employer indicates those specific skills needed for that job. The new employee then goes to the skill center, where he develops the required skills. Ideally, the skill center consists of a large cluster of laboratory-shop type areas where a multitude of skills at many levels can be taught, practiced and mastered. It would be an open-ended task oriented activity and the new worker would remain only long enough to master the skills demanded for his entering position. The skill center activities would be equated with academic credits which would be added to the student's school record.

The skill center would also be a "diagnostic clinic" for older workers, where they can be updated and/or upgraded in specific skills. At any given time, a truly effective center would likely have a greater number of older workers than new employees. If such a concept is completely accepted and truly integrated into the work community, the unemployment time between jobs for many persons could be reduced if not eliminated. Once business and industry know that the skill center is available for such tasks, perhaps they would assign a worker (who would otherwise be laid off) to the center and have him return to the prescribed new job with no period of unemployment. Such arrangements require relatively close liaison between the skill center and the business-industrial community.

Who will finance the skill centers? They are obviously expensive. If the center is professionally administered and a large enough number of workers are serviced by it, a long-term cost per student hour of instruction can be lower than what is now spent for traditional laboratory type courses. The key is maximum utilization, which requires some kind of original cooperative effort. The business-industrial community must be willing to hire new workers *before* they have specific skills, prescribe skills that they need, allow the new worker to acquire them at the skill center, and then have him report to the new job.

Who will manage the skill centers? There are several possibilities, and they can be managed differently in different locations: (a) the original institution; (b) a special consortium of school districts; (c) a proprietary school; and, (d) a profit-making learning corporation.

THE FOUR-YEAR MODEL

The two-year model, which is postsecondary in nature, can be expanded into a four-year model, as displayed in Figure 2. The last two years are essentially similar to the original model. The first two years extend into grades 11 and 12. The clearly nonacademically motivated students (potential dropouts and probable non-college bound high school graduates) would be counseled into the model at the start of grade 11. The first two years proposed here would be clearly exploratory for many, which helps the nonacademically inclined youngsters come to grips with their job decision dilemma. There would also be a general education common core, with about half the entire curriculum allocated to it.

The secondary school portion of the model would also have occupational cores (four are displayed in Figure 2). The number of occupational cores would vary with school size. There should be at least one occupational core that deals with clusters of low skill type jobs. This core would provide a unique type of educational treatment designed for potential dropouts, and would not attempt to keep them within the academic areas for too long. Youngsters in this core would move rather quickly into job placement. The sequence described earlier

THE FOUR-YEAR MODEL

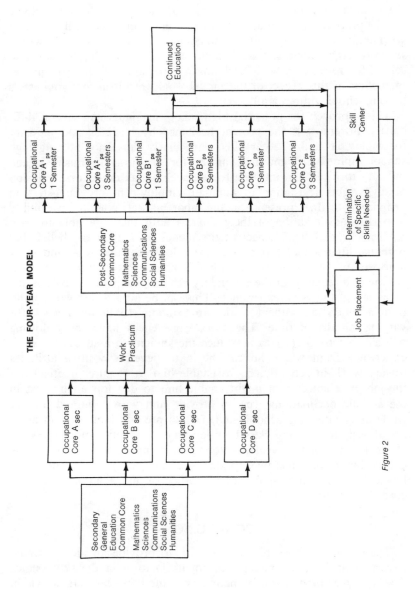

Figure 2

is then followed—the employer specifies the entry skills needed, the student obtains them at the skill center, and then reports to the first job fully qualified. The scheme extracts the potential dropout from the unsuitable academic situation as early as the 11th grade. Some can be prepared for job acceptance and entry into the skill center in six months and many will be functioning on their first job within seven or eight months. Later, these individuals will likely return to school for retraining, skills updating or upgrading. Successful implementation of this aspect of the model would result in few youngsters leaving school without a job.

This approach for potential high school dropouts has several difficulties. Foremost is the present hesitancy by business and industry to employ 16 and 17 year olds, particularly those not holding high school diplomas. Some mechanism for encouraging business and industry to hire them must be found, such as tax credit or expansion of civil rights legislation to mandate employment of youngsters in proportion to their presence in the labor market. Another possibility is partial subsidization of their salaries until they are able to earn a "living wage." This aspect of the model rests upon the belief that potential high school dropouts can develop into functional and valuable workers when provided with this kind of occupational shelter.

One difference from the secondary school occupational core is the provision of the work experience. This can be a part-time work situation in which the student works up to about 15 hours a week for varying lengths of time. The work experiences have the following overall objectives: (a) to introduce the student to a successful work experience from which he can begin to develop positive attitudes toward work in general; (b) to enable him to acquire practical on-the-job experiences that might enable him to develop an interest in the specific occupations; (c) to provide him with a limited income while he is attending school; and, (d) to provide him with an additional basis for making classroom-laboratory activities more relevant.

At the end of two years, a youngster completing any one of the occupational cores has two options—he can seek job placement followed by the sequence described earlier or enter an occupational core at the postsecondary level.

CONCLUSION

The major objective of the models is to provide an ideal learning environment for those youngsters not likely to enter the professions. The four-year model, which encompasses the two-year version within it, would act as the major "finishing" educational institution, since it would reach all but a small fraction of youngsters presently served by the traditional secondary schools and two-year colleges. This approach could reverse the present inequities in public education, where there is altogether too much emphasis upon preparation for the professions. The reality of the situation seems to be that while the average educational attainment will increase toward 14 years, the preparation of people earning the bachelor degree will not increase anywhere near the same rate. Judging from the continued increase in the number awarded (Hooper, 1971), the associate degree is replacing the high school diploma as the point of school departure for many Americans. This being the case, the two-year institution should be converted into "universal colleges" that encompass grades 11 through 14, with a large majority of students steered into occupational programs (Gillie, 1973).

The two-year model is a more practical approach since, in some places, it would evolve out of the present community junior colleges and area vocational schools. Admittedly, the two-year model also has certain elements that are sufficiently deviant from the run of the mill occupational programs to meet with almost instant opposition from some of the traditionalists. But the two proposed models do provide some alternatives to the present sources of occupational education.

REFERENCES

Gillie, A. C., Sr. *Principles of Post-Secondary Vocational Education.* (Columbus, Ohio: Charles E. Merrill Publishing Co. 1973)

Goldhammer, K., and Taylor, R. E. *Career Education: Perspective and Promise.* (Columbus, Ohio: Charles E. Merrill Publishing Co. 1972)

Hooper, M. E. *Associate Degree and Other Formal Awards Below the Baccalaureate: 1969-1970.* (Washington, D.C.: National Center for Educational Statistics. 1971)

Lerner, W. *Statistical Abstract of the United States: 1970.* 91st Annual Edition. (Washington, D.C.: U.S. Bureau of the Census. 1970)

U.S. Department of Labor. *Manpower Report of the President 1971.* 1971

U.S. Office of Education. *Vocational Education Amendments of 1968.* Pub. L. 90-576. 90th Cong. 1969

CAREER EDUCATION AND
HIGHER EDUCATION

Gilbert C. Fite

Higher education has been experiencing rapid and fundamental change in recent years, as have all institutions in the United States. Critics and reformers, including students, have challenged many of the traditional concepts surrounding postsecondary education. The idea that only a relatively few young people would attend college, that they would and should come mainly from middle and upper class white families, and that they should study principally to become teachers, businessmen, engineers, doctors, lawyers and other skilled professionals has been attacked and at least partially destroyed.

Historically, a college education supposedly has been the road to higher pay and more satisfying and fulfilling employment. Thus, the masses began to demand participation in the same educational advantages as the middle and upper classes. The result has been colleges and universities inundated with students, large numbers of whom had little interest in the traditional curriculum. To make matters worse, by 1970 there were so many college graduates that the labor market could not absorb them all in jobs for which they were prepared, or at salaries the graduates had come to expect. Out of this situation came the distressing news of graduating seniors taking janitorial jobs and postgraduate students tending bar or driving taxis.

The flood of people into the nation's colleges and universities, the inability of the labor market to absorb the graduates, and a growing awareness that many students were not prepared for the world of work gradually brought a reassessment of the programs and goals of postsecondary education. While many college faculties and administrators held that anything dealing with career education was somehow second class and hardly worthy of a respectable college or university, others saw it as a legitimate part of higher education and began to develop ways and means to implement additional programs for career education.

CAREER EDUCATION

Career education has been defined in a variety of ways. However, there has been rather general agreement that the term "career education" is based on the concept of preparing students for useful careers and satisfying lives in the worlds of work and leisure. It includes vocational education, but with a much broader connotation than earlier vocational training. For more than a century, preparation for a particular vocation has been a part of American higher education.

Establishment of the land-grant colleges was a part of the growing emphasis to prepare people for the world of practical work. Library shelves bulge with volumes on special career preparation—careers in banking and finance, rocketry, nursing, home economics, broadcasting, commercial art, hotel and restaurant management and scores of others.

But something new and important has now been added in the new career education movement. The modern concept of career education is to provide a wide variety of career preparation to students, while encouraging them to explore the alternatives, options and work opportunities at every level of their education. Thus, genuine career education begins in the early elementary grades and continues as long as the student stays in school. At the doctoral level, for example, students would be better served if their major professors would spend some time exploring with them alternative and satisfying employment rather than concentrating almost exclusively on teaching as a career.

CAREER EDUCATION IN COLLEGES AND UNIVERSITIES

The role of colleges and universities in training people for all aspects of the world of work has generated controversy for many years. In 1871, a little more than a century ago, a group known as the "Friends of Agricultural Education" met in Chicago where participants discussed many of the issues facing the fledgling agricultural colleges. Professor D. C. Gilman of the Sheffield Scientific School explained that there had been hostility between those who favored "bread-and-butter knowledge" with "learning left out," and those who believed that teaching classical subjects was what higher education was all about. "We have these two classes," Gilman continued, "on the one side a little suspicion on the part of classical men, and on the other a want of confidence on the part of practical men." But, according to Gilman, "We are beginning to reach such results that both parties are satisfied, and I think the war of hostility . . . is over, and the friends of education are agreed that both are good; the question being what you want" (Hatch, 1967).

But, Gilman was excessively optimistic if he thought the so-called practical men and the classical educators had already arrived at an understanding. In the late nineteenth century, most of the nation's leading educators who clustered in the great universities—Harvard, Yale, Johns Hopkins, Michigan, and others—emphasized strong academic programs that would prepare students for the highest level professions such as medicine, law and the ministry. Vocational education, regardless of its quality or emphasis, has been considered second class and never achieved the status enjoyed by the purely academic programs. Indeed, vocational training has been considered the poor relative in the college curricula, reserved for the less talented and poorer students. However democratic the American people may imagine themselves to be, a deep feeling of class consciousness has always persisted in United States society. Parents have wanted their children to avoid vocational programs if at all possible and concentrate on preparation for one of the "better" professions.

By the mid-twentieth century, the agricultural and mechanical colleges made every effort to alter their image and changed the emphasis from such practical subjects as home economics, agriculture and engineering to humanistic subjects and the social sciences. As the term "career education" entered educational vocabularies, many college faculties and administrators were alarmed, if not frightened. How would programs emphasizing career education affect academic standards? Would colleges and universities be transformed into high class trade schools? Were programs that included preparation for the world of work really deserving of university recognition? These and related questions were the subject of many faculty and administrative debates.

However, by 1970, American educators faced facts, not theory. The facts were that many college graduates with the traditional preparation could not get jobs. Not only did career education suddenly become respectable, it actually enjoyed popularity. Indeed, educators began to look at career education as a practical way to prepare men and women for life and work in an increasingly complex society.

Lawrence Davenport, chairman of the National Advisory Committee for Vocational Education, declared that, "Career education is a reform movement, which means that much of our traditional system of education—including vocational education—will have to undergo some pretty jolting changes" ("Traditional . . . ," 1972). The truth of this statement seems clear enough. While space does not permit a full discussion of the "jolting changes" alluded to by Davenport, there are at least three aspects of the problem that deserve consideration. These are the relationships between higher education and the secondary schools; the development and emphasis of career education in the colleges and universities; and, the training of personnel to carry out the continuing tasks of career education, particularly in programs of teacher education.

ARTICULATION BETWEEN HIGHER EDUCATION AND SECONDARY SCHOOLS

The long-standing basis for articulation between high school graduation and entrance into a college has been the transcript of credits, duly verified in terms of Carnegie Units and/or letter grades assigned by teachers. This information was intended to provide an intelligent evaluation on a particular individual's academic achievement, both past and potential. Many institutions of higher learning have modified their requirements for entry in efforts to seek more substantial bases for choosing prospective students—e.g., entrance and/or placement examinations, personal interviews and references from responsible persons outside the applicant's school environment. Whatever the means for screening applicants, the idea of academic orientation has normally been a consideration of highest priority. Educators wanted to know, "How can the applicant be expected to perform in a situation largely dependent upon classroom attendance, use of the library, private study habits and, to a lesser degree, laboratory work?"

As career development programs become more widespread and functional in American schools, there will be increasing numbers of high school graduates actively seeking and expecting educational experiences substantially different from passive listening to lectures, routine laboratory experiments and the carrying out of questionable study assignments. For some years now, jolting (or at least gentle) changes have been taking place at all levels of elementary and secondary schooling. Many local school systems have adopted the career education philosophy to some degree, and have either produced their own guides and materials or have secured them from outside sources. State and national governmental agencies, particularly in their vocational-technical departments, have been exceptionally active in collecting, organizing and disseminating career education literature and materials, as well as authorizing funds to support projects assigned to provide specific needs in the field. Sidney P. Marland, Jr. (1971) told a group in Houston that, "Career education is an absorbing topic at the Office of Education lately." In that same address, Marland indicated that career education would receive much more federal money.

At the 1971 American Vocational Association convention in Portland, Oregon, the House of Delegates moved to take advantage of the friendly attitude toward career education in Washington. They passed a resolution that asked for federal support for:

1. Programs at the elementary, middle school, secondary school, and postsecondary levels and continuing education, designed to develop an awareness of the world of work, develop career orientation and exploratory programs, provide assistance in decision making, provide specialized training for occupations and/or occupational clusters as needed at the secondary and postsecondary levels and provide for training or retraining of adults for new careers.

2. Programs to be jointly sponsored by business and industry and the public school system.

3. Programs for the career of homemaking and recognition of the role of the family in Education for Careers.
4. Programs involving the efforts of employers to provide observational, work experience, and work-study programs for present and prospective workers.
5. Programs of vocational guidance activities at all levels of the educational structure. . . .
6. Research and development programs and for exemplary programs designed to develop new models of Education for Careers, and
7. National, State, and Local Advisory Councils on Education for Careers (Hoyt, et al., 1972).

With increased federal financing subsequently forthcoming, new career education programs began to be developed on a broad scale. There is every reason to believe that there will be strong efforts to continue present programs and to create new possibilities for the development of a total career education program from elementary school through the university.

Even a cursory knowledge of the changes being brought about by career education in elementary and secondary schools is sufficient to indicate that the movement is much more significant than merely adding something extra to the curriculum. Something has been added, but there is also a stepped-up approach to the development of students' awareness of themselves, their perceptions of the immediate and extended environments, and their skills in dealing with decisions and feelings.

More and more students will be entering colleges and universities after having experienced in some way or other the career education pattern of increasing awareness, of exploration, of orientation and of tentative decision making with respect to what the next step will be in their own career development. If the school programs are reasonably successful, these young people will enter higher education with a stronger sense of self-direction and purposefulness than did many of their predecessors. They will have been active in becoming acquainted with themselves and with their own particular prospects for eventual entry into the world of work. Consequently, the idea of articulation between high school graduation and entry into college is going to require something more than the routine transcript, standardized tests and personal references. In this respect, college officials need to become aware of the kinds of career programs that prospective students are experiencing in high school, and what those students are likely to expect in the way of continuing education.

This is almost a complete reversal of the traditional pattern of having the colleges set up certain expectations to which high schools should and must adjust. The initial standards for "college prep" courses were more or less dictated by the colleges that prescribed certain kinds of academic content and skills. The present situation finds the "lower" schools taking a good bit of the initiative in curriculum changes, and the colleges are faced with adjusting to the effects of such changes. Those effects stem not only from a clearer realization of a need to relate school work to the real world, but also from experiences involving individualized instruction and active decision making.

CAREER DEVELOPMENT EMPHASIS IN HIGHER EDUCATION

Colleges and universities face the prospect of no small amount of internal turmoil with respect to both the selection of *what* they shall teach and *how* that content is to be taught. The effects of career education in public schools are already a force to be reckoned with, and institutions of higher learning are in a position that will require some measure of commitment to that impetus. Depending upon the imagination and leadership qualities of the persons who make such decisions on a given campus, the commitment to the career education concept may range from adding a token course in one or more departments wherein the demand may be reasonably overt, all the way to a reorganization of the institution in order that every department has an active role in the attitudinal as well as the content aspects of career education. Probably, most institutions will aim somewhere between the two extremes.

Whatever degree of commitment a college or university makes, there are certain large issues regarding curricular offerings that will need attention. What, for instance, shall be the relationship of career education to traditional liberal arts or general education programs? If, as appears to be the case in public school situations, career education is "for everyone K-12," to what extent does this continue at the college level? How does a curriculum, or a course, based on career development concepts differ from already existent college offerings in such fields as engineering, pre-medicine, or pre-anything? These and many similar questions will certainly arise as colleges and universities attempt to implement career education.

Besides the actual content and organization of curriculum, the varying points of view and levels of development of the students themselves are a major consideration. Presumably, if they have taken part in a career development curriculum in elementary and/or secondary school, these individuals have undergone a rather extensive range of exploratory and orientation activities directed toward their own eventual career choices. More specifically, at the critical point of leaving high school, they have opted for further formal education rather than immediate entry into the world of work or some other form of postsecondary training. They may or may not have definite ideas about what they want from their collegiate experiences. Some will know exactly where they want to go and why, while others will still be in some kind of exploratory stage. In any case, there appear to be some strong implications in this area for counseling and guidance as well as curricular offerings.

Perhaps, one of the key issues that colleges and universities face is a reassessment of the nature of their goals and objectives. What is their basic purpose? Almost everyone agrees that colleges and universities have certain common goals. These include broadening students' intellectual and cultural experiences by exposing them to a variety of academic subjects, and hopefully giving them a better understanding of themselves and their society. Also, most Americans have held that colleges and universities should prepare students for specific professions and careers, and place them in a position to earn a living.

The historic controversy within postsecondary education as to how practical or career-oriented the programs should be has been one more of degree than of kind. The main question has been one of emphasis and the *kind* of employment that a college graduate should pursue. No one ever suggested that a college student should give no thought to his or her future employment. As already mentioned, most Americans, including educators, expected that when a student had completed a college curriculum he would be prepared to fill a suitable job, or at least have the basic preparation for further study so that he could enter teaching, law, engineering, medicine or some other profession.

So long as only a relatively few young people went to college, and while trained personnel required for the country's industrial, agricultural and social needs could be provided in other ways (e.g., apprenticeship), this rather class-conscious and specialized role for the colleges and universities worked fairly well. College graduates from almost any and every program got jobs and, as late as the 1950s and early 1960s, the plea was to expand current programs and make them available to more students.

Meanwhile, the land-grant colleges had started out as a kind of peoples' institution. They grew out of a revolt against the emphasis on classical studies and the demand from both farm and labor spokesmen for institutions that would prepare students for jobs in agriculture and industry. Calvin M. Woodward of Washington University, St. Louis, declared in 1873 that "There has been a growing demand not only for men of knowledge, but for men of skill, in every department of human activity." Then he indicated that the colleges and universities had yielded "little else but candidates for Milton's class of 'gentlemen' inasmuch as they are fitted for no kind of work," except in the learned professions. Woodward concluded that the current college education "oftener *unfits* than *fits* a man for earning his living" (Cremin, 1961).

While they did not ignore the importance of humanistic subjects, the main purpose of the land-grant colleges was to provide practical, career-oriented training in agriculture and the scientific and mechanical arts. Students in chemistry, for instance, should be prepared to work in sugar refineries, brewing or starch making. Those in agriculture and mechanics should be able to fight noxious weeds or build bridges. The establishment of these new institutions emphasized the belief that a college education should be practical and career-oriented. By the 1890s, more than 25,000 students were enrolled in land-grant colleges and studying subjects ranging from metallurgy to dairy science. Other colleges and universities added industrial arts departments and expanded their vocational programs.

However, vocational education was never fully accepted by educators even within the land-grant colleges themselves. The image that the programs were somehow second class could never be overcome. Consequently, while the land-grant institutions continued to do outstanding work in agriculture and engineering, they gradually departed from the philosophy of the founders of the land-grant movement. This change came gradually, but by the mid-twentieth century its presence was evident as those institutions greatly expanded their liberal arts curricula, both at the undergraduate and graduate levels, and employed presidents and other top administrators who had no vocational education in their experience or background. Many of the land-grant institutions sought to leave their past as far behind as possible.

Although vocational and career programs expanded in the post-World War II period, their growth fell far behind that enjoyed by the liberal arts and sciences. The number of majors in industrial arts, for example, rose but at a much slower rate than those in history, English, physics and other academic subjects. Vocational educators talked about the need for more programs to train a wide variety of specialized personnel for industry, the health occupations and other fields, but few listened. Indeed, during the 1950s and 1960s, the popular critics of American education argued that one of the main weaknesses of the nation's schools was their failure to concentrate sufficiently on the basic academic disciplines. It could be argued that education had been subverted, and that the purpose of schooling was to cultivate the ability to think. This could be done best by studying arts and science subjects. In 1957, following Russia's launching of the first space satellite, many emphasized the need for stronger academic programs at every level of American education. Indeed, vocational and career programs seemed of minor concern as Americans determinedly set out to match the Russian feats in science and space technology.

This brief background is necessary to understand the difficulties, uncertainties and confusion that began plaguing colleges and universities around 1970 when they were confronted by new social and economic conditions. The situation that forced a painful reassessment of purposes and programs on many college campuses included a decline in the rate of increase of financial support, a surplus of teachers and other professional personnel, a reduction in the space program, and the lack of interest by many first generation college students in the traditional academic programs. As many institutions sought to reappraise their activities and seek new directions, former U.S. Commissioner of Education, Sidney P. Marland, Jr., gave a clarion call for the development of many more career-oriented programs.

Consequently, since about 1970, colleges and universities have implemented new and expanded career-oriented programs. These have included programs to train people in the health occupations, technology, computer sciences and many others. But there is still a question as to just what extent university faculties, administrators and governing boards are committed to career education. That many faculty members and administrators consider these programs second rate is still evident. The future of career education in postsecondary education will depend on the kind of financial support it receives, the degree to which the programs can shed the image of inferiority, and in general the place it is given among institutional priorities.

PREPARATION OF
CAREER EDUCATION PERSONNEL

Regardless of how well colleges prepare individuals for careers, postsecondary institutions have the added responsibility of preparing people who are capable and knowledgeable about the total concept of career education. This concept has extremely important implications for teacher education programs. Indeed, if career education ever achieves its rightful place in colleges and universities it must first have been fully developed at the primary and secondary levels. And, this will result if teachers are committed to all of the elements of career education.

As those postsecondary institutions that have a major responsibility for training teachers consider their approach to career education, they may make one of two possible mistakes. In the first place, there will be pressure to add a course or two in "Career Education" to the teacher training curriculum and let it go at that. Secondly, a few institutions may permit career education to overshadow most of what is done in the school or college of education. Neither of these approaches will achieve the desired results.

Hoyt, et al. (1972) have outlined some of the salient features that they believe are essential for a teacher education institution that develops and implements a comprehensive career education program. These include:

1. The undergraduate teacher education programs must be invested with a career education emphasis. Such an emphasis is now almost completely lacking. Work experience and work-study programs for prospective teachers should become as important to their preparation as student teaching.
2. Counselor education programs are in need of great revision. Not only must such programs contain a much heavier emphasis on career development, but they must also provide prospective counselors with broader concepts of career education and the means by which counselors can interact effectively with teachers, parents, and the business-industrial-labor community in a total career education program.
3. Prospective school administrators today have almost no emphasis on career education as part of their formal preparation. It must be made an integral and important part of the preparation of such personnel.
4. Teacher education institutions must assume responsibility for solving the need for support personnel in career education. Perhaps an even bigger responsibility for teacher education is the preparation of teachers as teachers, especially personnel who will work in the community college setting in training support persons for career education.
5. The need for research and evaluation in career education is an inescapable responsibility of teacher education institutions, particularly those located in universities.
6. Teacher education personnel must join with state departments of education personnel in assisting local school systems with the massive problems of in-service education that career education will bring. Faculty working in teacher education must be given time to do this job.

Obviously, administrative and staffing arrangements to implement these principles and suggestions would have to be determined by local needs and conditions.

Another area of activity by which a college or university can contribute directly to the enrichment of career education is in the development and dissemination of teaching-learning materials and other instructional aids for use by teachers in the field. These materials may include such items as audio-visuals, curriculum guides, units of activities, or manipulative objects.

If career education is to become a major emphasis during pre-service programs for teachers, it is essential that the university faculty itself be substantially reoriented both in its content and in its techniques. This changed perspective can be implemented by at least two major efforts in dealing with personnel matters. One, new personnel with career education competencies may be added to the staff as positions are vacated or created. Secondly, continuing faculty members will need sufficient in-service encouragement and direction to become knowledgeable and purposeful in arranging to include the career education orientation.

The idea of hiring new staff members specifically for enhancing an active incorporation of career education into a teacher preparation program offers intriguing possibilities for creative recruitment practices. New questions might well be asked as to just what kinds of skills, knowledge, and attitudes are needed for the desired emphasis. The accepted assumption has been that the main requirement is an advanced academic degree in order to qualify for faculty status. Sharlene Hirsch has pointed out clearly that past practices in the education profession may have been far from the best. She stated:

> The education fraternity is infamous for its inbreeding. Most of its executives have advanced in a typical pattern that begins with a degree from a college of education and moves on to teaching positions and ultimately to administrative assignments, probably with a break to pursue further education. Professional incest is, of course, practiced widely and perhaps prima facie does not constitute an automatic evil. However, if this practice operates to exclude capable, talented individuals just because they lack the requisite in-house training and experience, then the entire field is threatened with loss of able and gifted manpower (Pucinski and Hirsch, 1971:174).

No argument is being advanced here regarding the importance of degree requirements for faculty status. Rather it is only intended to point out that it might be useful to experiment with recruiting on the basis of performance-based competencies as an alternative to traditional academic credentials. It does not seem inappropriate that individuals who have been actively involved in "real world" careers could provide valuable perspectives as either regular or adjunct members of a university faculty that is geared to provide a program embracing career education.

Hirsch encourages just such considerations:

> If education were a strong self-sufficient profession with a substantial body of tested knowledge and a solid record of service to the nation's youth, then perhaps this narrow perspective could be tolerated more comfortably. However, education, despite some of its ancient ivy trappings, remains a very young, fragile, and incomplete discipline which has just begun to offer some hypotheses. As such, it could only stand to suffer at the critical juncture from perpetuating homogeneity and superficial exclusivity at the expense of encouraging cross-fertiliza-

tion—or what Donald P. Mitchell has called the 'necessary mix'—which could well provide the transfusion needed to suggest new directions. While still in its infancy, therefore, education has a unique opportunity to resist the dogmatism which has plagued so many other fields and major educational endeavors (Pucinski and Hirsch, 1971:175).

New personnel may also be sought among professional educators who have been specifically trained and are experienced in some aspect of career education. Many such people are already working as teachers, supervisors, counselors or administrators in public schools as well as in agencies at various levels of government. These individuals likely have some, if not all, of the traditionally required credentials for university employment, and could offer the advantages of whatever years of practical work in the field they may have experienced. A university committed to the career education concept should consider possible contributions from both outside and within the profession.

Besides attracting new types of individuals to faculty positions, the university also has the responsibility for directing and supporting the in-service growth of its continuing personnel. Those people who have served as members of a particular department or division of the university for any number of years will likely require positive encouragement if they are to adjust their competencies and perspectives to the new organizing principle of career education. Toward this end, the university will need to be ready to provide justification and direction for whatever new programs and/or administrative realignments may be instituted. It is reasonable to expect that some system of released time for consultation, committee work or workshop-type activities would be a part of the new order of things— at least during the early years of transition from traditional teaching to career education orientation.

CONCLUSION

There seems little doubt that colleges and universities will develop an increasing number of career education programs. However, two dangers exist. One is that the career education concept will be treated too lightly by the mere addition of a few practical or job-oriented courses and programs. On the other hand, there is a danger that career programs will receive so much emphasis that the arts and sciences will be weakened and some subjects even eliminated. Universities need to remove the dichotomy that has existed for so long between a liberal and a career-oriented education and strike a sensible balance that will preserve the best in all of postsecondary education.

REFERENCES

Cremin, Lawrence A. *The Transformation of the School.* (New York: Knopf. 1961)

Hatch, Richard A., ed. *An Early View of the Land-Grant Colleges.* (Urbana: University of Illinois Press. 1967)

Hoyt, Kenneth B., et al. *Career Education: What Is It and How To Do It.* (Salt Lake City, Utah: Olympus Publishing Company. 1972)

Marland, Sidney P., Jr. "Career Education." *Today's Education.* LX (October, 1971)

Pucinski, Roman C., and Hirsch, Sharlene Pearlman, eds. *The Courage to Change, New Directions for Career Education.* (Englewood Cliffs, New Jersey: Prentice-Hall Inc. 1971)

"Traditional Voc-Ed Can Not Be Plugged into CE, Davenport Warns." *Career Education News.* I, (December 15, 1972)

THE CLASSROOM EDUCATOR AND CAREER EDUCATION

Evelyn M. Robinson

If our schools are to be relevant, the foremost goal must be to provide, from kindergarten through postsecondary years, an integrated curriculum that relates to the world of work. Most educators, including guidance counselors and vocational teachers, will confirm the fact that the responsibility for counseling young people today should be determined by what is relevant to the student, not to his parents or teachers.

If students are allowed to take some initiative, they may make some mistakes, but will learn more quickly than if they are directed in every move. Many students, because of immaturity, resist criticism and may use lack of interest as an excuse. It is up to educators to try to understand these young people and to assist them as they learn by trial and error. Students need to understand that they should not be ashamed or feel guilty if they do not know the answer; but that if they make an error, they must try again, thereby gaining confidence.

It sometimes appears that parents no longer control their offspring and that children make their own decisions. Nevertheless, these young individuals are confused and lack experience. Educators must put forth extra effort to help these youth. The objectives of career education can help in guiding and directing these students as individuals. Teachers who really care will be able to make learning relevant to students.

REVISION NEEDED

In all education across the nation from kindergarten through postsecondary, educators must emphasize that everyone's future lies in career education. Many students have "missed the boat" because they were not at the right place at the right time. That is, they have not been able to get the necessary guidance and direction through practical individualized courses. An example of this would be a student who might have qualified for a better job through a cooperative program if he had been permitted to elect such a course rather than being referred to academic courses. There must be a revision of the present curriculum, especially at the high school level, to enable students to select courses that are relevant to their future needs and desires.

Guidance counselors must communicate and plan with the vocational teachers so that together they may meet the needs of students. With a better understanding among these educators and students, perhaps will come a better understanding among students and parents. This would provide a support to career education. Through career education, perhaps parents may understand that, for their son or daughter, vocational education may be a superior choice to a college education. The time has come for parents to recognize the importance of career education, of which vocational education is a part. They also must recognize that students need to be guided into a practical course of education that will help prepare them for future employment. It is well known that many students have graduated from college to discover that they have no skills, and are not actually qualified to enter the world of work.

The author believes that the primary objectives for all dedicated teachers in career education are to be enthusiastic and innovative; to motivate each student so that he will care enough to work toward a future goal; and, to help alleviate the present dropout problem.

Career education is influencing many students and, often, through cooperative programs, many have found jobs they really enjoyed and have been employed full-time upon graduation. Others, after working part-time through a cooperative program, have found that the particular job was not what they wanted as a full-time job. This experience provided them with the confidence needed to apply for a job more to their liking. Such experiences enable students to become more independent.

TEACHERS ON CAREER EDUCATION

How do teachers really feel about career education? What does career education really mean to the average classroom educator? The author questioned teachers at many grade levels throughout the United States. It is interesting, appropriate and timely to consider their comments.

> I'm wondering if a child centers down too soon on a single career aim if he might not close out possibilities that would limit future choices. Perhaps this is my own limited understanding of the term. . . . Career education is that education which is more oriented to the goal of making a living.
> *Ohio fifth grade teacher*

This does not mean that a child must decide to make choices, it just opens up to him the wonderful world of work and what can be available when he decides what he would rather do.

> It is my feeling that teachers often become so *busy* teaching a particular course that they forget to show their students the relevancy of the subject in preparation for their life's work. The development of a good rapport between student and teacher is so essential in gaining the confidence of students. This helps to create a situation whereby students feel free to ask questions about career education thus enabling communication to take place.
> *Business education teacher educator in a Western state*

> Career education sounds pretty ridiculous in kindergarten. Yet, we
> actually do start some thinking along that line.
> *Ohio kindergarten teacher*

The words *start thinking* are the key.

"What does your Daddy do?" the teacher asks. The child answers
almost invariably, "He makes money." Only a *few* children at this
age actually know what their fathers do at work. Maybe the time
has come for not only teachers, but parents to "show and tell" what
daddy does. Children are much smarter than they are often given
credit for. This kindergarten teacher continues:

> During the year we touch on many aspects of living—a trip to the
> farm, a record about a space flight, a movie about transportation. Many
> of the children express their personal views. One would be amazed at
> the number of potential teachers there are in kindergarten.
>
> Career education means preparing students to lead a useful, productive,
> and satisfying life. In administering a cooperative program, I am able to
> guide students in their adjustment to the world of work.
> *Ohio Cooperative Office Education coordinator*
>
> Career education means that a student will now have the opportunity
> to understand the meaning of work and enjoyment of working with
> both hands and mind. The student of all levels of competence and inter-
> est will have the chance to experiment and visualize the real meaning
> of occupation. In cooperative education, the career concept evolves im-
> mediately when the student is confronted with reality of the world and
> its societal methods of indoctrination. Within two months in the co-op
> program, the student is indoctrinated to responsibility and diverse
> occupations.
> *Indiana ICT coordinator and department chairman*
>
> Career education means preparation for a particular vocation.
> *Ohio occupational work experience coordinator*

Does it have to? In the OWE program, students have the opportunity to work at different jobs that give them the opportunity to
know what they like and don't like. He did mention that his students
are introduced to career education with an in depth look into careers
that are of interest to them. When asked how he might improve
methods of teaching or guiding students toward more exploration
of career education, he stated:

> This [career education] is not a teacher initiated function, in my opinion.
> It must be initiated as a community need through the administration
> with a proper curriculum written and adopted and then taught in a
> classroom.

The innovative teacher will get involved—this teacher will use
initiative and experiment. Educators at all levels in all subjects and
programs must be willing to try different methods to see which is or
can be most successful. To be satisfied and wait until the courses
come along is not the whole answer, but the participation of dedicated teachers is necessary to involve and help guide students today.

They must be prepared, and educators must help them—not only with skill knowledge, but with attitude, personal integrity, sense of responsibility and sense of initiative as well.

Career education means that education aimed toward preparation for skilled employment. All of my teaching is geared toward a better human understanding which is necessary for successful employment.
Ohio Technical College instructor

Career education means *orientation* in *junior* high schools to possibilities for training for future careers. I sincerely believe that the co-op programs in high schools are most valuable to students as they seem to achieve a greater maturity for their age than those who are just college bound. I will encourage students to enter the co-op programs.
Ohio Science and Planetarium director

Career education means learning that involves training for some particular vocation. It would involve ideas behind the vocation and practical application. It would probably be most beneficial to introduce career education to ninth graders early in the year and have a series of follow-up discussions throughout the year to keep them thinking about it.
English instructor

Basically, career education means preparing an individual to make a career choice. Career education may fit into teaching in two ways: (a) to teach graduate Business Education with the understanding that our people may still move in many different directions, (b) to prepare them to go back into the high school and aid in the establishment of the career education concept.
Mid-western Business teacher educator

Career education means to acquaint elementary and junior high school students with the field of work and to prepare high school students to enter the career of their choice.
Cooperative Office Education coordinator

Career education means preparing one for an occupation continuously from the elementary level through all other continuing education. The awareness of career education today is very important even though career education is not new. At the college level to work with prospective teachers to understand the importance of preparing all people for a vocation regardless of the choice of occupation is:
  1. alerting students continuously about the importance of the world of work,
  2. importance of being happy on the job and feeling a sense of achievement and accomplishment,
  3. importance of self-evaluation each year and updating oneself.
Wisconsin professor

My job is to motivate young people in the field of data processing and to create such a strong interest so that they will continue further study or will apply for a job to fit their personal skills—this is career education.
Technical College instructor

Career education is a total comprehensive educational program—kindergarten through adult—that provides for exploration and testing of self in relation to the world of work. Academic, vocational, and general subjects are sequenced to supplement one another so that a person moves from career awareness to fulfillment in life as a worker,

citizen, and person. At the University of . . . . , career education is stressed in all of the teacher education classes; several workshops have also been offered on the career education concept. Students definitely benefit from introducing the words career education as they see their role as part of a total education team and not just distributive education. The words career education may be introduced to students in many ways but some of the most effective ways would be through reading, handouts, committee reports, school observations, lectures, cassette tapes, student teaching, seminars, resource persons, and occupational experience. It is most important to relate to the real world!
Mid-western Distributive Education teacher educator

I feel it is most important that students in the elementary grades be acquainted with and oriented to the various jobs available in our big world of work. In my classes I encourage students to talk about what type of work their parents are doing and what they might like to do when they become an adult. Many have exciting ideas, many have no ideas, but at least they are thinking about career education and their future work. I hope they will become better citizens as a result.
Fifth grade teacher

Career education has an academic ring to it. We are involved in industrial education—training and retraining people for and in local industry. These people have had enough of English and career, etc. English for our industrial students is "Industrial Communication"—English in disguise but industrially and technically oriented. CAREER always reminds me of a position such as an ambassador to a foreign country! We are dealing with people that are fed up with the academic approach and just want to learn a good trade—industrial education—*not* CAREERS—just a good paying job!
Washington (State) community college instructor

Career education can fit into my way of teaching by re-emphasizing occupationally related information to the extent that it permeates all of our professional and technical (laboratory) experiences. In-service teachers must first be convinced of the value of career education because in the final analysis they are the ones who must be called upon to implement these programs. When more of the in-service school personnel (teachers, counselors, principals, etc.) are convinced, the benefits to be derived through relationships with students and their parents are forthcoming.
Florida College department chairman

What does career education mean to the author? The author would like to draw inference from the *different* points-of-view expressed. From reading the evaluations of career education given by these educators, one conclusion is obvious. One established meaning is implied in all definitions. Career education includes preparing everyone for a job in the world of work so that they may make a living and be happy. It is rather simple if one just stops to think about it. However, it is not so simple if one does nothing about it. Most people, at some time in their lives are obligated to make a living for themselves and possibly their family. Society does not owe *anyone* a living but should be willing to make it possible for every citizen to get the education to enable him to *earn* a living.

No longer should students take courses in school just for the "requirement" for graduation, but all courses in a curriculum should help prepare the student for the world.

RECOMMENDATIONS

As a classroom educator, the author makes the following recommendations:

1. Offer as many vocational educational programs in school today as possible.
2. Permit girls, and boys, from grades nine through 12 to take vocational home economics, both consumer and homemaking.
3. Permit and encourage boys, and girls, to take vocational shop and machine courses. Young people today are wanting to equalize roles.
4. Permit the disadvantaged and the handicapped to be educated to the best of their ability. Integrate them into regular classes wherever possible and advantageous.
5. Employ teachers who are willing to expand the Awareness Program for kindergarten through sixth grade so that these young people really know what is going on. At this age, individuals are frank and could be the best ambassadors for career education.
6. It is necessary to reach all seventh and eighth graders in the Career Orientation Program. These students are *eager* and *alive,* having more energy than they know what to do with. They must be given a chance to know what is ahead.
7. Ninth and tenth graders really need Career Exploration! They, too, are more than ready. Perhaps these students could be divided into interest categories with guidance counselors' help, and then be permitted to go on visitation tours to various training stations where cooperative students are at work.
8. For those students in the eleventh and twelfth grades who are in some type of vocational program—great! They will continue with proper guidance. For those who want more, college may fulfill the need.
9. Those who graduate from high school but do not go on to college or have not been in a vocational program will need encouragement to take adult night courses or attend a technical school to get necessary job preparation.
10. Postsecondary education students will most likely continue their education because they feel a need for further study. However, there will be some individuals who enter college

to find that they can't make the grade. They must have guidance to attend some school where they may get skill training and, hopefully, qualify for a job in the world of work.

CONCLUSION

Even though career education has long been advocated, there is no time like the present to really get everyone involved to make this a bigger and better world in which to live. There has been too much talk and not enough action!

All education must and will become more practical with "down to earth" methodologies if young people are really going to be helped. When everyone works together, leaders and followers alike, then great strides in career education will take place.

All educators must take another look at all of the various types of individuals in society today. Individualization is a key word in most of our classes today. The author has visited every state in the nation, talked with many teachers, visited many schools, and recognized the same need throughout to provide individualization to students and strive to maintain their interest. This interest must be held long enough to get some results. Students must be able to see some accomplishment if they are to continue being motivated.

It is up to all dedicated professional educators to train, guide and help students to help themselves. Education is imperative if an individual wants a career; therefore, career education can be the way to a future of happiness.

THE COUNSELOR'S ROLE IN CAREER EDUCATION

Duane Richins

It is assumed in mentioning the counselor's role in career education that much of the work of the counselor will be new and different, just as the concept of career education is new and different. This does not imply, however, that all parts of career education are virgin.

THE NEED FOR A CHANGE

An attempt will be made throughout this chapter to identify the present status of guidance, the acute need for a change and some of the methods currently used to foster these changes including career education. Finally, the role of the counselor in career education will be examined.

Causes for Alarm

Counseling is in need of revision. For years, counselors have sought to gain their own identity and firmly carve out for themselves a niche in education, but counseling today appears to be far from achieving its goal. Varying from school district to school district as it attempts to find its most needed and fulfilling place, counseling seems to be in real trouble and must have some basic revamping. This message seems to be coming from consumers, observers and those in the educational profession. Hays (1972) says:

> Just as government is concerned with costly management procedures and ineffectiveness, the public is concerned with the increasing costs of education and its lack of quality.
>
> If education in general is facing these problems, we can also assume that guidance programs and, more specifically, counseling programs are also. Indeed, those of us within the counseling profession probably are more susceptible to such criticism than the regular teaching staff. Why is this so? Because we have yet to convince the general public of the importance of guidance services and of counselors to the educational process.

What are the indicators that say change is necessary? First, the literature is replete with studies depicting counseling as being in desperate need of revision (DeFeo and Cohn, 1972; Hays, 1972; Humes, 1972; and, Glasser, 1969). Although this message has been published time and again, there appears to be too little being done relative to changing the counselor's role. There are a few schools and a few areas of our country where guidance programs have found favor. For the most part, what is coming forth loud and clear from administrators, the public and students is, "We want to know what the counselors can and will do that is beneficial to the educational process," and "We want to know to what extent he can deliver on these predetermined objectives."

DeFeo and Cohn (1972) put it this way:

Unless the questions raised here (how much and what kind of school and community involvement the counselor will be willing to assume) can be answered in the affirmative, I fear that economic pressures will result in decreased support for guidance and other pupil personnel services. The support guidance programs received from administration will be a direct result of the counselor's ability to demonstrate the value of his services.

A second indicator is evident in the expressed attitude of teachers. Many have been venting some negative feedback toward counseling.

A recurring criticism from the administrators centered around guidance counselors isolating themselves from other school personnel. Teachers felt no real relationship with the guidance counselors in some of the administrators' schools, and in some ways, resented them. They felt that counselors had no real understanding of the teachers' problems and efforts with children. Many teachers regarded the counselors more as filling an unreal, structural, or administrative need (i.e., Conant says, every secondary school of more than 500 students should have at least two counselors) rather than a real or carefully defined need (DeFeo and Cohn, 1972:320).

Students themselves have expressed the belief that a counselor is ineffective and many times wonder what his real purpose is.

To some students he is an extension of the principal; to others he is literally their counselor or their defender in truth or error, having identified his role by comparing the title of counselor with that of a legal counselor seen on T.V.; and to other students he is just another person in the administration office and they really don't know what he is for, what he does, or how he could possibly help them (Richins, 1972:1).

Third, the ever present dropout problem gives credence to the idea that counselors need to do things differently. Counselors are not the only ones who need to be concerned since all educators as well as students themselves must shoulder the blame; however, counselors do play a vital part in combating the dropout problem.

The attrition rate for the public schools in Mesa, Arizona, for example, amounts to about six percent per year for each grade, nine through 12, and has increased slightly each of the last five years. A serious problem discovered in Mesa was that of 400 students, grades seven through 12, who quit school in 1971-72, few had the benefit of counseling services. This was brought on by an oversized counseling load, "other assigned duties" such as substitute teaching, sponsoring of clubs, homeroom responsibilities, etc., which took most, if not all, of the counselors' time. Also, many students did not see the counselor as their advocate, but rather as the advocate of the "system." Regardless of the reasons, the needs of a large number of students were not and are not now being met under the present assignment of duties and allocation of time.

Most alarming, and certainly the most critical dropouts are those who remain in school, but who literally drop out of involvement in the learning process. They are "turned off" to education in its present form. These students merely go through the motions of being students while looking forward to the day they will be released from the need to put in an appearance at school.

Fourth, the counselor's own self-evaluation tells him that things are not right.

> A counselor can conscientiously work hard day after day and yet feel a definite rejection by his colleagues because they know little or nothing of his involvement with the students and of the goals and objectives he has in mind to achieve with them (Richins, 1972:1).

The counselor, too, feels isolated from his educational world and the educational world of the students with whom he counsels. This is mainly due to the nature of his duties, which generally confine him to his office, thus keeping him from the classroom area. This isolation is also due to his habit of not being in the classroom and associating with teachers in the formal educative process. It also may be attributed to a feeling of complacency brought about by the system that has "freed" him from the classroom.

Finally, the counselor has a basic desire to be free to perform the duties for which he is trained, that of counseling students.

> The counselors feel that they are victims of the system; when a new demand is placed on the school, the counselor receives the assignment because he is available. Therefore, the counselor feels that his role is of lesser importance than the new demand (that is probably true in the mind of the principal or he would not have assigned the task to him). Fundamentally the counselor should perform his function or be eliminated (Stinzi and Hutcheon, 1972:331).

These examples were designed to reveal some of the weaknesses now present in counseling. The next charge is to find possible remedies.

Alternatives

If it is agreed that a change in role is needed, the next logical questions may be, "What are the alternatives?" "Must a complete overhaul take place, or will a patch job suffice?" The following are ideas that appear plausible and, in some cases, have already been implemented by some school districts.

1. Do away with counseling.
2. Reassign counselors to "more productive" roles, i.e., deans, quasi-administrative functions, teachers, advisors, etc.
3. Let teachers do all of the guidance in the classroom.

4. Narrow the service offered by counselors to crisis counseling only.
5. Continue to add to the counselor responsibility spectrum without additional resources.
6. Establish greater specialization of counselor services with a resulting differentiation of staff responsibility. (One counselor might be assigned to handle all schedule changes, another all career counseling, another all testing, scholarships, and other personal problems.)
7. Use lay counselors from ethnic groups and/or environmental contexts.
8. Use counselor aides to take on additional responsibilities of counselors, i.e., career education materials, testing, attendance, schedule changes, registration, etc.
9. Make the needs of students the hub around which a new or revised counseling program is based.

After careful consideration of these and other alternatives, the counselors of Mesa Public Schools chose the alternative of truly becoming the advocate of the child. They are now in the process of taking deliberate steps to identify, validate, set priorities, deliver on, and be accountable for meeting specified needs of young learners in their charge. The first of this series of deliberate steps was a formal comprehensive needs assessment.

THE NEEDS ASSESSMENT SURVEY

In an attempt to analyze and redefine the counselor's role, the guidance department of Mesa Public Schools in Mesa, Arizona, initiated a project in February 1972 based on making the needs of the students the hub of the guidance program.

The American Institutes for Research in Palo Alto, California, was contracted as a consultant after which a formal, comprehensive assessment survey was conducted involving some 800 students at the sixth, ninth and twelfth grade levels. In addition, a significant number of parents, teachers, administrators and counselors were also involved in the survey. After determining the identified needs as expressed by the groups mentioned, these needs were then placed in priority order and teaching-counseling units developed by the guidance staff were constructed based on them. Teacher-counselor teams are now pilot testing these units in the classroom.

Because of the belief that guidance and counseling should exist for the benefit of students, a restructuring of the counseling program has continued. An effort is being made to use the findings of the needs assessment survey in an accountability model. Plans are to continue this restructuring, as well as to develop other periodic needs assessment surveys, in an attempt to make counseling, and school, more relevant to students. Additional needs assessments of minority populations will also be completed to give added support and data for modification of guidance units.

As this effort continues, Mesa counselors feel that some progress will be made toward creating a positive image for themselves. This will allow them to be recognized as a vital part in the educational process with specified responsibility. The machinery will be developed to give continuous feedback on how well counselors have succeeded in terms of student behavior changes.

In searching for ways to restructure guidance, many methods were considered. One theme in particular seemed to be critical to the new program, that of getting the counselor into the classroom so that he would be more available to assist students and teachers. As ways of accomplishing this task were being contemplated, career education and the national goals it brought with it were making themselves manifest. Consideration of some type of marriage between the new guidance objectives and those espoused by the career education program were entertained. The Comprehensive Career Education Model became a vehicle to help deliver the guidance units.

A COMPREHENSIVE
CAREER EDUCATION MODEL

Shortly before Mesa's involvement with the needs assessment survey, career education had gained prominence on a national scale. The Mesa Public Schools became one of the six school districts chosen nationally to participate in the development of the Comprehensive Career Education Model (CCEM). Some of the ideas for the restructuring of the guidance and counseling department for Mesa Public Schools have been developed jointly with this program at the local level.

One of several possibilities for restructuring of guidance came as a result of a particular CCEM need: having school personnel assigned as building coordinators to assume the responsibility for, and to assist teachers in, the implementation of career teaching units developed by the six national sites. The guidance department was looking for a way to change to a more effective role and to find a means to expose the new guidance units to the students. It was felt that one way to accomplish this would be to have counselors act as building coordinators so that they could: (a) have some input into the curriculum; (b) team with teachers as consultants and get a first-hand classroom experience with their counselees; (c) get out of their offices at least part of the time and become directly involved with students and teachers; and, (d) improve the setting where guidance units based on identified student needs could be introduced.

An agreement to do this was reached between the coordinator of guidance and the coordinator of staff development for the career project. One counselor at each school in the district was chosen as a building coordinator with all counselors assisting in the building coordinator function.

> The duties for which the building coordinators are responsible can be generally categorized into half a dozen meaningful functions.
>
> They are as follows: planning, assembling resources, organizing, communicating, directing, and controlling (Norton, 1972:17).

Planning

This entails making time available to plan with the teacher the details of the career or guidance unit.

Assembling Resources

An inventory of human and material resources, services and information, both in and out of the school setting, will be made.

Organizing

The input requests for resources and the output responses for those requests must be organized.

Communicating

The building coordinator must inform all personnel of the ongoing activities of CCEM.

Directing

The building coordinator has the responsibility for directing the program, both through the principal and through the teachers.

Controlling

The building coordinator has the responsibility to keep adequate records as to who, what, why, when, where and how to insure that the program runs efficiently and smoothly.

These building coordinator responsibilities have formed a link joining the counseling program with that of career education in such a way that new roles appear to be emerging. A review of the counselor in career education follows.

THE COUNSELOR'S ROLE IN CAREER EDUCATION

Different and more demanding responsibilities to the guidance and counseling staff came with the advent of career education and the redirected emphasis on the student as the center of the program. Now that students were to identify their needs, counselors could begin to structure goals and objectives to meet these needs. Since goals and objectives could be set up, some type of evaluation could be given and responsibility affixed for achieving those results.

Changes in the counseling role that seem most likely, and those that will tend to reshape or create new roles for the counselor as a result, are: use of a partnership situation; developmental counseling; accountability; demonstration or use of interpersonal and intrapersonal skills; and, the counselor's self-image. Each will be explored in more depth.

Partnership

> The counselor has a golden opportunity to work as a vital member of an educational team. If he helps to plan, provide, implement, and assist teachers with the career teaching units, his image has a chance of changing to a more positive position. When the counselor's talents are coupled with those of the teacher, the media specialist, the principal, and any member of other special services such as psychologist, speech or reading therapist, as well as resource speakers, and parents, he joins a very formidable and important team to assist in the education of young people and for the first time is consistently able to witness firsthand the actions of the counselees under his care and is able to use his skills and the resources of the school and district at his disposal in a more efficient and timely fashion than before (Richins, 1972:2).

Developmental Counseling

The cry from the counseling ranks has always been that the ratio of students to counselor is too high and that, generally, only crisis counseling can result. With career education, however, come new possibilities for the counselor to leave his office and, with the help of the teaming relationship cited earlier, become a firsthand observer and participant with counselees in their day-to-day educational experiences.

The counselor can be available to work with students in a more positive way than before. He is in a good position to see the need for, and to initiate, counseling in its earliest stages. Counseling in this type of setting can occur while the counselee is at his desk, in a corner of the room, or in the privacy of the counselor's office. It can be done with one student at a time, or in small, medium or large-sized groups. And, the counselor or some significant other person in the life of the counselee can manage it.

Counseling of this type should be considered "extra" as it is likely that there will always be a need to make time available for crisis counseling. It is hoped that the more developmental counseling the staff can do, the more students will be reached with the likelihood that severe crisis counseling can be decreased.

Accountability

Much has been said of late about education, in general, and guidance and counseling, in particular, being accountable for their actions. As mentioned earlier in this chapter, the public wants to know what educators can and will do for their children and appears to be searching for some means of evaluating educators to measure their output.

Mesa Public Schools has been developing an accountability model for counselors and this provides just such a measuring device.

> Basically, what it will involve will be counselors who will be committed by agreement or contract to bring about predetermined changes in the lives of students. This accountability may be charged to an individual counselor or possibly to the teacher-counselor team, but being able to measure the results and determine responsibility for those results is the name of the game (Richins, 1972:3).

If an adequate and acceptable accountability scheme can be devised, it could be one of the biggest boons ever to the counseling profession. It would allow the profession to know where and probably why it succeeds or fails and thus be able to improve consistently the quality of its work with the youth under its care.

Interpersonal and Intrapersonal Skills

Of all the school personnel, those who should be the best equipped with interpersonal and intrapersonal skills are the counselors. Due to the training they receive and the experience they have gained, the counseling staff should stand ready to lead in these areas. Such has not generally been the case. The counselors have not openly demonstrated these skills.

The use of the counselor in career education, at least as far as Mesa Public Schools is concerned, provides many more opportunities for the teacher-counselor team to make excellent use of these skills. If all counselors in a school are involved in the type of a developmental teaming relationship mentioned earlier, and all are willing to use these skills as needed or learn to use them as they go, counselors can soon show their value in a school setting. They will be actively involved in helping students and teachers.

Counselor Self-image

> As the emphasis shifts from crisis to developmental counseling through more exposure to students and teachers, the self-image of a counselor will also change from an image which shows him as neither administrator nor teacher and therefore sometimes without educational justification, to one of being a definite, helpful, important, vital member of the school staff who brings to bear much expertise, particularly in the areas of interpersonal and intrapersonal relations (Richins, 1972:4).

SUMMARY

The role of the counselor has needed changing for some time. Much has been written, but little has been done to bring about the necessary revisions. With the advent of career education on national, state and local levels came opportunities, resources and a desire to tackle the problem. To date, much has been accomplished in the way of planning guidance units and a rather ambitious pilot testing of these units is being implemented. However, little regarding actual changing of counselor roles is taking place yet. One significant event that is happening involves counselors making themselves accountable for agreed-upon changes.

The future looks bright. It appears as though some progress is being made toward making the guidance program an integral part of the educational process.

It is hoped that what has been tried by various school districts will be reported, scrutinized and evaluated and that which appears to be worthwhile will be adapted for use in other schools across the nation.

REFERENCES

Boy, Angelo V., and Pine, Gerald J. "A Sociological View of the Counselor's Role: A Dilemma and a Solution." *The Personnel and Guidance Journal.* XLVII (April, 1969)

DeFeo, Raymond A., and Cohn, Ben. "Budget Cut: Two Guidance Counselors." *The School Counselor.* XIX (May, 1972)

Glasser, William. *Schools Without Failure.* (New York: Harper and Row. 1969)

Hays, Donald G. "Counselor—What Are You Worth?" *The School Counselor.* XIX (May, 1972)

Herr, Edwin. *Review and Synthesis of Foundations for Career Education.* (Columbus: The Center for Vocational and Technical Education, The Ohio State University. 1972)

Humes, Charles W., Jr. "Program Budgeting in Guidance." *The School Counselor.* XIX (May, 1972)

Jones, G. Bryan, et al. *Development and Evaluation of a Comprehensive Career Guidance System.* Palo Alto, California: American Institute for Research in the Behavioral Sciences; and Washington, D.C.: U.S. Department of Health, Education, and Welfare. 1971.

——————. *Planning, Developing, and Field Testing Career Guidance Programs, A Manual and Report.* Palo Alto, California: American Institutes for Research in the Behavioral Sciences; and Washington, D.C.: Office of Education, U.S. Department of Health, Education, and Welfare. 1972.

Macy, Virginia. "Some Concerns About Counseling." *The School Counselor.* XIX (May, 1972)

Mozee, Elliott. "Counselor, Evaluate Thyself." *The Personnel and Guidance Journal.* LI (December, 1972)

Muro, James T. "Guidance Is Good—If and When." *Communique Resources for Practicing Counselors.* VI (February, 1972)

Norton, Robert E. *Staff Development Guidelines for Comprehensive Career Education.* (Columbus: The Center for Vocational and Technical Education, The Ohio State University. May, 1972)

Pulvino, Charles J., and Sanborn, Marshall P. "Feedback and Accountability." *The Personnel and Guidance Journal.* LI (1972)

Richins, Duane. "Possible Changes in the Professional Role of a Counselor."

Paper presented at the 1972 National Vocational and Technical Teacher Education Seminar, Columbus, Ohio, October, 1972.

Stinzi, Vernon L., and Hutcheon, William R. "We Have a Counselor Problem —Can You Help Us?" *The School Counselor.* XIX (May, 1972)

Sullivan, Howard J., and O'Hare, Robert W., eds. *Accountability in Pupil Personnel Services: A Process Guide for the Development of Objectives.* Los Angeles: California Personnel and Guidance Association. Monograph. Number 3. 1971.

LABOR LOOKS AT CAREER EDUCATION

Joseph V. Tuma

This chapter attempts to identify the essential points of interest and concerns of the contemporary American labor movement as these points relate to career education.

The reader will recognize that today's labor movement is neither monolithic nor ideologic. Indeed, labor leaders are pragmatic; but, as elected officials, they have developed a high degree of political and social skills. They must possess these to be reelected. At any given point in time, there are variations in opinions and official declarations of policy regarding educational concepts and strategies both within unions and among unions, within the leadership, and among the 20 million members. One cannot safely say that labor's perception of career education is diametrically opposed to that held by management, the minority community, or any other identifiable segment of the diverse American community.

In addition, to discuss labor and career education without mention of professional organizations as well as those whose working conditions are protected by civil service or tenure would deny consideration of a significant sector of labor (whether it is or is not a collective bargaining unit). This group numbers well in excess of 10 million. In fact most of the 81 million workers in the labor force either directly or indirectly, formally or informally, have an immediate interest in the economic as well as the educational process.

Within this broad heterogeneous representation, employees have common concerns and interests. However, these interests and concerns are not necessarily accompanied by a universality of agreement on solutions.

CAREER EDUCATION:
WHAT IT IS TO THE WAGE EARNERS

The term "career education" has intrigued, if not captured, the thinking of a significant portion of the educational fraternity. Of greater importance, the idea is now beginning to penetrate broad sections of the general working population.

Though still not a specific model (nor should it become one), career education is a concept that carries with it hope that educational offerings will emerge bringing with them a revival of education's historic leadership role, a role with which education has been identified since the founding of the Republic.

Perhaps, the reaction to career education can best be stated in the language of the working family, "We like the idea, because it says our children will have choices in getting jobs or even furthering their education. But if 'career education' doesn't work, then what we still want is a *good* education for our kids so that they can make a living in a job they like, or even go on to more schooling."

A superintendent of a medium sized school system in central Michigan said, "This idea will work—we have been doing it for 14 years. We just didn't put a label on it."

If these values are shared by workers and education, then career education already has a good deal going for it. Parents, irrespective of their work in life, seek a "better life" for their children. Educators and school officials are recognizing that simply awarding a diploma is not a fulfillment of the school's responsibility to either the student or society. An additional ingredient providing support to career education is the philosophical and positive concern of management. If school personnel handle their relationships with labor and management intelligently, career education can serve as a common denominator eliciting joint support of these effective powerful forces in the community.

It is the judgment of this writer that for career education to succeed, it requires: (a) a clear statement of purpose by educators and an understanding of that purpose; (b) support from labor and management through their respective organizations; and, (c) broad based parental and community support to which labor and management can contribute.

If career education is to succeed, the educational fraternity must consciously recognize that this is a nation of job holders. More than 90 percent of the employed population work for private or public organizations. Every job should in some way be part of a career. During the working span of life, individuals may be employed and reemployed from three to nine times. Each decade, the percentage of entrepreneurs declines, and the need for retraining will emerge at an increasing tempo.

To those who work for a living and live by the work ethic, career education serves as a launching pad to a job that is more than just income. It also serves as a stepping stone to satisfying employment, continued education and/or retraining for new endeavors.

Thus, what labor expects of career education is largely in consonance with the aspirations of most Americans. "If career education doesn't work, then what we still want is a *good* education for our kids so they can make a living in a job they like, or even go on to more schooling."

JOBS AS PROPERTY VALUE

The dramatic shift of the population from a self-employed status to an employer-employee status has belatedly forced a redefinition of property values. This is almost a 180 degree turn from the pre-Civil War period.

The days of home crafts and home industry have all but vanished. Agribusiness is consuming the family farm. Enormous shopping complexes leave little room for the corner merchant. City, state and federal governments have become some of our largest employers. Income, then, is generally derived from employment and not property holding. The *job* is a new form of property value.

Thus, such arrangements as labor-management contracts, personnel policies, civil service regulations, tenure and civil rights legislation are visible evidence of job-property protection. The job has all but replaced real property as a source of income. Aside from the legalisms as to who "owns" the job or the right to a job, workers (teachers, factory hands, the candlestick maker) have sought to build protection into their jobs through one device or another.

In the post-World War II period, as economic and social relationships have become increasingly complex, the interest in "job security" equates itself with jobs as a property value.

The greater number of jobs generated by our economy tend to reduce the man-made restrictions built around jobs, not the value of jobs. Thus, it follows that the greater the increase in output of goods and services *equitably distributed*, the greater the expansion in number of jobs and employment mobility. Full employment and high skill levels become handmaidens that can produce genuine security and high income levels.

Assuming that the job-property concept is a fact of life, can career education contribute to the institutional structures designed to enhance and enlarge the universe of "job property?" Can it accelerate the velocity of job-property exchanges to increase the expansion of goods and services? Can it provide the individual with sufficient skills and confidence to "trade off" one job for another in hopes that the trade will be more rewarding and self-satisfying?

WORKERS WANT A GOOD EDUCATION
FOR THEIR CHILDREN

Of more immediate concern now is the symbolic 5.5 economy: 5.5 percent unemployed and 5.5 percent annual income increment. Workers ask: "Is career education a Fifth Avenue term for traditional vocational programs? Is it a source of cheap, competitive labor? Is it a guise to direct minorities, already at the lower rung of the economic ladder, into undesirable, low-paying jobs? Is it the cutting edge for cheap 'child labor'?"

History has helped answer several of these questions for us. In the early days of our nation, free public education was supported by workers and their organizations. (Unions were then legally questionable and often considered conspiratorial.) Even when child labor was rampant in the 1800s, workers wanted night schools for their children, and teachers complained because the children were not sufficiently alert to learn after 12 hours in the mill (Schnapper, 1972).

The Morrill Act was designed to provide greater opportunities and freedom for workers, and veterans and commoners. Land grant colleges made it possible for those who broke the prairie to increase their efficiency and output after a divisive Civil War. It promoted economic independence, political freedom and, in some measure, reunification to a torn nation.

This historic step in education, combined with the Homestead Act, provided a 19th century version of career education and career opportunity for those who elected to till the soil.*

The Servicemen's Readjustment Act of 1944 (GI Bill) is unquestionably the largest single contemporary piece of educational legislation. In money terms alone, this investment in veterans has yielded a 50 percent return to the Federal Government. And, this does not take into account such elements as personal and family income, job satisfaction, social behavior and citizenship. There is no question about labor's support of this kind of educational legislation.

It can be generally concluded that labor's support can be enlisted for legislation having universal application. To interpret this support as paternalistic, fraternalistic or idealistic would be somewhat romantic. What workers and their leaders were saying then, as now, is this: "We want a good education for ourselves, as well as our children, so that we can make a living in a job we like, or even go on to more schooling."

UNIONS, THE EDUCATIONAL ESTABLISHMENT AND LABOR MARKET TRENDS

It is at this point that unions will critically examine career education. If it has universality and is open to all, it will be supported, provided funds are prudently spent. If, on the other hand, it is a new dressing for traditional vocational education, there will be careful scrutiny and, under certain conditions, resistance by segments of union leadership. If it is exclusively categorical in nature *and output,* it will not excite the leadership or command widespread support from the membership.

---

* According to some historians, the full fruit of the combined education and economic programs in the Morrill Act and Homestead Act was not realized because of the intervention of the "scalawags" who began dealing in homestead properties to the disadvantage of the under-equipped farmer.

From those within the labor movement committed to updating our educational programs into what we call career education, there are three areas of emphasis:

1. It is not vocational education, but vocational education is an appropriate component of career education; and, it should be melded into the total spectrum of contemporary education.
2. Freedom of choice must be available and based on effective demand (i.e., jobs). Education for the sake of education is not without value, but that's really not what workers want to buy for their children or themselves.
3. Career education, with a substantial vocational mix, can produce new forms of learning and new teaching styles that make schools more attractive to the student and add another dimension to the learning experience of the student. These fringe benefits to education can easily accrue to the teaching faculty when goals, objectives and terminology are exchanged within the context of career education.

Labor will look upon career education most favorably when it feels secure that a new employee has "performance capabilities" that do not dilute the occupational standards or hard won wage levels, and that the training received does not add to an overabundance of persons with available skills.

Labor market forecasters, therefore, will be asked by labor to develop more accurate and sophisticated data. The "occupational cluster" approach has more general approval of the labor movement than the single *Dictionary of Occupational Codes.*

Labor's support of career education can be enlisted in additional areas.

1. Participation on general craft advisory committees. The educational community badly needs to learn how to communicate effectively with the employer-labor community. The reverse is equally true. Much is to be gained in direct, concurrent and joint discussions with management and labor regarding the range of school offerings, its equipment needs, commercial and industrial processes, labor supply and demand, and most important, placement. Lamentably, the relationship between schools and labor can hardly be considered even a flirtation; a desirable and needed "love affair" waits to be discovered.
2. Job placement is a function that schools and their instructors are potentially better equipped to perform than any other institution. While all schools may not be equipped to assume the responsibility for placement, they should not abrogate the responsibility for insuring the performance of this function.

Teachers, counselors and instructors know the student and his strengths and weaknesses. Job placement may require specialized in-service training for faculty and staff, directed at labor and management needs. It may also require release time for personnel to develop a network of employment outlets and make continuous reassessment of curricula at each level. This is a small price to pay for placing a student in a suitable job or in a suitable work-training situation, cooperative program, or postsecondary education program.

To translate labor, management or community support of the career education concept into *active involvement* requires more than rhetoric. The need for this kind of involvement may be looked upon by educators as an intervention into "their" domain. This is a serious misconception; public schools are the public domain (Burt, 1971).

Many teachers, counselors and administrators still show reserve and sometimes trepidation in their communications with the public in general, and labor in particular. If educators open the door, labor can and should be ready to provide assistance in helping teachers to:

1. Identify community resources to reinforce the educational process. This may include understanding of job requirements, job standards, new and emerging job demands, improved technology, academic and physical requirements and economic benefits for particular occupations.
2. Gain an overview of the economic and social fabric of the community, i.e., transportation, manufacturing, commerce, agriculture.
3. Examine the social and economic strata of the community, including income levels, racial compositions, political forces and cultural imprints.
4. Strive for a common plane of communication among all segments of the community, with the public school as the loci.

The opposite side of the coin is that labor, once it is *welcomed* inside the schools, will react to facts and problems.

1. It will understand quite readily the dynamics, or sterility, of the administrative bureaucracy.
2. It will begin to relate to curriculum and, in laymen's language, distinguish the wheat from the chaff and say so.
3. It will begin to appreciate the specific problems of classroom teachers, such as, overloads, inadequate equipment, variations in learning capabilities, differences in home influence and even inequities in teacher salaries.

Teachers will find many benefits from this partnership. They will soon find their status in the community upgraded, professionalism respected and be called upon for extra hours of public service. (This, too, is a part of the teaching profession.)

Furthermore, labor will much more likely support school bond issues as really vital for the students, and not just to the school establishment. Most school children come from workers' homes. Here, votes count for the whole community!

Such approaches to joint cooperation should include other principal segments of the community. Labor, however, wants equal attention. No matter how worthy the cause, if public support is sought, and labor is an afterthought, it will show up in the "No" column.

The late Walter Reuther often said, "Labor will make progress *with* the community, not at the *expense* of the community."

So to educators and labor leaders alike, career education represents a common purpose that can serve every age group and population segment, and encourage the entire community to progress.

REFERENCES

Burt, Samuel M. *Strengthening Volunteer Industry Service to Public Education.* (Kalamazoo, Michigan: Upjohn Institute for Employment Research. 1971)

Schnapper, M. B. *American Labor.* (Washington, D.C.: Public Affairs Press. 1972)

YEARBOOK AUTHORS

Walter W. Adams (p. 141) is a research and development specialist at The Center for Vocational and Technical Education at The Ohio State University and unit chief for the Guidance, Placement and Support Systems Components of the Comprehensive Career Education Model. Mr. Adams has had experience as an assistant state supervisor in the Ohio Department of Education's Division of Guidance and Testing, working in the area of measurement and evaluation, and as state supervisor for guidance program development. He has also been a school counselor and a teacher of industrial arts and psychology.

Bela H. Banathy (p. 255) is a program director at the Far West Laboratory for Educational Research and Development, San Francisco, California (formerly in Berkeley). Prior to joining the Far West Laboratory, he was director of the East Europe-Middle East Division of the Defense Language Institute. He is a contributing author to *Trends in Language Teaching,* to the *Britannica Review of Language Education,* author of *Instructional Systems, A Design for Foreign Language Curriculum* and co-author of *The Educational Information Consultant: Skills in Disseminating Educational Information.*

Melvin L. Barlow (p. 30) is professor of education, Graduate School of Education, University of California, Los Angeles, and director of the Division of Vocational Education, University of California. Dr. Barlow is the Historian for AVA. In 1971, he was awarded the Ship's Citation, and will serve as editor for the 1974 Yearbook of the American Vocational Association.

Juliet F. Brudney (p. 266) has professional experience in the fields of community development, manpower training and adult education. She was executive director of Settlement Houses Employment Development, Inc. (SHED) of New York City from 1969-1971, director of special projects for the United Neighborhood Houses of New York City from 1962-1969, area director of the Neighborhood Conservation Program from 1959-1962, and a community organizer for the educational and health institutions at Columbia University.

Lowell A. Burkett (p. 65) is executive director of the American Vocational Association. Mr. Burkett, whose background includes trade experience, classroom teaching, and local and state administration, served as assistant executive secretary of AVA before being named to his present position. He is vice chairman of the National Advisory Council for Vocational Education and a member of the National Manpower Advisory Committee.

Joseph R. Clary (p. 280) is executive director of the State Advisory Council on Vocational Education in North Carolina and adjunct associate professor of education at North Carolina State University. Dr. Clary's professional experiences include work with the North Carolina State Department of Agriculture, teaching, and administration. He has written extensively for professional publications and co-authored the *Introduction to Vocations* Teachers' Guide used in the North Carolina Public Schools.

Curtis Dixon (p. 326) is the principal of Roosevelt High School in Atlanta, Georgia. Dr. Dixon has been a teacher, counselor, assistant principal, elementary principal, consultant and college lecturer. He has been active in professional, civic, religious and military organizations.

Harry N. Drier (p. 73) is unit head for staff development at The Center for Vocational and Technical Education at The Ohio State University. Mr. Drier has also been the Wisconsin coordinator for guidance and counseling, an area vocational high school and adult night school director, a counselor, physical education teacher and recreation director. He has authored or co-authored several books, booklets, papers and articles.

Jonah L. Fitch (p. 330) is Superintendent of the McMinnville (Tennessee) State Area Vocational-Technical School. Mr. Fitch has been a secondary school administrator and is a trustee of Middle Tennessee State University.

Gilbert C. Fite (p. 354) is president of Eastern Illinois University. Dr. Fite's main field of research is American economics and agricultural history. A recipient of both Ford and Guggenheim fellowships, he taught at the University of Oklahoma where he was research professor of history. Between 1962 and 1964, he taught at Jadavpur University in Calcutta, India, and was director of the American Studies Research Centre in Hyderabad. He is president of the Southern Historical Association.

Angelo C. Gillie, Sr. (p. 344) is professor of higher education and vocational education and associate in The Center for the Study of Higher Education at the Pennsylvania State University. He has also been on the faculty at Rutgers, University of Hawaii, Niagara County Community College (New York), University of Hartford, and New England Technical Institute. Dr. Gillie represents technical education as a vice president of the American Vocational Association. He has authored more than 73 books, monographs and journal articles.

Vivian M. Guilfoy (p. 266) has served as a staff member of several educational research organizations. Her experience includes work with

CONSAD Research Corporation of Pittsburgh where she was responsible for the preparation of proposals for development and applied research in education and manpower training; educational systems analysis for Puerto Rico's Department of Education; and, career development for minority adults and educational and manpower program development for the American Institute for Research. Ms. Guilfoy has also participated in the development of a variety of career education curricula.

Dallas Hardin (p. 337) is superintendent of schools in Washington County, Tennessee. Active in many school administrators' groups, he is vice chairman of School Superintendents of the Upper East Tennessee Area. He also is the public schools' representative to the First Tennessee-Virginia Development District and a director of the Washington County Drug Education Association.

Edwin L. Herr (p. 50) currently holds several positions at the Pennsylvania State University. He is professor and head, Department of Counselor Education; University Director, Vocational Teacher Education; and, acting assistant dean for Graduate Studies, College of Education. Dr. Herr has served as a business teacher, school counselor and director of guidance. He is currently editor of the *Journal of Counselor Education and Supervision,* and has published more than 75 articles, book chapters and reviews, in addition to seven monographs and books.

Kenneth B. Hoyt (p. 15) is professor of education and director of the Specialty Oriented Student Research Program at the University of Maryland. Dr. Hoyt authored the definition in *Career Education: A Handbook for Implementation* and co-authored *Career Education: What It Is and How To Do It; Career Education and the Elementary Teacher;* and, one of North Carolina State University's *Career Education Series.* He is past president of the American Personnel and Guidance Association.

Louise J. Keller (p. 173) is director, chairman and professor of the Department of Vocational Education at the University of Northern Colorado, Greeley. Her professional background includes work as a teacher-coordinator, high school department head, business education city supervisor, consultant, lecturer and workshop director. Dr. Keller is on the editorial board for Charles E. Merrill Publishing Company and is educational consultant for the National Cosmetology Accrediting Commission. Her latest publication is *Career Education In-Service Training Guide.*

Jean K. Kintgen (p. 157), assistant professor of Vocational and Technical Education at the University of Illinois in Urbana-

Champaign, is currently involved in the development and implementation of a health occupations teacher education program. Dr. Kintgen's professional experiences have included staff nursing, teaching and administration in nursing education and nursing service, a research associateship at The Center for Vocational and Technical Education, and chairmanship of the Division of Health Technologies at Columbus Technical Institute. She authored *Interpretation of Literature on Career Ladders and Lattices in Health Occupations Education.*

Aaron J. Miller (p. 241) is professor of education at The Ohio State University. He was an associate director at The Center for Vocational and Technical Education and project director for the school-based comprehensive career education model. Dr. Miller served as head of the Technical Education Department at Oklahoma State University and Director of Vocational, Technical and Adult Education for the Oklahoma City Public Schools. Among some 40 publications of Dr. Miller's are "Research in Vocational Education" in the *Encyclopedia of Education,* and "Vocational Education," in the *Teacher's Handbook.*

Jerry C. Olson (p. 293) is the assistant superintendent, System-Wide Programs and Services for the Pittsburgh Public Schools where he was formerly assistant superintendent of Occupational, Vocational, and Technical Education. Dr. Olson's professional experience includes public school teaching; instructorship at the Ohio State University; and, summer visiting professorships at Oregon State University, California State College, and The University of Minnesota. He has written numerous articles and co-authored the *Graphic Communications Series.*

Marla Peterson (p. 89) is director of the Enrichment of Teacher and Counselor Competencies in Career Education Project, Eastern Illinois University, Charleston, Illinois. Dr. Peterson was formerly the director of the OCCUPAC Project and a staff member of several other career education research projects.

Carl W. Proehl (p. 202) is professor of vocational education at the University of West Florida, Pensacola. Dr. Phoehl has been state director of vocational education in Florida, vice president for Adult and Vocational Programs at Pensacola Junior College, and Director of Education, U.S. Naval School, Pre-Flight, Pensacola, Florida. Dr. Proehl also has served on the faculties of Northern Illinois University, DeKalb, and the University of Illinois, Urbana. He is a member of the Florida State Advisory Council on Vocational-Technical Education.

Marvin Rasmussen (p. 114) is director of career education for the public schools in Portland, Oregon. He has taught and counseled on the secondary level and served 15 years as vice principal and principal of Benson Polytechnic High School. Mr. Rasmussen is chairman of the Governor's Advisory Council for Career Education and a member of the Governor's Manpower Commission. He spent 18 months on a special assignment to the Oregon Board of Education as director of a project for the development of career education in Oregon.

Duane Richins (p. 374) is a counselor in his fifth year at Mesa (Arizona) Junior High School, where he also taught eighth grade for four years before becoming a counselor. He was director of guidance and an acting high school principal in the South Pacific Islands of Tanga.

Evelyn M. Robinson (p. 367) is cooperative office education coordinator at Westlake High School in Ohio. Ms. Robinson was the first president of Classroom Educators in Business and Office Education, an affiliate of the American Vocational Association. She also has served as chairman of the Policy and Planning Committee of the AVA Business and Office Education Division and chairman of the Secondary Education Department, and been a contributor to the *American Vocational Journal.*

Richard G. Swails (p. 50) is the graduate student coordinator and principal author of a K-12 career development education syllabus being prepared for the Bureaus of Pupil Personal Services and Vocational, Technical and Continuing Education, Pennsylvania Department of Education. Prior to entering Pennsylvania State University as a doctoral student in counselor education, he served as director of the Career Resource Center, State College Area School District, State College, Pennsylvania. Mr. Swails has held positions as a high school teacher, school counselor and high school principal.

Gordon I. Swanson (p. 40) is professor of education and coordinator of international education at the University of Minnesota. A member of the UNESCO Advisory Committee on the role of science and technology in development, Dr. Swanson is also chairman of the Committee on International Education and a member of the NEA Commission on International Relations.

John E. Taylor (p. 121) is senior staff scientist with the Human Resources Research Organization (HumRRO) in Monterey, California. His recent projects, which have dealt with vocational education directly, include: a taxonomy for vocational instructional objectives; an occupational clustering system for the school-based Comprehensive Career Education Model; and, a career-oriented, peer-instruction model in the office cluster of business occupations. He has authored or co-authored more than 30 journal articles, technical reports and professional papers.

Robert E. Taylor (p. 213) has been director of The Center for Vocational and Technical Education, at The Ohio State University, since its inception in 1965. Also under Dr. Taylor's direction has been the ERIC Clearinghouse on Vocational and Technical Education. He is a professor in both the College of Education and the Department of Agricultural Education and reports directly to the provost and vice president of academic affairs of the university. Co-author of and/or contributor to five books, he has written numerous bulletins, manuals, reports and professional journal articles.

W. Wesley Tennyson (p. 100) is a professor of educational psychology, University of Minnesota, where he teaches in both the Division of Vocational-Technical Education and the Department of Counseling and Student Personnel Psychology. He is past president of the National Vocational Guidance Association and the Minnesota Association of Counselor Education and Supervision. Dr. Tennyson served as a high school teacher, counselor and director of guidance. He has been a frequent contributor to professional vocational publications.

Nicholas J. Topougis (p. 313) is director of the career education program in the Akron public schools. He has had extensive work experience with industry and business in sales and management. Mr. Topougis also has served as teacher, counselor and vocational guidance coordinator. In addition, he has served as a consultant to various state boards of education and local school districts.

Joseph V. Tuma (p. 384) is director of Manpower Education Programs, Institute of Labor and Industrial Relations, University of Michigan-Wayne State University. He also serves as director of the Area Manpower Institute for Development of Staff. He is in his fourth year as chairman of the Michigan Advisory Council for Vocational Education. His work experience includes almost a quarter of a century as a local union and international representative for the United Auto Workers. He is also a journeyman mechanic.

Darrell L. Ward (p. 213) is associate director for Field Services and Special Projects at The Center for Vocational and Technical Education, The Ohio State University. Dr. Ward's work at The Center has focused upon management systems, simulation materials for leadership development and leadership training for state and university personnel. He has served as a faculty member of the Oregon State System of Higher Education and on the staff of the Oregon State Department of Education.

Ralph C. Wenrich (p. 188) is professor of Vocational Education and Practical Arts at The University of Michigan. He also has served as department chairman. Dr. Wenrich was associate state superintendent of public instruction and state director of vocational education in Michigan, and held positions in the Pennsylvania State Department of Public Instruction, at the Pennsylvania State University, in several Pennsylvania public schools, and in foreign countries with US/AID and the Department of Defense. He is co-author of the book, *Vocational Education and Practical Arts in the Community School.*

Glenn White (p. 227) is the director of the Research Coordinating Unit, Missouri Department of Education. His background includes training as a counseling psychologist and elementary teacher. He has been a consultant and trainer for pilot dissemination projects in three states, and is presently a member of the National Steering Committee for Dissemination, and the Policy Committee for the Guidance Division of the American Vocational Association.